Architecture of Reliable Web Applications Software

Moh'd A. Radaideh
Abu Dhabi Police – Ministry of Interior, United Arab Emirates

Hayder Al-Ameed
United Arab Emirates University, United Arab Emirates

T0325222

IDEA GROUP PUBLISHING

Hershey • London • Melbourne • Singapore

Acquisition Editor:	Kristin Klinger
Senior Managing Editor:	Jennifer Neidig
Managing Editor:	Sara Reed
Assistant Managing Editor:	Sharon Berger
Development Editor:	Kristin Roth
Copy Editor:	Susanna Svidunovick
Typesetter:	Jamie Snavely
Cover Design:	Lisa Tosheff
Printed at:	Yurchak Printing Inc.

Published in the United States of America by
Idea Group Publishing (an imprint of Idea Group Inc.)
701 E. Chocolate Avenue
Hershey PA 17033
Tel: 717-533-8845
Fax: 717-533-8661
E-mail: cust@idea-group.com
Web site: http://www.idea-group.com

and in the United Kingdom by
Idea Group Publishing (an imprint of Idea Group Inc.)
3 Henrietta Street
Covent Garden
London WC2E 8LU
Tel: 44 20 7240 0856
Fax: 44 20 7379 0609
Web site: http://www.eurospanonline.com

Library of Congress Cataloging-in-Publication Data

Architecture of reliable Web applications software / Moh'd A. Radaideh and Hayder Al-Ameed, editors.
   p. cm.
   Summary: "This book presents new concepts regarding reliability, availability, manageability, performance, scalability, and secured-ability of applications, particularly those that run over the Web. It examines causes of failure in Web-based information system development projects, and indicates that to exploit the unprecedented opportunities offered by e-service applications, businesses and users alike need a highly available, reliable, and efficient telecommunication infrastructure"--Provided by publisher.
   Includes bibliographical references and index.
   ISBN 1-59904-183-9 (hardcover) -- ISBN 1-59904-184-7 (softcover) -- ISBN 1-59904-185-5 (ebook)
   1. Application software--Development. 2. Web site development. 3. Software architecture. I. Radaideh, Moh'd A., 1965- II. Al-Ameed, Hayder, 1969-
   QA76.76.D47.A7325 2007
   005.3--dc22
                              2006031365

British Cataloguing in Publication Data
A Cataloguing in Publication record for this book is available from the British Library.

Architecture of Reliable Web Applications Software

Table of Contents

Preface

This book is concerned with the issues and matters that relate to the reliability, availability, manageability, performance, scalability, and secured-ability of applications, particularly the ones that run over the Web. The importance of studying and exploring such issues is obvious.

This preface starts with a set of real-life experiences that lead me to realize the importance of the theme of this book. Then it provides an overview of the thirteen chapters that compose this book.

Experience I

Shortly after joining IBM Canada in 1997, I was introduced to an early release of the Java programming language, the SUN JDK 1.1.6. At that time, I was a member of the High-Performance Java team whose mission was to develop a tool for compiling the Java platform-independent pseudo code (.class) into platform-dependent executable modules (.exe). The tool was then named "High-Performance Java Accelerator". Things started well at the beginning; average win over the SUN JDK 1.1.6 was 300% speedup in terms of execution time. However, after SUN released the JDK 1.1.8, the previous win vanished. The average win of the accelerator-produced executables over the JDK 1.1.8 could not exceed the 10% speedup margin. That loss was simply due to the tremendous improvement made by SUN on their Java Just-In-Time (JIT) compiler. As a result, IBM decided to discontinue the project, but continued to support the few customers who leased licenses of the accelerator shortly after its release at the JDK 1.1.6 level. This project taught me the following lesson:

- A project will definitely fail if not enough careful planning and forecasting are made prior to starting the project. In the case of the above-mentioned project, if the people in charge had more serious efforts predicting the work carried out by SUN to improve the performance of their JIT compiler, the project would have progressed differently.

Experience II

In 1998, while working for IBM Canada, I submitted an early version of my Ph.D. thesis to my supervisory committee at McMaster University, Hamilton, Ontario, Canada. My supervisor, Professor David Lorge Parnas, was very supportive of my work. However, most of the other members of my supervisory committee were not familiar with the subject of my research (e.g., Organizing and Documenting Component-Oriented Toolkits). It was very unfortunate that most of them were unable to comment meaningfully on the practical application of my research subject, as they have almost no industrial exposure (i.e., non-practitioners). They were simply after the discrete-math formulas which I derived to represent the many rules and guidelines presented in my thesis for software design, organization, and documentation. Their thoughts were never satisfactory or convincing to me in terms of the real-life application of my ideas. This experience caused me to believe that it is problematic to rely on an academician to understand and provide resolutions to real-life problems unless he/she has real-life experience (i.e., practitioner).

Experience III

An interesting experience had to do with an assignment at American Airlines (AA) in Dallas, Texas. Verity assigned me on a six-week long project to integrate the K2 Enterprise Tool (Enterprise indexing and search) with AA's Oracle database server, BroadVision, and the front-end Apache Web server. The indexing tool had to index content from two different repositories: meta-content from their local Oracle database server and a set of html files stored on a remote machine. Each of these html files was associated with a single record in the database meta-content. The solution that we developed and implemented for AA consisted of two processes: the indexing process and the search process.

- The above-mentioned indexing process consisted of the following sub-processes:
  - o The first sub-process was to run on the remote machine to compress "tar" the entire folder of the to-be-indexed html files and place the resulting compressed file in a specific folder on the remote machine. Once it completes its job, this sub-process creates a semaphore empty file in the same specific folder as the compressed file. The semaphore empty file is to indicate that the compression job has been completed.
  - o The second sub-process was to run on the indexing machine itself. Its job was to telnet to the remote machine and check whether the semaphore file is there. Once the semaphore file is found, this sub-process performs a file transfer protocol (ftp) operation to download the compressed file from the remote machine and then uncompress it into a mirror folder on the local indexing machine. Then, this sub-process deletes the semaphore empty file on the remote machine and creates a similar file in a specific folder on the local indexing machine. This second semaphore file is to indicate that the remote html content has been mirrored on the local indexing machine and that it is ready now for indexing.

o   The third sub-process was to dump the to-be-indexed content from the Oracle database into a Verity-specific formatted file on the file system with each record linked to one of the above-mentioned html files.

o   The fourth sub-process was to insert a tag-line (i.e., metadata tag) into the header section of each html file based on the tag value available in the parent record in the Oracle database. The purpose of this was to indicate the importance of the associated html file as classified in the parent records (e.g., "Platinum", "Gold", "Silver", "Bronze", or "Public").

o   The fifth sub-process was to perform the indexing operation using the Verity mkvdk indexing tool and build the searchable collection (e.g., searchable index).

- The above-mentioned search process consisted of the following components:

o   The K2-BroadVision integration component: This component was written in C/C++, not Java, as the version of BroadVision at that time had a C/C++ API. This integration component was tuned to meet the AA requirements at that time, recompiled, and then placed on their system as a shared object.

o   A search page (i.e., a JSP page): This page was developed and used to encapsulate the above-mentioned integration component (shared object) to perform the search operations and then process their results (i.e., collect results and display them back to users).

The experience with the above-mentioned American Airlines project leads me to believe that:

- Reliability and availability of software systems highly depends on the reliability and availability of the infrastructures that they run on (i.e., networks, Web servers, database servers, etc.). Therefore, we cannot speak of software reliability in isolation from the overall system reliability and availability.

- Building systems by integrating software components from different vendors has side-effects on the overall reliability and availability of these integrated systems. Reliability of each component has to be investigated on its own before the overall system's reliability can be estimated.

- Having redundant components (i.e., Web-servers, database servers, etc.) always helps improve the overall reliability and availability of the system.

Experience IV

Another interesting experience had to do with a former dot-com company named BarPoint. com that was based in Florida. Verity asked me, around mid-2001, to visit that company to health-check their indexing-search system. It did not take me long to realize how unhappy the BarPoint executives were with the tools and solutions provided to them by Verity. The CEO was very cold, and I was hardly able to convince him to give me the opportunity to health-check their system. He demonstrated a sample problem by searching for the word "train". The results were totally incorrect and not related to the submitted search query (i.e., "train"). Also, it took that search operation about 3.5 minutes to bring back the search results, which is relatively too long for a typical search operation. After reviewing a few of the returned documents, I found them to contain the five letters "train" as part of other words such as "training", "trainee", etc. That observation led me to suspect the way in which the query was handled by the Java Server page (i.e., JSP) that wraps around the search server. After a quick review of the code in that JSP page, it was a very straightforward process to figure out the root cause of the problem. To explain, before communicating the query (i.e., "train") to the search server instance, the JSP page prefixes and suffixes the query with stars. In other words, the query "train" becomes "*train*". This query transformation caused the search server to perform a wild-search operation such that any document containing the five characters of "train" whether in the form of a separate word or as part of other words (i.e., as in "training") will be returned among the search results (i.e., a hit). After removing the prefix and suffix stars, it took only 1.5 seconds to perform the same search operation providing reasonable results. The CEO did not believe what happened. As a matter of fact, he seemed to suspect that I was faking things and playing tricks with him. In the end, I was able to win his confidence in my work by spending some time demonstrating other successful searches at reasonable search speeds, and as a result, that CEO approached Verity for further licenses of the same products (i.e., Enterprise K2) as well as licenses of other Verity products. This experience leads me to think of several reliability-related matters such as:

- Many software-related problems can be resolved by conducting careful and systematic thinking and analysis.

- Communications across the different layers "tiers" of a system must be well-defined and documented. This reminds me with the importance of formal documentation of software systems.

- Good design of software systems typically facilitates good testing of them before they are implemented, and that should reduce their chances to fail during their runtime cycles. In other words, this improves the mean time between the system's failures (i.e., MTBF).

- Reliability also has to do with the quality of a system's code, its structures, and organization.

- Documentation of a software system plays a crucial role in eliminating defects in that system by simply making it easy to point out the parts of the system's code that needs to be changed to fix the defects. This eventually improves the availability and reliability of systems.

Experience V

Another interesting experience had to do with a major telecom firm in Saint Louis. They required the indexing of about 12 million records of their Oracle meta-content to produce a searchable index within 10 hours. None of the commercial indexing tools that were available at that time, including the Verity ones, could satisfy their tough requirement. Their typical indexing process using Verity indexing tools took about 96 hours. The case was similar with other commercial indexing tools as the SBC staff indicated at that time. The challenge for Verity was obvious; the 96 hours of indexing time should be knocked down to 10 hours to win that deal. As a proof of concept engagement, I wrote a multiprocessing indexing tool that utilized their quad-CPU server. The following steps summarize what I did for them:

- On paper, I divided their meta-content into 20 blocks, each of about 500 thousand records.
- Twenty listeners were started on their Oracle database server, and each listener was associated with one of the above-mentioned 20 blocks.
- I wrote a short script (e.g., managing script) to trigger four instances of the indexer to start working, each on its associated block, and then sleep for a specific time.
  - o Once an indexer instance completed dumping its block, it indexed that into a distinct collection (i.e., mini searchable index).
  - o The managing script would then sleep for a specific time (i.e., 40 minutes) before it triggered the next four instances of the indexer to start their work. This wait-time was necessary to avoid congestion on the processing cycles of the four CPUs. The wait-time was determined based on a rough calculation that we made. It is important to mention that some intelligence can be employed to dynamically calculate this wait-time.
  - o Once a batch of four indexer instances were done, their produced four mini searchable collections would then be merged into a single intermediate searchable collection using the Verity merging tool.
  - o Once all five batches of the indexer instances were done (i.e., the 20 indexer instances were done), the merging tool would merge the five intermediate searchable collections into a single large one.

The solution as described above worked well. The overall indexing time of the 12 million records went from 96 hours down to 16 hours. Further tuning of the solution could have been performed to reduce that time to meet the required level of 10 hours. The above project leads me to believe that:

- Reliability of the indexing tool depends on the reliability of the indexing solution that is built around it (i.e., its wrapper).
- Reliability of the indexing tool also depends on the stability of the operating system and the database server.

In summary, the previous experiences conclude that reliability of software systems has to do with: (i) the reliability of the infrastructure, servers, and integrated components that compose these systems, and (ii) the skills and the quality of the people who developed the system.

Book Overview

This book is divided into twelve chapters. This section provides a quick overview of the subjects and content of these chapters. For details, readers will definitely need to read these chapters.

- The first chapter is entitled *"Database High Availability: An Extended Survey"*. It indicates that most of the available Electronic Services (e.g., e-services) represent database processing operations, and therefore it is important that we perform efficient and effective tuning on databases for performance improvement purposes. Reliability and availability of such e-services should be leveraged through the employment of advanced techniques such as clustering and distributed databases. In summary, this chapter is meant to present the definition, the background, and the typical measurement factors of database high availability. It also demonstrates some approaches to minimize database server's shutdown time.

- The second chapter is entitled *"Enterprise Metadata for Reliable Web Applications"*. It examines the critical task of governing the Web application environment with enterprise metadata methodologies. This chapter indicates that as organizations move to higher levels of maturity, the ability to manage and understand the entire environment is a very critical aspect of the architecture. It also indicates that successful metadata management requires a comprehensive strategy and framework which will be presented through historical, current-state, and future perspectives. This chapter defines "Metadata" as information pertaining to the Web application environment that the organization defines as critical to the business.

- The third chapter is entitled *"Architecture of an Information System for Personal Financial Planning"*. It presents a reliable application architecture and a corresponding system architecture of a system for personal financial planning. The presented application architecture is related to the business requirements and the system architecture is related to information technology. This chapter also presents an analysis model as part of the application architecture showing the granularity of an industry model. An intrinsic part of the proposed system architecture is the usage of Web technologies.

- The fourth chapter is entitled *"Approaches to Building High Performance Web Applications: A Practical Look at Availability, Reliability, and Performance"*. It introduces five practices to help build scalable, resilient Web applications. This chapter indicates that in 2004, IBM launched its expertise location system, bringing together two legacy systems and transforming the employee's ability to find and connect with their extensive network. It reviews five of the many issues that challenge enterprise Web applications: resource contention; managing transactions; application resiliency; geographic diversity; and exception perception management. It presents five key methods that mitigate these risks, achieving high-availability and high-performance goals.

- The fifth chapter is entitled *"The Demise of a Business-to-Business Portal"*. It describes the development and ultimate demise of the Bizewest portal in the Western

Region of Melbourne, Australia. This chapter indicates that no matter how good the portal software, the final success or failure of the portal is primarily related to how well it is adopted and used. It begins by discussing the concept and benefits of Web portals and especially those that are applicable to SMEs as the Bizewest portal was primarily aimed at SMEs. It describes how the portal was conceived and developed, and the difficulty that its proponents had in persuading regional SMEs to change their business processes to make best use of online trading with each other.

- The sixth chapter is entitled "*A Security Solution for Web-Services Based Grid Applications*". It introduces a Web services-based virtual organization solution, which is designed to enhance the security performance of WSGrid, which is a "Web services" based application for composing computational grids. This chapter indicates that the virtual organizations are formed by the joint of users and nodes. There is no central component in the system, and therefore every node is individual and has equal position.

- The seventh chapter is entitled "*Conceptual Model Driven Software Development (CMDSD) as a Catalyst Methodology for Building Sound Semantic Web Frameworks*". It introduces Hyper-services as a unified application model for semantic Web frameworks and proposes Conceptual Model-Driven Software Development as a means of easy adoption to them. This chapter indicates that hyper-services are based on agent societies, provided with structured information by the Semantic Web, and using Web services as a collaboration and communication interface, and that afterwards the WASP model is proposed as a framework for implementing Hyper-services. It separates the conceptual aspects from the technical details by automatically generating executable code from models while the implementation details are hidden to the end user, the service developer.

- The eighth chapter is entitled "*Automatic Replication for Web Applications*". It proposes a software architecture to enhance the availability of Web-based applications at a reasonable cost. It indicates that the architecture is pluggable to existing Web applications, and therefore no modifications are required to existing code. This chapter also indicates that availability is achieved by replication, and strong replica consistency is automatically guaranteed by using off-the-shelf group communication components. The most distinctive feature of the proposed architecture is that it explicitly addresses replica consistency, providing automatic strong replica consistency.

- The ninth chapter is entitled "*A Scalable QoS-Aware Web Services Management Architecture (QoSMA)*". It proposes a scalable QoS-aware architecture for the management of QoS-aware Web services to provide QoS management support for both Web services' providers and consumers. This chapter indicates that the proposed architecture is based on the commonly-used notion of QoS brokerage service that mediates between service requestors and service providers. Its responsibilities include performance monitoring of Web services, supporting users in Web services selection based on their QoS requirements, and the negotiation of QoS issues between requestors and providers. This chapter indicates that the proposed architecture provides several benefits, including the automation of QoS management and QoS monitoring for both providers and clients, allowing for better handling of the increasing demand while maintaining the pre-agreed-on QoS between service requestors and providers through the scalability of the architecture.

- The tenth chapter is entitled *"Information System Development Failure and Complexity: A Case Study"*. It examines the causes of failure in a Web-based information system development project and finds out how complexity can lead a project towards failure. This chapter indicates that learning from an Information System Development Project (ISDP) failure plays a key role in the long-term success of any organization desirous of continuous improvement via evaluation and monitoring of its information systems (IS) development efforts.

- The eleventh chapter is entitled *"SLA Monitoring of Presence-Enabled Services: A New Approach Using Data Envelopment Analysis (DEA)"*. It indicates that the concept of presence was initially associated with instant messaging service allowing an end user to recognize the presence of a peer online to send or receive messages, and that now the technology has grown to include various services like monitoring performance of any type of end user device and services that are accessible from anywhere, any time. IT indicates also that the need for enhanced value remains the driving force behind these services such as the Voice over Internet Protocol (VoIP) ones. It adds that monitoring service level parameters happens to be one of the most interesting application-oriented research issues because various service consumers at the customer companies/end users level are finding it very difficult to design and monitor an effective SLA (Service Level Agreement) with the presence-enabled service providers.

- The twelfth chapter is entitled *"All-Optical Internet: Next-Generation Network Infrastructure for E-Service Applications"*. It indicates that to exploit the unprecedented opportunities offered by the e-service applications, businesses and users alike would need a highly available, reliable, and efficient telecommunication infrastructure. This chapter provides an insight into building the next-generation network infrastructure, the All-Optical Internet. It discusses the dominant optical networks architectures in an attempt to show the evolution towards the ultimate all-optical packet-switching network.

Targeted Audience and Remarks

This book would be beneficial to IT practitioners, professionals, and professors. Also, it would be beneficial to IT graduate students.

Last, but not least, it is my personal honor to invite you to read through the 13 chapters which comprise this book. Should you have any questions or concerns, please do not hesitate to contact me at Radaideh@acm.org.

Dr. Moh'd A. Radaideh

Advisor/IT Expert, Office of the HR General Director

Human Resources General Directorate

Abu Dhabi Police GHQ – Ministry of Interior

United Arab Emirates

Email: Radaideh@uaeu.ac.ae Web: http://www.rad4me.com

Acknowledgments

Dr. Moh'd A. Radaideh would like to express his sincere thanks to His Highness, Sheikh Saif Bin Zayed Al-Nahayan, Minister of Interior in the United Arab Emirates, and His Excellency, Brigadier Mohd Bin Alawadi, the ADP HR General Director, for their ongoing help and moral support. He also would like to express his sincere appreciation to his beloved wife, Rawiah Radaideh, and beloved sons, Sa'eb, Ahmed, Saleh, Khaled, and Abdulkareem, and beloved daughters, Haneen and Ro'yah, for their patience, unlimited moral support, and understanding during these long years while being taken away from them.

Hayder Al-Ameed would like to express his sincere appreciation to his family for their ongoing encouragement and moral support, and for the understanding and patience which they have shown during the period of preparation.

Both authors wish to thank the colleagues who contributed to this book, and wish to express their sincere apologies to those colleagues of the chapters that could not make it through the evaluation process.

Both authors gratefully appreciate the help received from the following colleagues (in alphabetical order by first name) who participated in the evaluation process of the submitted chapters: Abdulrahman AlAli, Bernhard Ostheimer, Erdogan Dogdu, Fernando Diaz, Hong Lin, Jana Polgar, Joao M. Fernandes, John Goh, Jorge Carlos Marx Gómez, Michael Knapp, Mohamed Rousan, Paul Witman, Peter Fettke, Ricardo J. Machado, Theo Thiadens, and Yih-Jiun Lee.

Last, but not least, both authors would like to thank the support received from Idea Publishing Group of Hershey, PA, particularly Ms. Kristin Roth, during the course of developing this scholarly book.

Moh'd A. Radaideh
Hayder Al-Ameed

Chapter I

Database High Availability:
An Extended Survey

Moh'd A. Radaideh, Abu Dhabi Police – Ministry of Interior,
United Arab Emirates

Hayder Al-Ameed, United Arab Emirates University, United Arab Emirates

Abstract

With the advancement of computer technologies and the World Wide Web, there has been an explosion in the amount of available e-services, most of which represent database processing. Efficient and effective database performance tuning and high availability techniques should be employed to insure that all e-services remain reliable and available all times. To avoid the impacts of database downtime, many corporations have taken interest in database availability. The goal for some is to have continuous availability such that a database server never fails. Other companies require their content to be highly availabile. In such cases, short and planned downtimes would be allowed for maintenance purposes. This chapter is meant to present the definition, the background, and the typical measurement factors of high availability. It also demonstrates some approaches to minimize a database server's shutdown time.

Introduction

High availability of software systems has become very critical due to several factors that are related to the environment, processes and development strategies, hardware complexity, and the amount of dollars and human resources invested in the system. High availability cannot be achieved by just implementing a given service level or solution. Systems should be designed such that all factors that may lead the system to go down should be well-treated, if not eliminated.

In today's competitive business landscape, 24/7 operations become the standard, especially for the e-services-driven areas (e.g., e-commerce, e-government, e-learning, etc.) Downtime of applications, systems, or networks typically translates into significant revenue loss. Industry experts and analysts agreed on that in order to support e-service applications, typical network availability must reach 99.999%. In other words, networks must be at the "5-Nines" availability level (Providing Open Architecture, 2001). Reaching this level of availability requires careful planning and comprehensive end–to-end strategy. To demonstrate the impact of not being at the "5-Nines" availability level, a system with 97% availability will incur approximately 263 hours (6.6 days) of downtime per year. With 99 percent availability, downtime will be 88 hours (2.2 days) per year. Table 1 summarizes the impact of service downtime according to the availability ratings.

High Availability is not achieved through a single product or process. It is the result of an end-to-end analysis and reengineering of the entire service chain including the combination of people, processes, and technological factors (Otey & Otey, 2005). Every device or circuit in the path between client and server is a link in this service chain, and each must be considered separately. A chain is only as strong as its weakest link. As more applications are delivered via Web browsers, the emphasis for high availability is spreading from back-

Table 1. Downtime measurements at various availability rates

Availability Percentage	Downtime Percentage	Service Downtime (Minutes/Year)
95%	5%	50000
97%	3%	15840
98%	2%	10512
99%	1%	3168
99.5%	0.5%	2640
99.8%	0.2%	1050
99.9%	0.1%	528
99.95%	0.05%	240
99.99%	0.01%	53
99.999%	0.001%	5
99.9999%	0.0001%	0.51
99.99999%	0.00001%	0.054

end databases toward front-end and middleware devices like Web servers and firewalls. Database management systems (DBMS) play a pivotal role in much of today's business computing environment, underpinning electronic services operations, providing critical business support through data warehousing and mining, and managing the storage and processing of much of the world's financial data. As they are entrusted with the storage and processing of such critical data, one would assume that databases are designed to be reliable and highly available.

This chapter provides an overview of the high availability in general, and describes the business drivers behind it, or how it is measured. It focuses on the meaning of database high availability, its functionality and design strategies that emerge with the shift from technology-centric orientation of keeping the system running, to a more customer-centric focus on ultra-dependable services. The view of high availability provided in this chapter has no bias towards high availability practices offered today by the different DBMS vendors.

This chapter is organized into seven sections. The first section provides a generic introduction on the chapter's subject. The second section overviews the high availability-related issues. The third section discusses the model environment for highly-available systems. The fourth section discusses several strategies for database high availability. The fifth section discusses performance impact of high availability. The sixth section overviews several high availability solutions. The seventh section overviews a simple availability-benchmarking methodology.

High Availability Overview

A system is composed of a collection of interacting components. A system provides one or more services to its consumers. A service is the output of a system that meets the specification for which the system was devised, or agrees with what system users have perceived as the correct output values.

Service failures are incorrect results with respect to the specification or unexpected behavior perceived by the users of the service. The cause of a failure is said to be a fault. Faults are identified or detected in some manner, either by the system or by its users. Finally, an error is a discrepancy between the displayed output (e.g., computed, measured, or observed value or condition) and the correct or specified value or condition. Errors are often the result of exceptional conditions or unexpected interference. If an error occurs, then a failure of some form has occurred. Similarly, if a failure occurs, then an error of some form will occur. It is important to detect not only active faults, but also the latent faults. Finding and removing these faults before they become active leads to less downtime and higher availability. Availability is defined as the readiness for usage. The continuation of service, in the absence of failure, is called reliability. The nonoccurrence of catastrophic consequences or injury to the environment or its users is called safety.

Businesses have crossed geographical, cultural, and political boundaries in today's world. Information is the key for survival in the highly competitive global business environment. High availability of information requires information technology resources to be available round the clock, seven days a week, 365 days a year. Availability is generally understood as the percentage of the time a system is up and running.

Once the terms that describe availability are understood, it is then necessary to understand the various availability paradigms and solutions. Solutions include data redundancy, system failover, and network redundancy. These solutions can be combined to provide a highly available system that provides the necessary level of service to the users of the system. The paradigms involve the ways that these solutions are combined.

Achieving 5-Nines Availability

The 99.999% (5-Nines) availability standard specifies 24/7 service with a maximum of five minutes of downtime in a year. Generally, service availability depends heavily on the fault tolerance of the system, including hardware redundancy (Klein, 1988). The software components of the system use the redundant hardware to enable the service and application availability. 5-Nine implementations have its foundation in the set of principles. Some of these principles are related only to hardware, while other principles are related to software system components. The following list of issues focuses on providing the service high availability (Parikh, 2004):

- **Mitigation of risks:** Risk mitigation depends on monitoring (real-time and historical) trends, rules, and models to predict the occurrence of failures and to prevent them. Common risk mitigation techniques are:
  - o **Fault avoidance:** use of processes and tools to minimize the introduction of faults;
  - o **Fault minimization:** In spite of efforts to prevent or eliminate them, there will be faults in any system. Proper risk assessment and fault minimization can ensure uptime; and
  - o **Fault recognition and removal:** Monitoring and recognition can actively locate faults and assist with remediation of their root cause.
- **Resiliency:** the capability of a system to prevent degradation or failure as well minimize the damage or loss from a failure or malfunction; resiliency is affected by quality, design and stability
- **Redundancy:** the use of multiple redundant critical components, such as CPUs, network cards, electrical transmission, power supplies, disk drives, switches, routers, cooling systems, and other equipment used to support operations; redundancy is not limited to hardware, it can also include mirrored applications or databases, setup, and configuration files.
- **Inclusion:** including high availability through the entire application stack, including the client, middleware, and hardware

- **Serviceability:** the ability of the service to detect and rapidly correct problems and reconfigure itself online

- **Manageability:** the ease and ability to evaluate and tune for maintenance and availability, to identify critical resources, traffic patterns, and performance levels, and to configure business-critical applications

- **Methods and skills:** To achieve a 5-Nines environment, the administration, monitoring, and control of the high availability IT environment must be simple. Otherwise, installation issues, upgrades, human error, and customization will affect the system's availability. Because user error is a growing cause of outages, it needs to apply techniques to reduce the chance of user/administrator error.

- **Scalability:** Scalability of the system, network database, and applications is the key to availability. An available, well-defined, and properly-configured scalable platform is one that has enough capacity to handle the estimated or measured application's workload, with no bottleneck in the hardware. For software division, achieving the goal of scalability and therefore dependability and availability requires effort at all phases of development: design time, implementation time, execution time, and during maintenance.

- **System architecture:** Poor planning architecture or operational support can foster poor performance, impeded functionality, high cost of ownership, complex administration, lack of capacity and scalability, and poor reliability and availability. A properly developed system, on the other hand, is one that is of high quality, high performance, and high availability with a capacity for growth. Proper database system architecture requires understanding the business requirements. The points that should be considered in planning the architecture of any system might be the storage and I/O subsystem, ability to support growth, well-defined use and capacity planning, elimination of data redundancy, elimination of process redundancy, implementation and integration planning, and administration automation.

Maintaining Uptime and Availability

Uptime refers to the ability of conducting business in the event of partial system failure or unexpected demand. Organizations can prioritize, modularize, and segregate their business functions, provide redundancies, and establish processes to turn on or off pieces of their system and still continue to function. Availability is a measure of the ability of clients to connect with and use a resource at any point in time.

Carrier-class Information Technology (IT) infrastructures are the new standard for high-availability, zero-downtime, computing enterprises that serve a global customer base on 24/7/365 basis (Barraza, 2002). As the world becomes more wired and huge new global Web services become available, there will be no alternative to carrier-class services (Lemme & Colby, 2001). The impact of any downtime will simply become too traumatic for companies to opt for anything less than the most reliable quality service available. In order to improve the provided service uptime and availability, a set of maintaining issues should be taken into consideration:

- **Data protection:** Any data critical to business needs to be protected; backups are the easiest way to protect such data. Even with frequent backups, it should still employ data protection safeguards through the use of hardware, replication, or software to bridge backup periods.

- **Disaster recovery:** The capability to recover from natural disasters, such as fires, floods, earthquakes, or tornados, is as important as being able to recover from a hardware or software failure. Results of these disasters usually include physical damage or complete loss of systems, data, and even workplaces. Recovery time is directly related to how much upfront planning occurred and what procedures were established to restore the business locally. The impact and likelihood of a disaster and its cost to the business must be weighed against the cost of preventing the damage that results from such a disaster.

- **Application protection and recovery:** Web servers are an excellent example of why application recoverability is a critical issue. Most companies with e-commerce servers cannot afford the business impact of unplanned downtime. Companies should give careful consideration to the design and use of an application in a high availability situation, with the primary goal being to insulate the users from outages or system failures. Methods include employing client reconnect to an alternative server if a connection is lost, using error-handling, automating tasks, and setting up recoverable transactions.

- **Network management:** The network has become so ubiquitous in the computing environment. Proper network architecture, planning, maintenance, and monitoring are just as important as with any other system components or applications.

- **System management monitoring and measurement:** Database administrators often overlook the planning and selection of the architecture, procedure, and system-management processes. A vast majority of installations occur on an existing platform because of available space. Then, after the application is in production, performance and administration problems appear. To combat this cycle, systems must be properly planned, architected, and refined through a set of methods and processes. It is not enough to slap in a set of monitoring tools and expect them to take care of all deficiencies. True system management involves monitoring, measuring, altering, and reporting on the levels of availability, performance, and service. System-management tools can also provide real-time business applications for the many operational components. System management usually begins with taking measurements, setting baselines for uptime, and establishing performance metrics.

- **Automating processes:** Human errors are the leading cause of downtime; any effort to reduce human interaction with the system will reduce the risk of human errors. In order to eliminate downtime, tools should be employed to perform the systems' automation, control, or monitoring. Risk reducing might be implemented through the use of automation in the several areas like backups and recovery, upgrades, operations and administration, maintenance, usage, security, and control.

- **Training and support:** Training and support are critical to sustain and maintain availability. With technology and product updates, personnel must be able to quickly judge which features and upgrades map to existing business requirements. Annual training as well as participation in user groups can help users keep abreast of issues, features, and technologies.

- **Standards and documentation:** The written standards and procedures should provide the foundation for implementation. Without consistent standards and procedures, a project will decline into an indecipherable hodgepodge of unsupportable variations and techniques. Documentation is also important for employees new to the department or database. Standards, procedures, and documentation for the 5-Nines environment should include the following (Lemme, 2002):

  - o **Operating system (OS) standards and procedures:** These include file system layouts, kernel parameters, system backup/recovery, security, performance monitoring, installation, and upgrades of the operating system.

  - o **Database standards and procedures:** These include instance parameters, object sizing, storage and naming conventions, procedures for installation and upgrades, security guidelines, and backup/recover plans.

  - o **Application development standards:** These include techniques for managing change procedures, detailed coding standards including source code control, change control, naming conventions, and table/index creating.

  - o **Network standards and procedures:** These define network addressing and protocols supported for database and application communication.

High Availability (Reliability, Redundancy, and Service Availability)

Convergence of data communication, electronic, and Web services technologies has created demand for ever-increasing levels of availability. The 5-Nines (99.999%) system availability is no longer enough. Now network users, for instance, are demanding and expecting continuous delivery of voice, data, and multimedia services: They want always-on services and connections that are maintained without disruption regardless of any internal system faults or failures. A Service Availability solution is a customer-centric approach to meeting these demands (Service Availability, 2000).

Conceptualizing and design for availability have been technology-centric: Providing robust hardware, adding redundancy in case of failure, and improving switchover techniques to backup components have produced the current generation of high-availability strategies. These strategies provide higher levels of system uptime, but the service availability approach requires this and more. Undisrupted service means preserving application data and state across switchover scenarios. It requires aggressive optimization and integration of all system resources, and it requires a global perspective focused on the end-user experience of continuous service.

In the subsequent paragraphs, a discussion of the detailed meaning of reliability, redundancy, high and service availability are illustrated: in addition, the three switchover modes are mentioned, with the abstracted differences between them.

- **Reliability—Designing with integrity (hardware orientation):** Reliability is a measure of how dependable a system is once it is actually put into use (not breaking down). Designing for reliability aims at fault prevention. In designing for availability, it is predicted that components will fail, and systems are designed to mask and recover from the failure of individual resources. Originally, the reliability strategy was, first build great hardware that does not break down, and then, to be completely covered, supply a backup system just in case. Reliability, while effective for hardware, is not enough when complex software is also involved. Software is inherently less reliable, as every possible configuration of use and data cannot be tested prior to release; therefore, software glitches are often revealed only when the software is actually put into use. As systems become more and more software-driven, fault prevention has become an unrealizable standard, now replaced by fault management. The notion of reliability has had to be reconsidered in system design.

- **Redundancy—Replacement parts (component orientation):** Building with redundancy addresses potential failures by establishing a backup system for critical components. Full 2N redundancy is the duplication of components such that each active component has its own backup. It is the simplest redundancy configuration to manage, since processes can be mirrored on the redundant standby system for total system failover, if needed. But full redundancy is often prohibitively expensive, unnecessary, and impractical for complex systems (High Availability and More, 2001). Utilizing redundancy in complex systems requires dynamic system reconfiguration in order for the system to remain available. When redundancy is designed into a system, the system downtime is a factor of the frequency of failures multiplied by the time required to switchover to a standby component. Standby redundant components in the

Table 2. The main differences between the three switchover modes

Switchover mode	Technique Used	Recovery time	Maintain transaction state	Notes
Cold Switchover	Initialization of the standby component upon switchover	Slowest	NO	Conserves power and resources
Warm Switchover	Data can be saved to the standby component, but the application needs to be configured at the time of switchover, adding restart time to the switchover process.	Slow	NO	Cannot support uninterrupted connections during switchover
Hot Switchover	Application and transaction state data must be continuously checkpointed to the standby device, faults must be quickly detected and the system must be reconfigured	Fastest	YES	Complex to implement

2N design can be configured in one of the following three switchover modes. Table 2 summarizes the main features for the three switchover modes.

o   **Cold switchover:** This mode requires initialization of the standby component upon switchover. Of the three, this mode has the slowest recovery time, and it cannot maintain transaction state; however, it does conserve power and resources.

o   **Warm switchover:** Data can be saved to the standby component, but the application needs to be configured at the time of switchover, adding restart time to the switchover process. This mode cannot support uninterrupted connections during switchover (if an application has to be rebooted when a server fails, transactions in process at the time of the failure are lost).

o   **Hot switchover:** This mode has the fastest recovery time, but it is the most complex to implement: Application and transaction state data must be continuously checkpointed to the standby device, faults must be quickly detected, and the system must be reconfigured. Hot switchover redundancy designs support the higher levels of availability, but simply having redundancy obviously does not produce system availability; it is the management of hardware, software, and data redundancy; the management of faults; and the management of system reconfiguration that yields availability.

•   **High availability (system orientation):** Internet-based services and businesses need always-on availability. In availability management, hardware or software faults are unavoidable, and the system is designed to anticipate and work around faults before they become system failures. Thus, instead of counting on the hardware to avoid faults, availability and especially the high availability design relies heavily on management software to mask and manage faults that are expected to occur (Service Availability, 2000). Fault management takes practical precedence over designing for fault avoidance; the goal is to anticipate faults and execute fault recovery as quickly as possible. In the race towards ever greater levels of system availability, providing the quickest possible recovery times becomes the key. Availability management software must execute the fastest possible switchover to redundant resources and immediate reconfiguration of the system. In addition, 5-Nines levels of system availability cannot tolerate downtime for upgrading or maintenance. High availability management must be able to handle hardware and software upgrades without taking the system out of service. These requirements all are necessary to providing system availability, but they do not fully account for the needs of customers using the systems.

•   **Service availability—Customer-centric focus (service orientation):** The emergence of the Service Availability model as a driving concept in system design represents a shift from a technology-centric orientation to a customer-centric one. A service availability solution includes providing high availability at the level of 5-Nines or better, but it adds the requirement of service continuity, maintaining the integrity of customer connections and transactions without interruption despite any hardware or software failures in the infrastructure. Neither scheduled maintenance nor unexpected failure ought to prevent or disrupt provision of service to a customer. A service availability solution requires that a system be highly available and provide continuity of service. A system configured with redundant components that fail can switchover to the standby components without ultimately jeopardizing the metrics of reliability or availability, even though connections might be dropped or data lost or degraded. Thus, a service availability solution carries the caveat that, during switchover scenarios, customer data and application state must be preserved in order to provide continuity of service to the end-user. Service availability design requires a perspective that can account for and coordinate resources and technologies throughout the system. It requires real-time checkpointing of current data to hot standby resources and rapid, seamless switchover in case of active resource failure. Because the continuity of service ultimately depends on the resources and the functioning of the system as a whole, service availability management requires an integrated, total-system approach.

High Availability Environment

To understand availability, we first need to understand reliability. The reliability of an element is the conditional probability that the element will operate during a specified period of time. A system may be considered highly *reliable* (that is, it may fail very infrequently), but, if it is out of service for a significant period of time as a result of a failure, it will not be considered highly *available* (Singh, 2001). As another definition, high availability is more than excellent reliability. It is achieved through high service availability, the avoidance of downtime (including all maintenance downtime), and extreme data integrity, with no loss of stored data under any circumstances *(High Availability White Paper,* 2001).

Availability, usually measured on an annual basis, refers to the percentage of time which service is available to the users (Sauers, 1996). This covers mission-critical applications, e-mail, scheduling services, and other business solutions used by organizations and companies for their day-to-day operations.

There are two factors that determine system availability. The first factor is the reliability of the individual components that comprise the system. These components include server hardware, the server operating system, and the application itself. Other components may include data storage devices, network access devices, databases, file systems, and the data center infrastructure. The second factor is the time it takes for the application to be restored once a failure has occurred. The amount of time it takes to bring an application online again is dependent on the component that failed. If the application itself has failed, all that may be required for recovery is to simply restart the application (Bender & Joshi, 2004).

Levels of Availability

- **High availability:** This is a system or application designed to prevent a total loss of service by reducing or managing failures. The major goal of a highly available system is to provide a higher level of availability than a standard system. It achieves this goal by preventing Single Points of Failure (SPOF) through common hardware including CPU, disks, host adapters, network adapters, hubs, and routers.

- **Fault tolerance:** More expensive than a highly available system (by as much as five times), a fault-tolerance system contains multiple hardware components that function concurrently, duplicating all the computation incorporating redundant hardware components in a single system. However, a fault-tolerant system can fail when the system or application software fails.

- **Continuous availability:** As the name suggests, these systems are designed to provide continuous availability, which equates to non-stop service, with no planned or unplanned outages. Hardware and software failures can occur. However, the intention is to insulate the users from the failure and to reduce the time needed to recover from that failure to several minutes or less. In a continuously- available system environment, patches and upgrades can be performed with no impact on the users.

We can contrast the main difference in concept between fault tolerance and high availability. Fault tolerance provides additional resources that allow an application to continue functioning after a component failure without interruption (A Framework for System High Availability, 2000; Brown, 2000; Providing Open Architecture, 2001). Many of the high-availability solutions on the market today actually provide fault tolerance for a particular application component. Disk mirroring, where there are two disk drives with identical copies of the data, is an example of a fault-tolerant component. If one of the disk drives fails, there is another copy of the data that is instantly available for the application to continue execution. A fault-tolerant system would be used in a situation where no downtime can be tolerated at all, such as air-traffic-control systems, emergency-response systems, or financial-trading systems.

Metrics of High Availability

Availability is a function of system reliability and reparability, augmented and supported by redundancy. To quantify and identify the availability of any system, academic and industry sectors have defined two metrics that formalize the definition of a system's availability:

- **Reparability—Mean time To recover (MTTR):** Achieving high availability is also a factor of how quickly a system can be repaired when failures occur. Reparability is the measure of how quickly a failed device can be restored to service, expressed as a Mean Time To Repair (MTTR). The industry and the academic world today concentrate on finding solutions to reduce this time and to make it transparent to the users.

- **Reliability—Mean time between failures (MTBF):** Individual components have their own MTBFs. The MTBF of a system can be calculated by considering the failure rate of each component in the system. As systems have more and more components, the system MTBF will always go down. Today's industry has made significant progress in achieving very good MTBF through redundant hardware and software (e.g., clustered nodes to avoid single point of failure, application availability standpoint, etc.). Another way of expressing availability is referred to as number of Nines. This is expressed as a percentage of uninterrupted service per year and hence the downtime. A system is considered highly available when its availability is 99.9%, also called "3-Nines" (Arora, 2005; Bauer, 2001; Brien, 2000). For example, 528 minutes of system unavailability per year results in 99.9% or "3-Nines availability", and 5 minutes of system unavailability per year results in a 99.999% or "5-Nines availability". In the absence of any redundancy in the system platform, availability is given by a simple formula:

$$Availability = \frac{MTBF}{MTBF+MTTR}$$

Total Downtime in a year =
(Planned Shutdown + Unplanned Shutdown) in hours

Availability of a system =
$$\frac{(\text{Number of hours in a year}) - (\text{Total hours of downtime in a year}) \times 100}{(\text{Number of hours in a year})}$$

Achieving an acceptable level of availability in carrier-grade systems just by striving for high MTBFs and low MTTRs is generally not practical with today's technology, due to two factors. First, despite tremendous advances in the reliability of computer hardware, the system MTBFs of complex systems are too low because of the number of components they contain. This is particularly true since failures are caused by software errors as well as hardware faults. Second, most service providers are not willing to deploy a system which is subject to a multiple-hour outage while it is being repaired, regardless of how unlikely that outage may be. To attack both of these problems, high availability systems invariably contain redundant components (High Availability and More, 2001; Standards for a Service Availability, 2002).

- **Redundancy:** Redundancy augments the reparability of individual components by establishing a backup or standby for various components in the system. When there are multiple resources providing the same functionality, they can take over for one another very quickly in case of failure, driving the system MTTR toward zero. The effectiveness of redundancy is a function of how much redundancy a system contains, and how quickly backup components can be brought into service when failures occur.

Costs of Service Downtime

Uptime is usually the measurement of availability that refers to the time at which users can access the application. Downtime is the opposite of uptime; it is the amount of time that a database system or service becomes unavailable to users.

There are two ways to categorize system downtime. Some downtimes are results from a system failure and others are results from scheduled outages. Scheduled outages, such as those for repair and upgrades that have minimal impact on the business, are considered maintenance. For many applications, availability during business hours is required, but some downtime during non-business hours is acceptable. System failure outages can be caused by environmental causes such as loss of electricity, fires, floods, and earthquakes in addition to platform failures, application failures, or human errors. Although hardware failures are traditionally the major cause of downtime, software failures and user error are growing. Generally there are three types of downtime (Barraza, 2002; Kumar, 2005; Saito, Bershad, & Levy, 1999):

- **Planned downtime:** This is normal downtime that is planned and scheduled in advance. It is normally scheduled for patches, upgrades, and maintenance activities such as database reorganization, adding disk storage, performing offline backups, and installing patches, upgrades, or new application. It usually occurs during off-peak processing times such as off-hours or holidays.

- **Semi-planned downtime:** This includes software or hardware upgrades that are scheduled, but not entirely by the service provider. An example might be when a vendor releases security patches that must be applied quickly to avoid vulnerability. The schedule is largely driven by others.

- **Unplanned downtime:** Unplanned downtime is associated with unexpected events such as network, hardware, and software failures. A typical distributed application usually consists of a Web browser front-end and an application reliant upon servers, networks, and database. As a problem with any of these components can cause the application to become unavailable, all components need to be monitored equally.

Many harmful consequences may occur as a result of service downtime. The following set of instances illustrates the high impact of service downtime (Gribble, Brewer, Hellerstein, & Culler, 2000):

- **Downtime means down revenue:** When an application that runs a business is brought down by database failure, the most immediate and obvious cost is the loss of revenue. Typically, an e-commerce site may suffer losses from $10K to $100K every hour, depending on the volume of the online sales transactions. Large telesales businesses like airline reservations, catalog sales, and TV-based home shopping can easily miss sales opportunities of $100K per hour. In financial markets, losses total to millions of dollars per hour of downtime.

- **Downtime damages relationships:** Many organizations now offer Web-based applications and interfaces that provide access to databases. Some of these provide customers, in a self-service fashion, with information about their outstanding orders or account balances. Other applications give partners (e.g., suppliers and distributors) access to inventory levels and production schedules. Such applications are very valuable. Therefore, customers and partners develop dependencies and expect them to be available continuously. Database downtime thwarts these expectations, thus damaging important relationships. Customers and partners may shift their business elsewhere, perceiving downtime as a lack of dependability.

- **Downtime disrupts supply chains:** In the manufacturing sector, database downtime can hamper material management and resources planning, which, in turn, reduces yield on the production floor. Likewise, in the retail industry, database downtime halts just-in-time inventory, which depends heavily on database access. When a trade exchange suffers database downtime, it disrupts the supply chains of hundreds of companies.

- **Downtime erodes brand and share value:** For a company that operates largely online, all it takes is a well-publicized outage to tarnish the company's reputation. Once a brand is deemed unreliable, financial consequences usually follow on the perception-driven stock market, adversely affecting share price, financial evaluation, and market capital.

- **Downtime has legal repercussions:** When companies do business together online, they often strike a contract like a service-level agreement. A service outage can cost the provider dearly in fines and litigation. As protection from these legal repercussions, service providers and Web services companies need to ensure the highest availability possible for databases and applications.

Key Requirements of a Service Availability Solution

Continuous availability of voice, data, and multimedia communication services depends on each part of the multi-service networks working reliably to deliver these services without interruption. Hardware and software redundancy enables the management software to replace failed resources with the appropriate standby resources such that services remain available. Accomplishing this without downtime or loss of data and state requires a comprehensive and unified solution.

The entire availability management cycle must operate automatically, without human intervention and in real-time (High Availability and More, 2001). Information about the system must be collected and assessed in order to keep the system manageable. System resources must be represented, and their status, topology, and dependencies must be modeled and monitored. System faults must be quickly detected, diagnosed, and fixed.

Fault data must be provided to an intelligent availability-management service in order to have it to quickly and appropriately respond by initiating appropriate actions to reconfigure the status and the resources functioning. In other words, the system must be self-managing and self-reliant. Thus, implementation of a service availability solution requires management software that can:

- Collect system data in real-time
- Configure and maintain state-aware model of the total system
- Checkpoint data to redundant resources
- Detect, diagnose, and isolate faults
- Perform rapid and policy-based recovery
- Dynamically manage configuration and dependencies of all components in the system
- Provide administrative access and control

Strategies for Database Availability

There are two attributes of database availability. These are: (i) the severity of database downtime and the latency of database recovery that provide a context for understanding general categories like high availability, continuous availability, and disaster recovery; and (ii) specific strategies for database availability like maintenance, clusters, replication, and backup/restore (Russom, 2001).

Severity of Database Downtime

When it comes to database availability, continuous availability, where the database never suffers downtime, rises as the most important matter. This goes beyond the requirements of most users. Therefore many companies require their content to be of high availability in order to allow for planned downtime to maintain their databases. Planned downtime is not severe, because it is always scheduled for periods of low system activity. Even with the best-laid plans, some form of hardware or software failure is inevitable. When database availability strategy cannot recover automatically, unplanned downtime occurs; this is fairly severe, because it may require IT personnel hours to restore database operations. However, IT departments with well-designed plans can recover quickly and minimize unplanned downtime to provide a relatively high level of database availability.

Catastrophic downtime, the severest level of database downtime, occurs when hardware and facilities are damaged such that they cannot be repaired. Catastrophic events include hurricanes, tornados, flooding, earthquakes, fires, and explosions. When these destroy or damage a physical site, the strategy for disaster recovery must include a pre-prepared facility at a separate site. Ideally, the original site and the recovery site should be separated by a fair amount of geographic space. This is to ensure that both sites do not suffer downtime from the same catastrophic event. Note that multiple, geographically-dispersed data centers are not just for disaster recovery. This strategy can also ensure continuous availability when the primary data center is knocked out due to a disabling temporary event such as a rolling blackout.

Latency of Database Recovery

Latency has two meanings for database availability. The first refers to the amount of time it takes to return to full operation after a failure. Technical people sometimes use temperature as an analogy for quantifying the recovery period. For instance, clusters are hot; in that case, failover is instantaneous and seamless, whereas the time-consuming process of restoring a database from a backup tape is cold. Somewhere between these extremes, replication technologies are considered warm.

The second meaning of latency is how up-to-date the database meta-content is after the failure, as compared to before. For example, when a database is corrupted at noon, and is restored from a backup from the previous midnight, twelve hours of inserts and updates are lost. Likewise, with asynchronous forms of replication, the standby database may be a few minutes behind the primary one, simply because it takes time to collect and communicate data over a network.

Strategies for Database Availability

Online and Offline Maintenance

Maintenance is the main factor to determine the database availability. For instance, most planned downtime is devoted to database maintenance or reconfiguration. Although planned, bringing down the database for maintenance is, nonetheless, a downtime that cannot help but impact someone in businesses that operate 24x7. Furthermore, many database administrators and IT managers confess that maintenance tasks sometimes go awry, thus extending planned downtime into unplanned downtime.

For these reasons, modern database administrators insist on performing maintenance operations online whenever possible. With some databases, it is now possible to execute online backups, table reorganization, reindexing, fault isolation, and so forth. This reduces planned downtime, as well as the probability of that it may extend into unplanned downtime (Lumpkin, 2004). Furthermore, online maintenance enables database administrators to lightly adapt to change, without waiting for a window of planned downtime.

Related to maintenance is the issue of configuration. In the early days of database management systems, the smallest change of data structure or operating environment required the database administrator to halt the database and restart it with new parameters. That is unthinkable in today's fast changing business environment. Restart is a form of downtime. Therefore, a database that supports dynamic reconfiguration is an important and integral component of any high availability strategy.

High Availability Clusters

Hardware clusters with database servers are the preferred strategy for achieving the shortest period for recovery after a hardware or database failure. A cluster typically has two or more nodes with a database server active on each to create a hot standby capability (Low Cost High Availability, 2004). If a database server fails, another can take its load instantaneously, assuring continuous availability to client applications.

Although the hot standby capability of a high availability cluster provides the least latent path to recovery, clustering has serious geographic limitations. Communication between nodes usually takes place via some form of Small Computer System Interface (SCSI(or other protocol that is not suited to Wide Area Network (WAN) or Internet communications. Therefore, nodes of a cluster must sit in close proximity, usually in the same data center. This works well until an event makes the data center unusable, whether temporarily or on a longer term. Thus, a cluster must be complemented by another database availability strategy that involves multiple and geographically-dispersed data centers to ensure continuity when the primary cluster fails.

Warm Standby Replication and Switching

Replication is a software strategy for duplicating data from a primary database to a standby. Warm standby replication means that the standby is kept online and fully operational such that it can take over immediately and automatically when the primary database fails. To keep the two databases synchronized, transactions are replicated on a continuous or scheduled basis. The two databases run on separate servers, writing to separate disk devices. Therefore, a failure on one leaves the other unaffected.

On the upside, failover is fairly immediate because the replicated warm standby database is always online. The servers for the primary and standby databases can be physically located in different geographies communicating via WAN; thus losing one site brings down only one server. The replication process does not affect application performance because it executes asynchronously after a transaction is committed. Replication software can operate in tandem with clustered and/or fault-tolerant hardware achieving higher levels of availability.

On the downside, however, the warm standby database tends to be latent because it takes time to communicate data additions and changes. During peak times, the load on the primary server may starve the replication process, causing the standby to be several minutes behind.

Although warm standby replication is excellent for automatic database server failover, it is of no help with client failover. In general, client applications must restart to connect to the new server after failover. To get around this limitation, warm standby replication can be complemented with a switching mechanism, which ensures that clients do not need to reconnect in the event of a failover. With switching technologies, automatic client failover is transparent to most end-users who see only a slight delay while the switch is made.

In short, warm standby replication (combined with switching) approaches the low data latency, and seamless server and client failover of a cluster. However its geographic flexibility makes warm standby replication ideal for disaster recovery after the catastrophic loss of a data center.

Cold Standby

As a low-end strategy for database availability, many companies depend on backup and restore. After all, the utility programs that come with a database management system as well as assistant tools have reached a mature stage where they are feature-rich, robust, and fast. Plus, the best practices for backup and restore are easy to grasp and straightforward to implement.

But there is a catch. It takes time to restore a database after a failure or corruption. The restore process could last for hours, while end-users sit idle. Hence, with a backup and restore strategy, there is considerable latency, as well as latency in the sense of a delta between the content of the backup and the primary database at the moment of failure (Disaster

Recovery Package, 2004). The latency of backup and restore can be reduced considerably by implementing a so-called cold standby which simply extends the backup process by an extra step that restores backups to a standby database server. Since the standby database is cold, it takes a few minutes to bring it online, but this is a fraction of the latency of a restore process. If the scenario periodically sends transaction logs from the primary to the standby, it will serve to reduce the latency of database content. Hence, a cold standby extends tried-and-true backup-and-restore procedures to achieve database high availability with a level of data loss that is acceptable for lower-valued transactions.

Performance Impact on Availability

Downtime is not the only concern when dealing with high availability. Most large applications encounter diverse processing needs. On one hand, the online users require good response time from many short transactions. On the other hand, large batch jobs (e.g., reports and complex extracts) expect high throughput of a handful of very large transactions. These conflicting needs cause response time to fluctuate, decreasing the reliability and availability of the application. This is especially a concern with applications that provide services directly to end users and consumers such as in e-commerce applications.

Redundancy is the Key to Availability

The logical solution for increased availability is to maintain the data in more than one place. Coincidentally, one of the best solutions for improving the application response time is to separate the batch reporting and extract processing from the Online Transaction Processing (OLTP). This solution also requires a redundant database. This means that owners of large critical applications are seeking a solution that provides both high availability and the ability to offload non-critical processing from the main system (Aronoff, 2003).

The criteria for a comprehensive high availability and high performance solution include existence of a full copy of the primary database, which should be accessible even when there is no emergency, mainly for reporting and extracts. Furthermore, the copy of the database should be an up-to-date image of the primary database. When a disaster occurs, the copy should be capable of becoming the primary database (failover). After the disaster, the solution should take into account the switch back to the primary system. Certainly, failover practice to the secondary database should be very fast, and no data should be lost during the process.

Range of Common Solutions

There is a wide range of solutions to the high availability problem. The most common approaches are (Aronoff, 2003):

- **Local disk mirroring:** This approach provides protection against many disk-related failures, but the mirror is usually not breakable under normal circumstances. Once broken, the mirror becomes stale relative to the copy that is still operational. To re-synchronize, many disk mirror solutions perform a complete copy of the data from the operational copy to the stale copy. If the database is large, this process can take a long time. Such an approach does not provide a resolution for a local disaster. It also does not provide protection against physical block corruption or accidental loss of data due to a database administrator's (DBA) error.

- **Remote disk mirroring:** Remote disk mirroring provides the protection of disk mirroring, but to a remote location. Remote disk mirroring comes in two flavors: *synchronous* and *asynchronous*. With asynchronous mirroring, the primary system does not wait for the data to be committed to the remote disk. With synchronous mirroring, the application waits for the data to be committed to both the local and the remote disk. In asynchronous mirroring, when a switchover is required, the DBA will not be able to open the remote database. For this reason, most remote mirroring implementations use the synchronous method. However, with this method, a wide bandwidth is needed between the source and destination. Otherwise, the network will slow the primary system.

- **Standby databases:** This solution provides some protection against a catastrophe that makes the primary database unavailable. This solution has some shortcomings. The copy is only as current as to when the last log was applied. Once the database is opened and modified, a complete image is required to reconstruct the standby database. Additionally, there is some administration required for the standby database as the structure of the source database changes, such as adding data files or auto-extending table spaces. Also, the standby database does not provide protection against certain types of database block corruption.

- **Local clustering:** Local clustering is a hardware solution that enables multiple computers to share a set of disks. Applications on these computers are written such that they can freely migrate between the machines in the clusters using a technology known as *floating IP addresses*. This approach provides good protection against most common failures. However, since there is only one copy of the database, there should still be consideration for protection of the disks. Moreover, since there is only one copy of the database, any physical block corruption or accidental dropping of a database object will cause the application to fail.

- **Replication:** Replication provides the ability to have a live remote database that can be used both to reduce the workload of the primary system and for failover when a disaster happens. The live database on the remote site does require database administration, and application of patches to the application is not straightforward.

- **Local clustering with oracle parallel server:** Database Parallel Servers offers another alternative for high availability systems. Using this facility, many instances of database running on different hardware can access the same database on shared disks. This does permit the hardware that would be allocated for a standby system to be actively used in production.

The difficulty in using such approach for highly available solutions is that the application needs to be designed such that transferring blocks between instances (pinging) is minimized. If not, application performance can be severely degraded. Also, there is only one copy of the database that is not protected from disk failures, block corruption, or human errors such as accidental table drop.

Database Availability Solutions
Available from DBMS Vendors

The explosive growth in e-services and other Internet-based applications, along with the increased demand for 24/7/365 global operations, has placed a greater emphasis on the need for continuous data and system availability. There are two main hardware concerns with respect to maintaining a highly available database environment: *server high availability* and *storage availability* (Arora, 2005). High availability of the database tier is achieved by the implementation of clustering. Operating system vendors and database vendors have devised their own methods to implement clustering for the database server.

As many of today's enterprise applications rely on commercial databases, this section is intended to demonstrate and review the current best practice regarding their design and configuration. Although there are many similarities between database products, we base our discussion on the different practices offered by today's database management systems.

The primary technological consideration in a database high-availability environment is protection against server failure. Server failure can be defined as an unplanned event that causes the server system to be inaccessible by users (Otey & Otey, 2005). A number of different factors can cause server failure due to both hardware and software causes including:

- Hardware failure (CPU, RAM, storage, I/O, or power supply)
- Operating system or device driver failure
- Database server failure

The protection approach against hardware failure is to invest in a hardware platform that provides redundancy of key components. Whilst for the software side, this is done by keeping operating system, device drivers, and application software up-to-date with the most recent service packs (DB2 Operation, 2000).

Regarding the highly available database platforms, the technological advantages of clustering technologies, database replication, and database log mirroring are the main implementation issues towards protection against database server failure. Clustering essentially uses multiple servers in an environment where one or more backup servers can seamlessly take over the workloads of a failed primary server. This section will examine each of these alternatives and discuss how they are implemented by each of the enterprise database products.

Database Clustering

With database clustering, each physical server in the cluster is called a *node*. The entire group of nodes work together to form a *cluster*. These clustering nodes can be viewed as a single node/server. The showcasing of a single server instead of multiple clustered nodes is accomplished by sharing common resources. These resources can be disk storage, Internet Protocol)IP(addresses, and application instances. All of the nodes in a cluster are in a state of constant communication. If one of the nodes in a cluster becomes unavailable, another node will automatically assume its duties and begin providing users with the same services as the failed node. Typically, each node will have active resources simultaneously. In such cases, synchronization among database content and transactions is an important aspect. This is accomplished by means of the database replication feature. In the event that one of the nodes is failing, the other node will immediately take over active ownership of all the resources from the other node. This process is called *failover*.

Each node in a cluster needs to keep other nodes in that cluster informed of its health and configuration. This is done periodically by broadcasting a network message, called a *heartbeat*, across a network. The heartbeat signal is usually sent over a private network (e.g., the cluster interconnect), which is used for inter-node communications (Chandrasekaran & Kehoe, 2003).

The failover process for a database cluster should require a short interval of a few seconds to complete, depending on the hardware employed. In addition, the database on the failover node must be recovered to maintain transactional consistency. The length of this recovery period depends largely on the level of database activity that was occurring at the time of failover and the type of hardware used. Clients connected to the failed node are disconnected. When they attempt to reconnect, they are able to access the cluster resources on the backup node. Different database clustering solutions might offer the following advantages:

- **Automatic failover:** When a failure is detected, the cluster automatically switches from the primary node to the secondary node.

- **Transparent to clients:** After the failover is complete, clients can reconnect to the cluster using the same virtual name and/or IP address.

- **Transactional integrity:** All committed transactions are saved and made available after the failover process completes.

- **Rapid failover:** The failover process for the system can be completed in a few seconds. The subsequent database availability depends on the number of transactions that need to be rolled forward or rolled back.

Recently, most commercial database management system providers have started to address cluster architectures using numerous approaches. While other providers use solutions offered by third-party companies with limited support for scalability and high availability (Cecchet, Marguerite, & Zwaenepoel, 2004).

Database clusters are designed to support additional nodes, with two primary architectures (Tendulkar, 2005). These are the Shared Storage (usually called *Shared-Disk*) and the Shared None (usually called *Shared-Nothing*).

Although, there have been many papers written on the features obtained by these two database architectures, it still seems to be confusing. It is important to understand both the concepts and the different acquired features by implementing each approach, especially in the database high availability area of deployment. The following paragraphs illustrate the main issues regarding shared-disk and federated databases as a step towards shared-nothing database clusters.

•   **Shared-disk cluster database architecture:** The shared storage type of architecture stores the entire database on storage disks that can be directly accessed by each node. This model has typically been the best for scaling the database to handle a large

Figure 1. Basic database clustering structure

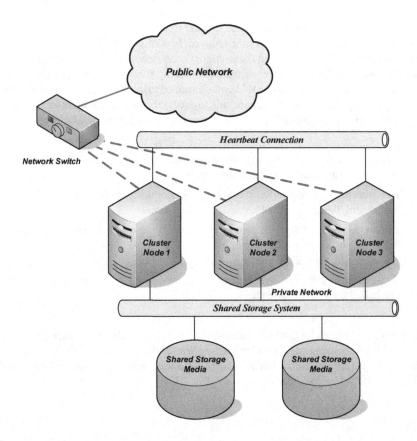

number of concurrent clients, especially in an Online Transaction Processing (OLTP) environment. Transactions running on any instance can directly read or modify any part of the database. Such systems require the use of internode communication to synchronize update activities performed from multiple nodes. When two or more nodes contend for the same data block, traditional shared disk database systems use disk I/O for synchronizing data access across multiple nodes (i.e., the node that has a lock on the data writes the block to the disk before the other nodes can access the same data block) (Chandrasekaran & Kehoe, 2003).

A node can be made up of multiple processors. A common type of node is a Symmetric Multi-Processor (SMP) node. Each node has its own dedicated system memory as well as its own operating system and database instance. Shared disk database architectures run on the top of hardware clusters that give every participating server equal access to all disks. However, servers do not share memory; clustered database combines the memory in the individual nodes to provide a single view of the distributed cache memory for the entire database system (Cai & Leung, 2002). Figure 1 demonstrates the basic structure of the database clusters.

The primary cluster components are the processor nodes, a cluster interconnect, and a shared storage subsystem. The nodes share access to the storage subsystem and resources that manage data, but they do not physically share main memory in their respective nodes. Clustered databases have a single data dictionary and a single system image. Each cluster node requires the following hardware:

- **A hard disk for the server's operating system:** This disk is not shared and is not connected to the controller that is used to connect to the shared storage. Instead, the disk uses its own controller and should be mirrored for improved availability.

- **High speed connection adapters (i.e., Network Interface Card (NIC)) that connect to the cluster's shared disk storage:** One NIC is used to connect the cluster node to the external network. The second NIC is used for the private cluster network, which maintains the heartbeat of the cluster (a signal indicating that a node is available).

Because the nodes in a cluster use a shared storage subsystem, they typically need to be in relatively close proximity to one another. The distance between nodes depends on the connection that the nodes use for the storage subsystem. Geo-clusters (multi-site clusters) are formed by separating the cluster nodes geographically. Such structure is accomplished by synchronously mirroring the quorum disk between the different locations. Generally a cluster is essentially unaware of the geographic distance between its nodes, so these solutions must be implemented at the network and storage levels of the organization's infrastructure.

- **A database instance that runs on every node of the cluster:** Transactions running on any instance can read or update any part of the database. There is no notion of data ownership by a node. System performance is based on the database effectively utilizing a fast interconnect between cluster nodes.

With the concept of using an N+1 configuration (N active nodes with 1 spare node), it provides a very flexible and cost effective clustering scenario to enable highly available applications. As an instance, with a four-node cluster in an N+1 configuration, you can have three of the four nodes set up to actively provide different services while the fourth node is a passive node that is ready to assume the services of any of the three active nodes in the event of a server failure.

Clustering is powerful, but not all database clustering is the same. There are as many implementations as there are databases. The costs of these vary significantly, and many vendors leave too many of the practical issues of clustering up to the application programmers, which significantly impacts the cost and complexity of the solution (Choosing the Right Database, 2004). Even among databases that provide clustering, many of the challenges of clustering are not addressed in the design of the database. Instead, the expectation is that application designers will do the necessary programming to make it to work. Primary key generation, for instance, can be a serious problem in clustered databases. If the connection between clustered databases goes down and they are forced to operate independently, the databases may generate the same primary key and use it to insert a different record at each location. If this happens, the cluster will completely fail when the link comes back up and the keys conflict. Another often-overlooked issue is auto-failover, or the ability for clients to automatically connect to a second database server when the primary server goes down. The problem is that with most databases, this is not automatic. Therefore, application programmers need to build their application with clustering in mind.

- **Shared-nothing (federated database) cluster database architecture:** The shared nothing (federated database) architecture is a logical unification of distinct databases running on independent servers, sharing no resources, and connected by a local area network (LAN). Thus, a federated database is a distributed database (Buch & Cheevers, 2002). The concept is known as database replication and is used to maintain the same copy of database content across each node in the cluster. Replication helps the slave node in maintaining a duplicate copy of the data from the master node of that cluster.

Database files are partitioned among the instances running on the nodes of a multi-computer system. Each instance or node has ownership of a distinct subset of the data, and all access to this data is performed exclusively by this owning instance. In other words, a shared nothing system uses a partitioned or restricted access scheme to divide the work among multiple processing nodes. A transaction executing on a given node must send messages to other nodes that own the data being accessed. It must also coordinate the work done on the other nodes to perform the required read/write activities. Such messaging is commonly known as *function shipping*. However, shared nothing databases are fundamentally different from distributed databases in that they operate one physical database using one data dictionary (Chandrasekaran & Kehoe, 2003).

For both the DBA as well as the application developer, there is a clear distinction between local data, which is on the disk attached to a particular server, and the remote data, which is owned by another server in the federated database. Applications see a logical single view of

Figure 2. Shared nothing database clustering architecture

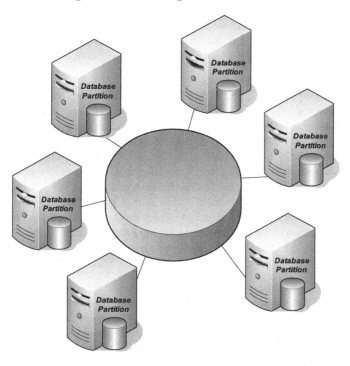

the data through UNION ALL views and distributed SQL (Microsoft calls this technology Distributed Partitioned Views DPVs) (Otey & Otey, 2005). The DPV is constructed differently at each node. It must explicitly consider which partitions are local and which are remote. Figure 2 shows the overall structure of the shared nothing database clusters architecture.

Shared Disk vs. Shared-Nothing Storage

This section will try to demonstrate the main variations in implementation aspect between the shared and shared nothing storage approaches. The discussion will focus on application development and database high availability concerns.

- **Application development:** Generally, database clusters appear just like a regular database, which means there are no additional constraints on the application developer. An application, even a complex OLTP for a Symmetric Multiprocessing (SMP) platform, runs with no modification on a shared-disk cluster. The single database image, with no data partitioning, carries over from the SMP to the cluster.

In contrast, federated databases do not have a single database image, which means they are multiple independent databases. Data must either be distributed across participating databases (for large, frequently updated transaction tables) or replicated (for reference data tables that can be accessed equally from every node). Dividing data entities across databases requires creating distributed partition views, which are distinct on every node.

- **High availability:** Before going into details of the availability framework for cluster systems, it seems valuable to understand the differences between availability within a single node and within a cluster. In a single node, database system availability refers to the ability to survive various application and operation failures within the database instance. In the worst case of the failure of the node, availability refers to the ability to recover the database to a transaction consistent state as fast as possible. For a cluster system, aside from handling failure scenarios in a single node, it needs to handle failure scenarios associated with a node, a group of nodes, or a network, while providing required performance. A cluster database builds on top of the fault-tolerant capabilities of the single instance database and enhances the database server to handle failure scenarios unique to a cluster system.

Another main advantage of the cluster architecture is the inherent fault tolerance provided by multiple nodes. Since the physical nodes run independently, the failure of one or more nodes will not affect other nodes in the cluster. In the extreme case, a cluster system can still be available even when all but one node survives, making a system based on cluster highly available. This architecture also allows a group of nodes to be taken off-line for maintenance while the rest of the cluster continues to provide services online.

When a node in a shared-disk cluster fails, all data remains accessible to the other nodes. In-flight transactions spanning nodes are rolled back. Thus, no data remains locked as a result of the failure. In most offered database clusters with shared-disk, recovery after node failure is automatic. After detecting node failure, the cluster is automatically reconfigured and the same roll-forward/roll-back recovery processes that work in the SMP environment are applied.

Another benefit of the shared disk approach is that it provides unmatched levels of fault tolerance with all data remaining accessible even if there is only one surviving node. If a node in the shared disk cluster fails, the system dynamically redistributes the workload among all the surviving cluster nodes. This ensures uninterrupted service and balanced cluster-wide resource utilization.

On the other hand, data in federated databases is divided across databases, and each database is owned by a different node. The only way to access data owned by a node is to request the data from the node, and have the node service the request. Thus, when the node fails, the data that it owns becomes unavailable, and the entire system becomes unavailable as well. Also, any in-flight distributed transactions controlled by that node might have locked data on other nodes. Therefore, recovering from node failures requires additional work in resolving these in-flight transactions.

As instances of a recently-provided database clustering commercial solutions, Oracle Real Application Clusters have started to address cluster architectures using shared storage systems such as SAN (Storage Area Network). Sybase offered Adaptive Server Enterprise with efficient auto-failover capability. The IBM DB2 Integrated Cluster Environment also uses a shared storage network to achieve both fault tolerance and performance scalability. Open-source solutions for database clustering have been database-specific. MySQL replication uses a master-slave mechanism as a solution offered by a third-party company with limited support for transactions and scalability (Cecchet et al., 2004). Postgre does not have a database clustering option, although some experiments have been reported using partial replication. These extensions to existing database engines often require applications to use additional APIs to benefit from the clustering features.

Database Replication

In many Internet applications, a large number of users that are geographically dispersed may routinely query and update the same database. In this environment, the location of the data can have a significant impact on the application response time and availability. A centralized approach manages only one copy of the database. This approach is simple, since contradicting views between replicas are not possible. The centralized approach suffers from two major drawbacks (Amir, Danilov, & Miskin-Amir, 2002):

- Performance problems due to high server load or high communication latency for remote clients
- Availability problems caused by server downtime or lack of connectivity; clients in portions of the network that are temporarily disconnected from the server cannot be serviced

Figure 3. Database replication overall structure

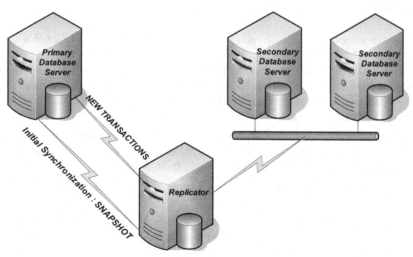

The server load and server failure problems can be addressed by replicating the database servers to form a cluster of peer servers that coordinate updates. If the primary server fails, applications can switch to the replicated copy of the data and continue operations. Database replication is different from file replication, which essentially copies files. Database-replication products log selected database transactions to a set of internal replication-management tables. The software then periodically checks these tables for updated data and moves the data from the source to the target systems while guaranteeing data coherency and consistency. Many database-replication products even have built-in tools to allow updating the primary database with any changes that users made to the backup database while the primary database was offline. Figure 3 shows the main components of the database replication environment.

The database replication process is usually done by three primary components:

- **Primary database server (*Publisher*):** The source of the data being replicated;
- **Secondary database server (*Subscriber*):** The destination of the replicated data; there can be one of more Subscribers; and
- **Replicator:** This handles sending the data from the Publisher to the Subscriber(s).

Database replication uses a snapshot of the source database to initially synchronize the databases at the publisher and the subscriber. As transactions are committed at the publisher side, they are captured and sent to the subscriber(s).

Transactional replication mainly is not designed for high availability; the process of promoting the secondary server to assume the role of the primary server is manual, not automatic. In addition, returning the primary server to its original role after a failure requires a complete database restoration.

Database Log Mirroring

The database mirroring is another option that enables database-level failover against unplanned downtime caused by server or database failures. In the event that the primary database fails, database mirroring enables a second standby database server to be almost instantly available with zero data loss. The secondary database will always be updated with the current transaction that is being processed on the primary database server. The impact of running Database Mirroring to transaction throughput is minimal.

Unlike clustering services which works at the server level, database mirroring is implemented at the database level. Database mirroring provides nearly instant failover time, taking only a few seconds, while clustering typically has longer failover times.

Database Mirroring provides added protection against disk failures as there is no shared quorum disk as there is in a clustering solution.

Unlike clustering, which requires specific hardware configurations, database mirroring works with all standard hardware that support most of today's DBMS systems. Figure 4 demonstrates the overview of how database mirroring works.

Figure 4. Database mirroring overview

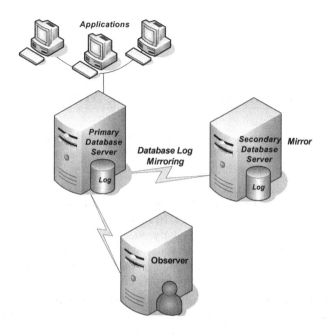

Database mirroring is implemented using three systems: the primary server, the secondary server, and the observer. The primary database server usually provides the database services. By default, all incoming client connections are directed to the primary server. The job of the secondary server is to maintain a copy of the primary server's mirrored database. The secondary server is not restricted to just providing backup services. Other databases on the secondary server can be actively supporting other unrelated applications. The observer essentially acts as an independent third party with the responsibility of determining which system will assume the role of the primary server.

The applied strategy in database mirroring is usually done by sending transaction logs between the primary and secondary servers. Such practice leads to database mirroring of a real-time log shipping application. When a client system writes a transaction to the primary server, that request is written to the primary server's log file before it is written into the data file. That transaction record then gets sent to the secondary server where it gets written to the secondary server's transaction log. After the secondary server has written the record to its log, it sends an acknowledgement to the primary server. This lets both systems to know that the record has been received and that the same data now exists in each server's log file. In the case of a commit operation, the primary server waits until it receives an acknowledgement from the mirroring server before it sends its response back to the client saying that the operation is completed. The secondary server should be in a state of continuous recovery to keep the data files up-to-date with the incoming transaction log data.

To facilitate high availability for client applications, database mirroring works in conjunction with the Transparent Client Redirection (TCR) layer, which in turn enables end-user systems to be automatically redirected to the secondary server in the event that the database on the primary server becomes unavailable.

Availability Benchmarking Methodology

In this section, a sample of ad-hoc measurement of availability in database management systems is illustrated by Brown who worked on the software Redundant Array of Independent Disks (RAID) availability benchmarking (Brown, 2000; Brown & Patterson, 2000).

Brown's technique quantifies availability behavior by examining the variations in delivered quality of service as the system is subjected to targeted fault injection. The availability benchmarking methodology consists of four parts: (i) a set of quality service metrics that measure the test system's behavior; (ii) a generator that produces a realistic workload and provides a way to measure the quality of service under that workload; (iii) a fault-injection environment used to compromise the test system's availability; and (iv) a reporting methodology based on a graphical representation of the test system's availability behavior.

The first step in the availability benchmarking methodology is to *select appropriate quality of service metrics*. These metrics must be chosen so that they can reflect degradations in system availability, in the broadest sense of the term. The choice depends on properties of the system being benchmarked. For example, performance degradation would be seen as a decrease in availability in most systems. Thus, a performance-based quality of service metric is typically an appropriate choice for an availability benchmark. But other metrics can be considered as well, including, for example, the consistency or accuracy of results delivered by the test system.

The second component of the availability-benchmarking methodology, the *workload generator*, typically takes the form of a traditional performance benchmark. The role of this component is to produce a realistic workload that places the test system under the kind of load conditions that it typically experiences in practice. Using a performance benchmark since a great deal of existing work has been carried out to construct realistic workloads in that context. In addition, it requires that the workload generator be able to measure the desired quality of service metrics defined in the first step of the methodology. Since quality of service is typically closely tied to performance, a standard performance benchmark often has the desired measurement capability built-in. The availability benchmarking methodology specifies that, while the workload generator is running, the test system should be subjected to targeted faults designed to mimic real-world failure cases that may compromise availability.

The third component of the methodology is a *fault-injection environment*. A key point here is that the injected faults must be chosen to be realistic, either based on a priori knowledge of failure-prone design flaws of some part of the system, or based on historical knowledge of typical failure cases for the system and the kinds of faults that provoke these cases.

Finally, the last component of the availability-benchmarking methodology *specifies the way that results are collected and presented*. Essentially, this component defines the procedural aspects of carrying out an availability benchmark. First, the system is run under the generated workload with no faults injected. The quality of service values collected during this run are statistically processed to produce a 99% confidence interval demarcating the normal quality of service behavior of the system. Then, the experiments are repeated multiple times with different combinations of faults injected during those runs; the methodology specifies both single-fault micro benchmarks in which a single fault is injected and the system is left untouched until it stabilizes or crashes, and multiple-fault macro benchmarks in which a series of faults designed to mimic a complex real-world scenario is injected, with human intervention allowed for system maintenance purposes. The results of these faulty runs are reported graphically, with quality of service plotted versus time, overlaid with both an indication of when the faults were injected as well as with the 99% confidence interval computed from the normal run.

Conclusion

High availability does not just happen. It is only achieved through strengthening the combination of people, processes, and technology. A plan that focuses purely on technology will never achieve high levels of availability because many of the significant factors that affect availability stem from the interaction of people and processes. Preparing the proper hardware and software platform is only a starting point. From that point on, high availability is the result of good planning and practices in combination with the appropriate technologies.

Designing a cost-effective high-availability environment for an information system(s) requires understanding the causes of outages, the critical elements for application execution, and the impacts of application outages on the business. With today's technology, there is a range of solutions to support business-critical applications. Although outages may occur, recovery is likely to be quick. If an application outage lasts for more than a few minutes, it will severely impact business. In such cases, a clustering solution may be necessary. For constant 24-hour availability, or applications where outages either are life-threatening or will directly affect the survival of the business, it will be required to have high-end and fault-tolerant solutions. Good operational procedures can make an enormous difference between theoretical availability and the actual availability of a solution.

Finally, an organization must have an enterprise vision for high availability to gain and sustain its competitive advantage. A strategy must be developed to effectively respond to unanticipated events or disruptions. Demands, risks, and opportunities abound, ranging from market fluctuations to employee error and misconduct to earthquakes and terrorism.

References

A framework for system high availability. (2000). CA: Intel Corporation, Inc.

Amir, Y., Danilov, C., & Miskin-Amir, M. (2002). *Practical wide-area database replication* (Tech. Rep. No. CNDS-2002-1). Baltimore: Johns Hopkins University.

Aronoff, E. (2003). *Building a 24x7 database.* Saint Johns, MI: Quest Software, Inc.

Arora, R. (2005). *High availability strategies of an enterprise.* Uttar Pradesh, India: TATA Consultancy Services.

Barraza, O. (2002). *Achieving 99.9998+% storage uptime and availability.* Carlsbad, CA: Dot Hill Systems Corp.

Bauer, M. (2001). *Oracle8i Parallel Server Concepts Release 2.* Redwood City, CA: Oracle Corporation, A76968-01.

Bender, W. J., & Joshi, A. (2004). *High availability technical primer.* McLean, VA: Project Performance Corporation.

Brien, M. O. (2000). *GoAhead Availability Management Service Technical Brief.* Bellevue, WA: GoAhead Software, Inc.

Brown, A. (2000). *Availability benchmarking of a database system.* Berkeley, CA: University of California at Berkeley, EECS Computer Science Division.

Brown, A., & Patterson, D. A. (2000). Towards availability benchmarks: A case study of software RAID systems. In *Proceedings of the 2000 USENIX Annual Technical Conference* (pp. 263-276). San Diego, CA.

Buch, V., & Cheevers, S. (2002). *Database architecture: Federated vs. clustered.* Redwood Shores, CA: Oracle Corporation

Cai, J., & Leung, S. (2002). *Building highly available database servers using Oracle real application clusters.* Redwood Shores, CA: Oracle Corporation

Cecchet, E., Marguerite, J., & Zwaenepoel, W. (2004). C-JDBC: Flexible database clustering middleware. In *Proceedings of USENIX Annual Technical Conference, Freenix Track*, Boston (pp. 9-18).

Chandrasekaran, S., & Kehoe, B. (2003). *Technical comparison of Oracle real application clusters vs. IBM DB2 UDB ESE.* Redwood Shores, CA: Oracle Corporation

Choosing the right database: The case for OpenBase SQL. (2004). Concord, NH: OpenBase International, Ltd.

DB2operation: The challenge to provide 24x365 availability. (2000). Houston, TX: BMC Software, Inc.

Disaster recovery package for SYBASE adaptive server enterprise. (2004). Dublin, CA: Sybase Inc.

Gribble, S. D., Brewer, E. A., Hellerstein, J. M., & Culler, D. (2000). Scalable, distributed data structures for Internet service construction. In *Proceedings of the 4th Symposium on Operating Systems Design and Implementation (OSDI 2000)*, San Diego, CA (pp. 319-332).

High Availability and More: Achieving a Service Availability™ Solution. (2001). Bellevue, WA: GoAhead Software, Inc.

High availability white paper. (2001). San Jose, CA: BlueArc Corporation.

Klein, D. (1988). *Architecting and deploying high-availability solutions.* USA: Compaq Computer Corporation, Inc.

Kumar, S. (2005). *Oracle Database 10g Release 2 High Availability.* Redwood City, CA: Oracle Corporation, Inc.

Lemme, S. (2002). IT managers guide: Maximizing your technology investments in Oracle. *Database Trend and Application Magazine.*

Lemme, S., & Colby, J. R. (2001). *Implementing and managing Oracle databases* (1st ed.). New York: PRIMA Publishing.

Low cost high availability clustering for the enterprise. (2004). Burlington, MA: Winchester Systems Inc. and Red Hat Inc.

Lumpkin, G. (2004). *Oracle partitioning—a must for data warehouse and OLTP environments.* Redwood Shores, CA: Oracle Corporation, Inc.

Otey, M., & Otey, D. (2005). *Choosing a database for high availability:An analysis of SQL server and Oracle.* USA: Microsoft Corporation.

Parikh, A. (2004). *Trustworthy software.* Unpublished master of science dissertation, Stevens Institute of Technology, Castle Point on Hudson, Hoboken.

Providing Open Architecture High Availability Solutions. (2001). Bellevue, WA: GoAhead Software, Inc.

Rosenkrantz, B., & Hill, C. (1999). *Highly available embedded computer platforms become reality.* Chicago, USA: Motorola Computer Group, issue of Embedded Systems Development.

Russom, P. (2001). *Strategies and Sybase Solutions for Database Availability.* Waltham, MA: Hurwitz Group Inc.

Saito, Y., Bershad, B. N., & Levy, H. M. (2000). Manageability, availability, and performance in Porcupine: A highly scalable, cluster-based mail service. In *Proceedings of the 17th Symposium on Operating System Principles (SOSP): ACM Transactions on Computer Systems, August, 2000, Vol. 18*(3), (pp. 298-332). Kiawah Island, SC.

Sauers, B. (1996). *Understanding high availability.* USA: Hewlett-Packard Company, Inc.

Service availability: A customer-centric approach to availability. (2000). Bellevue, WA: GoAhead Software, Inc.

Singh, H. (2001). *Distributed fault-tolerant/high availability systems.* Los Angeles, CA: TRILLIUM Digital System, Inc.

Standards for a Service Availability™ Solution. (2002). USA: Demac Associates for Service Availability™ Forum.

Tendulkar, V. S. (2005). *MySQL Database Replication and Failover Clustering.* Mumbai, India: Tata Consultancy Services Ltd.

Chapter II

Enterprise Metadata for Reliable Web Applications

R. Todd Stephens, BellSouth Corporation, USA

Abstract

This chapter examines the critical task of governing the Web application environment with enterprise metadata methodologies. As organizations move to higher levels of maturity, the ability to manage and understand the entire environment is one of the most critical aspects of the architecture. Metadata can be defined as information pertaining to the Web application environment that the organization defines as critical to the business. Successful metadata management requires a comprehensive strategy and framework which will be presented through historical, current-state, and future perspectives The author expects that by understanding the role of metadata within the Web application environment, researchers will continue to expand the body of knowledge around asset management and overall architecture governance.

Introduction

Hardly a book or magazine can be picked up that does not mention the focus to achieve enterprise effectiveness or share information which allows the organization to react in an effective manner. Terms used to describe this process include organizational learning, institutional memory, and knowledge management. Organizations have the tools and techniques to share and disseminate information throughout all levels of the firm. What does it take to become a knowledge-based organization in a Web-enabled environment? More specifically, how will an organization that is deploying Web-based applications integrate the level of knowledge required in order to manage and govern the environment as a portfolio of assets? A solid metadata management strategy is a great start.

Today's business competitive landscape requires information systems to be operational 24 hours a day. Downtime can result in a significant amount of revenue to be lost; this is especially true in the online environment. This chapter is not about knowledge management, but rather building an environment to support reliable Web applications. Building applications requires a complete understanding of the entire information technology environment. The first generation of applications required only a limited understanding of the environment since most applications were built in a stovepipe fashion and required only low levels of integration. That is to say, applications performed simple data processing or reporting without concern of the disparate areas of the business. These data feeds moved around the company in a point-to-point fashion without much concern for the integration or reuse at an enterprise level. Many of the major functions that metadata can provide revolve around the integration of technology assets. Projects like a data warehouse or Enterprise Application Integration (EAI) provided excellent opportunities to push the metadata philosophy into the main stream of information management. Today, service oriented architecture (SOA) and the push toward a Web-enabled environment provide a great deal of opportunity for integrating metadata at the enterprise level.

Metadata has traditionally been defined as "data about data" or "information about information". Pöyry, Pelto-Aho, and Juha Puustjärvi (2002) define metadata as a discipline that is descriptive and classifying information about an object. Metadata describes data, information, and knowledge within various levels of context (Tannenbaum, 2001). Today, with the advent of technologies such as hypermedia and heuristically-based searching and indexing, a new, broader, more generic definition of metadata is needed. This definition should include the traditional concepts, but it should add the concepts of existence, perspective, modeling, and topicality. A new definition should recognize that much, if not most, of enterprise data is not found in traditional relational database management systems (RDBMS), but rather, it is found in the myriad technological assets and views of those assets that exist at any point in time. The enterprise definition of metadata is as follows:

Metadata is structured, semi-structured, and unstructured data which describes the characteristics of a resource (external source of information) or asset (internal source of information). Metadata is about knowledge, which is the ability to turn information and data into effective action.

Metadata can provide abundant information about where an asset is located, what primitive elements make up the asset, how the asset was developed or created, where the asset is physically located, who the steward of the asset is, and, of course, an inventory of what assets exists. Scientists, researchers, and business practitioners continue to redefine, re-scope, and re-purpose the basic utility of metadata. So, what is metadata and how can it help? Metadata is defined within many fields of study including:

- Vocabulary of metadata information
- Relationships between assets
- Information retrieval
- Information presentation
- Knowledge management
- Information architecture
- Data architecture
- Architecture standards

Metadata is as much a philosophy as it is a technology. The process of managing information continues to be a hot button for most organizations, and the interest continues to grow. Take the following two quotes:

Knowledge assets, like money or equipment, exist and are worth cultivating only in the context of strategy and architecture. (Thomas A. Stewart, 2003, p. 212)

The fact that information has replaced physical assets as the driver of value, leads one to believe that the management of those information-based assets is critical to the future growth of business. (Daniel Gross, 2002, p. 7)

Although the data, information, and knowledge argument has been stated many times, the reality is that metadata puts data into context which forms the foundation for information and knowledge. The technical world is changing and continuous to introduce new technologies at a rapid pace that most of us have trouble keeping up. Extensible Markup Language (XML) standards, net centricity, Web services, and many other innovations are forcing us to rethink our ability to manage the complexities of the technology environment. The business world is also changing and demanding 24-hour availability, communication across business units, integration with external partners, and an element of speed that can only be delivered by an agile organization. Why is metadata emerging as a critical technology today in areas such as grid computing, SOA, Web services, and knowledge management? The reality is that we simply have too much information, and metadata can help organize, manage, and allow us to govern the environments as we once were able to do.

The objective of this chapter is to lay out a framework of how to develop and deploy an enterprise metadata strategy by which the organization can reach the higher levels of maturity. After reading this chapter, you should be able to:

- Identify the key principles of enterprise metadata and contrast this with historical implementations of metadata
- Describe the components of implementing metadata in a SOA environment
- Distinguish between management, measurement, and governance of the information technology portfolio
- Explain the role of metadata in deploying Web-based applications and the importance of governance
- Define an integration maturity model for enterprise metadata
- Define key business and technical services that can be delivered via the metadata repository to a Web-enabled environment

Background

Overview

The word "metadata" is derived from the Greek word "meta" meaning beside or after and from the Latin plural of the word "datum", meaning something given. At the basic core, metadata will answer the following in reference to the assets within the organization: What do we have, what does it mean, where is it, how did it get there, and how do I get it? Metadata includes the descriptive information but also includes the overall information management of metadata within the organization (Tannenbaum, 2001). Marco (2000) defined metadata as all of the physical data and knowledge-containing information about the business and technical processes, and data, used by the corporation. Rarely are the concepts of metadata placed on the front end of a project or systematically addressed during the design process. Yet, every project at some point will ask the very questions that metadata can address. In the data warehouse world, metadata focuses on the data definitions, transformation rules, and logical entity/attribute definitions. In the Web world, Hypertext Markup Language (HTML) utilizes the Metatag to add metadata definitions to Web pages. Office documents add metadata through the file properties, and metadata is no stranger to the library science field of study either. Librarians define metadata as structured information that describes a resource where the resource could be a book, journal, newspaper, corporate report, or any other element within the library. At the most basic definition, metadata simply describes objects where the level of detail, utility, and functionality varies from one implementation to another.

The background section will establish a foundation of past implementations of metadata where value has been defined by various organizations and academic research efforts. The emerging world of enterprise metadata will be reviewed where the enterprise semantic metadata model opens the door to universal acceptance of this technology. In addition, terms used within the metadata environment will be defined in order to gain a greater understanding of the environment. Finally, we will describe why this chapter is critical to the deployment of a large-scale Web environment based on SOA standards.

Metadata and the Data Warehouse

According to Bill Inmon (1996), the father of the data warehouse, a warehouse is a subject-oriented, integrated, time-variant, and nonvolatile collection of data supporting management's decision-making process. Generally, the warehouse is populated from a collection of data sources with an extraction, transform, and load (ETL) tool. These data sources are often application data stores such as customer relationship management (CRM), legacy, or an online transaction processing (OLTP) system. Usually, data marts are fed from the data warehouse with ETL tools where analytical functions can be performed on specific subsets of the data.

From the very start metadata has played an integral role in the development of the data warehouse. Business metadata helps the user to understand the meaning of the data and how the data is being used within the corporation in relation to the business processes. Business metadata can be generated at the time of design, architecture, data population, and process analysis. Examples of business metadata include information models, logical models, quality metrics, report definitions, terms, rules, and many other elements that help the business user understand what the data is and how it is being used (Do & Rahm, 2000). Technical metadata describes the physical data components, which include tables, fields, structures, relationships, and transformation rules. While not a perfect classification, technical metadata is used by the information technology staff, and the business metadata is used by the business and analyst community. The data warehouse is a very successful implementation of metadata management for several reasons:

- Metadata management provides an end-to-end solution, from the logical definition of data to the physical transformation of the data.
- Metadata is at the heart of the operational process. By defining the source, target, and transformation information, metadata is the main driver of the application itself.
- Metadata provides the core documentation of the processes.
- System integration is supported by building a semantic understanding of the data sources.
- Control and reliability are increased within the data warehouse development effort.
- Flexibility is improved by integrating metadata as control mechanism.
- Data analysis is improved by utilizing the conceptual, logical, and physical metadata to understand the process and results.

The metadata repository allows developers, data analysts, and data administrators to view, modify, and manage the application end-to-end. Metadata is the central point of administration of the data warehouse. Since a data warehouse reflects the business model of an enterprise, an essential element for warehouse architecture is metadata management. The repository enables the sharing of metadata among tools and processes for designing, setting up, using, operating, and administrating a warehouse (Chaudhuri & Dayal, 1997).

The Library Card Catalog

Library and information science (LIS) is the field of study related to the issues of library management. This includes academic studies about how library resources are used and how people interact with library systems. These studies tend to be specific to certain libraries at certain times. The organization of knowledge for efficient retrieval of relevant information is also a major research goal of LIS. Basic topics in library science include the acquisition, classification, and preservation of library materials. In a more present-day view, a fervent outgrowth of LIS is information architecture. LIS should not be confused with information theory, the mathematical study of the concept of information. The field of library and information science is not defined by the output of its information specialists, but by the "information specialists" who remain in academia, teaching and doing research, by its literature, its journals, and all the other ways in which an academic discipline is defined. The usual comment from metadata experts is that true metadata expands far beyond simply cataloging data or other assets. True, but on the other hand, library science goes far beyond simply sticking a number on the cover of a book and ensuring it is placed in the correct location. A card catalog not only indexes books but also journals, microfiche, magazines, newspapers, government documents, and annual reports. The vast majority of the information is based on a simple ontology of information architecture called the Dewey Decimal System. Classification provides a system for organizing knowledge and may be used to organize knowledge represented in any form, for example, books, documents, and electronic resources. The Dewey Decimal System provides a means to classify the resources by utilizing a tiered classification where the first tier defined the main classes spanning a range from 000 to 999: generalities, philosophy and psychology, religion, social science, language, natural science and mathematics, technology (applied sciences), arts, literature, and geography and history. The second tier continues to break down the topic into further defined sub-categories which are referred to as divisions. Each major category is divided into nine sub-categories spanning a range of 10 to 90. Each sub-category is further divided into nine specialized topics ranging from 1 to 9. This produces a three character code of classification which can then be organized into further details by adding decimals to the code. For example:

500 Natural sciences & math (Tier 1)

  520 Astronomy & allied sciences (Tier 2)

    523 Specific celestial bodies (Tier 3)

      523.7 Sun

        523.71 Constants and dimensions

        523.72 Physics of

        523.73 Motions

        523.74 Photosphere

523.75 Chromosphere and corona

523.76 Solar interior

523.78 Eclipses

The Dewey Decimal System is a hierarchical system, in which the arrangement of books on the shelves moves from the general to the specific. The system works wonderfully and has been in use for over 100 years. Invented by Melville Louis Kossuth Dewey, the Dewey Decimal System created a revolution in library science and set in motion a new era of librarianship.

HTML Metadata: Meta-Tag

Within the Internet technology, the number one standard protocol is the Hypertext Markup Language (HTML). HTML is a type of document that is interpreted by a browser which presents the images and text to the end user. HTML documents are often referred to as "Web pages". The browser retrieves Web pages from Web servers that, thanks to the Internet, can be pretty much anywhere in the world. While a discussion of the syntax, usage, and methodology of Web-based applications would be interesting, our main focus is the management of the Web page asset itself. Most development organizations utilize a source type tool or integrated environment to manage the back end, while the front end was originally to be managed by the use of metadata. The metadata element of HTML is a documentation type tag known as a metatag. Metatags can fall into two categories. Site tags define characteristics for the entire site and are usually found on every page with identical values, while page tags are specific for each page being described. Metatags can assist in the process of knowledge management by cataloging information and organizing content. This information can document the relevance of the document without actually reading the content and attempting to interpret the meaning. This, in turn, allows for greater management of the Web site (Watchfire, 2000). Unfortunately, many organizations utilized the metatag, not as a means of management, but one of deceit. Tagging the contents in one context and then providing alternative content forced search engines to basically ignore the metadata and focus on interpreting the actual content.

Enterprise Metadata

Enterprise metadata has received a lot of attention and press over the past few years, as many organizations have attempted to push data warehouse success to the enterprise level. Unfortunately the integrated tools, controlled environment, and high degree of quality assurance are much harder to find at the enterprise level. Enterprise data architects are looking for alternative methods of data integration. Perhaps, enterprise metadata holds the key. In this chapter, we are attempting to lay the foundation of a new definition of metadata, as well as review the different perspectives on the role and value of metadata within the or-

Figure 1. Extended metadata landscape

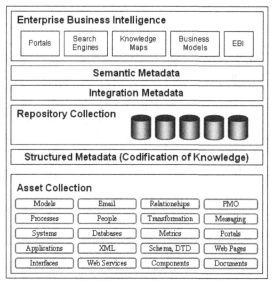

ganization. Enterprise metadata and business intelligence come together to provide one of the most powerful communication tools within the organization. The rationale of enterprise business intelligence is to discover the utilization of capital assets within the organization. The current level of technology can deliver knowledge to the end user, but more advanced methods are needed in the areas of taxonomies, ontologies, standards, and automation. Most researchers will agree that a broadly-based approach is needed, including consideration of how users understand, navigate, and communicate knowledge embodied in computer-based vocabularies and metadata classification schemes. Implementations of structured metadata solutions must overcome a variety of problems including: mixed vocabularies, content and structure of the meta-model, the variety of asset structures, and integration of less structured knowledge placed in documents, business processes, and Web pages.

Figure 1 presents a layered view of the role enterprise metadata plays in the communication of knowledge via enterprise business intelligence. The enterprise architecture defines a universe that consists of assets that are created by the technical community in a variety of forms (Layer 1). An asset is any person, place, or thing within the technological community. Examples of assets include: databases, logical models, physical models, XML structures, components, documents, metrics, systems, interfaces, and so forth. A resource would be similar to an asset with the exception that resources come from outside of the organizational walls. Resources could include research services, Web services, and packaged models. Enterprise business intelligence (EBI) is built upon this foundation of assets.

Structural Metadata

Structural metadata (Layer 2) is the category where the context-specific meta-model information will be stored and knowledge is codified. Each type of asset, as well as the context
of the asset, will have different data collection points. Static databases will have different
metadata components from the logical view of the data, which will be different than the
transformation of that data from one source to another. At the heart of any repository is the
core constructs that make up the meta-model. The meta-model is simply the elements that
are used to describe the asset. The same principles that exist for an entity-relationship model
apply to a meta-model as well. While we indicate entity-relationship (ER) diagramming
as the technique, any modeling type language could work: Universal Markup Language
(UML) diagrams, class-objects, and so forth. For example, the elements in Table 1 can be
used to describe a table asset.

While meta-models vary from implementation to implementation, we can categorize them
into four distinct models: closed models, standards-based models, functional, or industry-
based models.

Just about every tool out there has an underlying physical meta-model that requires a proprietary model for integration. These meta-models are designed to work with the specific
tool. Logical or UML models for these tools are much harder to acquire. The real question
is, can the model be described as open, extensible, and open to metadata interchange? Closed
models, or proprietary models, are built based on the individual application requirements,
without consideration of standard models. These models are driven by the technical and
business requirements that deliver a flavor of uniqueness into the metadata strategy. These
models provide the basic utility required by the structural metadata. There has been a lot of
research focused on trying to create a standards-based meta-model. ISO 11179, common
warehouse model (CWM), and metadata object facility (MOF) are all efforts at creating meta-
models that allow meta-exchange through a collection of standards. Developing standards
is a response to the enterprise need to integrate valuable data that is spread across organizations from multiple sources. More and more standard schemas or industry models are being

Table 1. Basic metadata components for data

Name	Description
Table Name	The name of the table
Database Name	The name of the parent database
Keywords	Specific keywords and phrases about the table
Description	Detailed description of tables utility
Date	Date the information was published
Schema	Related source schema
Logical Model	Parent logical model
Owner	Owner of SME of table
Server	Physical location of table

developed in order to share information between the corporations. New standards like the reusable asset specification (RAS) or the interactive data definition (IDDU) are emerging that are forcing the industry to look beyond the internal proprietary data structure environment. The XML.org Registry is a community resource for accessing the fast-growing body of XML specifications being developed for vertical industries and horizontal applications. The XML.org Registry offers a central clearinghouse for developers and standards bodies to publicly submit, publish, and exchange XML schemas, vocabularies, and related documents. Operated by OASIS, the non-profit XML interoperability consortium, the XML.org Registry is a self-supporting resource created by and for the community at large. Industry and functional meta-models are part of this movement, although an XML representation is not required. Industry models will focus on a specific industry, like telecommunications, while functional models focus on a specific business element like customer. Irregardless of model specification, the basic purpose is to hold the structured information specifically pertaining to the object being described.

Repository Collection

The main reason that employees come to the repository (Layer 3) is to locate and gather information. The content of a repository is not limited to the metadata content which is provided. Rather, content includes the solutions and strategies employed to make it easy for the user to accomplish important tasks, such as information retrieval, search, and navigation required in creating knowledge feedback (Calongne, 2001). Becker and Mottay (2001) define information content to include timely and correct error messages, prompts, button labels, textual description, help, and customer service information. For a global perspective, repository designers should be careful not to lose specific meaning in the translation or the use of specific symbols, such as the shopping cart. The repository site gives an organization the ability to present almost limitless information on their assets. This information or content should include the metadata and service quantity, quality, and relevance to the customer (Palmer, 2002). The repository services and design structure will be covered later in this chapter.

Integration Metadata

While structural metadata focuses on the asset-specific information, integration metadata (Layer 4) focuses on the generic information that can describe each asset. Information elements like name, description, type, and author are generic in nature and could describe any asset within the enterprise. The current Web environment can support a single threaded keyword search of textual information. Unfortunately, the volume of information is making this model more and more unusable (Decker, Mitra, & Melnik, 2000). The efforts under the Semantic Web umbrella are working toward providing a better method of searching the Web via the use of vocabularies like the Dublin Core framework. This framework describes the schema of metadata that can be embedded in Hypertext Markup Language (HTML) or resource definition framework (RDF) (Lassila, 2000).

Table 2. Dublin core metadata set

Element	Description
Title	A name given to the resource
Creator	An entity primarily responsible for making the content of the resource
Subject	The topic of the content of the resource
Description	An account of the content of the resource
Publisher	An entity responsible for making the resource available
Contributor	An entity responsible for making contributions to the content of the resource
Date	A date associated with an event in the lifecycle of the resource
Type	The nature or genre of the content of the resource
Format	The physical or digital manifestation of the resource
Identifier	An unambiguous reference to the resource within a given context
Source	A reference to a resource from which the present resource is derived
Language	A language of the intellectual content of the resource
Relation	A reference to a related resource
Coverage	The extent or scope of the content of the resource
Rights	Information about rights held in and over the resource

The key to providing semantic knowledge is an agreement on the standards of documentation. The Dublin Core Metadata Initiative (DCMI) is an organization that is working on creating a standard set of descriptive tags through an open source type organization. The standard summarizes the updated definitions for the Dublin Core metadata elements as originally defined by the DCMI. These definitions are officially known as Version 1.1. The definitions utilize a formal standard for the description of metadata elements. This formalization helps to improve consistency with other metadata communities and enhances the clarity, scope, and internal consistency of the Dublin Core metadata element definitions (Dublin Core, 2005). There are 15 basic elements defined by the DCMI, which are presented in Table 2.

Each of these elements can provide vital information pertaining to the usage, purpose, content, and structure of the Web page or any other Web-based object. Some of these elements are broken down into further qualifications such as the "Date" element. The qualifiers of the "Date" element include valid date, issued date, modified date, available date, and created date. These qualifiers provide additional semantic definitions that enable a closer definition of the semantic meaning of the object. In addition, expansion of these basic elements is encouraged in order to expand the utility and value for each organization.

Semantic Metadata

Semantic metadata (Layer 5) is the assembly of assets based on explicit or implicit elements. Explicit assemblies could include hierarchal structures, such as the ones found within search engines like Yahoo. Implicit assemblies could include inference engines that traverse the corporation looking for relevant assets. Keyword-based search engines provide a basic example of how this process might work in the future. Currently, a user types in a few keywords, and the search engine returns a set of documents that contain some or all of the keywords. This functionality should be expanded to include any asset within the corporation, and not just the ones documented in a Web page or document. In the future, agents will be able to traverse operating systems, XML constructs, interfaces, and other assets that can be viewed by the computer system. Assets will then be able to be grouped by context, usage, time, and various other constructs. Semantics takes data and information and applies the behavior of the user in order to define meaning (McComb, 2004). Semantics take metadata above and beyond the simple descriptive definition to providing the basis for understanding the business model itself. In order to achieve this level, applications must move beyond the simple catalog to an integrated semantic architecture. When we bring together the structured definitions, the unstructured content, and the relationships, then we can create a semantic understanding of the environment. With semantics, the agility of the technology community will be taken to a new level unseen by any organization to date.

Core Value of Reuse

Reuse, software reuse, and code reuse are three terms that are often misused and confused by the general practitioner. Reuse is has been tossed around since 1994 where many organizations jumped all over the reuse bandwagon without much success. Software reuse goals and practices are not new, but full scale success has been hard to find. That being said, effective reuse of knowledge, processes, and software has been proven to increase productivity and quality of the Information Technology organization. McIlroy (1969) published one of the earliest references to software reuse in 1969 at the New York NATO Conference on Software Engineering. Early reuse efforts were primarily focused on reusing algorithms to ensure the consistency of calculations. Companies with scientific and engineering computing needs were early proponents of "function reuse" to ensure that a specific engineering calculation across all of their systems computed the same value. The initial goal was not to reduce costs to build systems nor quicker time-to-market. In 1995, Gamma, Helm, Johnson, and Vilissides (1995) published their unique approach to reuse in a book called *Design Patterns: Elements of Reusable Object-Oriented Software*. The result was a recognition that reuse must include much more than just code. Spanning from architecture to test-cases, reuse must be looked at in a holistic fashion in order to produce economic benefits. Organizations spend more time on the architecture, design, analysis, and specification than on actual coding. Therefore, any improvements in reuse can result in enormous gains in the efficiency of the SDLC process

Roles within Reuse

There are several different roles within a reuse environment. Most are fairly obvious and present a wide collection of analogies. The reuse producer is the person, community, or application that creates a reusable asset. As described in the previous section, the producer may or may not design reuse into the asset from the very beginning. Nonetheless, they have produced an asset that can and will be reused in one form or another. The reuse consumer is responsible for locating and accessing the reusable asset information, assessing the ability to reuse the asset, adapting to the asset reuse environment, and integrating the asset into the framework. The role of the broker is to manage the information about the asset and act as a third party for the use and functionality of the asset. A portion of this functionality will be performed by the repository which provides discovery, access, and documentation services.

Benefits of Reuse

There are various benefits of reuse defined in the industry including: reduction of cost, higher productivity, improved software quality, shortened time to market, and consistent applica-tion functionality. Grady (1997) indicates that organizations can expect a 10-35% reduction in overall cost by implementing a reuse strategy. Reduction of cost has more of an impact than just the bottom line. Reuse allows developers to produce more with less and improve product maintainability. Improved quality, in turn, reduces the total cost of ownership. GTE had a 14% reuse percent with an overall savings of $1.5million. Implementing reuse allows developers to focus on the business functionality and not be distracted by infrastructure, database, and other reusable functions. At Phillips, they reported that design for large-scale reuse addresses the need for higher productivity in a domain-specific architecture (for a product family), design for reuse, reuse guidelines, and rules. The studied organization has achieved more than 70% reuse within a product family and more than 40% on a different product family. AT&T reported a ten-fold improvement in software quality by implementing a reuse program. Enabling the ability to discover and access reusable assets is a primary responsibility of the repository.

Contribution of This Study to the Field

Although there have been many research studies and books involving SOA, Web Services, and development frameworks, none have specifically looked at the actual implementation, governance, and large-scale portfolio management of the technology environment. This chapter contributes to the field in several ways. First, it adds to the literature on the strategic governance of the Web application environment. It places the concepts of accountability, management, and strategic architecture on the front end of the processes versus the back end, as most implementations view the concepts of metadata. This section focused on the background of metadata in order to establish a foundation of concepts that will be built upon in the remaining text of this chapter. The next section will provide a framework of imple-mentation and support model based upon the experience of a Fortune 500 company. The repository design will include business services, technology services, integration points, and a comparison to the current Web service registry framework. The metadata maturity model will describe an evolutionary path that organizations can take in order to enable metadata within the Web-enabled environment. The future of enterprise metadata section will follow and describe various trends that will impact metadata in the near future. The final section will describe the conclusions, implications, recommendations, and summary of this chapter on enterprise metadata.

Enterprise Metadata in the
Web Application Environment

Overview

Up to now, this chapter has focused on establishing the foundations of metadata, defining the basic building blocks of metadata management, and the principles of reuse at the enterprise level. This section will take those guiding principles and apply them to the Web application environment in hopes to not only expand the body of knowledge, but to lay the foundation of success for any implementation desiring to manage the Web application environment as a portfolio of assets. First, the problems and issues must be reviewed by any large-scale implementation of enterprise metadata or an enterprise integration effort. These problems must be addressed in order to create an architecture environment that can be governed and moved to the highest levels of maturity. The Zachman framework will be used to establish the breadth and depth of the architecture environment. The Web application environment will be simplified in order to communicate how the enterprise repository can be implemented into a large-scale organization, followed by a detailed design of the repository itself. Finally, the Metadata Maturity Model will describe how technology organizations can use the repository to actually govern the Web-enabled environment.

Issues and Problems

Implementing Web applications on a large scale presents many problems that can be addressed with solid metadata principles. This section will review several of the problems that need to be addressed in a large-scale deployment of a SOA.

Managing the Environment

How many assets are held within the corporation or large organization? Obviously, the way in which we define an asset can increase or decrease that number. Suppose we have 2,000 systems or applications within the corporation, with an average of 10 databases per system. This would indicate that we would have 20,000 databases being supported by the operations organization. Assuming we have an average of 10 tables per database and 10 fields per table, the end result would be estimated at two million data fields. While this number may seem enormous, we have not added the relationships between the assets, schema definitions, components, programs, interfaces, Web pages, metrics, or business rules. The problem we face is not just the quantity of assets, but also the diversity, methodology, standards, and integration of tools. The diversity issue addresses the reality that the assets within the environment are different. They are modeled differently, designed differently, and deployed differently. Much of the work developed by John Zachman addresses the environment from an architecture point of view. Zachman is credited with creating a vision of the enterprise architecture in the 1960's. Zachman (1987) designed a two-dimensional model that requires the integration of models for each of the functional components: data, function, network, organization, schedule, and strategy. Generically speaking, enterprise architecture has five major layers: (a) scope, (b) business model, (c) system model, (d) technology model, and (e) components. The purpose of the layers is to align an organization's strategy with its information technology. Two basic assumptions are that a strategy exists and the result is a functioning enterprise. A centralized strategy may not be defined for large organizations, which makes developing models difficult. Enterprise architects often start building information technology from the bottom up, because they cannot see the relevance of strategy and modeling. It is important to realize what is in-scope and out-of-scope, especially for a large enterprise (Rico, 2004). The Zachman model presents a high-level view of the diversity of assets within the technology community. The message is actually much worse, since each of the classifications can be broken down into multiple layers. For example, computer programs can be classified as components, programs, Web services, and so forth. In addition, the rapid pace of change within these classifications continues to evolve. This creates an environment where classification and definition will be increasingly a challenge for even the most advanced organizations.

Integration Issues within Information Technology

As the Zachman framework illustrates, the enterprise must determine how these assets are going to be integrated at a logical, physical, and knowledge layer. Enterprise application architectures and SOA are efforts to integrate the physical layer of the environment by exposing data and services to the enterprise. Integration at this level is accomplished by using operational data stores, or enterprise databases, which are the cornerstone of an enterprise application architecture from the data perspective. SOA integrates the physical layer with shared messaging infrastructures and common services. The gap in the design is the integration of information within the environment. Systems communicate with services, access common components, and read data stores which operate over an enterprise infrastructure. This environment must be documented and integrated within the tool environment as well as the knowledge management environment.

Structured vs. Unstructured Content

Within the computing environment, there exists a classification methodology based upon the structure of the information. On one end of the spectrum is data that can be placed into simple constructs of structure. Examples of structured data include XML structures, taxonomies, airline schedules, parts catalogs, and customer information. Information that can be classified in a structured format has a defined format that can be easily stored in databases, typically linked together by logical relationships like keys or indices. On the other end of the spectrum where information cannot be easily classified under the structured umbrella is

Figure 2. Structured and unstructured information

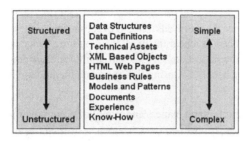

information classified as unstructured. Examples of unstructured data include documentation, contracts, and video. The reality is that there is really no such thing as pure structure nor pure un-structure, for that matter. Figure 2 provides a view of how data moves from a structured format to the unstructured information held within the organization.

The issue that must be addressed is the integration of these different types of information formats. By definition, information stored within a repository is structured since that information is stored in databases and defined by the meta-model. However, this structured information must be accompanied by the unstructured supporting artifacts. For example, a repository built to house XML artifacts would need the structured definitions of the vocabulary and naming conventions, the design documents, use cases, and associated assets. Solutions in the Web application space that support the SDLC, governance, and architecture must integrate the structured and unstructured information held within the environment.

Impact Analysis

Impact analysis is the process of identifying or estimating the impact of a change in the environment. Impact information can be used when planning changes, making changes, or tracking the effect of changes implanted within the environment (Apiwattanapong, Harrold, & Orso, 2003). Traditionally, impact analysis was done at the data layer by the use of a field-to-field mapping technology known as ETL. Within the data warehouse environment, data must be mapped from external sources and loaded into the data warehouse. Traditionally, an ETL tool was required to extract data from a source system, transform the information into a warehouse format, and then load the data into the target tables; this means that the processing work was done outside of the database system itself. The ETL tool is integrated into the application suite where metadata can be used and reused within the environment. In the process of mapping, the application will identify, define, and store the metadata information for each field that is being mapped. The application will also capture the transformation rules that must be applied as data moves from one application to another. For example, the gender code of system A may utilize numeric representations which need to be converted to alphanumeric codes of "M" and "F". The transformation rule would be something along the lines:

"If Source-Gendor = 1 then Move "M" to the Target-Gendor Else Move "F".

This type of information has an enormous amount of reuse since once a system or database is integrated; you do not need to repeat the work the next time. Once the source and target definitions are captured, the definitions can be reused until the system owners modify the underlying structures. The benefits of using this approach include the following:

- Reduces build, support, maintenance, and troubleshooting overhead
- Data Warehouse projects take less time to develop, and allows for an iterative development style, reducing the risk of failure
- Documentation and metadata is simplified as only one area needs to be documented and managed
- One processing environment reduces cost, leverages skills, and simplifies management
- Integration occurs external to the operational applications

Organizations that have any size to them are going to have an enormous amount of data within the legacy applications, operational data stores, CRM systems, and enterprise resource planning (ERP) systems. Impact analysis could only be done on the specific data elements that were brought into the warehouse environment. In addition, data was generally loaded from the golden source or from the operational store that had update or origination rights over the data element. Unless the warehouse included an element data consolidation, the various sources of the data were never captured.

While field-to-field mapping of the data warehouse provides enormous benefits, logical impact analysis has been gaining ground in the past few years. Logical impact analysis utilizes the models within the environment and follows the linkages that are implied or explicitly stated. In a simple example, ER tools provide linkages between the logical entities and attributes, physical tables and fields, and the actual database instances of the model itself. Traditional metadata repositories have been built around this linkage between the three layers of data designation: logical, physical, and implementation. UML and other higher-level modeling languages are looking into this impact analysis at the model level. Most research of impact analysis in the software environment has focused on the code, but recent research has extended this to the modeling environment. In the context of UML-based development, it becomes clear that the complexity of design and analysis requires impact analysis at a higher level. In addition, model-based impact analysis allows for value to be gained before the system is actually constructed (Briand, Labiche, O'Sullivan, & Sowka, 2005).

Other research efforts are mapping data definitions to a single enterprise model standard. As seen in Figure 3, we can map data definitions to a single definition or standard. For example, suppose we define customer account as the standard for our primary account number definition. Now each and every instance of the customer account field, irregardless of definition or transformation rule, is mapped to this single definition. While impact analysis utilizing this method is not as exact as the field-to-field mapping alternative, the implementation is far simpler.

Figure 3. Mapping strategies

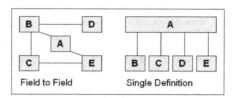

The mapping to a single standard works equally well in the logical or model area as it does in the physical data environment. While there are many alternatives at the data layer, moving impact analysis across the entire asset portfolio has been problematic. The lack of standards, metadata architecture, and integrated tool set has kept most organizations from implementing impact analysis across the enterprise portfolio. The inability of relating the entire enterprise portfolio creates an environment where total architecture governance is impossible. In order to address this issue, additional research and published case studies are required.

Summary of Issues and Problems

The issues and problems discussed in this section simply reflect the complexity of the environment itself. The reality is that businesses have large-scale environments where the collection of assets is enormous. Managing the environment is a challenge due to the lack of standards and common tools currently available on the market today. Establishing an adaptive architecture involves change for people, process, and technology. By planning evolutionary change and implementing reusable elements, the architecture will permit consistent integration between applications, increase the overall adaptability of the Information Technology environment, increase the speed of solution delivery, and maximize technology investments. None of this transition can occur without addressing the issues in totality.

Web Application Environment

Throughout this chapter, the authors have painted a picture of the environment by which Web applications operate. This environment can be described by the various architectures which include technical, data, functional, and application. Organizations that are deploying Web applications will need to update, integrate, or replace much of their infrastructure. This section will simplify the environment in order to apply the basic metadata principles described in the earlier sections. The idea is that we can use these principles as building blocks and thus apply them to the entire technology environment.

Figure 4 provides an image of this simplified environment. The following paragraphs will focus on where and how the issues of metadata should be addressed at each level.

Figure 4. Simplified Web application environment

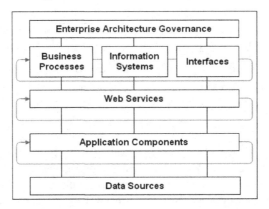

Enterprise Architecture Governance

Enterprise architecture defines the rules of engagement, standards, best practices, and support models within the technology community. Standardizing on a particular tool or language allows the organization to gain economies of scale as well as buying power from the vendor partners. Architecture is the basic building block or raw material of the metadata environment. Organizations must review, document, and deploy architectures that support the business objectives and strategic direction. Enterprise architecture planning is the process of defining architectures (data, application, technology, and function) for the use of information in support of the business and the plan for implementing those standards (Spewak, 1993). Data architecture focuses on the data quality, data management, data content, data usage, modeling, storage, and traditional metadata management. Technical architectures review the hardware, software, and vendor relationships, while the functional architecture documents the business processes. The final architecture is the application architecture, which works as a conduit between the functional and technical specifications. Architectures define the rules of the game within the corporate environment, and these rules can make or break the Web application implementation. Spewak (1993) defines a collection of benefits of implementing enterprise architecture:

- Focus is on a strategic use of technology for managing data as an asset
- Standard vocabulary facilitates communication and reduces inconsistency and data redundancy
- Documentation increases understanding of the business
- New systems and integration concerns are melded
- Architecture allows for a comprehensive, objective, and impartial approach

- The long range system plan complements the business plan
- Enterprise Architecture allows easier accommodation of dynamic business changes such as mergers, acquisitions, new products, lines of business, and technology transformation

Business Processes

At the cornerstone of all applications are the business processes or functions that solve problems. A business process is simply any activity in which the business is engaged in order to deliver the product, service, or experience to the end customer. Business process engineering is often called re-engineering since each business process is evaluated in order to reduce the cost, time, and complexity. For example, the business process for order fulfillment within a collaborative Web space might include the following steps:

- Receive the order
- Log the order
- Schedule the production build
- Build the site from the standard template
- Update the order log
- Notify the customer

Each of these processes requires resources and technology in order to complete. Any improvements with the use of technology will increase the turnaround time for the procurement of the internal assets. The term "procure" is used to indicate that a reusable asset is integrated into technology environment. The ideal business process is one that is automated and provides a complete self-service type of environment. As business process modeling continues to evolve, new requirements are emerging for developing an enterprise business process repository as well as integrating the process itself with the other assets in the collection that perform the specific business functions.

Information Systems

At the most basic level, an information system is a combination of people, hardware, communication networks, and data resources that collect, transform, and disseminate information within an organization (O'Brian, 2003). People resources will include the employees, consultants, contractors, customers, and suppliers. The hardware resources will include the physical devices that are used in order to operate the system, which would include computers, hardware, wiring, software, printers, and so forth. The network and communications include the physical and electronic resources required to move data from point A to point B. The final area is the data resources which are described later in this section. Information systems create a plethora of enterprise assets that can be cataloged in the repository including:

hardware, machine configurations, open source software, release levels, network IP addresses, and many other elements that need to be tracked and managed across the enterprise.

Application Interfaces

An interface is defined as a communication connection between two systems. Although programs may communicate within a system, only external communications are described as an interface. In an organization that is relatively small, there may not be a significant number of interfaces. However, in a large enterprise there may be thousands of systems that communicate within the organization. Executive management is looking for a high level view of how these systems communicate. The Interface Repository is the system that will collect the information and provide an interface for viewing. For example, assume that the organization only has three systems. The expense system sends a daily feed to the general ledger system, which communicates with the accounting package with remote procedure calls (RPC). The value of an interface repository goes far beyond the simple collection of information. In the past few years, disaster recovery and security have been hot topics of discussion and investment. When a failure or security breach occurs, most organizations do not have a clear understanding of the impact of that failure point. The interface and system repository can tell you exactly which systems have failed and the impact to the business applications. According to Amjad Umar (1997) an interface repository is a dynamic representation of available object interfaces. This repository represents the interfaces of all objects in the distributed environment. The clients access the interface repository to learn about the server objects and determine what type of operations can be invoked on an object. The elements captured about the interface could include: type, payload, technology, message structure, frequency of use, protocol, processing period, and routing instructions.

Web Services

A Web service can be described as a collection of software components that performs business functions across a variety of technologies and standards. Specifically, a Web service is a URL-addressable software resource that performs the business functions over the Internet protocol. The Web service is at the top of the program stack since this chapter is discussing a Web-enabled environment. The Web service enables other systems to access the functionality by wrapping the service in standard technologies like Extensible Markup Language (XML), Universal Description, Discovery and Integration (UDDI), Simple Object Access Protocol (SOAP), and HTTP. Web services attempt to remove the hardware and software requirements of integration that many of the current systems are developed under. Traditional implementations of a Web service repository have been focused on the UDDI standard, and are more commonly referred to as a registry. Later in this chapter, the author will discuss the specific differences between the two containers.

Application Components

In most organizations, the business logic is embedded into the program logic of the software application. These application components may also be described as common business services, since they perform a wide degree of application integration. The service may access multiple data sources across multiple infrastructures. The service is not a Web service but rather a CORBA or .Net type application that runs on a middleware infrastructure. Functional architecture focuses on the collection of components by mapping them to the domain model. The domain model is a representation of the basic business functions or business processes. This mapping, where one business process is mapped to the application component, insures that only a single enterprise component is built and reused by the entire corporation. The reuse repository is the primary container for holding the application component metadata. Every component contains metadata that can be abstracted before, during, and after the development process. Some of the basic elements of component metadata include keywords, description, author, and classification vocabulary. The reuse repository may also contain the class diagrams, UML models, actual code, downloads, and implementation instructions. Software reuse is the most discussed and least implemented within the software quality improvement area. An estimated 75% of all application development organizations operate at level one of the software process capability maturity Model (Hunter, 1997). The Reuse Repository can provide the tools needed to overcome most of the technical barriers that keep reuse from being implemented industry wide. The repository can provide the basic storage, retrieval, and organization needed in order to enable reuse within the organization.

Data Sources

Ultimately, all business processes require data in some form or fashion. The components will need to access data across the business in real-time. Legacy application, operational data stores, and warehouses hold the vast majority of enterprise information. Keys here are the models, definitions, and data management systems. The models may very well be in a UML format as opposed to the traditional entity relationship (ER) format. Data is one of the top assets of a corporation. Many decision-makers require only "data and fact" to solve problems which a corporation faces. However, these decision-makers cannot easily make decisions when there are inconsistencies in data. Therefore, the goal of data architecture is to provide the framework where data quality is improved by managing data as an asset. Data architecture is the blueprint for the lifecycle of business information. The lifecycle includes the structure of the information (as represented by data models and databases) as well as the business events and movement of the information. This view of data provides a better foundation for transforming a silo-oriented set of existing applications into systems that fit into the organizational model. Data Architecture is the corporation's expression of strategy for creating and managing the use of data in order to transform data into information. Recognizing that data is a strategic asset that is expensive to handle and easy to waste, the data architecture must assure:

- Standardization of data structures (logical and physical)
- Definition and protection of the data resource
- Consistency and quality of the data resource
- Judicial use of corporate resources (e.g., personnel) in managing the data asset
- Credible and timely data is delivered throughout the enterprise at a reasonable cost
- Driven by the needs of business and can adapt to changes in the business
- Implemented in any technical environment

The metadata repository for the data environment will capture the logical and physical models, entities, attributes, tables, fields, files, domains, vocabularies, stewards, and data transformation rules. Moving beyond the traditional data field, the data sources can be extended to message structures, XML vocabularies, Extensible Style sheet Language Transformation (XSLT) documents, and many other emerging technologies used to describe data structures. The common component of each of these classifications is the repository itself. As described, each and every asset classification can have its own repository or a more universal repository can be constructed that can hold different types of assets with variable meta-models. Figure 5 replaces the asset map from Figure 4 with the matching repository.

As described, each of these elements has a corresponding repository or registry. The following section lays out a framework of design for developing a universal asset repository, including business functions and client support methodologies that cross the entire technology portfolio.

Figure 5. Distributed repository architecture

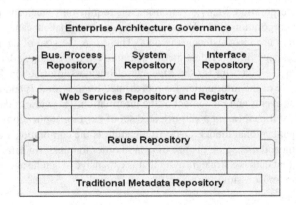

Metadata Repository Overview

The repository should be designed as a universal repository where all assets can be described irregardless of core metadata model. The main reason that employees come to the repository is for the information. The content of a repository is not limited to the metadata content provided. Rather, content includes the solutions and strategies employed to make it easy for the user to accomplish important tasks, such as information retrieval, search, and navigation required in creating knowledge feedback (Calongne, 2001). Becker and Mottay (2001) define information content to include timely and correct error messages, prompts, button labels, textual description, help, and customer service information. For a global perspective, repository designers should be careful not to lose specific meaning in the translation or the use of specific reserved for online retail applications. The repository site gives an organization the ability to present almost limitless information on their product or service. This information or content should include the information related to service quantity, quality, and relevance to the customer (Palmer, 2002).

Writing for the repository is an important aspect of Web-based content. Nielsen (2000) defined three core guidelines for writing for the repository. First, information content should be succinct. Information provided on the repository should be about 50% less than the information printed in the supporting documentation. If additional information is required, the user should link to a document or another repository page. Second, the designer should write for scan-ability and not require the user to read long continuous blocks of text. Morkes and Nielsen (1997) reported that 79% of users simply scanned repository pages versus actually reading line by line. Based on this research, repository pages should be structured with two to three levels of headlines. Finally, repository designers should use hypertext to break up information into multiple pages. Keevil (1998) indicated that users prefer writing that is concise, easy to scan, and objective in style. In addition, the following guidelines can enhance a user's experience within a usable repository site:

* Adding tables of content and section summaries
* Adding bullets, numbered lists, and headings
* Using boldface and colored text to highlight keywords
* Writing shorter paragraphs
* Removing buzzwords and marketing objectives

Effective content writing is one of the most critical aspects of repository page design. Most users will simply scan online content, rather than carefully reading each line (Nielsen & Tahir, 2002). Many people in the Information Technology field look at the metadata repository as an application which provides a limited set of value points for the organization. The reality is that the repository itself is just one part of a much larger collection of products, services, tools, processes, and customer support components. Figure 6 provides one view of the repository environment that attempts to pull in some of these components into a single framework.

Figure 6. The asset portal and corresponding components

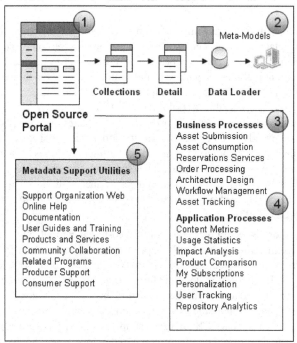

The structure of this diagram includes components labeled one through five.

1.   The asset portal
2.   The traditional repository
3.   Business processes
4.   Application processes
5.   Customer support environment

The Asset Portal

Varon (2005) indicated that an enterprise portal gives end users access to multiple types of information and applications through a standard interface. The vertical portal addresses one aspect of a business, such as a human resources site that lets employees sign up for training classes and view pay stubs. Others define a portal as an interface for people to access and exchange information online. It is usually customizable and can be designed to provide employees, customers, or trading partners with the information that they need, when they need it. Aiken and Finkelstein (2002) indicated that enterprise portals will be the primary method used by organizations to publish and access business intelligence and knowledge management resources. These definitions provide the foundation for an asset portal (Figure 6, label #1). The asset portal is a vertical portal that focuses on the information technology assets and the metadata representations of these assets. The asset portal is the desired starting point for the user base. The main portal page should contain some of the following functionality:

- Basic overview, user guide, and online help
- Semantic and advanced boolean search
- Multiple hierarchal structures for asset classification
- Usage-based listings: latest additions, coming soon, top ten
- Key business functions
- Service provider support
- Personalization
- Related programs

These components provide links to the entire metadata environment from a single point of access. The portal framework fundamentally changes how information systems are built, designed, and implemented. Reuse is imperative when new technologies like SOA enable the asset-based environment.

The Traditional Repository

The traditional repository (Figure 6, label #2) is similar to the traditional data warehouse, only extended to the entire inventory of assets. The collection image describes the various methods of grouping assets. Grouping assets into collections is a natural activity that has been done ever since the computer was created. Four basic collection schemes can be defined: classification, assimilation, semantic, and activity-based. The classification relationship is a basic domain-based relationship. For example, all ".xls" files on a personal computer are related by the classification that they are Excel files. Suppose the content classification scheme contains categories customer, product, order, billing, and finance. The librarian can classify entities in the customer classification taxonomy, irregardless of the originating logical model. The most obvious relationship between assets is the assimilation relationship, which basically states that one asset is directly, systematically, and purposefully related to another. The relationships between logical, physical, and database constructs is an example of an assimilation relationship. The semantic relationship could be considered a classification relationship on steroids. However, the classification focused on a specific match under a metadata domain, the semantic search moves beyond this and allows for a variety of semantic techniques. The simple search will take a term, search the entire collection of metadata fields, and locate the term within a text structure. Semantics allow for associations based on a percentage or predicted matching methodology. The final collection method is the activity-based method. Here, we review the actual usage of the repository in order to create the collection. Examples of activity-based collections include: top ten, most used, recently added, and coming soon. From the simple search to the activity-based list, these collections simply group assets together.

The detail page provides the metadata that describes the asset itself. This metadata includes the generic meta-model, which is a structure that contains common elements such as name, description, or keywords. The Dublin Core standard is an emerging standard which can form the basis of a generic meta-model. The context specific meta-model describes a specific asset within a specific context: the Object Management Group (OMG), common warehouse model (CWM), reusable asset specification (RAS), and Web Service Definition Language (WSDL). These standards focus on specific types of resources or assets (structural metadata). Presenting this information in a single, usable, and functional page is critical to the success of the repository. The modern enterprise environment is a collection of technical, functional, application, and data-related assets loosely connected within a heterogeneous environment. Communicating the inventory, meaning, and eventual understanding of the knowledge held within the corporation can be a daunting task.

The final area is the data loader utility which actually loads the metadata information into the meta-model. Vendors provide a large collection of utilities that can harvest metadata from tools, databases, and a wide variety asset types. In addition to the automated loading utility, most applications provide librarian tools for versioning, data quality, integration, and data entry.

Business Processes

The essence of electronic commerce is to move 100% of business processes (Figure 6, label #3) online. Few concepts have revolutionized business more profoundly than e-commerce. E-commerce is changing the shape of competition, the speed of action, and the streamlining of interactions, products, and payments from customers to companies and from companies to suppliers (Seybold, 1998). Organizations are also looking internally; Human Resources (HR) have made major moves toward employee self-service. Information technology must begin to move toward self-service, and this applies to the repository as well.

Asset Submission and Status Tracking

Metadata must be collected on each and every asset submitted to the repository. Even when the majority of metadata is collected through an automated tool, basic information must be collected in order to initiate the process. An online form or a series of forms can provide self-service for collecting the information from the asset producer. In addition, the form can also begin the process of tracking assets. Enterprise assets cannot just be submitted and loaded into the repository without a governance review by the architecture community. By moving this function online, the asset producer can check the status of the asset as it moves through the process. At some point, the asset submission could trigger a collection of services that integrate the architecture community, designers, developers, and many other groups within the technical community.

Asset Consumption

The repository can also provide services for the consumers of assets. Consumers work on the front end of projects to integrate reusable assets into the technology environment. One of the biggest problems with implementing enterprise architectures is the understanding of the environment from a usage point of view. While it may sound simple, knowing who is using what naming standard, vocabulary, domain model, pattern, or any other asset is critical to impact analysis and version control. Not to mention, reuse, return on investment, and other success criteria that could be addressed. Online forms can trigger the engagement process for utilizing assets, as well as track the relationship between user/application and the asset.

Application Processes

Application processes are products and services based on the application data produced from content and usage. Think of application processes as business intelligence for the repository. Some of these services include content metrics, usage metrics, impact analysis, user tracking, and subscription services.

Subscription Services

Subscription services are simply processes for notification when an enterprise asset is modified within the technology environment. The user may want to be notified when a specific asset is changed or reloaded. They may also want to subscribe to an entire category of assets which allows them to get notification on a more global scale. In the past, notification was accomplished by a librarian sending an email from a list or posting the information on a Web site. This method is commonly referred to as pull strategy, which forces the user to come to the site without any notification. This will cause a random delay in proliferating information throughout the enterprise. The system being described here provides an automatic notification of update when new assets are modified or added to the collection. The value of sending an automatic notification cannot be underestimated since this may decrease the time required to implement new functionality. In the world enterprise application integrations, this utility can be extremely valuable.

Product Comparison

The idea of product comparison is simple; place assets in a side-by-side framework where similar metadata elements can be compared. A good example of this utility is Dell and their laptop comparison pages. The customer can see the various laptops, images, prices, configurations, and support options. The product comparison function allows the customer to make an educated selection of the products offered. The essence of the online customer experience is the perception of complete control, and that is exactly what needs to be done with enterprise assets. Imagine how this kind of utility could be used with the enormous collection of XML vocabulary standards, or the volume of Web services that will be available in the next few years.

Customer Support Environment

While technology and new architectures get the majority of the headlines, at the implementation level, it still all comes down to the customer (Figure 6 label #5). The customer is the person or group that receives products or services of the Metadata group. Building a great company on the Web is not about "aggregating eyeballs," "increasing stickiness," or embracing any of the other slogans that masquerade as strategy. It is about rethinking the most basic relationship in business: the one between you and your customers (Kirsner, 1999). How well do you meet their needs? How smoothly do you solve their problems? How quickly do you anticipate what they will want next? The real promise of the Web is a once-and-for-all transfer of power: Consumers and business customers will get what they want, when and how they want it, and even at the price they want. Adding customer support utilities to the product mix is a positive step in creating a customer experience. Some of the basic components should include: user guides, online help, product and service overviews, FAQ, and training programs. In addition, producer and consumer communities can be created with a wide variety of collaboration tools in order to add value to the relationship. The Metadata Services Group is not only a development, delivery, and integration organization; they are also a support organization. Support organizations should have online brand sites that support one-way communications, which is similar to the traditional Intranet. These sites

Figure 7. The repository and registry

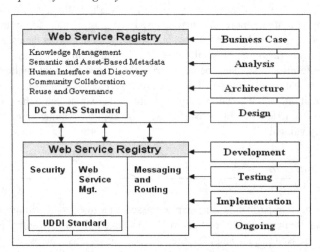

should include service functions like "*about us*", contact information, process definitions, project plans, and detailed descriptions of products and services. In addition to the brand site, the support organization should begin to integrate more collaboration and interactive technology. The bottom line is that success in the world of metadata will be defined by the customer, not by the technology. The repository environment is a complex collection of communications that are one-way, collaborative, and interactive by nature. Delivery of enterprise metadata must be effective, efficient, and dependable if it is to have value in the customer's eyes. The customer must be able to depend on the consistency of the technology, processes, and the relationship. Building the entire repository environment will ensure that you can deliver that value each and every time.

Integration of the Repository and Registry

For each of the elements in the model described in the prior section, a repository could be constructed, and in many cases, vendors have emerged to fill the basic requirements. This section will review the integration of a structured data environment with an unstructured information environment. More specifically, we address the question: Is there a difference between a repository and a registry?

Most organizations have been using the terms interchangeably for years. In today's environment, they are two different methodologies that serve the development and analyst communities. Figure 7 presents a layered approach for integrating the repository framework with the IDDU-based Web service registry. The repository serves a different user base than does the registry. Namely, the repository focuses on the early stages of the system development framework (SDLC), while the registry focuses on the latter stages. Information technology professionals simply have different information requirements depending on what their role and responsibility is within the business unit. The repository serves the higher levels of the organization like architecture, design, analysis, and even development. Employees at this level want to review the documentation, user guides, implementation, and service level agreements. They want the repository to be easy to use and easy to access. They demand value-add services like subscription services, semantic search, multiple classifications, and community collaboration: none of which can be found in the current service registry standard. The repository contains the assets, metadata elements, and unstructured supporting documents.

The Web service registry is based on the UDDI model and basically serves to categorize information about businesses and the services that they offer, and it associates those services with technical specifications of the Web service. These technical specifications are usually defined using Web Services Description Language (WSDL). WSDL describes what a Web service does, how it communicates, and where it lives. A Web service consumer queries the UDDI registry to find the WSDL descriptions to determine how to use the Web service. A UDDI registry is itself a Web service. The UDDI specification defines an API based on simple object access protocol (SOAP) messages, with a WSDL description of the registry service. Most UDDI registries also provide a browser-based human interface. A UDDI registry consists of the following data structure types: *Business Entity (businessentity), Business Service (businessService), Binding Template (bindingTemplate), and T-Model (tModel).* Descriptions of specifications for Web Services or taxonomies that form the basis for technical fingerprints; its role is to represent the technical specification of the Web Service, making it easier for Web Service consumers to find Web Services that are compatible with a particular technical specification. That is, based on the descriptions of the specifications for Web services in the tModel structure, Web Service consumers can easily identify other compatible Web Services. For instance, to send a purchase order to a business partner's Web service, the invoking service must know not only the location/URL of the service, but what format the purchase order should be sent in, what protocols are appropriate, what security is required, and what form of a response will result after sending the purchase order (Duncan, 2004).

By combining these two environments, the user can be presented with a seamless application that guides them to the required business function. The overall principle of building the Web application environment on top of the metadata architectures is to provide a complete picture of the knowledge held within the space itself. Why is the convergence of the traditional metadata repository and the Web service registry needed? The reason is surprisingly simple: the evolution from innovation to the migration into the mainstream. While Web services were solely for the technical community, all that was needed was the IDDU standard registry. This is no different than the observed behavior of database administrator's (DBA) resistance to the metadata repository. They simply prefer the low-level technology tools they are accustomed to. As the body of knowledge and utility of Web services continues to expand, the more complex and service-based repository is needed. Unfortunately, the simple act of having a repository available does not guarantee success, which is why a maturity model is needed. The following section describes the role of the repository and the additional elements required in order to guarantee success in the transition to a Web-enabled environment.

Governance by Maturity Model

In order to define the processes for architecture governance, we must first define a maturity model for the progression of metadata integration. Maturity models are simple classifications of how well an organization adheres to a defined set of standards. In 1986, the Software Engineering Institute (SEI), with assistance from the Mitre Corporation, began developing a process maturity framework that would help organizations improve their software process. The capability maturity model for software (CMM) presents sets of recommended practices in a number of key process areas that have been shown to enhance software process capability. The CMM is based on knowledge acquired from software process assessments and extensive feedback from both industry and government. At one point, the SEI was supporting five different versions of CMM. Champlin (2005) has identified over 180 maturity models currently in use today. Effective information technology governance does not just happen; top performing enterprises carefully design governance, and managers throughout the organization make daily decisions putting that design into practice. This governance process provides an accountability framework for encouraging desirable behaviors and outcomes (Ross & Weill, 2005). The following paragraphs will review the concepts around technology governance and the integration of the business strategy with the metadata architecture. The majority of this section will define the metadata maturity model which focuses on the level of metadata integration within the environment.

Figure 8. Metadata management maturity model

Metadata Maturity Level	Program Basics			Program Basics		
	Senior Management Commitment	Professional Support	Architecture Governance	Participation	Information Integration	Eco-System
Self-Governed	No	No	No	No	No	No
Supported Self-Governed	Partial	Partial	No	No	No	No
Centrally Governed	Partial	Yes	Partial	No	No	No
Enterprise Awakening	Yes	Yes	Yes	Yes	No	No
Planned Growth	Yes	Yes	Yes	Yes	Yes	No
Synergistic	Yes	Yes	Yes	Yes	Yes	Yes

Metadata Maturity Model

As described in the opening paragraph, the CMM is a model for judging the maturity of the software processes of an organization and for identifying the key practices that are required to increase the maturity of these processes. The CMM is organized into five maturity levels: initial, repeatable, defined, managed, and optimizing. Predictability, effectiveness, and control of an organization's software processes are believed to improve as the organization moves up these five levels. While not rigorous, the empirical evidence to date supports this belief. Figure 8 presents the metadata maturity model.

The Metadata Maturity Model is broken into three vertical sections: metadata maturity level, program basics, and program development. The maturity definition describes the level obtained by an organization as they mature along the natural progression of metadata management. Program basics will describe the support structures required in order to reach the higher levels of maturity. Program development will describe the levels of integration. Horizontally, the rows depict the natural progression from one level to the next with the indication that an organization has achieved one or more of the six vertical classifications. The reader will note that the domain has been simplified to "Yes," "No," and "Partial" as the base value. Clearly, this can be extended to a numerical ranking which could extend the utility of the model as a metric type dashboard. However, this chapter will utilize the simple domain in order to provide a clearer picture of how the model can be utilized in a large-scale organization.

Program Basics

The program basics review the three major support components of a metadata implementation. By support, we mean the different organizations that need to understand the importance of having an integrated metadata architecture. Some of these organizations include: the support of senior management, a support organization for the products and services, and the architecture support for enterprise governance.

Senior management commitment is required for any project requiring the resources and commitment from the technology community. Projects often fail because their sponsors have under-emphasized or have simply been unable to obtain senior management commitment. Simply stated, without commitment or demonstrated leadership, initiatives will stall, fall substantially short of expectations, or just plain fail. The most important aspect of senior level commitment is to translate that commitment to the organization in the form of goals and objectives that can be executed against in the form of a project or program. In order to gain this commitment, organizations must be able to present a solid business case and a clear message of criticality. The business case must address the tangible and intangible benefits, along with the total cost of ownership. Metadata programs are more successful when they are part of an over-arching program of organizational change, business improvement, or operational excellence. If metadata cannot stand on its own merit, then integration into current initiates is the key. The measurement under senior level commitment includes no support (No), limited support (Partial), or full support (Yes).

Professional support is a designated measurement of the experience, tools, and support model in place for the metadata program. Experience is the key for organizations implementing metadata at any level. The majority of concepts under the metadata environment are fairly well known and defined within the following fields of study: knowledge management, information science, library science, and information systems. However, bringing that type of knowledge into the organization is critical for long- term success. Finding resources that are dedicated to the quality, integration, and usage of the metadata information must be placed on the forefront of the requirements when building an organization that will support metadata at the enterprise level. One aspect is the ability of the team to demonstrate adaptability, flexibility, creativity, and passion. These behavior-oriented aspects are also critical to the success of the program, since you can teach technology, but developing passion can be a challenge. Many firms are looking beyond the technical skills and researching the behavior aspects that deliver a high performance workforce. Researchers in this space (Abell, 2004) indicate six core competencies that are essential in the information space:

- **The ability to learn:** being curious and seeking new knowledge, being responsible for self development
- **Self-initiation:** acting like a business of one; not waiting to be told
- **Collaborative:** being a team player, having positive regard for other people, not status driven
- **Intellectual linking:** seeing the big picture and making connections
- **Humility:** recognizing that other people know things, learning from mistakes
- **Ability to think and do:** having a focus on outcomes

The world of information technology is changing at a rapid pace, where tools for metadata acquisition, storage, and utilization are falling behind the demand. The same is true for the standards required to integrate the vast amount of knowledge. A support model strategy is based upon leveraging open and active lines of communication between technically-adept staff and the ultimate consumer or producer of the metadata information. This strategy will empower users to enable long-term, scalable and stable use of metadata technology. The Metadata support model asks five basic questions of the technology environment:

- What metadata products and services are available to me?
- How can I utilize these products and services within my environment?
- Who can help me in case I need some professional guidance?
- Are the metadata applications ready for enterprise usage?
- How am I doing in comparison to others and against best practices?

Success in metadata is not about deploying software packages or writing white papers. Success comes from offering deep support and laying the foundation for an evolutionary value-add environment. This requires us to offer not just products, but services and experiences as well. Deep support is about owning the customer experience and metadata's role within the enterprise environment. Chief executives recognize that technology, effectively planned, implemented, and supported, can measurably contribute toward the realization of business objectives. The support model simply allows the metadata world to evolve and produce additional value over time.

The architecture environment can act as a governance body for the enterprise asset collection. Governance requires the organization to know what assets they have and how they are being used. Assets can and should be mapped to a domain model which also requires an association with the repository environment. Enterprise architecture provides the tight cohesion and loose coupling between the business and information technology strategies. It is the "glue" that allows both business and information technology strategy to enable and drive each other. Business and technology are changing rapidly. For these changes to be reflected in the information technology architecture, there must be a well-defined process in place to ensure the continual reexamination and alignment of the business and information technology strategies. Establishing an adaptive Information Technology architecture involves change for people, process, and technology. By planning evolutionary change and implementing reusable elements, the architecture will permit consistent integration between applications, increase the overall adaptability of the information technology environment, increase the speed of solution delivery, and maximize information technology investments. Architecture is just one example of an organization that should utilize the enterprise asset catalog. While metadata focuses on the world of data architecture the vast majority of time, metadata will play a pivotal role in application, functional, XML, and technical architectures. The state of measurement here is the definable support from the standard bodies within the enterprise. These three main functional categories define the program basics. Noticeably missing from the program basics is any technology or standards. Much of this is assumed within the architecture and tools environment.

Program Development

The program development areas review the functional integration of the metadata archi-tecture within the organization. These integration classifications include the participation with the business and technology communities, process integration, and functional metadata ecosystem where the entire environment is controlled by the physical metadata.

The metadata environment exists within a business model to bring producers of the meta-data information together with the consumers. The relationships between these groups create a type of metadata integration map. From this map, the organization should be able to determine:

- Which organizations influenced the metadata strategy and vision
- Which organizations provide data to the repository collection
- Which customers utilize the repository collection
- Who is on the side of metadata management, and who is not
- Where the organization fits into the enterprise structure
- How metadata utilizes other organizations to expand the level of services
- How well metadata is branded and marketed within the enterprise

These questions illustrate the importance that metadata has throughout the organization. The map should not only indicate that a relationship exists between the various entities, but also determine the strength of that relationship. The strength of the relationship can be measured by the level of integration, dependencies, governance utility, and metrics of usage and content for the repository collection. One additional note that needs to be understood is that not all relationships are positive. While rare, competitive environments may emerge where the success on one architecture, software, or group will hurt another; this competitive environment needs to be understood, and the implications need to be defined.

The level of integration defines how the metadata and the repository collection are integrated into the day-by-day activities of the organization. Many of the major support functions that metadata can provide revolve around integration projects. Projects like a data warehouse or EAI provide excellent opportunities to push the metadata philosophy. Metadata can be used in an active or passive nature. While most implementations stress the active use of the information in configuring and managing assets, we cannot overlook the utility and value that comes from the structured and unstructured sources of information delivered in a passive fashion. The divergence of thought comes from the value generated from the passive and active utility built around the asset. Passive utility can be defined as the utility of publishing, indexing, searching, and result generation of metadata information. Many experts argue on the limited value of the passive metadata, but we have many examples of where this type of utility is not only valued but demanded. It is widely recognized that an organization's most valuable knowledge, its essential intellectual capital, is not limited to information contained in official document repositories and databases: scientific formulae, "hard" research data, computer code, codified procedures, financial figures, customer records, and the like (Bobrow, Whalen, & Yamauchi, 2003). However, in order to develop the know-how, ideas, and insights of the community at large, metadata must be managed at every stage of the asset. Since passive utility is the discovery and knowledge-based reuse of metadata information, it stands to reason that passive utility must be delivered first. Active utility without information is simply pointless. Success in metadata means that getting accurate, complete, and contextual information from an asset and then providing access to this information across the organization.

The final column in the model describes a metadata ecosystem that reviews the level at which organizations are utilizing metadata on an active basis. Active usage of metadata is taking metadata to the next level of value, beyond reference and context building that is used in the prior section. Active usage does not control the metadata, but uses that metadata to drive change within the organization. At the lowest end of active utility is using database metadata systems to control the structure of the physical database, or using ETL metadata to control the transformation between two systems. Advanced active utility will utilize the metadata portfolio or ecosystem to control, manage, and govern the entire technology environment.

Maturity Levels

Six maturity levels have been identified within the metadata maturity model shown in Figure 8. Each of these levels is a natural progression of growth and expansion of the products and services described in the previous sections. Since the model has two distinct vertical sections, the progression from one level to the next will not be as simple as moving across the horizontal cross-sections. In addition, the levels of the six functional elements are not as simple as "yes, the organization has the capability" or "no, they do not." In the following paragraphs, the author will describe in general terms the organizational attributes that define the classification.

Self-Governed Level

The self-governed organization will have a limited amount of program basics and program development components. This does not mean that they do not have metadata. There is never a question whether or not an organization has or produces metadata; the question is, do they manage the information effectively? Metadata at the self-governing level simply exists without much guidance or oversight. Governance here is a random event, since leadership does not actually use information to drive change or to measure performance of the business or technology community.

Supported Self-Governed Level

Supported organizations will have some support from the senior management as well as someone who understands the value of metadata to the organization. This expert may be home-grown or a hired consultant. Organizations that have a knowledgeable metadata resource can find solid value by deploying their skills in the database organization, Web development group, or the document management organization. Participation is still limited to a few organizations with little or no integration between the efforts.

Centrally-Governed Level

On this level, central governance has been established by an enterprise metadata group. This group will require some level of commitment from senior management as well as the support from the architecture community. This support can simply be an acknowledgement from the different architecture segment teams of the importance of metadata or a fully functional metadata management segment team. The principles of metadata are universal and should fall under an architecture guidance model. Having metadata centrally governed opens the door for the development of an enterprise metadata program. Programs will encourage organizations to share best practices and experiences, and collaborate on how metadata can have value across all business units or technology environments. At this point, the organization has mastered the program basics, and now the program development activities need to be addressed.

Enterprise Awakening Level

The ability to reach this level may be as much as result of the skills of the leadership within metadata. Support from senior management, centralized customer support, and a defined architecture are the cornerstones where the program can be developed and extended to the entire organization. Since metadata can be deployed in a distributed, centralized, or federated at the physical level, integration is critical. Most organizations will need to experience some level of local success before moving toward an integration strategy. The program needs solid participation across the business lines in order to achieve the enterprise awakening level.

Planned Growth Level

At this point, each and every project has addressed the metadata issue, and there are no exceptions. Most organizations have no problem ensuring that architecture, design, development, database design, and many other areas are addressed within the software development cycle. Metadata should be integrated across the enterprise as a passive information source. This level is extremely valuable since the entire portfolio of assets have been accounted for and documented. In addition, the relationships between the assets have been identified, and the information can be used for reporting applications like a dynamic hub and spoke application for the systems and interfaces.

Synergistic Level

Each and every possible function of metadata is now addressed, from the database metadata to the Web page and XML tag management. Each and every dimension of metadata is managed at the enterprise level and support for a true corporate index of information, a virtual asset catalog of all the content within the enterprise. This information is being used to actually govern and drive technology changes throughout the SDLC. Very few organizations have reached this level of maturity due to the lack of tools and standards.

Model Summary

The model presented here is just one of the many maturity models within the information technology environment. The model does not address specific processes and products required to reach the different levels. If you take a look at the vertical elements, you really see some basic questions that need to be asked about any metadata project or group.

- Is the project supported, endorsed, or promoted by senior executives?
- Do you have the necessary knowledge of metadata in your organization?
- Does your architecture support metadata management, and to what extent?
- Is everyone participating?
- Is metadata being used to document and provide informational utility?
- Is metadata being used to manage, govern, and change the technical environment?

The purpose of the metadata maturity model is to provide guidance for improving an organization's processes and its ability to manage the development, acquisition, and main-tenance of products and services as they relate to the metadata environment. The model helps an organization review its organizational maturity, process area capability, establish priorities for improvement, and guide the implementation of these improvements. The model describes an evolutionary improvement path from an ad hoc, immature process to a mature, disciplined process of managing metadata at the enterprise level.

Managing the Environment with Metrics

Metrics have always been an important part of information technology. Unfortunately, for the most part, metrics are an afterthought of the project itself. The natural progression of a system that moves from innovation, incubation, and migration is to eventually measure the impact and value-add to the business. Metrics tend to create absolutes where performance is defined by numerical standards which are not easily manipulated. Of course, there are more things than strict numerical analysis that defines success, but organizations had bet-ter be sure that the implementation includes a solid collection of metrics. Many metrics are simply irrelevant to the metadata work being done or do not have a direct impact on the long-term success of the program. Information is gathered, but no action is taken as a result. Take a look at the performance metrics in the repository and ask yourself, "When was the last time we took an action, based on this number?" Many times, metrics are used as a weapon against the staff member. Dr. Edward Deming often said, "We need to drive fear out of the workplace", but most performance measurement systems do exactly the opposite. When management does act on a metric, they do not always look at the business process. Instead, they focus on someone, some other department, or some outside factor to "blame", causing people to play the system and to point their fingers elsewhere when problems arise. Many times the metrics selected are too high-level to provide information where someone can take action to address problems before they develop. In other cases, an important result gets looked at, but it is impacted by so many variables that it is difficult to determine the degree of correlation. For example, is a three percent decrease in the rate of content due to improvements in the process or variability in the measurement system? The metrics show a result, but it may be too late to take any corrective action, which leads us to understand that by the time a problem is discovered, it is too late to do anything about it. In the world of metadata, there are an infinite number of possible metrics. This section will define the foundation metrics that each and every metadata implementation should review in detail: content and usage.

Content Metrics

Content metrics describe what information is housed inside the repositories. Without considering how the data is used, content focuses on the what. Perhaps the most obvious example of content metrics is the object count. An object count sounds like a simple concept except for the fact that there are multiple methods for defining what classifies as an object. In the database world, there are plenty of options to consider when counting objects: entities, attributes, tables, databases, fields, and specific component of metadata descriptors. Should a table count as one asset or do we break down the object by the number of fields within the table? When counting logical assets, do we count the logical model, add the entities and attributes, or is that considered double counting? There is no real answer here, other than it depends on the organizational requirements. The essential element for content metrics is the consistency of delivery and definition.

We can measure the breadth and scope of these metadata elements for each object type as well as the percentage of completeness for the model itself. Some objects may have an extended meta-model with 20 metadata elements while others may only contain only a few. The number of attachments is another measurement that can be taken on a specific asset. The thinking here is that objects that have extended unstructured documentation are better understood than those with only a few attachments. Examples of attachments could include logical models, UML models, user guides, and installation instructions.

Content metrics should be captured on a monthly basis and reviewed by utilizing trend analysis software which evaluates the information over an extended period of time. Ideally, the process of collection should be automated and have the ability to capture metrics at any point in time. What growth percentage should be applied to the content metrics? Again, long-term success is not defined by the explosion of growth in the first year but by the subsequent three to five years. The first few years may very well have triple digit growth, but sustaining this is near impossible over the long term.

Usage Metrics

The other key metric is usage. Remember, you can have all of the content in the world, but without usage you have not done much more than build a nice inventory. Usage is the key to delivering long-term value-add to the organization. The first usage metric class is focused on the user. Many Web-based applications utilize three high-level classifications for user traffic. A "hit" is each individual file sent to a browser by the Web server. A "page view" can be described as each time a visitor views a Webpage on your site, irrespective of how many hits are generated. Web pages are comprised of files. Every image in a page is a separate file. When a visitor looks at a page (i.e., a page view), they may see numerous images, graphics, pictures, and so forth, and generate multiple hits. For example, if you have a page with 10 pictures, then a request to a server to view that page generates 11 hits (10 for the pictures, and one for the HTML file). A page view can contain hundreds of hits. This is the reason that most organizations measure page views and not hits. Additionally, there is a high potential for confusion here, because there are two types of "hits". The hits we are discussing in this article are the hits recorded by log files, and interpreted by log analysis. A second type of "hits" are counted and displayed by a simple hit counter. Hit counters record one hit for every time a Webpage is viewed, which is also problematic because it does not distinguish unique visitors. The third type of class is a visitor which is an individual user; Web analytics can distinguish between a return visitor and a unique one. While not perfect, page views offer the best trending metric available. Organizations should utilize the 10% bar to measure progress over a 12-month period. If the traffic grows at or above 10%, then the organization has exceeded their objective. Those repositories that fail to deliver 10% must be reviewed in order to determine the viability of the application itself. The key is that both content and usage must grow in order to deliver that business value over the long term.

An organization can also track the length of time that a person stays on the repository, what time of day is most popular, and which day compromises the heaviest traffic. These time-based metrics are important to ensure that the repository is up and operational 100% of the time, especially during high-traffic periods. Now, if they move away from the user and focus the attention on the actual page or artifact, other metrics provide insight. The administrator can tell which of the asset pages is viewed the most and which artifact has the highest download rate. These simple metrics may alter the way you present artifacts and even generate new classifications. Having links on the repository that represent "Most Popular," "Most Downloaded," or "Latest Additions" add value to the metadata environment. These classifications are defined as usage-based classifications. In other words, the use of the repository actually defines the classification of the assets. Assuming the repository has some advanced features, one can measure how many subscriptions per asset you have, how many transactions may be processed by the component, or what is the reuse level within the application. Remember, the application can generate any number of metrics, but organizations should only focus on the ones that can generate action, support the expansion of the brand, and help managers understand the environment.

Summary of Web-Enabled Governance with Metadata

Enterprise architecture is the driving force to establish a roadmap to achieve the objectives of the business via technology investments and the utilization of current information technology environments. The California Information Technology Council (2005) recently published a framework describing a collection of principles that represent the criteria for investment and governance. First, the business must drive the technology decisions, and architecture must enable this activity by minimizing unintended effects on the business due to technology changes. Utilizing enterprise repositories for impact analysis will ensure that proposed changes will not create catastrophic events within the business itself. Technology communities should build what the business needs, not what technology experts think is important. Metadata provides the means for inventory management to see what is already built, which ensures that duplicate efforts do not occur. In addition, efforts like domain analysis help understand how the inventory maps to the business processes. Enterprise architecture ensures that all decisions are made across business units where no single organization declares a standard that is incompatible with the current infrastructure. By focusing on enterprise assets, metadata solutions work seamlessly with the frameworks and base activities of the architecture community. Deploying this enterprise view and treating technology investments as assets, organizations can ensure that common solutions are built and reduce the level of investment within the technology community.

The Future of Enterprise Metadata

Overview

The previous sections of this chapter focused on building the ideal environment for governing the current Web application environment. Unfortunately, the Web-enabled environment tomorrow will not look like the one defined by current standards. Just as traditional metadata operated effectively within the data warehouse, most of the principles, standards, and best practices did not scale to the enterprise level. The issue of scalability and the lack of standards must be addressed by the innovation of new tools for integration. While we cannot predict that these issues will be completely addressed in the near future, the long-term view is that the vast majority of these issues will be resolved. What remains to be discussed are the advancing technologies and trends that will need to be integrated into the design and architecture strategy. This section will include discussion on three major trends: RSS technology, Semantic Web, and the Information Worker.

Really simple syndication (RSS) is a lightweight XML format designed for sharing headlines and other Web content. Originated by UserLand in 1997 and subsequently used by Netscape to fill channels for Netcenter, RSS has evolved into a popular means of sharing content between sites. RSS solves myriad problems that Webmasters commonly face, such as increasing traffic, as well as gathering and distributing news. RSS can also be the basis for additional content distribution services (Eisenzopf, 2002). The typical use of the RSS feed is within the WebLog (blog) environment. Once the author updates their blog with an entry, the system will update the RSS file and send a "ping" message to the "Aggregation Ping Server" indicating that the site has updated. Several organizations like Feedster and Technorati monitor the feeds and publish in a centralized location. The other option is that end users can simply purchase or download a news aggregator application (reader) which allows the user to subscribe to any blog that supports the RDF/XML feed. The application can check the blog for updates once an hour or once a day, depending on the configuration of the reader. This eliminates the need to engage search engines or news collection sites in order to read the content from a specific source of information.

The implications for the metadata environment are enormous. Taking a closer look at the RSS standard reveals that the standard is fairly simply and consistent irregardless of the context. This indicates that a simple meta-model, such as the Dublin Core, could be easily exchanged by the use of RSS technology. News readers could replace the majority of the functionality currently held within the centralized metadata repository. Publishing new content is very similar to the information required for publishing technology asset meta-data or will be in the future. Advancements in the RSS technology will allow code objects, analysis documents, modeling artifacts, and other system development lifecycle products to publish information about the assets automatically. This will eliminate the need for the extraction of information by hand or forcing integration into a single methodology. RSS already has search functionality and personal taxonomies where the end user can catalog their own content, which may prove to be much more valuable than the traditional information technology-based taxonomies and onotologies.

As the vendor community converts their product lines to the XML-based standards, a whole new world will open up to the possibilities of the Semantic Web-enabled applications. W3C (2001) defines the Semantic Web as an extension of the current Web in which information is given well-defined meaning, better enabling computers and people to work in cooperation. The mix of content on the Web has been shifting from exclusively human-oriented content to more and more data content. The Semantic Web brings to the Web the idea of having data defined and linked in a way that it can be used for more effective discovery, automation, integration, and reuse across various applications. For the Web to reach its full potential, it must evolve into a Semantic Web, providing a universally-accessible platform that allows data to be shared and processed by automated tools as well as by people. By definition, the Semantic Web will integrate the different technologies like XML, RDF, RSS, name-spaces, and ontologies. These technologies will come together to radically change the way in which we collect information. The Semantic Web is more than just standards and technologies. Marshall and Shipman (2003) indicate that the promise of the Semantic Web has raised a number of different expectations. These expectations can be traced to three different per-spectives on the Semantic Web. The Semantic Web is portrayed as: (1) a universal library, to be readily accessed and used by humans in a variety of information use contexts; (2) the backdrop for the work of computational agents completing sophisticated activities on behalf of their human counterparts; and (3) a method for federating particular knowledge bases and databases to perform anticipated tasks for humans and their agents. McComb (2004) defines the killer application in the Semantic Web as a radical improvement over search and agent technology. An agent is a program to which an individual delegates some authority to act on the individual's behalf and then releases to act autonomously. The Semantic Web and accompanying technologies will produce an environment where a universal repository is possible and should be on the market. From the perspective of a librarian, cataloger, publisher, or content provider, the Semantic Web is a metadata initiative; at the heart of the Semantic Web is the assumption that adding formal metadata that describes a Web resource's content and the meaning of its links is going to substantially change the nature of the way that computers and people find material and use it. Because there are a variety of metadata efforts underway (the Semantic Web is one metadata initiative among many), it is important to evaluate the Semantic Web in this context (Marshall & Shipman, 2003).

Assuming that a syndicated repository comes to fruition, then the question remains, what else will alter the future of the enterprise metadata environment? Research that currently falls under the umbrella of information worker may provide an indication. Business models of individual workers and organizations will revolve around the ability to create and integrate knowledge. This may occur by assembling new constructs of information and data. Perhaps these new constructs will holistically change the way we think about work. It is hard to imagine a world where 90% of what we do day by day will be eliminated or automated. Wave one of the information world was the codification of data, information, and knowledge. The industry is about 70% complete with our ability to translate objects, elements, and transactions into core structures. Success stories can be found in a myriad of systems: operational data stores (ODS), expert systems, online transaction processing applications, business intelligence, and many more. Our ability to move from classic data processing to information technology has been nothing but remarkable. However, like most waves, as problems were solved, others were created. The volume of data and information is staggering, and our ability to understand the context, meaning, value, and usage is getting more difficult every day. Take, for example, the Internet, 50 billion Web pages which grow an estimated 20% a month. Over 30 million documents or pages pass over the communication lines each and every day; not to mention the 2,000 research reports which are published. Yet, trying to find anything out on the Internet today remains a challenging task. Whiting (2003) estimate that Radio Frequency Identification (RFID) tags could generate 7.7 million terabytes of data a day. Generating, storing, and building a system to manage this volume of data will get easier, but our ability to understand and generate business value may not. The second wave of information was the desire to integrate our systems, data, and information in order to reduce the complexity and redundancy. Our efforts to solve this problem have produced a huge collection of technologies like Enterprise Integration Application (EAI), Semantic Web, portal technology, search engines, content integration, and on and on. The third wave describes the integration of the business model where the basic tasks of information technology have all been automated. Investments in information technology, while profoundly important, are less and less likely to deliver a competitive edge to an individual company (Carr, 2004).

The role of metadata within the world changes from an active or passive role to one that is basically essential to the success of the business itself. Automation and integration into the basic business model will require an entirely new view on the importance of metadata. While our prior sections described metadata as the glue that holds the systems together, now metadata holds the business itself intact. Organizations will move away from employers and business process owners to outsourcing the vast majority of the business functions. Business will evolve to a coordinator of effort or assembler of resources. Business models will emerge as value-add only for a short period of time, which will require the assemble process to happen instantaneously. While this vision may seem far-fetched, the reality is that many businesses are already moving in this direction with outsourcing, service architectures, and dynamic business models. The evolution of the information worker will literally transform the way in which we work and provide value to the business. The change in focus from information work to knowledge work requires a shift in the way we conceptualize what we do. We should expand our focus on technology to creating corporate and operational value through our efforts. This conceptual shift, in addition to representing a new common sense about the work we do, may be the key to gaining acknowledgment and appreciation within the organization, and it should open up new possibilities for career development.

The future of metadata is clear, and organizations must begin to embrace this technology in order to ensure universal acceptance. Some organizations are already paving the way: The DCMI Global Corporate Circle Core promotes the use of the Dublin Core standard by enterprise organizations for both internal and external information. These organizations coordinate with developers and information providers to ensure interoperability with enterprise-wide applications.

Conclusion, Implications, Recommendations, and Summary

Overview

The meanings, impact, and future environments of enterprise metadata were researched, documented, and applied to the Web-enabled environment within this chapter. A universal repository design was laid out, including a wide variety of functions that address the needs of the business as well as the technology community. The environment was integrated into the Web-enabled architecture in order to deliver a tool for governing the entire lifecycle of asset development. This section will address the conclusions of the author, implications for researchers and architects, recommendations for further research, and a summery statement of accomplishment.

Conclusions

The impact of the enterprise metadata environment is being felt by every organization that is attempting to integrate a Web-based environment. The establishment of an architecture governance process, along with a collection of tools for managing the environment, is critical to the success of any large-scale effort. In this chapter, the author has described the need for a universal strategy for asset management across the Information Technology infrastructure. The findings imply that organizations that wish to reach the higher levels of maturity must begin to review and deploy enterprise metadata frameworks. Architects must ensure that assets are cataloged, documented, and reused within the system development lifecycle. In addition, developers must ensure that they utilize the services defined by the architecture community within the domain model. The asset catalog or repository must be the first step in application architecture, design, and development.

The repository must extend beyond traditional database assets and begin to integrate the entire collection of assets within the organization. These assets must not only be documented but related, based on a wide variety of relationships. Examples include call structures, model relationships, and interfaces between systems and information stewards. By focusing on the enterprise or shared assets, the volume of assets will be reduced to a manageable environment which will enable not only integration but an efficient deployment process. The repository is not only for the consumer of the metadata information but for the producer as well. Implementations must understand the role and responsibilities for each of the players in order to continue to deliver value over the long term.

The future of metadata will revolve around its ability to move beyond the core assets and into new technologies like RSS, Semantic Web, and the migration toward the information worker. Technology and the business environments continue to evolve, and metadata must adapt to this change in order to continue to add value. Ultimately, the business world will define the utility and requirements for the long-term adaptation of metadata technologies.

Implications

Theoretical Implications

While many previous works (Aiken & Finkelstein, 2002; Marco, 2000; Tannenbaum, 2001) addressed the need for metadata within the data space, this research focused on taking these concepts to the Web-enabled environment. It is believed that this research will encourage additional studies in the areas of asset management, enterprise architecture, and full-system lifecycle integration. While this study focused on the high-level design and business value, researchers should continue to look at how metadata can be integrated into emerging integration strategies like Information Technology Infrastructure Library (ITIL) which provides the foundation for quality Service Management. Metadata management is a complex and evolving methodology that should continue to be reviewed by both corporate and academic researchers. This research should be improved by finding casual relationships between the capturing and utilization of metadata and the success of the overall Web-enabled environment.

Future studies and frameworks should integrate metadata and the repository as part of the overall vision and strategy. Metadata must be addressed and enabled on the front end of the program. This research attempted to establish a design strategy where organizations can tailor the system for their individual needs. In addition, the research took a giant leap forward to integrate the entire asset collection into a single repository instead of the isolated implementations currently in place. Organizations that can recognize the value to collecting, storing, retrieving, and utilizing metadata in this type of environment will outperform those organizations that fail to document their environments.

Implications for the Architecture Community

The results of this research suggest that architecture-based organizations need to move beyond simply defining standards and ignoring the success or failure of the implementations. Architects must understand the implications of their decisions and the standards they set. By implementing enterprise metadata, the architecture can play an integral part of governing the Web-enabled environment. Governance ensures that the information technology environment is supervised, controlled, monitored, and guided toward the strategic direction of the organization. In doing this, Information Technology enables the business and can create that elusive competitive advantage.

Recommendations

Clearly, the enterprise metadata environment has evolved over the past few years. Although sporadic, the environment has progressed since the beginnings of EAI or SOA. The technology, standards, and design frameworks evolution will continue as more and more organizations embrace XML, taxonomies, ontologies, and many of the Semantic Web standards. Integration continues to be the basis of most technology investments within the organization. There is a convergence of technology, implementations, and standards which will speed the acceptance of this technology in the coming years. Organizations should continue to push the industry as well as the vendor community to develop solutions to address the issues of asset management at the enterprise level. While standards like ITIL are emerging, the vendor community is not investing enough capital to address the gaps in the software environment. Most organizations still build their own solutions or try to patch a variety of software applications.

Researchers should take a look at helping to fill in the gaps and supporting the various standards that are converging. Enormous investments are being made in XML and the Semantic Web; these efforts need to be applied to the metadata environment in order to move to the highest level of maturity. This research did not have the space to address the design to the levels of data standards, visual design frameworks, nor application technologies. This high-level design needs to be taken to the implementation phase, and clearly define requirements based on research and the emerging standards. The research could also be applied to other software applications within the Web-enabled environment, including the Web service registry and business intelligence reporting required by organizations implementing these technologies.

The final recommendation is for organizations that have not addressed the integration, either at the data or service layer, to begin the process as soon as possible. The industry is moving closer to a borderless business environment where transactions will flow, not within businesses, but between them. Dynamic business models are built upon the utilization of Internet technologies to literally redefine how business gets done. The new business models require integration, not within the organizational technical environment, but between organizations. Organizations that do not invest in these external integration technologies and adopt the emerging standards will be left behind and unable to compete under the new business model.

Summary

Section one of this chapter focused on the basic definition of metadata from the traditional data perspective. The objectives were laid out to describe the impact of enterprise metadata to the technology community. Section two provided a more detailed historical perspective of metadata by focusing on the various success stories of metadata implementations. The main contribution of this section was the enterprise metadata layered framework that describes how the separate meta-models need to be integrated into a universal asset repository in order to continue to bring value-add to the organization. Enterprise metadata-related terms and a basic overview of reuse was provided to understand the utility that metadata will play in the larger scale of enterprise architecture. Section three focused on the specific high-level design of the repository that is required within the Web-enabled environment. A metadata maturity model defined a methodology to measure the progression of implementation within the organization, which provides a simple-to-use process for measuring success. This research concludes that the basic development of an enterprise metadata strategy is an imperative to the success of any Web-enabled environment.

References

Abell, A. (2004). *The war for your talent*. Retrieved March 22, 2005, from http://www.tfpl.com/assets/applets/warfortalent.pdf

Aiken, P., & Finkelstein, C. (2002). *Building corporate portals with XML*. New York: McGraw-Hill.

Ambler, S., & Constantine, L. (2000). *The unified process inception phase*. Gilroy, CA: CMP Books.

Apiwattanapong, T., Harrold, M., & Orso, A. (2003). Leveraging field data for impact analysis and regression testing. In *Proceedings of the 11th European Software Engineering Conference and 11th ACM SIGSOFT Symposium on the Foundations of Software Engineering* (pp. 128-137). Helsinki, Finland: The Association of Computing Machinery.

Becker, S., & Mottay, F. (2001, January). A global perspective on Website usability. *IEEE Software, 18*(1), 61-54.

Bobrow, D., Whalen, J., & Yamauchi, Y. (2003). Information use of service technicians in difficult cases. In *Proceedings of the SIGCHI Conference on Human Factors in Computing Systems 5*(1) (pp. 81-88). New York: The Association of Computing Machinery.

Briand, L., Labiche, Y., O'Sullivan, L., & Sowka, M. (2005). Automated impact analysis of UML models. *Journal of Systems and Software, 79*(3), 339-352.

California Information Technology Council (2005). *California Enterprise Architecture Framework*. Retrieved August 3, 2005, from http://www.cio.ca.gov/ITCouncil/Committees/PDFs/California_EA_Framework_Final.pdf

Calongne, C. (2001, March). Designing for Website usability. *Journal of Computing in Small Colleges, 16*(3), 39-45.

Carr, N. (2004). *Does IT matter.* Boston: HBS Press.

Champlin, B. (2005). What makes people trust online gambling sites? In *Proceedings of the 13th.Annual Conference on Business Process Management* (pp. 10-11). London: Association of Business Process Management Professionals.

Chaudhuri, S., & Dayal, U. (1997). An overview of data warehousing and OLAP technology. *SIGMOD Record, 26,* 65-74.

Decker, S., Mitra, P., & Melnik, S. (2000). Framework for the semantic Web: An RDF tutorial. *IEEE Internet Computing, 4*(6), 68-73.

Do, H., & Rahm, E. (2000). *Metadata interoperability in data warehouses* (Tech.Rep. No. 01-2000). Department of Computer Science, University of Leipzig.

Dublin Core (2005). *Dublin Core Elements.* Retrieved January 5, 2005, from http://www.dublincore.org

Duncan, S. (2004). *UDDI publishing using the browser interface.* Retrieved April 12, 2005, from http://www.oracle.com/technology/products/jdev/howtos/10g/WS_UD-DIPublish/uddi_HowTo.html

Eisenzopf, J. (2002). *Making headlines with RSS using rich site summaries to draw new visitors.* Retrieved July 16, 2005, from http://www.newarchitectmag.com/archives/2000/02/eisenzopf/

Gamma, E., Helm, R., Johnson, R., & Vilissides, J. (1995). *Design patterns: Elements of reusable object-oriented software.* Reading, MA: Addison-Wesley.

Gilbert, D., Powell-Perry, J., & Widijoso, S. (1999). Approaches by hotels to the use of the Internet as a relationship marketing tool. *Journal of Marketing Practice: Applied Marketing Science, 5*(1), 21-38.

Grady, R. (1997). *Successful software process improvement.* Englewood Cliffs, NJ: Prentice Hall.

Gross, D. (2002, March). Data mine. *Stern Business,* New York University.

Hunter, R. (1997, March). Once is not enough. *CIO,* 27-31. Retrieved April 27, 2001, from http://www.cio.com/archive/030197_gartner_content.html

Inmon, W. (2002). *Building the data warehouse.* New York: Wiley Computer Publishing.

Keevil, B. (1998). Measuring the usability index of your Web site. In *Proceedings of the CHI '98 Conference* (pp. 271-277). Los Angeles, CA: The Association of Computing Machinery.

Kirsner, S. (1999). The customer experience. *FastCompany, 01*(12), 12-14.

Lassila, O. (1998). Web metadata: A matter of semantics. *IEEE Internet Computing, 30*(7), 30-37.

Marco, D. (2000). *Building and managing the metadata repository: A full lifecycle guide* New York: Wiley Computer Publishing.

Marshall, C., & Shipman, F. (2003). Which semantic web? In *Proceedings of the 2003 International Conference on Hypertext,* (57-66). Nottingham, UK: The Association of Computing Machinery.

McComb, D. (2004). *Semantics in business systems: The savvy manager's guide.* Boston: Morgan Kaufmann Publishers.

McIlroy, M. (1969). *Mass produced software components.* NATO Scientific Affairs Division, Garmisch, Germany, 138-155.

Morkes, J., & Nielsen, J. (1997). *Concise, scannable and objective: How to write for the Web.* Retrieved January 20, 2003, from http://www.useit.com/papers/webwriting/writing.html

Nielsen, J. (2000). *Designing Web usability.* Indianapolis, IN: New Riders Publishing.

Nielsen, J., & Tahir, M. (2002). *Homepage usability: 50 Websites deconstructed.* Indianapolis, IN: New Riders Publishing.

O'Brian, J. (2003). *Management information systems: Managing information technology in the e-business enterprise.* Columbus, OH: McGraw-Hill.

Palmer, J. (2002). Designing for Website usability. *Computer, 35*(7), 102-103.

Pöyry, P., Pelto-Aho, K., & Puustjärvi, P. (2002). The role of metadata in the CUBER. In *Proceedings of the 2002 Annual Research Conference of the South African Institute of Computer Scientists and Information Technologists on Enablement through Technology* (Vol 30, pp. 172-178). South Africa: University of South Africa.

Rico, D. (2004). *ROI of software process improvement: Metrics for project managers and software engineers.* Fort Lauderdale, FL: J. Ross Publishing.

Ross, J., & Weill, P. (2005). *Recipe for good governance.* Retrieved July 19, 2005, from http://www.cio.com.au/index.php/id;824342129;fp;4;fpid;56484

Seybold, P. (1998). *Customers.com: How to create a profitable business strategy for the Internet and beyond.* New York: Random House.

Spewak, S. (1993). *Enterprise architecture planning: Developing a blueprint for data, applications, and technology.* New York: Wiley Computer Publishing.

Stewart, T. (2003). *The wealth of knowledge.* New York: DoubleDay Publishing.

Tannenbaum, A. (2001). *Metadata solutions: Using metamodels, repositories, xml, and enterprise portals to generate information on demand.* Boston: Addison Wesley Professional.

Umar, A. (1997). *Object-oriented client/server Internet environments.* Upper Saddle River, NJ: Prentice Hall, Inc.

Varon, E. (2002). Portals finally get down to business. *CIO Magazine, 12.*

WC3 (2001). *Semantic Web.* Retreived June 22, 2005, from http://www.w3.org/2001/sw/

Watchfire. (2000). *Metatags: They're not just for search engines anymore.* Retrieved June 17, 2001, from http://www.watchfire.com/resources/metatagswhite.pdf

Whiting, R. (2003). RFID backers, privacy advocates seek common ground. *Information Week, 11,* 10-11.

Zachman, J. (1987). A framework for information systems architecture. *IBM Systems Journal, 26,* 37-68.

Chapter III

Architecture of an Information System for Personal Financial Planning

Oliver Braun, Saarland University, Germany

Günter Schmidt, Saarland University, Germany

Abstract

We present a reliable application architecture and a corresponding system architecture of a system for personal financial planning. The application architecture is related to the business requirements, and the system architecture is related to information technology. We will present an analysis model as part of the application architecture, showing the granularity of an industry model. An intrinsic part of the proposed system architecture is the usage of Web technologies.

Introduction

The architecture of an information system influences just about everything in the process of developing an information system. The *system architecture* gives the rules and regulations by which the information system has to be constructed. The architecture's key role is to define the set of constraints placed on the design and implementation teams when they transform the requirements and analysis models into the executable system. These constraints contain all the significant design decisions and the rationale behind them.

The mission and concern of this chapter is to present a reliable *application architecture* and a corresponding *system architecture* of a system for *personal financial planning*. The application architecture is related to the business requirements, and the *system architecture* is related to information technology. We base the discussion of the business requirements on the application architecture, LISA, where four views on models are defined in Schmidt (1999):

1.   The granularity of the model differing between industry model, enterprise model, and detailed model

2.   The elements of the model differing between data, function, and coordination

3.   The life cycle of modelling differing between analysis, design, and implementation

4.   The purpose of modelling differing between problem description and problem solution

We will present an *analysis model* as part of the application architecture showing the granularity of an industry model. It contains *data*, *function*, and *coordination models* related to the purpose of modelling. The language we use to develop the analysis model is the Unified Modeling Language (UML). An intrinsic part of the proposed system architecture is the usage of Web technologies, as the global Internet and the World Wide Web are the primary enabling technologies for delivering customized decision support. We refer to the reference model as a combination of the analysis model and the system architecture. We believe that combining analysis model and system architecture could enhance the usability of the reference model.

We understand *personal financial planning* as the process of meeting life goals through the management of finances (Certified Financial Planner's (CFP) Board of Standards, 2005). Our reference model fulfils two kinds of purposes: First, the analysis model is a conceptual model that can serve financial planners as a decision support tool for the analysis of requirements. Second, system developers can map the analysis model to the system architecture at the design stage of system development. Furthermore, the reference model serves as a capture of existing knowledge in the field of IT-supported personal financial planning. The model also addresses interoperability assessments by the concept of platform-independent usage of personal financial planning tools.

State of the Art

Personal Financial Planning

The field of personal financial planning is well supplied with a lot of textbooks, among them: Böckhoff and Stracke (2003), Keown (2003), Nissenbaum, Raasch, and Ratner (2004), Schmidt (2006), and Woerheide (2002), to name just a few. Most books can be used as guides to handle personal financial problems, for example, maximise wealth, achieve various financial goals, determine emergency savings, maximise retirement plan contributions, and so forth. There are also papers in journals ranging from the popular press to academic journals. Braun and Kramer (2004) give a review on software for personal financial planning in German-speaking countries.

We will start our discussion with some definitions related to the world of personal financial planning. Certified Financial Planner's (CFP) Board of Standards defines *personal financial planning* as follows:

Definition 1: *Financial planning* is the process of meeting your life goals through the proper management of your finances. Life goals can include buying a home, saving for your child's education, or planning for retirement. Financial planning provides direction and meaning to your financial decisions. It allows you to understand how each financial decision you make affects other areas of your finances. For example, buying a particular investment product might help you pay off your mortgage faster, or it might delay your retirement significantly. By viewing each financial decision as part of a whole, you can consider its short and long-term effects on your life goals. You can also adapt more easily to life changes and feel more secure that your goals are on track. (Certified Financial Planner's (CFP) Board of Standards, 2005)

The draft ISO/DIS 22 222-1 of the Technical Committee ISO/TC 222, Personal Financial Planning, of the International Organization for Standardization, defines *personal financial planning* as follows:

Definition 2: *Personal financial planning* is an interactive process designed to enable a consumer/client to achieve their personal financial goals. (ISO/TC 222, 2004)

In the same draft, *Personal Financial Planner, consumer, client,* and *financial goals* are defined as follows:

Definition 3: A *Personal Financial Planner* is an individual practitioner who provides financial planning services to clients and meets all competence, ethics, and experience requirements contained in this standard. A *consumer* is an individual or a group of individuals, such as a family, who have shared financial interests. A *client* of a Personal Financial Planner is an individual who has accepted the terms of engagement by entering into a contract of services. A *financial goal* is a quantifiable outcome aimed to be achieved at some future point in time or over a period of time. (ISO/TC 222, 2004)

Certified Financial Planner's (CFP) Board of Standards and the Technical Committee ISO/ TC 222, Personal Financial Planning, of the International Organization for Standardization define the *personal financial planning process* as follows:

Definition 4: The *personal financial planning process* shall include, but is not limited to, six steps that can be repeated throughout the client and financial planner relationship. The client can decide to end the process before having passed all the steps. The process involves gathering relevant financial information, setting life goals, examining your current financial status, and coming up with a strategy or plan for how you can meet your goals given your current situation and future plans. The financial planning process consists of the following six steps:

1. **Establishing and defining the client-planner relationship:** The financial planner should clearly explain or document the services to be provided to the client, and define both his and his client's responsibilities. The planner should explain fully how he will be paid and by whom. The client and the planner should agree on how long the professional relationship should last and on how decisions will be made.

2. **Gathering client data and determining goals and expectations:** The financial planner should ask for information about the client's financial situation. The client and the planner should mutually define the client's personal and financial goals, understand the client's time frame for results, and discuss, if relevant, how the client feel about risk. The financial planner should gather all the necessary documents before giving the advice that the client needs.

3. **Analyzing and evaluating the client's financial status:** The financial planner should analyze the client's information to assess the client's current situation and determine what the client must do to meet his goals. Depending on what services the client has asked for, this could include analyzing the client's assets, liabilities, and cash flow, current insurance coverage, investments, or tax strategies.

4. **Developing and presenting financial planning recommendations and/or alternatives:** The financial planner should offer financial planning recommendations that address the client's goals, based on the information which the client provides. The planner should go over the recommendations with the client to help the client understand them so that the client can make informed decisions. The planner should also listen to the client's concerns and revise the recommendations as appropriate.

5. **Implementing the financial planning recommendations:** The client and the planner should agree on how the recommendations will be carried out. The planner may carry out the recommendations or serve as the client's "coach," coordinating the whole process with the client and other professionals such as attorneys or stockbrokers.

6. **Monitoring the financial planning recommendations:** The client and the planner should agree on who will monitor the client's progress towards his goals. If the plan-

ner is in charge of the process, he should report to the client periodically to review his situation and adjust the recommendations, if needed, as the client's life changes.

Systems, Models, Architectures

Models are simplifications of reality. Models exist at various levels of abstraction. A level of abstraction indicates how far removed from the reality a model is. High levels of abstraction represent the most simplified models. Low levels of abstraction have close correspondence with the system that they are modelling. An exact 1:1 correspondence is no longer a model, but rather a transformation of one system to another. *Systems* are defined as follows:

Definition 5: A *system* is a collection of connected units organized to accomplish a purpose. A system can be described by one or more models, possibly from different viewpoints. The complete model describes the whole system. (Rumbaugh, Jacobson, & Booch, 2005, p. 635)

The personal financial planning process can be supported by financial *Decision Support Systems* (DSS). In general, a Decision Support System can be described as follows:

Definition 6: A *Decision Support System* (DSS) is an interactive, flexible, and adaptable computer-based information system, specially developed for supporting the solution of a non-structured management problem for improved decision-making. It utilises data, provides an easy-to-use interface, and allows for the decision-maker's own insights. (Turban, 1995)

Continuous interaction between system and decision-makers is important (Briggs, Nunamaker, & Sprague, 1997). Interactive decision-making has been accepted as the most appropriate way to obtain the correct preferences of decision-makers (Mathieu & Gibson, 1993; Mukherjee, 1994). If this interaction is to be supported by a Web-based system, then there is a need to manage the related techniques (or models), to support the data needs, and to develop an interface between the users and the system. Advances in Web technologies and the emergence of the e-business have strongly influenced the design and implementation of financial DSS. As a result, improvement in global accessibility in terms of integration and share of information means that obtaining data from the Internet has become more convenient. Growing demand in fast and accurate information sharing increases the need in Web-based financial DSS (Chou, 1998; Dong, Deng, & Wang, 2002; Dong, Du, Wang, Chen, & Deng, 2004; Fan, Stallaert, & Whinston, 1999, 2000; Hirschey, Richardson, & Scholz, 2000; Li, 1998; Mehdi & Mohammad, 1998).

The application of DSS to some specific financial planning problems is described in several articles. In Schmidt and Lahl (1991), a DSS based on expert system technology is discussed. The focus of the system is portfolio selection. Samaras, Matsatsinis, and Zopounidis (2005) focus on portfolio selection. They propose a DSS which includes three techniques of investment analysis: Fundamental Analysis, Technical Analysis, and Market Psychology. Dong, Du, Wang, Chen, and Deng (2004) also focus on portfolio selection, and report on the implementation of a Web-based DSS for Chinese financial markets. Zahedi and Palma-dos-Reis (1999) describe a personalised intelligent financial DSS. Zopounidis, Doumpos, and Matsatsinis (1997) give a survey on the use of knowledge-based DSS in financial management. The basic characteristic of such systems is the integration of expert systems technology with models and methods used in the decision support framework. They survey some systems applied to financial analysis, portfolio management, loan analysis, credit granting, assessment of credit risk, and assessment of corporate performance and viability. These systems provide the following features:

- They support all stages of the decision-making process, that is, structuring the problem, selecting alternative solutions, and implementing the decision.

- They respond to the needs and the cognitive style of different decision-makers based on individual preferences.

- They incorporate a knowledge base to help the decision-maker to understand the results of the mathematical models.

- They ensure objectiveness and completeness of the results by comparing expert estimations and results from mathematical models.

- Time and costs of the decision-making process is significantly reduced, while the quality of the decisions is increased.

Special emphasis on Web-based decision support is given in Bhargava, Power, and Sun (in press). Even though the above efforts in developing DSS have been successful to solve some specific financial planning problems, these do not lead to a general framework for solving any financial planning problem. There is no DSS which covers the whole process of financial planning. *Models* can be defined as follows:

Definition 7: A *model* is a semantically-complete description of a system. (Rumbaugh, Jacobson, & Booch, 2005, p. 461)

According to that definition, a model is an abstraction of a system from a particular viewpoint. It describes the system or entity at the chosen level of precision and viewpoint. Different models provide more or less independent viewpoints that can be manipulated separately. A model may comprise a containment hierarchy of packages in which the top-level package corresponds to the entire system. The contents of a model are the transitive closures of its containment (ownership) relationships from top-level packages to model elements. A model may also include relevant parts of the system's environment, represented, for example, by actors and their interfaces. In particular, the relationship of the environment to the system elements may be modelled. The primary aim of modelling is the reduction of complexity of the real world in order to simplify the construction process of information systems (Frank, 1999, p. 605). Mišić and Zhao (1999) define *reference models* as follows:

Definition 8: A *reference model* describes a standard decomposition of a known problem domain into a collection of interrelated parts, or components, that cooperatively solve the problem. It also describes the manner in which the components interact in order to provide the required functions. A reference model is a conceptual framework for describing system architectures, thus providing a high-level specification for a class of systems. (Mišić & Zhao, 1999)

Reference modelling can be divided into two groups (Fettke & Loos, 2003): Investigation of methodological aspects (e.g., Lang, Taumann, & Bodendorf, 1996; Marshall, 1999; Remme, 1997; Schütte, 1998), and construction of concrete reference models (e.g., Becker & Schütte, 2004; Fowler, 1997; Hay, 1996; Scheer, 1994). To the best of our knowledge, there is no reference model for personal financial planning. Our reference model for personal financial planning consists of an analysis model for the system analysis of a personal financial planning system and of corresponding system architecture of an information system for personal financial planning.

Analysis Model

Surveys of reference models at the analysis stage of system development (i.e., conceptual models) are given in various papers, for example, Scholz-Reiter (1990), Marent (1995), Mertens, Holzer, and Ludwig (1996), Fettke and Loos (2003), and Mišić and Zhao (1999). For the construction of models, languages are needed. We will use the *Unified Modeling Language* (UML) for our analysis model.

Definition 9: The *Unified Modeling Language* (UML) is a general-purpose modelling language that is used to specify, visualize, construct, and document the artefacts of a software system. (Rumbaugh, Jacobson, & Booch, 2005, p. 3)

UML was developed by the Rational Software Corporation to unify the best features of earlier methods and notations. The UML models can be categorised into three groups:

- **State models** (that describe the static data structures)
- **Behaviour models** (that describe object collaborations)
- **State change models** (that describe the allowed states for the system over time)

UML also contains a few architectural constructs that allow modularising the system for iterative and incremental development. We will use UML 2.0 (Rumbaugh, Jacobson, & Booch, 2005) for our analysis model.

System Architecture

In general, *architecture* can be defined as follows:

Definition 10: An *architecture* is the organizational structure of a system, including its decomposition into parts, their connectivity, interaction mechanisms, and the guiding principles that inform the design of a system. (Rumbaugh, Jacobson, & Booch, 2005, p. 170)

Definition 11: The term *system architecture* denotes the description of the structure of a computer-based information system. The structures in question comprise software components, the externally-visible properties of those components, and the relationships among them. (Bass, Clements, & Kazman, 1998)

IBM (Youngs, Redmond-Pyle, Spaas, & Kahan, 1999) has put forth an *Architecture Description Standard* (ADS), which defines two major aspects: functional and operational. The IBM ADS leverages UML to help express these two aspects of the architecture. This standard is intended to support harvesting and reuse of reference architectures.

For a comprehensive overview of architectures, languages, methods, and techniques for analysing, modelling, and constructing information systems in organisations, we refer to the Handbook on Architectures of Information Systems (Bernus, Mertins, & Schmidt, 2005)

The reference architecture we use to derive our *system architecture* is a service-oriented architecture (SOA) proposed by the World Wide Web Consortium (W3C) (Booth, Haas, McCabe, Newcomer, Champion, Ferris, et al., 2005) for building Web-based information systems. According to the Gartner group, by 2007, service-oriented architectures will be the dominant strategy (more than 65%) of developing information systems. The architecture we propose supports modular deployment of both device-specific user interfaces through multi-channel delivery of services and new or adapted operational processes and strategies. Service-oriented architectures refer to an application software topology which separates business logic from user interaction logic represented in one or multiple software components (services), exposed to access via well-defined formal interfaces. Each service provides its functionality to the rest of the system as a well-defined interface described in a formal mark-up language, and the communication between services is both platform- and language-independent. Thus, modularity and re-usability are ensured, enabling several different configurations and achieving multiple business goals. The first service-oriented architecture relates to the use of DCOM or Object Request Brokers (ORBs) based on the CORBA specification.

A *service* is a function that is well-defined, self-contained, and does not depend on the context or state of other services. Services are what you connect together using Web Services. A service is the endpoint of a connection. Also, a service has some type of underlying computer system that supports the connection that is offered. The combination of services, both internal and external to an organisation, makes up a service-oriented architecture. The technology of Web services is the most likely connection technology of service-oriented architectures. Web services essentially use XML to create a robust connection.

Web Services technology is currently the most promising methodology of developing Web information systems. Web Services allow companies to reduce the cost of doing e-business, to deploy solutions faster, and to open up new opportunities. The key to reach these goals is a common program-to-program communication model, built on existing and emerging standards such as HTTP, Extensible Markup Language (XML - see also Wüstner, Buxmann, & Braun, 2005), Simple Object Access Protocol (SOAP), Web Services Description Language (WSDL) and Universal Description, Discovery and Integration (UDDI). However, the real Business-to-Business interoperability between different organisations requires more than the aforementioned standards. It requires long-lived, secure, transactional conversations between Web Services of different organisations. To this end, a number of standards are underway (e.g., Web Services Conversation Language (WSCL), and the Business Process Execution Language for Web Services (BPEL4WS)). With respect to the description of services' supported and required characteristics, the WS-Policy Framework is under development by IBM, Microsoft, SAP, and other leading companies in the area. On the other hand, no other standard languages and technologies have been proposed for composing services and modelling transactional behaviour of complex service compositions. Such proposals include the Unified Transaction Modeling Language (UTML) and the SWORD toolkit.

Requirements for a Reference Model for Personal Financial Planning

Our reference model for personal financial planning should fulfil the following requirements concerning the *input*, *data processing*, and *output*: The input has to be collected in a complete (that is, adequate to the purpose) way. The *input* data have to be collected from the client and/or from institutions that are involved in this process. Such institutions may be Saving Banks, Mortgage Banks, Life Insurance Companies, Car Insurance Companies, Providers of Stock Market Quotations, Pension Funds, and so forth. This stage is time-consuming, and the quality of the financial plan is dependent on the completeness and correctness of the collected input data. *Data processing* (i.e., data evaluation and data analysis) have the task to process the input data in a correct, individual, and networked way. Correct means that the results have to be precise and error-free according to accepted methods of financial planning. Individual means that the concrete situation with all its facets has to be centred in the planning, and that it is forbidden to make generalisations. Networked means: All of its data's effects and interdependencies have been considered and structured into a financial plan. The *output* has to be coherent and clear.

Analysis Model

The main task of an analysis model for personal financial planning is to help financial planners to consult individuals to properly manage their personal finances. Proper personal financial planning is so important because many individuals lack a working knowledge of financial concepts and do not have the tools they need to make decisions most advantageous to their economic well-being. For example, the Federal Reserve Board's Division of Consumer and Community Affairs (2002) stated that "financial literacy deficiencies can affect an individual's or family's day-to-day money management and ability to save for long-term goals such as buying a home, seeking higher education, or financial retirement. Ineffective money management can also result in behaviours that make consumers vulnerable to severe financial crises".

Furthermore, the analysis model should fulfil the following requirements:

- **Maintainability** (the analysis model should be understandable and alterable)
- **Adaptability** (the analysis model should be adaptable to specific user requirements)
- **Efficiency** (the analysis model should solve the *personal financial planning* problem as fast and with the least effort possible)
- **Standards-oriented** (the analysis model should be oriented at ISO / DIN /CFP- board standards; it should fulfil, for example, the CFP financial planning practice standards (Certified Financial Planner's (CFP) Board of Standards, 2005)

System Architecture

An architecturally-significant requirement is a system requirement that has a profound impact on the development of the rest of the system. Architecture gives the rules and regulations by which the software has to be constructed. The architect has the sole responsibility for defining and communicating the system's architecture. The architecture's key role is to define the set of constraints placed on the design and implementation teams when they transform the requirements and analysis models into the executable system. These constraints contain all the significant design decisions and the rationale behind them. Defining an architecture is an activity of identifying what is architecturally-significant and expressing it in the proper context and viewpoint.

The system architecture for an IT-based personal financial planning system should fulfil the following requirements:

- **Maintainability** (the architecture should be understandable and alterable)
- **Adaptability** (the architecture should be adaptable to specific user requirements)
- **Efficiency** (the architecture should deliver a framework that allows a Personal Financial Planner to solve *personal financial planning* problems as fast and with the least effort possible, for example, by automatic data gathering)
- **Standard-oriented** (the architecture should be oriented at well-established standards, for example, service-oriented architectures)
- **Reliability and robustness** (the architecture should support a reliable and robust IT-system)
- **Portability** (the architecture should support a platform-independent usage of the personal financial planning system)

In the following sections, we describe a reference model for personal financial planning which meets the requirements specified in this section. The whole reference model is elaborated in more detail by Braun (2006b).

Architecture of a Reliable Web Application for Personal Financial Planning

Our architecture for personal financial planning consists of two parts (see Figure 1):

1. **Analysis model** as part of the application architecture, which can help financial planners to do personal financial planning; and
2. **System architecture**, which can help system developers to develop logical models at the design stage of system development.

Our reference model for personal financial planning has two purposes: First, the analysis model can help financial planners to do personal financial planning in a systematic way.

Figure 1. Analysis model and system architecture

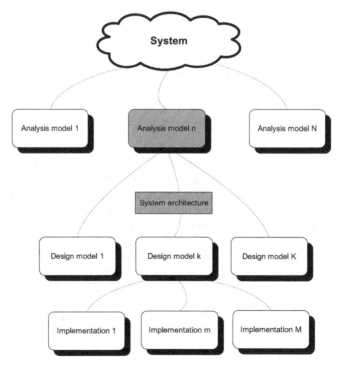

Second, at the design stage of system development, system developers can take the analysis model produced during system analysis and apply the system architecture to it. An intrinsic part of our reference model at the architecture level is the usage of Web technologies, as Web technologies have already and will strongly influence the design and implementation of financial information systems in general.

Design starts with the analysis model and the software architecture document as the major inputs (q.a. here and in the following Conallen, 2002). Design is where the abstraction of the business takes its first step into the reality of software. At design level, the analysis model is refined such that it can be implemented with the components that obey the rules of the architecture. As with analysis, design activities revolve around the class and interaction diagrams. Classes become more defined, with fully qualified properties. As this happens, the level of abstraction of the class shifts from analysis to design. Additional classes, mostly helper and implementation classes, are often added during design. In the end, the resulting design model is something that can be mapped directly into code. This is the link between the abstractions of the business and the realities of software.

Analysis and design activities help transform the requirements of the system into a design that can be realized in software. Analysis begins with the use case model, the use cases and their scenarios, and the functional requirements of the system that are not included in the use cases. The analysis model is made up of classes and collaborations of classes that exhibit the dynamic behaviours detailed in the use cases and requirements.

The analysis model and the design model are often the same artifact. As the model evolves, its elements change levels of abstraction from analysis to detailed design. Analysis-level classes represent objects in the business domain. Analysis focuses on the functional requirements of the system, ignoring the architectural constraints of the system. Use case analysis comprises those activities that take the use cases and functional requirements to produce an analysis model of the system. Analysis focuses on the functional requirements of the system, so the fact that some or all of the system will be implemented with Web technologies is beside the point. Unless the functional requirements state the use of a specific technology, references to architectural elements should be avoided. The analysis model is made up of classes and collaborations of classes that exhibit the dynamic behaviours detailed in the use cases and the requirements. The model represents the structure of the proposed system at a level of abstraction beyond the physical implementation of the system. The classes typically represent objects in the business domain, or problem space. The level of abstraction is such that the analysis model could be applied equally to any architecture. Important processes and objects in the problem space are identified, named, and categorised during analysis. Analysis focuses on the functional requirements of the system, ignoring the architectural constraints of the system. The emphasis is on ensuring that all functional requirements, as expressed by the use cases and other documents, are realised somewhere in the system. Ideally, each use case is linked to the classes and packages that realise them. This link is important in establishing the traceability between requirements and use cases and the classes that will realise them. The analysis model is an input for the design model and can be evolved into the design model.

System Architecture

Architecture influences just about everything in the process of developing software. Architecture gives the rules and regulations by which the software has to be constructed. Figure 2 shows the general architecture of our prototype FiXplan (IT-based Personal Financial Planning), and the data flow between the *User Interfaces*, the *Application Layer*, and the *Sources* (Braun & Schmidt, 2005).

Basically, the system contains the following components:

- **Clients:** Used by Personal Financial Planners or clients to access our main financial planning system and our Web Services; User Interfaces may be Web browsers such as the Internet Explorer or Mozilla, or applications such as Microsoft Excel.

- **Server:** As described in detail in the analysis model; the Web Services Toolbox provides useful tools for personal financial planning.

- **Sources:** Used as a repository for the tools of the personal finance framework.

The three-tier architecture of FiXplan supports modular deployment of both device-specific user interfaces through multi-channel delivery of services and new or adapted operational processes and strategies. All connectivity interfaces are based on standard specifications.

Reliable Messaging

One of the first attempts to deliver guaranteed and assured delivery for Web Services was Reliable HTTP (HTTPR) from IBM. HTTPR aimed to provide reliable message delivery for

Figure 2. General three-tier architecture of FiXplan

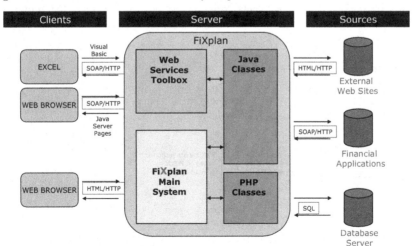

Web Services, providing a "send and forget" facility through a guaranteed messaging model. It provided guaranteed delivery because it automatically retried requests if a link or a server was down. However, "OASIS WS-Reliability and WS-ReliableMessaging proposed by IBM, BEA, TIBCO, and Microsoft (submitted to the W3C) are the new competing protocols for reliable messaging" (Watters, 2005, p.24).

At the client side, the Web browser and PHP-scripts handle the user interface and the presentation logic. At the server side, the Web server gets all *http* requests from the Web user and propagates the requests to the application server, which implements the business logic of all the services for personal financial planning. At the database server side, transactional or historical data of the day-to-day operations are stored in the system database by RDBMS. The application server sends the query to the database server and gets the result set. It prepares the response after a series of processes and returns to the Web server to be propagated back to the client side. A registered user can log in and pick an existing session or create a new session of his preference, such as a level of user protection, access rights, and level of complexity. Based on the three-tier structure, FiXplan can run on both Internet and intranet environments. The user can, for example, use a Web browser to access a Web server through HTML language and HTTP protocol. The kernel of the system is placed on the web server. FiXplan uses a collection of Web Services. These services communicate with each other. The communication can involve either simple data passing, or it could involve two or more services coordinating some activity. Some means of connecting services to each other is needed.

Figure 3 illustrates a basic *service-oriented architecture*. It shows a service consumer below, sending a service request message to a service provider above. The service provider returns a response message to the service consumer. The request and subsequent response connections are defined in some way that is understandable to both the service consumer and the service provider. A service provider can also be a service consumer.

All the messages shown in the above figure are sent using SOAP. SOAP generally uses HTTP, but other means of connection such as Simple Mail Transfer Protocol (SMTP) may be used. HTTP is the familiar connection we all use for the Internet. In fact, it is the pervasiveness of HTTP connections that will help drive the adoption of Web services. SOAP can be used to exchange complete documents or to call a remote procedure. SOAP provides

Figure 3. Basic service oriented architecture

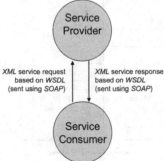

the envelope for sending Web Services messages over the intranet/Internet. The envelope contains two parts: an optional header providing information on authentication, encoding of data, or how a recipient of a SOAP message should process the message; and the body that contains the message. These messages can be defined using the WSDL specification. WSDL uses XML to define messages. XML has a tagged message format. Both the service provider and service consumer use these tags. In fact, the service provider could send the data shown at the bottom of this figure in any order. The service consumer uses the tags and not the order of the data to get the data values.

FiXplan is both Web Service Provider and Web Service Consumer, as shown in Figure 4.

In this example, a browser (e.g., INTERNET EXPLORER) requests a static Web page with a form from a Web server (e.g., TOMCAT). After submitting the form, the Web page containing the desired results will be dynamically generated using Java Server Pages (JSP). In order to build up the Web page from JSP, the JSP calls a special Java method in a proxy class. As a result of this call, a SOAP message is sent to the corresponding Web service of the JAVA WEB SERVICES TOOLBOX. The Web service extracts the input data (in our example *accNr1, accNr2*) needed to compute the output data (in our example *balance*) from the received SOAP message. Because of the fact that our Web services are written in Java, looking for an answer means calling one of the methods of our JAVA CLASSES.

The design allows the Web service to be a consumer of another Web service: One of the Java classes called by the Web service to calculate the output data (in our example *balance*) is a proxy class which sends SOAP messages to external Web services (in our example a BANK GIRO SERVICES) and receives the results from these Web services (in our example *balance1* and *balance2*). In our example, this Java class computes also the sum of *balance1* and *balance2*.

The output data of the Java method (in our example *balance*) is packed in a new SOAP message and sent back. On the client side, the searched result is extracted from the SOAP

Figure 4. Service provider and service consumer

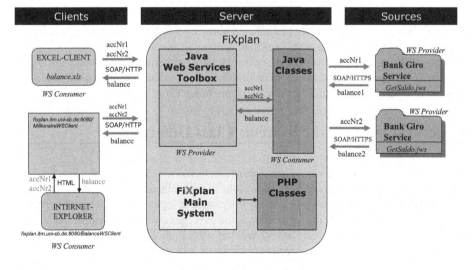

message and given to the JSP by the proxy class. Finally, the JSP code includes the result in the Web page which is sent back to the browser.

If you have an Excel client, you have an Excel sheet instead of a Web page. When you want to calculate a result, you call a Visual Basic function which corresponds to the JSP in the example above. The Visual Basic function uses a Microsoft object which does the same as the proxy class: sending a SOAP message to the server and receiving the answer. The result is given to the Visual Basic function which writes it in the Excel sheet.

Analysis Model as Part of the Application Architecture

The *analysis model* of our reference model for *personal financial planning* consists of the following parts: *Use Cases* build the dynamic view of the system, and *class diagrams* build the structural view of the system. Both are combined in the behavioural view of the system with *activity diagrams* and *sequence diagrams*.

Dynamic View on the System: Use Cases

Use cases, use case models, and *use case diagrams* are defined as follows:

Definition 12: A *use case* is the specification of sequences of actions, including variant sequences and error sequences, that a system, subsystem, or class can perform by interacting with outside objects to provide a service of value. A use case is a coherent unit of functionality provided by a classifier (a system, subsystem, or class) as manifested by sequences of messages exchanged among the system and one or more outside users (represented as actors), together with actions performed by the system. The purpose of a use case is to define a piece of behaviour of a classifier (including a subsystem or the entire system), without revealing the internal structure of the classifier. A *use case model* is a model that describes the functional requirements of a system or other classifier in terms of use cases. A *use case diagram is a diagram* that shows the relationships among actors and use cases within a system. (Rumbaugh, Jacobson, & Booch, 2005, pp. 668-677)

Structural View on the System: Class Diagrams

The hierarchy of the dynamic view of the system (use cases) may provide a start but usually falls short when defining the *structural view* of the system (classes). The reason is that it is likely that certain objects participate in many use cases and logically cannot be assigned to a single use case package. At the highest level, the packages are often the same, but at the lower levels of the hierarchy, there are often better ways to divide the packages. Analysis identifies a preliminary mapping of required behaviour onto structural elements, or classes,

Figure 5. Structural elements

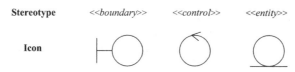

in the system. At the analysis level, it is convenient to categorise all discovered objects into one of three stereotyped classes: *«boundary»*, *«control»*, and *«entity»*, as suggested by Jacobson, Christerson, Jonsson, and Overgaard (1992); see Figure 5.

Definition 13: *Boundary classes* connect users of the system to the system. *Control classes* map to the processes that deliver the functionality of the system. *Entity classes* represent the persistent things of the system, such as the database. (Jacobson, Christerson, Jonsson, & Overgaard, 1992)

Entities are shared and have a life cycle outside any one use of the system, whereas control instances typically are created, executed, and destroyed with each invocation. Entity properties are mostly attributes, although operations that organise an entity's properties can also often be found on them. Controllers do not specify attributes. Initially, their operations are based on verb phrases in the use case specification and tend to represent functionality that the user might invoke. In general, *class diagrams* can be defined as follows:

Definition 14: A *class diagram* is a graphic representation of the static view that shows a collection of declarative (static) model elements, such as classes, types, and their contents and relationships. (Rumbaugh, Jacobson & Booch, 2005, p. 217)

Use Case Realisation: Sequence and Activity Diagrams

Construction of behavioural diagrams that form the model's use case realisations help to discover and elaborate the analysis classes. A use case realisation is an expression of a use case's flow of events in terms of objects in the system. In UML, this event flow is expressed with *sequence diagrams*.

Definition 15: A *sequence diagram* is a diagram that shows object interactions arranged in time sequence. In particular, it shows the objects participating in an interaction and the sequences of messages exchanged. (Rumbaugh, Jacobson & Booch, 2005, p. 585)

A sequence diagram can realise a use case, describing the context in which the invocation of the use case executes. The sequence diagram describes the objects that are created, executed, and destroyed in order to execute the functionality described in the use case. It does not include object relationships. Sequence diagrams provide a critical link of traceability between the scenarios of the use cases and the structure of the classes. These diagrams can express the flow in a use case scenario in terms of the classes that will implement them.

An additional diagram that is useful for mapping analysis classes into the use case model is the *activity diagram*.

Definition 16: An *activity diagram* is a diagram that shows the decomposition of an activity into its constituents. (Rumbaugh, Jacobson, & Booch, 2005, p. 157)

Activities are executions of behaviour. Activities are behavioural specifications that describe the sequential and concurrent steps of a computational procedure. Activities map well to *controller classes*, where each controller executes one or more activities. We create one activity diagram per use case.

Figure 6. Basic use case model

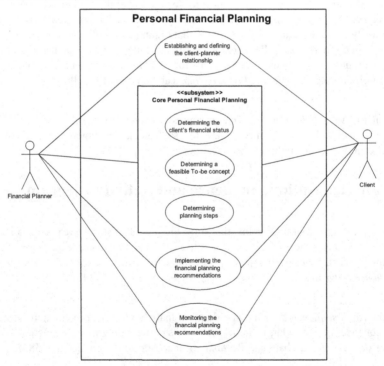

Example Models

The basic analysis *use case* model (see Figure 6) is oriented to the Certified Financial Planner's (CFP) Board of Standards and ISO/TC 222 definition of the *personal financial planning* process (see Definition 4).

In the following, we will describe the subsystem *Core Personal Financial Planning* in detail. *Core Personal Financial Planning* includes three use cases, *determining the client's financial status, determining a feasible to-be concept,* and *determining planning steps,* that are elaborated in more detail in the following sections.

Determining the Client's Financial Status

Determining the client's financial status means answering the question *"How is the current situation defined?"* We will pick the following scenarios as the main success scenarios.

Determining the client's financial status includes:

1. **Data gathering:** The Financial Planner asks the client for information about the client's financial situation. This includes information about *assets*, *liabilities*, *income*, and *expenses*.
2. **Data evaluation:** The Financial Planner uses two financial statements: *balance sheet* and *income statement*.
3. **Data analysis:** The Financial Planner analyses the results from balance sheet and income statement.

He can investigate, for example, the state of the provisions and pension plan, risk management, tax charges, return on investments, and other financial ratios.

In the following, the scenario is described in more detail:

*   **Data gathering—assets and liabilities:** The first category of assets is *cash,* which refers to money in accounts such as checking accounts, savings accounts, money market accounts, money market mutual funds, and certificates of deposit with a maturity of less than one year. The second category of assets is fixed assets, fixed-principal assets, fixed-return assets, or debt instruments. This category includes investments that represent a loan made by the client to someone else. Fixed-return assets are primarily corporate and government bonds, but may also be mortgages held, mutual funds that invest primarily in bonds, fixed annuities, and any other monies owed to the client. The third category of assets is equity investments. Examples of equity investments are common stock, mutual funds that hold mostly common stock, variable annuities, and partnerships. The fourth category of assets is the value of pensions and other retirement accounts. The last category of assets is usually personal or tangible assets, also known as real assets. This category includes assets bought primarily for comforts, like home, car, furniture, clothing, jewellery, and any other personal articles with a resale

value. *Liabilities* are debts that a client currently owes. Liabilities may be charge account balances, personal loans, auto loans, home mortgages, alimony, child support, and life insurance policy loans. In general, assets are gathered at their market value, and debts are gathered at the amount a client would owe if he were to pay the debt off today.

- **Data gathering—income and expenses:** *Income* includes wages and salaries, income from investments such as bonds, stocks, certificates of deposit, and rental property, and distributions from retirement accounts. *Expenses* may be costs for housing, food, and transportation. Expenses can be grouped by similarity; for example, one can choose insurance premiums as a general category, and then include life insurance, auto insurance, health insurance, homeowner's or renter's insurance, disability insurance, and any other insurance premiums one pays in this general category. The acquisition of personal assets (buying a car) is also treated as an expense.

- **Data evaluation—balance sheet:** A *balance sheet* has three sections. The first section is a statement of *assets* (things that one owns). The second section is a statement of *liabilities* (a list of one's debts). The third section is called *net worth*. It represents the difference between one's assets and one's liabilities. Businesses regularly construct balance sheets following a rigorous set of accounting rules. Personal balance sheets are constructed much less formally, although they should follow some of the same general rules incorporated into business balance sheets. The assets on a personal balance sheet may be placed in any order. The most common practice is to list assets in descending order of *liquidity*. Liquidity refers to an asset's ability to be converted to cash quickly with little or no loss in value. Liabilities are normally listed in order of increasing maturity. The *net worth* on a balance sheet is the difference between the total value of assets owned and the total amount of liabilities owed. Net worth is the measure of a person's financial wealth.

- **Data evaluation—income statement:** Where the personal financial balance sheet is like a snapshot of your net worth at a particular point in time, an *income statement* is a statement of income and expenses over a period of time. The time frame is usually the past year. The first section of an income statement is the *income*. The second section is a statement of *expenses*. Expenses are usually listed in order of magnitude, with the basic necessities being listed first. The third section is a summary that represents the *contribution to savings*. Contribution to savings is the difference between the total of income and the total of expenses. A positive contribution to savings would normally show up in the purchase of investments, a reduction in debt, or some combination of the two. A negative contribution to savings shows up in the liquidation of assets, an increase in debt, or some combination of the two.

- **Data analysis:** The *net worth* number is significant in and of itself, since the larger the net worth, the better off a person is financially; however, the balance sheet and the income statement contain even more useful information that a financial planner should consider. The traditional approach for analysing financial statements is the use of *financial ratios*. Financial ratios combine numbers from the financial statements to measure a specific aspect of the personal financial situation of a client. Financial ratios are used:

1. To measure changes in the quality of the financial situation over time
2. To measure the absolute quality of the current financial situation
3. As guidelines for how to improve the financial situation

We will group the ratios into the following eight categories: liquidity, solvency, savings, asset allocation, inflation protection, tax burden, housing expenses, and insolvency/credit (DeVaney, Greninger, & Achacoso, 1994; Greninger, Hampton, & Kitt, 1994).

For example, the Solvency Ratio is defined as:

Solvency Ratio = Total Assets / Total Liabilities

and the Savings Rate is defined as:

Savings Rate = Contribution to Savings / Income

Determining a Feasible to-be Concept

The use case scenario is as follows.

Determining a feasible to-be concept includes:

1. **Data gathering and feasibility check:** The financial planner asks for information about the client's future financial situation. This includes information about the client's *future incomes and expenses* and the client's assumption on the *performance* of his assets. Future incomes and expenses are determined by *life-cycle scenarios*.

   The financial planner asks the client for his *requirements* on a *feasible* to-be concept.

   A to-be concept is feasible if and only if all requirements are fulfilled at every point in time.

2. **Data evaluation:** The financial planner uses two financial statements: (planned) *balance sheets* and (planned) *income statements*.

3. **Data analysis:** The financial planner analyses the results from balance sheets and income statements. He can investigate, for example, the state of the foresight and pension plan, risk management, tax charges, return on investments, and other financial ratios.

Data evaluation and data analysis have to be done in a very similar way as in determining the client's financial status. In this section, we will concentrate our discussion at the first step: *Data gathering*.

Future incomes and expenses are determined by *financial goals*. Financial goals are not just monetary goals, although such goals are obvious and appropriate. Goals can be short-term, intermediate-term, and long-term.

Short-term goals refer to the next twelve months. What does a client want his personal balance sheet to look like in twelve months? What would he like to do during the coming year: Where would he like to spend his vacation? How much would he like to spend on the vacation? What assets, such as a new computer or a new car, would he like to acquire?

Intermediate goals are usually more financial in nature and less specific in terms of activities and acquisitions. As one thinks further into the future, one cares more about having the financial ability to do things and less about the details of what one will do. Most intermediate goals would likely include more than just wealth targets. For example, a client may target a date for buying his first home. Intermediate goals often address where one wants to be in 5 or 20 years.

For most people, *long-term goals* include their date of retirement and their accumulated wealth at retirement. What sort of personal balance sheet does a client want to have at retirement?

The *goals* of a system for personal financial planning consist in helping a personal financial planner to handle the financial situation of a client in a way that the client can maximise his/her quality of life by using money the best way for him/herself. Goals are about the management, protection, and ultimate use of wealth.

There is a strong propensity to associate wealth or standard of living with quality of life. Wealth is normally defined as assets owned less any outstanding debts. Standard of living is measured in terms of annual income. For some people, wealth or standard of living may be the correct measure of their quality of life. For many, that is not the case. First, many people give away substantial amounts of wealth during their lifetimes (places of worship, charities, non-profit organisations such as alma maters). People give gifts because they derive pleasure from it or because they have a sense of obligation. Second, many people hold jobs noted for low pay (religious professions such as priests) and earn low pay compared with what their level of educational training could earn them in other professions. A lot of people pass up lucrative corporate incomes in order to be self-employed. Some people seek jobs with no pay. Full-time, stay-at-home parents are examples of people who accept unpaid jobs based on the benefits they perceive from managing the household. Obviously, many people regularly make choices that are not wealth- or income-maximising, and these choices are perfectly rational and important to their lives. Proper financial planning seeks only to help people make the most of their wealth and income given the non-pecuniary choices they make in their lives, not just maximise their wealth and income.

Life-cycle scenarios (Braun, 2006a) are, for example, applying for a personal loan, purchasing a car, purchasing and financing a home, auto insurance, homeowner insurance, health and disability insurance, life insurance, retirement planning, and estate planning.

Requirements to a feasible to-be concept as introduced in Braun (2006a) are primarily requirements to balance sheets such as the composition of the entire portfolio, a cash reserve, and so forth. According to the financial goals of a company, a client may have the following two main requirements to a feasible to-be concept: assurance of liquidity (i.e., to always have enough money to cover his consumer spending) and prevention of personal insolvency (i.e., to avoid the inability to pay).

Assurance of liquidity (liquidity management) means that one has to prepare for anticipated cash shortages in any future month by ensuring that enough liquid assets to cover the deficiency are available. Some of the more liquid assets include a checking account, a savings account, a money market deposit account, and money market funds. The more funds are maintained in these types of assets, the more liquidity a person will have to cover cash shortages. Even if one has not sufficient liquid assets, one can cover a cash deficiency by obtaining short-term financing (such as using a credit card). If adequate liquidity is maintained, one will not need to borrow every time one needs money. In this way, a person can avoid major financial problems and therefore be more likely to achieve financial goals.

Prevention of personal insolvency can be carried out by purchasing insurance. Property and casualty insurance insure assets (such as car and home), health insurance covers health expenses, and disability insurance provides financial support in case of disability. Life insurance provides the family members or other named beneficiaries with financial support if they lose their bread-winner. Thus, insurance protects against events that could reduce income or wealth. Retirement planning ensures that one will have sufficient funds for the old-age period. Key retirement planning decisions involve choosing a retirement plan, determining how much to contribute, and allocating the contributions.

If the *feasibility check* fails, personal financial planners can apply their knowledge and experience to balance the financial situation. They can take actions which adjust to the financial structure by changing requirements to a feasible to-be concept, by changing future expenses (such as expenses for a car), or by alternative financing expenses (for example, by enhancement of revenues). These actions may be necessary to ensure that the main financial goals are fulfilled.

Measures to Take

Financial goals of a client determine the planning steps as gathered in the section "Determining a Feasible To-Be Concept" and activities to achieve a feasible to-be concept.

Figure 7. Basic use case analysis model elements

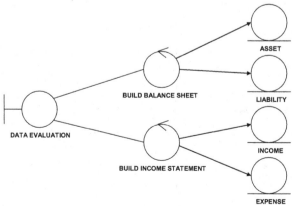

UML Diagrams

In this section, we will elaborate the use case, *Determining the client's financial status: Data evaluation,* as an example of the UML diagram.

The *class diagram* in Figure 7 shows a first-pass analysis model for the use case, *Determining the client's financial status: Data evaluation*. The most important elements are the class names, the types, and the relationships.

This basic class diagram can be elaborated with the operations and attributes as described in the use case specification to an elaborated class diagram (Figure 8).

Figure 9 shows a simple *sequence diagram* that indicates a basic flow of the use case, *Determining the client's financial status: Data evaluation*. Messages corresponding to operations on the classes are drawn to correspond to the main narrative text alongside the scenario.

Figure 8. Elaborated analysis model elements

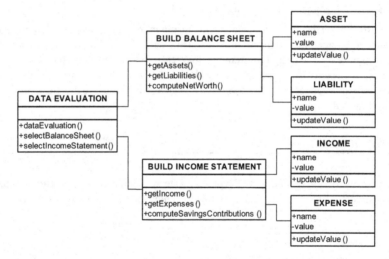

Figure 9. Basic sequence diagram

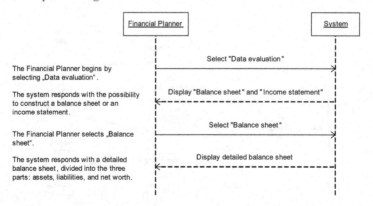

Figure 10 shows the same use case scenario, *Determining the client's financial status: Data evaluation,* as depicted in the sequence diagram in Figure 9, with *System* expressed in terms of the analysis classes in Figure 7.

Figure 11 shows the basic *activity diagram* for the use case, *Determining the client's financial status: Data evaluation,* elaborated with classes from Figure 7.

Figure 10. Sequence diagram elaborated with analysis objects

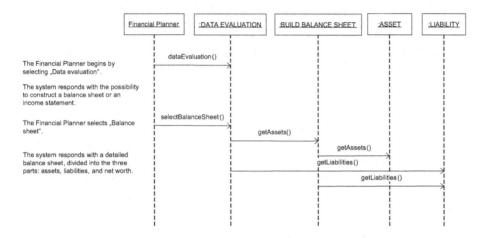

Figure 11. Basic activity diagram

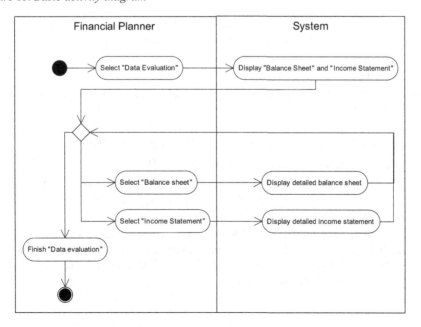

Conclusion and Future Trends

We gave an architecture for a reliable *personal financial planning* system consisting of an *system architecture* and a corresponding *analysis model* (conceptual model) as part of the application architecture. An intrinsic part of our *system architecture* is the usage of Web technologies. Our model for personal financial planning fulfills two kinds of purposes: First, the *analysis model* is a conceptual model that can help financial planners to do their job. Second, at the design stage of system development, system developers can take the *analysis model* and apply the *system architecture* to them. The model combines business concepts of *personal financial planning* with technical concepts from information technology. We evaluated the model by building an IT system FiXplan (IT-based personal financial planning) based on the model. We showed that our model fulfills *maintainability*, *adaptability*, *efficiency*, *reliability*, and *portability* requirements. Furthermore, it is based on ISO and CFP Board *standards*.

Further research is needed to enlarge the model with respect to an automatisation of the to-be concept feasibility check. Here, classical *mathematical programming models* as well as *fuzzy models* may deliver a solution to that problem. While in the case of classical models the vague data is replaced by average data, fuzzy models offer the opportunity to model subjective imaginations of the client or the personal financial planner as precisely as they will be able to describe it. Thus the risk of applying a wrong model of the reality, and selecting wrong solutions which do not reflect the real problem, could be reduced.

References

Bass, L., Clements, P., & Kazman, R. (1998). *Software architecture in practice. The SEI series in software engineering*. Reading, MA: Addison Wesley.

Becker, J., & Schütte, R. (2004). *Handelsinformationssysteme*. Frankfurt am Main: Redline Wirtschaft.

Bernus, P., Mertins, K., & Schmidt, G. (2005). *Handbook on architectures of information systems*. Berlin: Springer.

Bhargava, H. K., Power, D. J., & Sun, D. (in press). Progress in Web-based decision support technologies. *Decision Support Systems*. (Corrected Proof), 2005.

Böckhoff, M., & Stracke, G. (2003). *Der Finanzplaner*. Heidelberg: Sauer. 2 Auflage.

Booth, D., Haas, H., McCabe, F., Newcomer, E., Champion, M., Ferris, C. et al. (Eds.). *Web services architecture, W3C*. Retrieved August 5, 2005, from http://www.w3.org/TR/ws-arch/

Braun, O. (2006a). Lebensereignis- und Präferenzorientierte Persönliche Finanzplanung—Ein Referenzmodell für das Personal Financial Planning. In G. Schmidt (Ed.), *Neue Entwicklungen im Financial Planning,* Hochschulschriften des Instituts für wirtschaftsinformatik. Hochschule Liechtenstein.

Braun, O. (2006b). *Web-basierte Informationssysteme in betriebswirtschaftlichen Anwendungs-umgebungen am Beispiel IT-gestützter Persönlicher Finanzplanung.* Habilitations-schrift. Saarland University, Saarbrücken, in preparation.

Braun, O., & Kramer, S. (2004). Vergleichende Untersuchung von Tools zur Privaten Fi-nanzplanung. In S. Geberl, S. Weinmann, & D. F. Wiesner (Eds.), *Impulse aus der Wirtschaftsinformatik* (pp. 119-133). Heidelberg: Physica.

Braun, O., & Schmidt, G. (2005). A service oriented architecture for personal financial planning. In M. Khosrow-Pour (Ed.), In *Proceedings of the 2005 IRMA International Conference, Managing Modern Organizations with Information Technology* (pp. 1032-1034). Hershey, PA: Idea Group Publishing.

Briggs, R. O., Nunamaker, J. F., & Sprague, R. H. (1997). 1001 Unanswered research ques-tions in GSS. *Journal of Management Information Systems, 14,* 3-21.

Certified Financial Planner's (CFP) Board of Standards, Inc. (2005). Retrieved August 14, 2005, from http://www.cfp.net

Chou, S. C. T. (1998). Migrating to the Web: A Web financial information system server. *Decision Support Systems, 23,* 29-40.

Conallen, J. (2002). *Building Web applications with UML (2nd ed.).* Boston: Pearson Edu-cation.

DeVaney, S., Greninger, S. A., & Achacoso, J. A. (1994). The Usefulness of financial ratios as predictors of household insolvency: Two perspectives. *Financial Counseling and Planning, 5,* 5-24.

Dong, J. C., Deng, S. Y., & Wang, Y. (2002). Portfolio selection based on the Internet. *Sys-tems Engineering: Theory and Practice, 12,* 73-80.

Dong, J. C., Du, H. S., Wang, S., Chen, K., & Deng, X. (2004). A framework of Web-based decision support systems for portfolio selection with OLAP and PVM. *Decision Sup-port Systems, 37,* 367-376.

Fan, M., Stallaert, J., & Whinston, A. B. (1999). Implementing a financial market using Java and Web-based distributed computing. *IEEE Computer, 32,* 64-70.

Fan, M., Stallaert, J., & Whinston, A. B. (2000). The Internet and the future of financial markets. *Communications of the ACM, 43,* 82-88.

Federal Reserve Board Division of Consumer and Community Affairs (2002). *Financial literacy: An overview of practice, research, and policy.* Retrieved on October 24, 2006 from http://www.federalreserve.gov/pubs/bulletin/2002/1102lead.pdf

Fettke, P., & Loos, P. (2003). Multiperspective evaluation of reference models—towards a framework. In M. A. Jeusfeld & Ó. Pastor (Eds.), *ER 2003 Workshops* (LNCS 2814, pp. 80-91). Heidelberg: Springer.

Fowler, M. (1997). *Analysis patterns: Reusable object models.* Menlo Park, CA: Addison-Wesley.

Frank, U. (1999). Conceptual modelling as the core of the information systems discipline—Perspectives and epistemological challenges. In W. D. Haseman & D. L. Nazareth (Eds.), *Proceedings of the 5th Americas Conference on Information Systems (AMCIS 1999)* (pp. 695-697). Milwaukee, WI.

Greninger, S. A., Hampton, V. L., & Kitt, K. A. (1994). Ratios and benchmarks for measuring the financial well-being of families and individuals. *Financial Counselling and Planning, 5*, 5-24.

Hay, D. C. (1996). *Data model patterns—conventions of thought*. New York: Dorset House Publishing.

Hirschey, M., Richardson, V. J., & Scholz, S. (2000). Stock price effects of Internet buy-sell recommendations: The motley fool case. *The Financial Review, 35*, 147-174.

International Organization for Standardization (ISO/TC 222). (2004). *ISO/DIS 22 222-1 of the Technical Committee ISO/TC 222, Personal financial planning.*

Jacobson, I., Christerson, M., Jonsson, P., & Overgaard, G. (1992). *Object-oriented software engineering: A use case driven approach*. Boston: Addison-Wesley.

Keown, A. J. (2003). *Personal finance: Turning money into wealth*. Upper Saddle River, NJ: Prentice Hall.

Lang, K., Taumann, W., & Bodendorf, F. (1996). Business process reengineering with reusable reference process building blocks. In B. Scholz-Reiter & E. Stickel (Eds.), *Business process modelling* (pp. 264-290). Berlin: Springer

Li, Z. M. (1998). Internet/Intranet technology and its development. *Transaction of Computer and Communication, 8*, 73-78.

Marent, C. (1995). Branchenspezifische Referenzmodelle für betriebswirtschaftliche IV-Anwendungsbereiche. *Wirtschaftsinformatik, 37*(3), 303-313.

Marshall, C. (1999). *Enterprise modeling with UML: Designing successful software through business analysis*. Reading, MA: Addison-Wesley.

Mathieu, R. G., & Gibson, J. E. (1993). A methodology for large scale R&D planning based on cluster analysis. *IEEE Transactions on Engineering Management, 30*, 283-291.

Mehdi, R. Z., & Mohammad, R. S. (1998). A Web-based information system for stock selection and evaluation. In *Proceedings of the International Workshop on Advance Issues of E-Commerce and Web-Based Information Systems*, p. 81, Washington D.C.: IEEE Computer Society.

Mertens, P., Holzer, J., & Ludwig, P. (1996). *Individual- and Standardsoftware: tertium datur?* Betriebswirtschaftliche Anwendungsarchitekturen mit branchen- und betriebstypischen Zuschnitt (FORWISS-Rep. FR-1996-004). Erlangen, München, Passau.

Mišić, V. B., & Zhao, J. L. (1999, May). Reference models for electronic commerce. In *Proceedings of the 9th Hong Kong Computer Society Database Conference—Database and Electronic Commerce*, Hong Kong (pp. 199-209).

Mukherjee, K. (1994). Application of an interactive method for MOLIP in project selection decision: A case from Indian coal mining industry. *International Journal of Production Economics, 36*, 203-211.

Nissenbaum, M., Raasch, B. J., & Ratner, C. (2004). *Ernst & Young's personal financial planning guide (5th ed.)*. John Wiley & Sons.

Remme, M. (1997). *Konstruktion von Geschäftsprozessen—Ein modellgestützter Ansatz durch Montage generischer Prozesspartikel*. Wiesbaden: Gabler.

Rumbaugh, J., Jacobson, I., & Booch, G. (2005). *The unified modelling language reference manual* (2nd ed.). Boston: Addison-Wesley.

Samaras, G. D., Matsatsinis, N. F., & Zopounidis, C. (2005). Towards an intelligent decision support system for portfolio management. *Foundations of Computing and Decision Sciences, 2,* 141-162.

Scheer, A. W. (1994). *Business process engineering—reference models for industrial companies* (2nd ed.). Berlin: Springer.

Schmidt, G. (1999). *Informationsmanagement.* Heidelberg: Springer.

Schmidt, G. (2006). *Persönliche Finanzplanung - Modelle und Methoden des Financial Planning.* Heidelberg: Springer.

Schmidt, G., & Lahl, B. (1991). Integration von Expertensystem- und konventioneller Software am Beispiel der Aktienportfoliozusammenstellung. *Wirtschaftsinformatik, 33,* 123-130.

Scholz-Reiter, B. (1990). *CIM—Informations—und Kommunikationssysteme.* München, Wien: Oldenbourg.

Schütte, R. (1998). *Grundsätze ordnungsmäßiger Referenzmodellierung—Konstruktion konfigurations- und anpassungsorientierter Modelle.* Reihe neue betriebswirtschaftliche Forschung. Wiesbaden.

Turban, E. (1995). *Decision support and expert systems* (4th ed.). Englewood Cliffs, NJ: Prentice-Hall.

Watters, P. A. (2005). *Web services in finance.* Berlin: Springer.

Woerheide, W. (2002). *Core concepts of personal finance.* New York: John Wiley and Sons.

Wüstner, E., Buxmann, P., & Braun, O. (2005). The extensible markup language and its use in the field of EDI. In P. Bernus, K. Mertins, & G. Schmidt (Eds.), *Handbook on architectures of information systems* (2nd ed., pp. 391-419). Heidelberg: Springer.

Youngs, R., Redmond-Pyle, D., Spaas, P., & Kahan, E. (1999). A standard for architecture description. *IBM Systems Journal 38.* Retrieved on October 16, 2006 from http://www.research.ibm.com/journal/sj/381/youngs.html

Zahedi, F., & Palma-dos-Reis, A. (1999). Designing personalized intelligent financial decision support systems. *Decision Support Systems, 26,* 31-47.

Zopounidis, C., Doumpos, M., & Matsatsinis, N. F. (1997). On the use of knowledge-based decision support systems in financial management: A survey. *Decision Support Systems, 20,* 259-277.

Chapter IV

Approaches to Building High Performance Web Applications:
A Practical Look at Availibility, Reliability, and Performance

Brian Goodman, IBM Corporation, USA

Maheshwar Inampudi, IBM Corporation, USA

James Doran, IBM Corporation, USA

Abstract

In this chapter, we introduce five practices to help build scalable, resilient Web applications. In 2004, IBM launched its expertise location system, bringing together two legacy systems and transforming the employee's ability to find and connect with their extensive network. This chapter reviews five of the many issues that challenge enterprise Web applications: resource contention, managing transactions, application resiliency, geographic diversity, and exception perception management. Using the IBM expertise location system as context, we will present five key methods that mitigate these risks, achieving high availability and high performance goals.

Introduction

In this chapter, we introduce five practices for building scalable, resilient Web applications. First, we briefly review the context in which IBM launched its internal expertise location system in 2004. We then introduce the challenges we faced in implementing the business requirements and present five key methods that mitigated risks to achieving our high availability and performance goals.

Specifically, we will look at:

- caching strategies for high availability Web applications: beyond storing copies of HTML (Challenger, Dantzig, & Iyengar, 1998; Iyengar & Challenger, 1997);

- asynchronous task processing within Web applications: removing non-essential linear logic from high-volume transactions (Grand, 2002);

- building self-reliant autonomous behavior: encapsulating through services achieving tight integration with *true* loose coupling (Birman, van Renesse, & Vogels, 2004);

- client-side Model View Control (MVC): moving MVC to the browser supercharging the response times and getting a "wow" user experience (Murry, 2005; Sun Microsystems, 2002);

- graceful degradation: keeping users thinking and feeling "fast," "reliable," and "always on" (Florins & Vanderdonckt, 2004).

Caching Strategies

Caching strategies are a core part of high-performing Web experiences. In many cases (Amiri, Park, & Tewari, 2002; Candan, Li, Luo, Hsiung, & Agrawal, 2001; Liebmann & Dustdar, 2004; Rodriguez, Spanner, & Biersack, 2001), the assumption is that caching occurs at the edge of the network, the closest point to the consumer and the furthest from the data or application. Another somewhat overlooked approach is object caching.

Davison (2001) provides a wonderful primer on Web caching that illustrates the principles of caching and highlights some of the issues that may arise due to its use. Edge caching, or Web caching, is focused on storing and managing Web pages (static or dynamic) to help speed up transaction times. As the complexity of Web architecture evolves, applications have become more distributed. Edge solutions exemplify this, placing caches of content, sometimes fragments of executable code, in multiple geographical locations.

In recent years, object caching has enjoyed a revival and is now seen as a more desirable component of Web application architecture. Caching objects and sharing them across an infrastructure is a compelling capability. Often, the cost associated with building an object is considered quite high. The difference with an object cache mechanism is that it often resides at the Web server (Jadav & Gupta, 1997), the Web application, or as a middleware between the data and the Web application logic. Once an object is built, it can be cached, distributed, and managed for future reuse; it delivers performance at the application layer, whereas edge caching offers performance benefits to the delivery of data.

The strategies and issues found in edge caching are very similar to those encountered in object caching, and understanding their roles can offer a more complete view of a caching strategy. If it is possible to reuse an object (whether it is HTML or an object created from multiple data sources), an opportunity exists to increase performance. Caching takes advantage of predicting what resource might be required in the near future and storing a copy for later use. Later in the chapter, we explore approaches to managing custom object caches and situations where they can provide impressive benefits.

Asynchronous Processing

Asynchronous processing is often thought of as multithreaded computing or parallel computing, both of which are far more technical than intended. A common trap in transaction processing is the preconceived notion that all processing has to be linear. There are opportunities to move non-critical or batch-oriented logic out of the critical path of handling a transaction. However, this often introduces a level of complexity that surrounds the execution of tasks that are not time-critical. For example, Reynal (2005) offers a palatable introduction to failure detectors, a common component of an asynchronous system. Failure detectors help the system decide when activity is not behaving as it should. For instance, an asynchronous task might connect to an XML feed to refresh a local data cache. Obviously, a simple rule such as *all transactions must take no longer than one minute* to be considered healthy might suffice. At the other end of the spectrum, a failure detector might consider many variables such as historical averages or current operating features like a process' memory usage. Asynchronous processing offers the opportunity to offload activities that are less time-sensitive and speed up a given transaction. While it introduces a different level of management, it can be done very effectively and contributes to the overall performance of a system.

Resilient and Autonomic Behavior

In recent years, resilient and autonomic behavior has been posited as one of the next great evolutions in computing, driven primarily by the need to reduce maintenance and administration of increasingly large and distributed systems (Kephart, 2005). The goal is to embed the capability for an entire system, including hardware, middleware and user facing systems, to take a proactive approach towards maintaining a level of performance and reliability with little or no human intervention. At the core of this motivation is the need to build resiliency and autonomic capability into the component portfolio itself. Service-oriented architecture (SOA) is seen as an opportunity to provide systems with more resilient and autonomic features (Gurguis & Zeid, 2005). The increased dependency on Web services as a critical part of an application's building blocks introduces a new requirement of availability. Birman et al. (2004) discuss making Web services highly available through extending the base standards with high assurance, enhanced communication, and fault detection, an insightful collection of capabilities that enable more consistent performance. While SOA offers loose coupling, problems in one part of the system can have ripple effects on others. Availability, resiliency, and self-management are core attributes to a high performance system.

Client-Side Model View Control

Within the last year, a great deal of focus has been placed on richer Web application front ends (Paulson, 2005; Weiss, 2005). Web 2.0 or Ajax (Asynchronous JavaScript and XML) offer compelling user experiences by delivering the model view control (MVC) design paradigm to the browser. The Web client can update its data without end user action or refreshing the user experience. The current page does not need to reload to pull new data. It uses JavaScript and the browser's XMLHttpRequest object to connect back to the server. The server might be running a Web service, but it is not required. The document format does not have to be XML, though it often is. Using the Ajax approach to build user interfaces for Web applications delivers a more responsive user experience. Later in the chapter, we examine the use of the Web 2.0 model to deliver a high performance Web experience to bandwidth-constrained geographies. Delivering a fast end-user experience can be the key to persuading users that they are working with a superior application.

Graceful Degradation

Andoni and Staddon (2005) offer a unique approach to notifying users that their status with application is about to change. They describe how a user might have access to a certain level of content, but are delinquent on the payment of a bill, thus jeopardizing access to the service. Andoni and Staddon offer an example of graceful degradation where the service not only delivers a less optimal experience, but links the warning of their eminent status change to the content that they are viewing. The idea is that the user gets less and less value out of the content; for example, video content becomes choppier (Andoni et al, 2005). The key to graceful degradation is in altering the user experience to communicate that some features are not available while maintaining the overall performance and availability of the application. All too often, applications are built with hard dependencies on certain features that do (but should not) prevent users from benefiting from the other unaffected capabilities. Building high performance applications involves offering a system that can temporarily modify itself to maintain an acceptable level of performance while setting expectations, so that end users are subtly aware of any issues but are not helpless.

Using each of these approaches, we will identify the circumstances that lead the architectural and design changes, review the relevant design patterns, discuss the real-world implementation, and consider the before and after results. While IBM's expertise solution offers many opportunities for innovative thinking, the concepts discussed in this chapter are generally applicable when reviewing or designing Web applications for high load, high availability and fast performance.

Setting the Context

Web application design and architecture have matured greatly in recent years. Numerous books and articles discuss everything from design patterns and enterprise architecture to solution deployment strategy and high availability infrastructure (Alur, Crupi, & Malks, 2001; Eckstein, 2003; Fowler, 2000; Gamma, 2002; Grand, 2002; Schmid & Rossi, 2004). The current art grew out of the need to provide highly scalable and fast Web experiences to match the growing sophistication of end users (Burns, Rees, & Long, 2001; Goodman & Kebinger, 2004; Iyengar & Challenger, 1997; Malveau & Mowbray, 2001; Schmid & Rossi, 2004; Zhang & Buy, 2003). One area lacking in the current literature is a real-world strategy for applying appropriate design patterns and architectural approaches that improve the performance and reliability of today's enterprise Web experiences. In addition, intranets often impose additional constraints, budgets, legacy systems, network bandwidth limitations, and the general desire to do more with less (Appel, Dhadwal, & Pietraszek, 2003).

Intranets are a fertile ground for trying new approaches in the hope of solving real problems. The payoff for finding the right architecture or design is that it often leads to solutions that perform to expectations, are easily maintained and, most importantly, help transform the business. Popular examples of this are expertise location systems (AskMeCorp, 2005; Autonomy, 2005; Entopia, 2005; Tacit, 2005). These systems allow users to find people or answers to questions in a fast and efficient way. Helping employees in an enterprise to find each other or other knowledge repositories has a direct impact on the company's ability to draw from its network in real-time.

Example: *Amy is a sales representative with Acme, Inc., and is at a client's location pitching her products. The client has introduced a new requirement, integrating two technologies with Acme's solutions. Amy quickly does a search across the company for people with knowledge of the technologies in question. She gets twenty results, including three senior level technical architects and two that have actually worked with the client in the past. Amy holds her own, saying that there are experts in the company with those technologies, and we could certainly revisit and explore how it might come together. During the break, Amy chats with her colleagues to get more background, sends email to a few of them, and creates a group so she can refer to them at a later time. Amy is able to demonstrate responsiveness and strong ties to her company for the rest of the client visit.*

In 2004, IBM redesigned its internal corporate directory, "BluePages," to include extensive profiling information, updated search capabilities, real-time connection and common Web services. Some of the challenges included managing an increase in data (10-fold), a demanding world-wide target population, and a geographically-dispersed infrastructure. These are the somewhat typical issues architects face today, and the 2004 redesign proved several best-practice approaches to high performance Web application design.

Challenges in Building High Performance Web Applications

Data-Driven Web Applications Drive Contention to the Data Source

Over the last few years, Web applications have moved from basic content presentation with a few dynamic elements to more advanced content personalization and collaboration capabilities. Regardless of where a given application lives on that spectrum, most aggregate data and every request to the Web application incurs at least one hit to a data source. This introduces some obvious opportunities to manage transactions, while ensuring that the contention to the data source is minimized. Among the many ways practitioners address this space are connection pooling, data source replication, and resetting expectations to redefine requirements.

Pooling

Connection pooling is the primary tool for ensuring fast transactions to data sources. Object pools are collections of already created and initialized objects (Grand, 2002). The pool often limits the number of possible objects to maintain resource predictability and force a level of resource management. Objects are created beforehand to eliminate the performance cost associated with creating and initializing the objects for use. In the case of a database connection pool, a series of database connection objects are created that maintain a connection to the database. This eliminates the need to create a connection or initialize any required parameters. Many application platforms provide database connection pooling as part of their design: however, object pools are fairly straightforward to implement and are required when there is no "out of the box" solution. In the end, connection pooling is all about making the transaction perform so well that any contention for a managed resource is minimized.

Replicate the Data Source

Enterprises often have guidance and standards for reuse and data mart creation and management. The goal is often to minimize redundant data in multiple places. The side affect of centralizing data is that many exploiting applications are requesting the same data source. If deployed properly, this is a suitable strategy: Each exploiter is given access to a specific number of connections, reducing one application's impact on another. An issue is still not resolved when databases are geographically separate from the exploiting application. Database connection pools and database connection tools usually connect to databases over a network protocol that carries all the risk of network latency and instability. One method of mitigating this variable is to replicate the data source to the same subnet as the application server (Pacitti & Simon, 2000). By collocating the data source with the Web application, the number of issues introduced by the network is greatly reduced. If there was an issue with contention or network performance, they are addressed. As with many of these solutions, contention can still exist (Abbadi & Toueg, 1989; Pacitti & Simon, 2000), but by addressing the performance of every link, contention is minimized.

Do Less, Simplify Views, Reduce Functionality

A requirements document is an architect's best friend. It clearly specifies both functional requirements (i.e., users need to be able to send pages from the Website) and non-functional requirements (i.e., needs to handle 200 concurrent users per second). Therefore, the client has a clear understanding of what he/she/it is asking and what the service provider is committing to deliver. There are times when requirements are accepted even with little knowledge of what will be required to fulfill the commitment. This is very common when the team either lacks the experience necessary to size appropriately or when it is breaking new ground. During these times, practitioners often return to their customers, presenting the issues of the moment and convincing everyone that the right thing to do is revisit the requirements document. If there is too much occurring in a given user scenario (impacting the ability to support a certain service level), the team must consider whether it should be doing less, simplifying view or reducing functionality. Sometimes this *really* is the only option; after all, ambitious customers ask for the world, and it is the service provider's job to help realize that vision as best he/she/it can.

Transaction-Based Systems Tend to Do Too Much

In the early days of the Web developer, applications were often created as Fast-CGIs hooked into Web servers, persistent in memory and performing functions on each request. The more promising applications often provided considerable value, but increased in complexity. Application design went through a period of linear programming and with the maturation of application models such as J2EE, developers were able to branch out into an object-oriented world where solutions were created by pulling together modular components. Unfortunately, the practitioners did not evolve at the same rate as the technology. All this is to say, developers of transaction-based systems often do too much in one area of the application, reducing flexibility and manageability.

The Servlet Controller

One of the common approaches to structure a Web application is to use a servlet controller (Alur et al., 2001), which handle all the requests into an application. They often perform some very basic request preparation and then forward the transaction to other servlets to perform specific tasks. Servlet controllers act as the gate keepers to the application, providing a single face to the end user while maintaining the flexibility and modularity of specialized servlets that handle only the function required at any one time.

STRUTS

One of the most popular implementations employing a servlet controller is STRUTS from the Apache Software Foundation (Apache Foundation, 2005). STRUTS is a very robust framework that allows Web applications to be built based on some of the best design patterns (Sun Microsystems, 2002). STRUTS includes several features that address the transition from a single bloated application to a highly modular system.

Deal with Slow Performance by Adding Servers /Over-Scale

There are times when a change to the requirements document is not an option. The next favorite solution is to scale the application horizontally. "We will just add more hardware" is what we often hear. This traditional approach usually means you have enough servers to handle peak loads, and during the lower traffic hours the application is over-provisioned. Adding hardware to solve an architectural or design problem is a tactical solution which only masks the problem. Adding hardware often helps address load issues, but the increase in resource brings an increase in complexity. There is a balance to be found between budget, hardware capability, and application architecture and design.

Complex Applications Need Tender Loving Care

Even the simplest applications have a tendency to become complicated. Companies often have legacy systems, a variety of existing hardware, software and processes, and the integration task can therefore be daunting. Even the most skilled, well-funded projects have weak points. These Achilles heels often require constant monitoring.

Some systems integrate with in-shop or third-party monitoring systems, allowing systems administrators to be notified when issues arise. The basic checks include making a request to the application, and as long as there is a response, trouble goes unnoticed. Some systems are more proactive, looking for errors and response times. However, with the desire to mask errors or erratic behavior from end users, monitoring tools have a difficult time relying on the basic tests. The Web application may be performing fine, while the database is down.

Savvy developers build in special servlets that perform end-to-end tests of their Web application. These test servlets make a series of calls to ensure that all is right from the application's perspective. However, this level of development is often unfunded because the value it provides is seen only when there is a problem, and even then it simply quickens the time to resolution instead of eliminating it. Applications with a myriad of dependencies, network files stores, LDAP (Lightweight Directory Access Protocol) servers, databases, and Web services require monitoring as well. To an end user, an unresponsive or non-functioning application is as good as no application (Goodman et al., 2004).

The Platform and Plumbing Can Impact Perceived Performance

Managing end user perception is a key task in achieving high customer satisfaction. With the continual push for a service-oriented architecture and componentization, the dependency list keeps growing. Exposing services also means providing consistent, reliable service; impacting and exploiting applications in acceptable ways. One of the problems is that not everything is managed in the application architecture layer. Platform and network plumbing can have serious impacts to perceived performance.

Applications are often made up of many components and software stacks. Each component contributes to the overall application platform, and it is possible to combine modules that work better or worse. This fact often drives solution providers into single-silo approaches, embracing a single vendor or a specific recipe of vendors to deliver solutions. A more mature approach is to realize the need for standards-based solutions to ensure that components are easily mixed and matched without impacting the exact implementation of the application.

Network conditions have an obvious effect on applications, especially when a global audience is considered. A fast application in North America (.25 - .50 ms response time) can become slow in Asia Pacific (5-15 sec). Some of these challenges arise simply because of the amount of content being shuttled across networks. Some delay can be minimized through caching edge servers, better network backbones, and globally-distributed solutions.

Unexpected Errors Happen, but Who Needs to Know?

Application developers are told to handle errors with grace, but the definition of "grace" often varies in meaning and context (Nielsen, 2003; Preece, 1994; Raskin, 2000). If an application supports a very small audience, it might be preferred not to spend a lot of time on exception handling. In most cases, though, applications are meant to benefit a larger population and, often, a demanding user.

The most basic approach to handling errors is to employ custom error pages, so that at least the error looks like it was intended to be read and responded to. This is the minimal amount of effort required to keep up appearances.

Table 1. Sample non-functional requirements (NFR) for an enterprise application

	Target	Measured By
Scalability	Up to 250 requests per second	Application stability
Performance	- For 95% of the transactions < 7 seconds - For 5% transactions < 10 seconds	Probe tools measuring response times at different geographies
Availability	99.96% during schedules service hours	Tools measuring availability metrics

Some developers have resorted to irrational behavior to confuse the user. If an error occurs when submitting a form, some applications redirect the user to a different page, possibly unrelated, in the hopes of confusing or at least giving the appearance that the user might have actually been at fault. "When in doubt, redirect to the home page" is a motto no one should be fond of, but it happens.

More sophisticated developers include a clear and direct message acknowledging the error. Sometimes an alert is generated for the benefit of the systems team; other times, the Web applications present the message to stop any further complaint. These approaches often tailor errors with reasonably coherent messages. Instead of ERROR 500, it might read "We're sorry! The application is currently having difficulty handling your request."

Approaches to Building More Resilient Web Applications

Numerous challenges face application developers and architects developing scalable Web applications that also maintain performance and reliability. In the previous section, we covered five scenarios that often plague Web applications: data source contention; performing too many tasks; care and maintenance; platform and network capability; and exception handling. With each of these areas, we explored some of the popular approaches for addressing the problem space.

In this section we examine alternative approaches to these problems that have proven best practices in our own architecture and application design. We will cover:

- Caching strategies for high-availability Web applications: beyond storing copies of HTML (Challenger et al., 1998; Iyengar et al., 1997)

- Asynchronous task processing within Web applications: removing non-essential linear logic from high-volume transactions (Grand, 2002)

- Building self-reliant autonomous behavior: encapsulating through services achieving tight integration with *true* loose coupling (Birman et al., 2004)

- Client-side Model View Control (MVC): moving MVC to the browser supercharging the response times and getting a "wow" user experience (Murry, 2005; Sun Microsystems, 2002)

- Graceful degradation: keeping users thinking and feeling "fast," "reliable," and "always on" (Florins et al., 2004)

High-Availability Application Layer Caching

One of the challenges that busy Web applications and Web portals face is the need to perform data source queries to deliver features and functions to end users. As we reviewed earlier, this often drives contention to the data source. One overlooked approach is to design smart caching strategies to minimize calls to the data source. This aversion is well warranted, as the decision to cache often has implications in terms of high availability, data freshness, synchronization challenges, and real-time management. The following section reviews two strategies for caching: database-driven caching and more dynamic LDAP caching.

Database-Driven Caching

Typically, relational databases comprise a mix of static lookup-type tables and dynamic or updatable data sets. Each of these offer opportunities for application layer caching. To help provide context to these situations, we will use the IBM expertise location system as an example.

Static Table Data Cache

One of the popular aspects of an employee's profile is the contextual information which we display alongside the more central content. A drastic change from the previous version is the area of the profile that depicts organization structure. When this profile view was initially designed, the pages were getting response times around 850-1000 milliseconds and were driving, on average, six times more LDAP operations to our enterprise directory than the second most common function of viewing employee records.

While there are several factors contributing to the performance attributes, the primary one was the introducing of the reporting structure on every profile. To help address both of these

Figure 1. Example of a BluePages profile view with reporting structure (right)

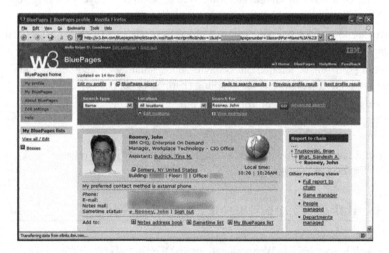

undesirable characteristics, we designed a cache holding reporting structure information for all users, using a local database as the source. Obviously, there is huge performance gain by replacing three LDAP operations with three lookups in a local memory object. Reusing the application data source to build the data structure alleviated any additional work from the corporate LDAP directories.

Caching lookup tables and other relatively stable areas of the database is easy and reduces the workload on the database and the application. It is a simple way of maintaining the user experience while improving performance.

Dynamic Table Data Cache

Static data is an easy and obvious caching opportunity, one that many architects and developers can easily apply to existing or new applications with very little investment. Obviously, things get challenging when caching occurs at the application layer, and the data has the possibility of being updated. Suddenly, maintaining appearances to an end user has to be well thought-out.

With the move to a modern Web application, IBM's expertise location exposed several common services and introduced an unexpected load. Caching at the service layer played a very important role in sustaining the growing popularity of service-oriented architecture and Web services.

In this type of cache, we need to deal with a table data which gets updated continuously by the Web application.

There are three key parts of this design (Figure 2): the scheduler, cache manager (Grand, 2002), and high-availability data structure. The scheduler initiates the cache manager and,

Figure 2. Highly-available data cache

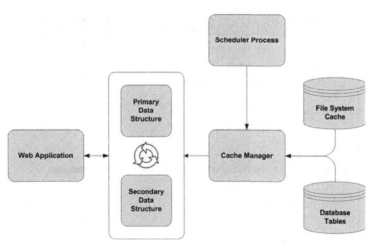

in follow-on versions, also manages any message queues and events that trigger cache management features, such as changing the schedule for refresh. It performs most of the critical operations managing the cache data structures. Obviously, the cache manager is responsible for making calls to a Data Access Object (Alur et al., 2002) to load the cache. This might be from the database or from the file system, depending on the configuration. The file system was used to eliminate start-up lag at risk of displaying stale data. For example, the reports-to chain cache (organizational) data object in BluePages is approximately 18MB size. It takes enough time that cycling the application produces undesired load and delay. By automatically committing the data structures in memory to disk, the cache manager can load instantly and update as needed.

The cache manager works with two data structures, the primary and secondary caches. Various data structures operate slightly differently and, often, some level of synchronization is required when performing manipulations. To eliminate contention of the data cache, a second one is created by the cache manager. It uses the second one to perform any management operations (add, update, delete) and sets a Boolean flag to immediately put it into play. The other cache can then be deleted or saved depending on the refresh strategy. For example, if the database is designed with time-stamps on changing data, deleting the cache is somewhat wasteful. There might be only five changes, and there is really no need to transfer all of the other data. By selecting only the items that changed and updating those in memory cache, updates can happen frequently and take effect more promptly with less resource churn.

One of the major undertakings for BluePages was the introduction of Web-based management for key subsystems (Figure 3). The cache management is one example of these Web-based management systems.

Figure 3. Data cache Web-based administration

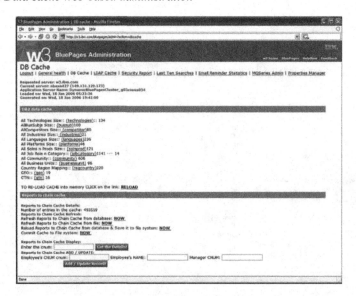

Web-based management of the cached object allows us to monitor the data that is in memory. For the reports-to chain cache, it shows data for an employee's reporting structure. It also allows an administrator to manage the data in memory (create, update, delete), commit those changes to the file system or database, and reload the cache, if necessary. Providing administrators with management capabilities to key subsystem components removes the specialists from having to perform more risky manual tasks in support of an application. It also allows the application to appear more responsive by supporting more real-time management instead of code changes or manual application restarts.

By using strategic caching, BluePages was able to see a reduction of 800 milliseconds in response time. Approximately 750 milliseconds were due to the reports-to chain cache and ~50 milliseconds were associated with database calls. Currently the same page delivers a 70ms server-side response time.

Another situation in which dynamic data caching plays an important role is the design of service implementations. Most services (Web services, XML-RCP, URL APIs, etc) take a considerable amount of overhead to process a request. For example, in Web services, a decent amount of XML is being manipulated; this in turn creates a considerable amount of garbage. Consider that overhead on top of the need to actually service the request by hitting data sources or performing calculations. BluePages receives approximately 3.2 million service calls per day and supports a response time of a few milliseconds for service exploiters. To achieve this level of efficiency, caching was employed to enable smarter transaction processing.

The key to smarter transaction processing is providing a proxy between the transaction request and the service logic, or process. The proxy determines if the request should pass into the process stage or if the request for whatever reason deserves a cached, static, or predefined response.

In the BluePages architecture, this "service cache layer" pre-fetches basic information related to the service and decides if it has enough information to respond. More specifically, BluePages offers a URL API to access a user's personal photo. The cache layer stores all

Figure 4. Using caching to avoid unnecessary transactions

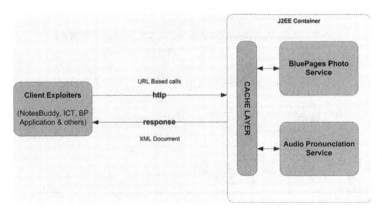

the unique IDs and uses this information to short-circuit the request. If the request is for a user that does not have a photo, a redirect to a default image can be sent. The redirect is used instead of a full photo to keep the transaction light and to ensure that browsers get an opportunity to cache the default image for faster rendering.

In BluePages, this cache avoids over one million service calls from reaching the processing phase of the service. That translates into over one million database calls while improving overall response times.

Dynamic LDAP Caching

Sometimes caching all the data in RAM is just a waste of space. LDAP caching with some level of detail is probably not the best candidate to load into RAM. Presumably there is a high level of caching at the LDAP server, so it is best not to add another layer. Therefore, a cache is needed that builds based on usage, and some general rules about how memory can be reclaimed and which entries are always a "good idea" to have.

The typical reporting view includes a list of individuals related to the current profile. While one LDAP connection can be established with multiple queries executed, the transaction itself is still somewhat intensive. We think of the transaction time with LDAP as being very fast, and it is; but when you deal with so many transactions, general queuing theory and rendering speed tend to get the better of us. A read from RAM is simply much faster than a transaction to LDAP.

This view is supported with the lazy loading (Grand, 1999) dynamic LDAP cache. At least three levels of the chain already exist, and the subsequent entries are cached for future use.

Figure 5. BluePages reporting structure tab

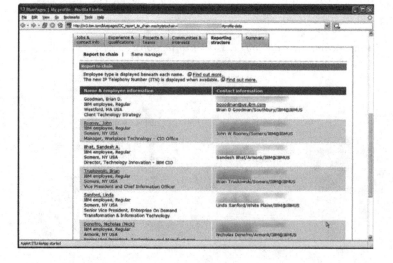

Figure 6. Dynamic LDAP cache

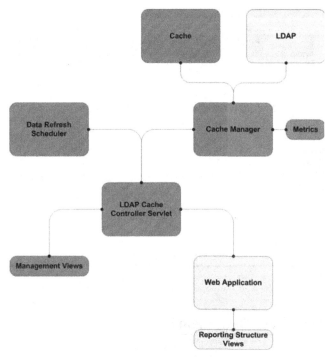

The LDAP Cache Controller servlet acts as the central management point. It delivers the subsystem management views, and Web applications use a static method to access the Cache Manager (Grand, 2002). The Cache Manager is the object that populates the cache and fails over to LDAP as needed. It keeps track of metrics and performs any regular updates based on the Data Refresh Scheduler.

As with the other cache subsystem, the LDAP cache has a management interface. The main difference is the cache statistics view. With a database view, the hit rate is not relevant. In many cases, it is 100%. In the case of a dynamic cache where you are building it based on usage, hit rates are everything. When you consider that the only views driving this usage are organization structures (the third most accessed view), it is astounding that we experience an 80% hit rate.

In order to avoid the added traffic, caching was used. On some pages, we save up to 6 seconds—an eternity in Web time.

- Cache hit rate is 80% with a peak size of 80K entries stored
- Total LDAP call reduction by ~792K per day (240K queries vs. 48K queries)
- Avoiding up to ~6-10 LDAP operations and a response time of ~1000-1500 milliseconds on each organizational page

Figure 7. Dynamic LDAP cache Web administration

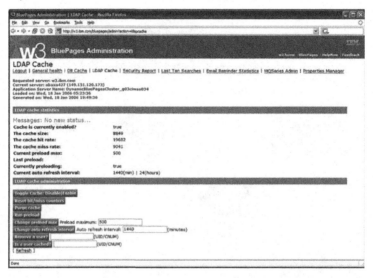

Asynchronous Task Processing

Making Transactions Non-Linear

One of the themes that this chapter raises is the notion that many operations can happen asynchronously (Grand, 2002). However, many architects and developers do not take the time to think about how to build their system to support it. Often implementing function wins out over responsible use of resources. A typical Web transaction is performed through a GET or a POST to a servlet or CGI. The servlet or CGI processes the request and returns a response. In many ways this is linear programming. If you use message queuing systems in your Web applications today, then you might already know the wonders of responding without necessarily completing the entire transaction. To help illustrate this design point, BluePages offers a couple of examples, all based on the same pattern.

One of the design criteria for the online administration page was to track operation statistics in real-time: Who were the last ten users to log-in (success/failure), what were the last ten searches, and so forth. One of the more costly aspects of collecting such performance statistics is that it takes cycles away from performing the user facing operations. The problem to solve was how to perform the tasks as part of a transaction without constantly having a locked state around a data structure, or processing requests while we should be sending back results.

The basic solution is based around a blocking queue design pattern (Grand, 2002; Kabutz, 2001) dequeueing only when there are objects present in the queue. This avoids spinning extra cycles with no operation. In the class diagram (Figure 9) below, SampleBlocking-

Figure 8. BluePages Web administration view of last ten searches

Figure 9. Blocking queue class diagram

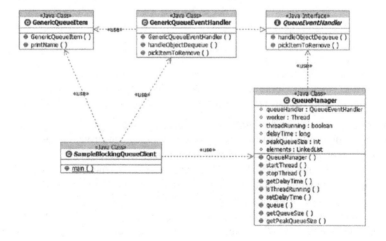

QueueClient is a client/component exploiter of QueueManager. QueueManager manages the thread and message brokering. QueueManager is initialized with a QueueEventHandler and uses that interface to interact with other implementations of handling the queue. For example, some queues need to be priority-sorted or dequeued based on some other criteria. The GenericQueueItem happens to be the object being enqueued and dequeued. It is a very simple and effective design pattern.

An example from BluePages illustrates the real-world use further. BluePages provides a keyword search to employee profiles. A user might search for other employees in the company who know about a certain client and a technology. The servlet processes the request and enqueues a value object to the queue with minimal amount of data (i.e., the query terms, the URL, the user ID, a time-stamp, etc.) and then respond with the search results. Asynchronously, a thread uses a QueueEventHandler object to decide which item in the queue should be dequeued and then passes that object to get handled. The object performs any calculations (number of searches, list management, and clustering or trend-type calculation) and stores the data to be presented and used in other ways. An example of where this data can be used is in the popular, "what are other people searching for right now" capability. Even though the insert is synchronized (we used a Java ArrayList), they take more precedent because there are more enqueues than dequeues at any given time. You can see in the sample screen shot of the BluePages administration interface that the peak queue size for this specific server instance is 268, so we know the approach is working.

In some cases, a soft-queue is not sufficient, and a real message queue subsystem is required. The proposal of this section is simply to raise the issue that not all aspects of a transaction need to complete during the duration of handling a request. There are times when it is not encouraged, and specifically for J2EE, it is suggested to be incorrect. For example, when performing database transactions asynchronously, a transaction is preferred for all the security context concerns (Brown, 2005). Asynchronous beans helps alleviate some of this limitation, as discussed in the next section.

Asynchronous Beans in J2EE

Spinning new threads from a servlet for asynchronous task processing is a common design approach until recent times. Some of the drawbacks of this approach include: The transaction loses container security, transaction scope, and lack of failover during critical failures.

J2EE came up with a standard solution to solve this problem, in which the servlet request places the task information as a message in queue, and message-driven beans (MDB) read this message. A *message-driven bean* is an enterprise bean that allows J2EE applications to process messages asynchronously. It acts as a JMS message listener, which is similar to an event listener except that it receives messages instead of events. The messages may be sent by any J2EE component, an application client, another enterprise bean, or a Web component, or by a JMS application or system that does not use J2EE technology. MDBs process the task in an asynchronous way within the container, taking advantage of all the container's built-in features. As soon as the request message is processed, the MDB can place a response on the response queue. Servlet requests can keep polling the response queue for the status of the request submitted to let the end user know the results of the asynchronous task.

Business Grid Computing

Web application architectures often require batch processing of some of the maintenance tasks. It is not uncommon to have developers rewriting code with stand-alone applications or scripts to perform these operations outside of the Web container. This results in code redundancy and, obviously, such implementation loses the application server container advantages. Advanced J2EE containers such as IBM WebSphere Extended Deployment, allow asynchronous task processing by allowing batch, long-running or compute-intensive tasks to run within the container; the best application is chosen for this task based on resource utilization.

The business grid function in WebSphere Extended Deployment extends the WebSphere Application Server to accommodate applications that need to perform long-running work alongside transactional applications. Long-running work might take hours or even days to complete, and consumes large amounts of memory or processing power while it runs.

While IBM and other companies have advanced application platforms to help with the task of batch processing as an architect or application designer, it is important to ensure that your applications have a strategy to minimize the duplication of code and fragmentation.

Application Resiliency

As more applications are designed to participate in Service-Oriented Architectures, they increase their dependency on resources outside of their control. Applications make calls to external interfaces, such as databases, LDAP, messaging servers, SOAP-based Web service calls, or even HTTP-based services. Suddenly, the performance of an application depends on the external interfaces of other applications and services (Krishnamurthi & Bultan, 2005). The availability or poor performance of external services potentially impacts the availability of the dependent exploiting applications. This section will look at how applications can employ a more autonomic, resilient approach to these situations.

Human Required: The SOAP Fault Specification

For Web Services, W3C built the SOAP Fault (W3C, 2003) to represent the availability status of the service providers. The information provided by SOAP Fault is similar to the reason-phrase provided by HTTP (Internet Society, 1999) which underscores the nature of the problem (Table 2). One of the problems with these approaches is that system designers end up using generic issue codes, making it almost impossible to know what is really going wrong. Issues can be detected, but a human is still required. What if the dependant hosting environment has problems? This could result in Web application servers accepting requests, filling queues, and in turn affecting the entire infrastructure. This becomes even more unattractive if the hosting environment provides shared hosting or manages entry through proxy

Table 2. Example of SOAP fault

```
<?xml version="1.0" encoding="UTF-8"?>
<soap:Envelope
xmlns:soap="http://schemas.xmlsoap.org/soap/envelope/" >
 <soap:Body>
  <soap:Fault>
    <faultcode>-1000</faultcode>
   <faultstring>Database is unavailable.</faultstring>
   <detail/>
   </soap:Fault>
  </soap:Body>
 </soap:Envelope>
```

servers. A SOAP Fault indicates that an issue occurred with that transaction; however, it places the next step back onto the calling application, which may very well keep making service calls and impacting the overall application performance.

Communicating Availability

Transaction or session-specific errors often indicate that something is wrong, but a hung socket connection or a cascading error may never return a satisfactory message to allow an exploiting application to respond appropriately. In order to provide a higher level of resiliency, real-time status is required. UDDI servers can identify several end points, which may allow a Web service client the opportunity to use a different system to accomplish the same task. The problem is that any one of those services may be having problems. To help address this situation, system availability is included as part of the interaction between the service consumer, service discovery, and service provider.

This model (Figure 10) provides a level of service availability above and beyond the typical transaction-based error. Service clients can be advised of issues through simple calls to an independent third party, which allows appropriate logic to take place to maintain a higher level of service. This technique is similar to network dispatcher models, where a single service provides a feedback loop to ensure that servers in a cluster are available before being dispatched. For example, an asynchronous process may test the availability of an externally-dependant service through the central availability system. The response will provide information similar to typical faults; however, it is received outside of a transaction with the provider. This eliminates hung sockets or other variables that are only visible to the provider. Updates to availability status can be made from other enterprise monitoring tools, allowing for an integrated knowledge base of service availability.

In Figure 11, Enterprise Directory is a service provider. In this case, the service provider makes use of Tivoli Service Management to monitor its services. ED Monitor is one such

Figure 10. Service availability system for more predictable operations

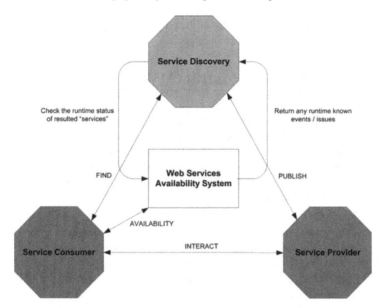

Figure 11. BluePages system checking availability of enterprise directory

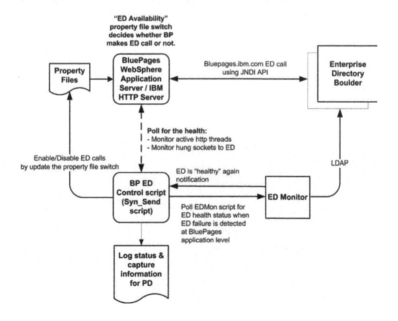

service monitoring tool. BluePages monitors the health of the enterprise directory to failover or degrade service as necessary. Applications cannot perform in autonomic ways without being informed about their state, the state of the environment and, more importantly, the state of the systems and services on which it depends.

Client-Side Model View Control (MVC)

The Model View Control (Sun Microsystems, 2002) design pattern is a very popular approach to Web application design. Its one limitation is that the view is created server-side and must be transmitted to the client for interpretation. Moving MVC to the client truly separates the view from the middleware. The need for such activity is rooted in the desire for richer interactions and faster transactions. This section addresses client-side MVC and getting that "wow" user experience.

Common challenges for any enterprise Web application include internationalization and a variety of hosting issues that may impact responsiveness. While there are frameworks for addressing language translation among a diverse group of end users, the system deployment is often centrally located, resulting in poor performance for locations with limited bandwidth or congested links. BluePages is a real-world example of an enterprise application offering internationalization while being hosted from a single geography.

Figure 12 charts response times for the same page for Asia Pacific, Europe, and the United States. BluePages is deployed in the United States and, as the chart depicts, the performance of the application degrades as the end user's location moves further away.

The problem with the traditional (server-side) MVC design pattern is that it renders the entire view at the server, and makes the application and infrastructure components transmit the data to the Web clients. Web applications end up sending a considerable amount of HTML back to the client Web browsers to achieve a rich user interface.

Figure 12. BluePages response time comparison

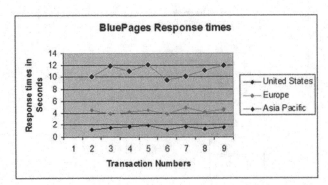

Consider users that rely on client-installed applications (VB-based, Lotus-based, or even Oracle forms), which query for information from a server. The amount of data transferred is the smallest possible, as it is no longer transmitting the view. The client-side applications display the data using the front-end logic held at the client. The client server model helps illustrate the benefits of a client-controlled view; however, it brings all the negative issues that drove the Web revolution. The ideal situation is a richer client side view that is managed via the Web.

The decision regarding whether to use client-side MVC or server-side MVC may depends on several factors, including the kind of application, end user connectivity, or even how much data is being transferred to the client browser and what impact it has on the overall performance of the Web application. There are two approaches to client-side MVC: JavaScript Templates and the XMLHttpObject.

Client-Side MVC: Using JavaScript Templates

Using the JavaScript Template design pattern places all the rendering of the user interface into client-side cacheable assets. In this design pattern, the Controller Servlet invokes a Model Servlet. The Model code executes business logic, including actions such as retrieving information from database systems or other external services. The Model servlet passes values to the View Controller to render an XML document or HTML/plain text response. The View Controller decides which JavaScript template should be invoked for a particular service response. Once the response reaches the client browser, the JavaScript template specified by the View Controller renders the information retrieved by the service call. All the necessary HTML logic needed to display a rich GUI Web page is already built into the JavaScript templates.

This design pattern is dependent on how JavaScript files are cached by the Web browsers. When a JavaScript file is requested through the browser, it is also accompanied by HTTP header directives that tell the browser how long the object can be considered fresh. Freshness

Figure 13. Client-side MVC, JavaScript templates

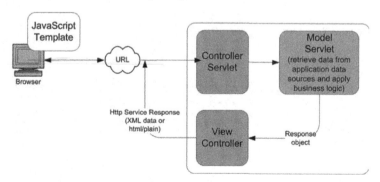

Table 3. Sample search results response time comparison

Search Keyword	Number of Results	Server-Side MVC Design Response Times	Client-Side MVC Design Response Times
Smith, Chris	30	14.12	1.482
Linda	28	8.32	1.803
Kline	42	8.47	2.093
Kile	8	6.43	1.172
Inampudi	3	6.17	1.042

translates to how long the resource can be retrieved directly from the browser cache instead of making calls to the originating end point. Since the browser represents the cache closest to the end user, it offers the maximum performance benefit whenever content can be stored there. Another consideration is that the JavaScript templates need to change infrequently to support a longer client-side timeout. Using this design pattern, BluePages shows a ten-fold improvement.

Client-Side MVC Using XMLHttpObject

Every modern Web browser has some form of XMLHttpObject that provides a socket connection to the originating server. This provides the opportunity to make subsequent asynchronous calls. Coupled with Dynamic HTML (DHTML), the user interface can be updated without a browser refresh. Avoiding the browser refresh provides a richer user experience because the context of the interaction is maintained. This is a popular approach and is often referred to as "Asynchronous JavaScript and XML" (AJAX) (Murry, 2005). The most popular examples are found from Google (GMail, Google Suggest, and Google Maps) (Google, 2005a, 2005b, 2005c).

In this design, pattern applications make asynchronous HTTP calls using XMLHttpObjects via JavaScript. A server-side service returns a response object. The response could be SOAP,

Figure 14. Client-Side MVC using XMLHttpObject

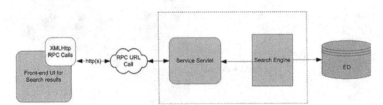

Figure 15. BluePages type ahead engine using XMLHttpObject

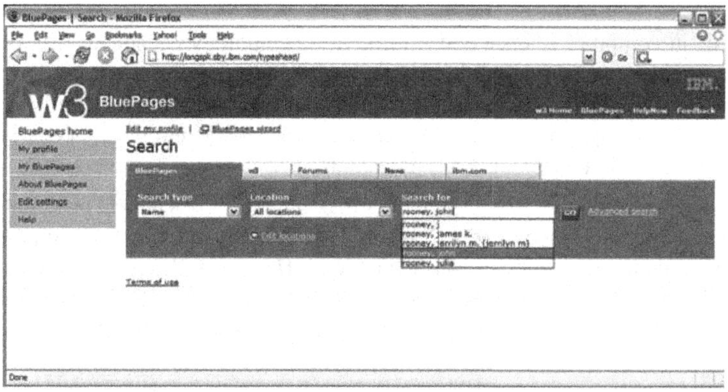

XML, plain text, or JavaScript. The response text is then processed by the logic in JavaScript methods. Using DHTML, the content is displayed on the Web page.

Another use of this design pattern is depicted in Figure 15. As the user enters the employee's name for the search, the type-ahead engine makes a service call to retrieve matches from BluePages user dictionary. The list of potential names is displayed in the pull-down list based on the retrieved matches. As the user types more characters, the search is refined. In this scenario, it is important that the list retrieval is faster than the end user's typing speed.

Network Bandwidth Savings

Client-side MVC has another important advantage: network bandwidth savings. Since client-side MVC makes use of static templates to render the user interface, the look and feel for an application can be cached in the client browser. The data that gets transferred to the client browser becomes much smaller.

While client-side MVC introduces some additional design complexity for Web applications, it can be worthwhile to achieve richer interfaces and more responsive Web experiences. There are sure to be many perspectives on the advantages and disadvantages of client-side MVC before it is universally accepted, but it has the potential to address some of the long-standing issues of Web application architecture.

Table 4. BluePages search performance using JavaScript template design pattern

ED Search	Current Implementation	BPv6 Implementation
Page size	77.9KB (Search on "kline" 25 results/page)	18.7KB (Search on "kline" 25 results/page)
Data transfer / day	77.9 GB	18.7 GB

Graceful Degradation

Most degrees in computer science and information technology do not require a class in human-computer interface design. It is not uncommon for an application to let the end user know that there was an error, for example, that it could not write to the memory and thus had to halt. The developer might have thought that the error would never occur, but even some of the common issue messages are unfriendly.

While there has been plenty of discussion over making exceptions appear informative and friendly (Nielson, 2000; Preece, 1994; Raskin, 2000), there is less focus around graceful degradation (Andoni et al., 2005; Florins et al., 2004; Herlihy & Wing, 1987). The driving principal is that an application can go beyond responding with friendly errors and actually disable features and functions until the environment stabilizes. Web applications in particular are vulnerable to an increasing number of dependencies: Web services, databases, LDAP directories, and file systems. Any single dependency can bring a Web application to a halt, and an unresponsive Web application might as well be a dead application. A simple method to address some of these issues is to place a timeout on the transaction, forcibly breaking the process to return an error to the end user. It is better to say something is broken than to be truly unavailable. This is really the first step. The second step is to prevent future access to the resource until a successful transaction indicates that the resource is again available. The challenge is to monitor your dependencies and code against the availability of those resources. If a database becomes unavailable, a backup might be used or menu items might be disabled, with ample indication to the end user that some of the features to which they may be accustomed have been disabled temporarily.

The BluePages Web application has many dependencies on external resources, and this provides an excellent real-world example. As part of the application, a service interface exposes read access to a back-end data store. Simple requests to the service return a person object in the form of a DSML XML document. It happens that the full-text search engine requires XML documents to be written on a file system. This allows the file system to be the primary data source with the database as a backup. The added resources and processing required for reading a record from the database and returning an XML document are less preferable than serving up a static XML document. A simple servlet proxies requests to the appropriate data handlers by referencing a Boolean flag. This flag is used as an availability indicator of the primary data source. This indicator is set in two ways. First, any transaction which fails accessing the file system will set the flag so subsequent calls are routed to the secondary method. Second, an asynchronous process periodically checks the primary resource and proactively sets the flag in the hope that it will catch the issue before a failing request does. Additionally, this process sets the flag back when its periodic test no longer fails. From an exploiter's perspective, the service rarely fails. At most, there is a slight slowdown in performance, which is undesirable, but better than failing altogether. Adding a proxy layer between the requestor and the actual data access method lets the application short-circuit a potentially grave situation early, preserving the rest of the application.

Another example includes a typical dependency on a database or LDAP directory. BlueP-ages provides both directory lookup and free text search. The truth is that the free text search can provide similar search results to that of the directory query, but the results are not exactly the same. Based on the previous example, it is easy to imagine the monitoring system provided in the application. The difference here is that if there is a problem with the LDAP resource, the current deployment has no effective way for failover. Instead of simply sending an error or notifying the user that the LDAP servers are causing a problem (not exactly something the average user understands), a subsequent query is automatically performed using the free text search. An unresponsive directory message might imply that the Web application itself can no longer perform any useful function. In our case this is not accurate, but end users should not have to figure this out. The search results are not perfect, but often they will suffice. Moreover, it is a single step to an end user; they cannot use the application improperly. Even if they do not see the general message that some features are disabled, the query is handled and results are provided as best as possible. The results are labeled appropriately, and the error messages are well communicated, while the user maintains access to the information. In this case we alter the behavior of the application slightly to support a more satisfying application experience. Failure is communicated, and next steps are clearly provided.

The principal of graceful degradation means that, as an application begins to fail, it does so in a way that is not jarring to the end users or other components or subsystems. If a single feature is broken, disable the components that rely on that feature, provide a method for resuming work, or failover to a backup method. There are times where budget, design limitations, or schedule restrict the ability to implement applications in this way, but the benefits are quite significant. Applications that gracefully degrade and re-enable as possible are easier to manage and maintain. They change the mode of application instability to monitoring, instead of scrambling to reboot and provide service. In some ways, we are talking about building smarter systems. At the heart of any autonomy is a core system that can indicate for it and others that a problem exists.

Future Trends

Just as software design and architecture continue to evolve, underlying infrastructure and middleware continue to provide an ecosystem within which applications can execute. Key to maximizing future infrastructure advances is the ability for an application to tolerate and to exploit many of these advances. Recently, autonomic computing technologies have advanced to the point where grid-like technologies can be delivered, without the need for disruptive approaches to be embedded within application designs. By having a middleware environment that provides the needed abstraction layer around the underlying physical deployment topology, applications can be managed against a set of predetermined policies. These policies, while enforcing against a breach of their predefined goals, will provision and de-provision instances of an application, all without having the application or pre-mediation of the event.

Given today's large dynamically-configurable operating systems/hardware, applications should provide ample opportunities for the hypervisor to capitalize on parallelism. Key to this ability is having applications designed with clear units of work spawning threads which are then separately managed and driven to their logical conclusion. Just as loosely coupled applications need to understand their dependencies on downstream processing, highly threaded applications need to understand and take steps to ensure that they provide exception handling, for the non-serialized processing that is likely to occur.

In focusing on the maturing of the infrastructure and middleware, a key strategy within the industry is to deliver computing resources as a dependable, scalable, and transparent commodity which applications exploit through standard development and interface models. This strategy is squarely focused at delivery of the infrastructure as a utility.

Utility Computing

Utility computing is a provisioning paradigm in which a service provider makes computing resources available to a consumer as needed. Infrastructure management and the ability to charge for specific usage, rather than the traditional fixed rate model, are central to the value proposition.

The utility computing vision makes several promises revolving around reducing IT complexity, pricing based on usage and decreasing operating, and capital costs to the enterprise. Adapting an infrastructure to a utility computing model is not simply about making changes to IT infrastructure; people and business process changes are also critical for future success (Whatis.com, 2005)

A sub-strategy of utility computing is directly associated with consolidation. In a shared utility computing model, a service provider looks to centralize its computing resources to serve a large audience reducing overhead while maintaining business resiliency. The value proposition for utility computing can be difficult to express, but the following points to help articulate it:

- **Efficiency yields cost savings:** In accordance with industry observations, the average machine utilization of datacenter systems is between 15 and 25 percent (Coulter, 2005).

- **Abstraction and virtualization yields flexibility:** A dynamic infrastructure allows the environment to proactively respond to changing application loads (Chase, Anderson, Thakar, Vahdat, & Doyle, 2001). Through virtualization, transparent provisioning of system resources is performed against a constantly reevaluated set of policies. As load decreases and the likelihood of a policy breach is diminished, systems are de-provisioned and reallocated to other services. This increases the overall utilization of assets and saves money through less upfront infrastructure.

- **Standardizing the infrastructure stack speeds implementation:** By having a utility computing mindset, individual applications are freed from the overhead of having to procure, setup, and test dedicated infrastructure, which typically has long lead times and capital expenditure associated with it. This process is typically repeated numerous times within an enterprise portfolio, and little if any economies of scale are leveraged. By driving standardization into the infrastructure stack and a predictable set of services, applications can execute against a set of assumptions and deploy into a shared resource pool without unique and dedicated resources.

Figure 16. Dedicated resources vs. shared utility

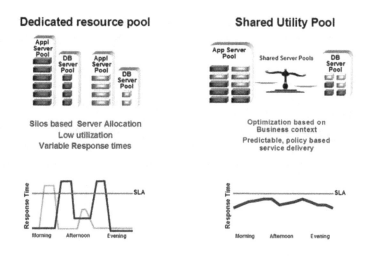

In order to support this utility computing services model, many fundamental infrastructure services are needed, such as the ability to meter, bill, provision, and de-provision the infrastructure. Niche industries will focus on these core services with much of the discussion around virtualization centers on increasing the utilization of assets. Standardization is key to a successful business in utility computing.

As the industry continues to move toward the utility delivery model, application architectures will need to evolve to a platform agnostic perspective where the MIPS and GIGs are of interest, rather than which level of operating system or service pack exists. Additional planning and specification will be required to externalize how an application is to be scaled, depending on the real-time operating characteristics.

Today's visualization tools allow the management of entire resource pools and proactively manage its utilization (IBM, 2005b). Virtualization is a journey in which applications and middleware are abstracted from progressively greater layers of the machine physical characteristics.

In a utility computing environment characteristic, workloads are highly distributed; applications instances must be allocated and de-allocated frequently and with minimal overhead and latency. Without this on-demand provisioning scheme, it will be difficult to maximize the efficiency of the core infrastructure. Currently, low utilization rates continue as a result of massive infrastructure build-outs. These build-outs are a direct result of static, fixed computing limitations and, quite frankly, over-funded approaches to guarantee application availability; maintaining high utilization rates in all resources is critical if utility providers are to be profitable. Understanding how utility computing impacts their work is critical to architects, developers, and strategists catching the wave the first time around.

Conclusion

Every enterprise application has special considerations to achieve functional and non-functional requirements. As practitioners, we all look for a common platform to help alleviate some of our woes. It is not uncommon for people to say, "We will just add more servers," or "CPUs are getting faster and RAM is getting cheaper." It is true that application platform and server management can contribute substantially to success. The key to successful Web applications is the approach taken to application design and architecture while providing the necessary abstraction layers to allow exploitation by an ever-maturing systems management set of technologies. A well-designed application will thrive in future computing environments, but no amount of autonomics will efficiently deliver a poorly-designed application.

This chapter reviewed five common challenges in enterprise Web application design: resource contention, managing transactions, application resiliency, geographically-diverse and exception/perception management. Using our experiences with IBM's expertise location system, we presented five key methods:

- High-availability application layer caching
- Asynchronous task processing
- Self-reliant, autonomous behaviors
- Client-side MVC
- Graceful degradation

Finally, looking at trends that will continue to change and impact enterprise application design and architecture offers some insight to upcoming challenges. While the approaches in this chapter are somewhat generic, they are by no means the only way to address these issues. However, over the last 18 months, we have witnessed their immense contribution to the resilience, scalability, and overall performance from transaction time to network throughput and bandwidth usage.

References

Abbadi, A. E., & Toueg, S. (1989, June). Maintaining availability in partitioned replicated databases. *ACM Trans. Database Syst., 14*(2), 264-290.

Alur, D., Crupi, J., & Malks, D. (2001). *Core J2EE patterns: Best practices and design strategies, pp. 172-407*. Palo Alto, CA: Prentice Hall.

Amiri, K., Park, S., & Tewari, R. (2002, November 4-9). A self-managing data cache for edge-of-network Web applications. In *Proceedings of the Eleventh International Conference on Information and Knowledge Management, CIKM 2002*, McLean, VA (pp. 177-185). New York: ACM Press..

Andoni, A., & Staddon, J. (2005, June 5-8). Graceful service degradation (or, how to know your payment is late). In *Proceedings of the 6th ACM Conference on Electronic Commerce, EC 2005,* Vancouver, BC, Canada (pp. 9-18). New York: ACM Press.

Apache Foundation (2005). *The Apache Struts Web Application Framework.* Retrieved September 10, 2005, from http://struts.apache.org/

Appel, A., Dhadwal, A., & Pietraszek, W. E. (2003). More bang for the IT buck. *The McKinsey Quarterly, 2*, 130-141.

AskMeCorp Inc. (2005). *Knowledge Management Software and Services | AskMe.* Retrieved June 7, 2005, from http://www.askmecorp.com

Autonomy Inc. (2005). *Autonomy.* Retrieved June 7, 2005, from http://www.autonomy.com

Bates, M., Davis, K., & Haynes, D. (2003). Reinventing IT services. *The McKinsey Quarterly, 2*, 144-153.

Birman, K., van Renesse, R., & Vogels, W. (2004, May 23-28). Adding high availability and autonomic behavior to Web services. In *Proceedings of the 26th International Conference on Software Engineering* (pp. 17-26). Washington, DC: IEEE Computer Society.

Brown, K. (2005). Asynchronous queries in J2EE. *JavaRanch.* Retrieved from http://javaranch.com/newsletter/200403/AsynchronousProcessingFromServlets.html

Burns, R. C., Rees, R. M., & Long, D. D .E. (2001). Efficient data distribution in a Web server farm. *Internet Computing, IEEE, 5*(4), 56-65.

Candan, K. S., Li, W., Luo, Q., Hsiung, W., & Agrawal, D. (2001, May 21-24). Enabling dynamic content caching for database-driven Web sites. In T. Sellis (Ed.), In *Proceedings of the 2001 ACM SIGMOD International Conference on Management of Data,* Santa Barbara, CA (pp. 532-543). New York: ACM Press.

Challenger, J., Dantzig, P., & Iyengar, A. (1998). A scalable and highly available system for serving dynamic data at frequently accessed Web sites. In *Proceedings of ACM/IEEE Supercomputing 98 (SC 98).* New York: ACM Press.

Chase, J. S., Anderson, D. C., Thakar, P. N., Vahdat, A. M., & Doyle, R. P. (2001, October 21-24). Managing energy and server resources in hosting centers. In *Proceedings of the Eighteenth ACM Symposium on Operating Systems Principles, SOSP '01,* Banff, Alberta, Canada (pp. 103-116). New York: ACM Press.

Coulter, T. (2005). *Utility computing reality.* Retrieved September 10, 2005, from http://www.line56.com/articles/default.asp?ArticleID=6467

Davison, B. D. (2001). A Web caching primer. *Internet Computing, IEEE, 5*(4) 38-45, Jul/Aug 2001

Eckstein, R. (Ed.). (2003). *Java enterprise best practices.* Sebastopol: O'Reilly & Associates, Inc.

Entopia (2005). *Entopia—solutions for information discovery.* Retrieved June 7, 2005, from http://www.entopia.com/

Florins, M., & Vanderdonckt, J. (2004, January 13-16). Graceful degradation of user interfaces as a design method for multiplatform systems. In *Proceedings of the 9th International*

Conference on Intelligent User Interface (IUI '04), Funchal, Madeira, Portugal (pp. 140-147). New York: ACM Press.

Fowler, M. (2000). *Refactoring: Improving the design of existing code.* Upper Saddle River, NJ: Addison-Wesley.

Goodman, B. (2002). *Accelerate your Web services with caching: Drive your solutions into the fast lane.* Retrieved June 7, 2005, from http://www-106.ibm.com/developerworks/webservices/library/ws-cach1/?ca=degrL19wscaching

Goodman, B., & Kebinger, J. (2004). *Increase stability and responsiveness by short-circuiting code: Keep your Web applications running when tasks lock up.* IBM Developer Works. Retrieved June 7, 2005, from http://www-106.ibm.com/developerworks/web/library/wa-shortcir/?ca=dgr-lnxw09ShortCircuit

Google (2005a). *Google Gmail Beta.* Retrieved September 10, 2005, from http://mail.google.com/

Google (2005b). *Google Maps Beta.* Retrieved September 10, 2005, from http://maps.google.com

Google (2005c). *Google Suggest Beta.* Retrieved September 10, 2005, from http://maps.google.com

Gamma, E., Helm, R., Johnson, R., & Vlissides, J. (1995). *Design patterns.* Upper Saddle River, NJ: Addison-Wesley Professional.

Grand, M. (1999). *Patterns in Java, (vol. 2): Lazy initialization* (pp. 233-237). New York: John Wiley and Sons, Inc.

Grand, M. (2002). *Java enterprise design patterns, pp 159-500.* New York: John Wiley and Sons, Inc.

Gurguis, S. A., & Zeid, A. (2005, May 21-21). Towards autonomic Web services: Achieving self-healing using Web services. In *Proceedings of the 2005 Workshop on Design and Evolution of Autonomic Application Software (DEAS '05),* St. Louis, MO (pp. 1-5). New York: ACM Press.

Hammar Cloyd, M. (2001). Designing user-centered Web applications in Web time. *IEEE Software, 18*(1), 62-69.

Hassan, A. E., & Holt, R. C. (2002, May 19-25). Architecture recovery of Web applications. In *Proceedings of the 24ᵗʰ International Conference on Software Engineering, ICSE '02,* Orlando, FL (pp. 349-359). New York: ACM Press.

Herlihy, M. P., & Wing, J. M. (1987, August 10-12). Specifying graceful degradation in distributed systems. In F. B. Schneider (Ed.), In *Proceedings of the Sixth Annual ACM Symposium on Principles of Distributed Computing (PODC '87),* Vancouver, BC, Canada, (pp. 167-177). New York: ACM Press.

IBM. (2005a). *IBM Software: WebSphere Extended Deployment.* Retrieved September 10, 2005, from http://www.ibm.com/software/webservers/appserv/extend

IBM. (2005b). *IBM Tivoli Provisioning Manager—Product overview.* Retrieved September 10, 2005, from http://www.ibm.com/software/tivoli/products/prov-mgr/

Internet Society (1999). *Hypertext Transfer Protocol—HTTP/1.1*. Retrieved September 10, 2005, from http://www.w3.org/Protocols/rfc2616/rfc2616.html

Iyengar, A., & Challenger, J. (1997). Improving Web server performance by caching dynamic data. In *Proceedings of the Usenix Symposium of Internet Technology and Systems*, Usenix Association: Berkeley, CA (pp. 49-60).

Iyengar, A., Challenger, J., Dias, D., & Dantzig, P. (2000). High performance Web site design techniques. *IEEE Internet Computing, 4*(2), 17-26.

Jadav, D., & Gupta, M. (1997). Caching of large database objects in Web servers. In *Proceedings of the Seventh International Workshop on Research Issues in Data Engineering, April 7-8, 1997*, (pp.10-19).

Kabutz, H. (2001). *Blocking queue. The Java™ Specialists' Newsletter* (016). Retrieved September 10, 2005, from http://www.enterprisedeveloper.com/developers/javaspecialist/Issue016.html

Kaplan, J., Loffler, M., & Roberts, R. (2004). Managing next-generation IT infrastructure. *McKinsey on IT, 3*.

Kephart, J. O. (2005). Research challenges of autonomic computing. In *Proceedings of the 27th International Conference on Software Engineering, ICSE '05, St. Louis, MO, May 15-21, 2005* (pp. 15-22). New York: ACM Press

Krishnamurthi, S., & Bultan, T. (2005). Discussion summary: Characteristics of Web services and their impact on testing, analysis, and verification. *SIGSOFT Softw. Eng. Notes, 30*(1) (Jan. 2005), 5.

Liebmann, E., & Dustdar, S. (2004). Adaptive data dissemination and caching for edge service architectures built with the J2EE. In *Proceedings of the 2004 ACM Symposium on Applied Computing, SAC '04, Nicosia, Cyprus, March 14-17, 2004* (pp. 1717-1724). New York: ACM Press.

Liu, Y., Ngu, A. H., & Zeng, L. Z. (2004). QoS computation and policing in dynamic Web service selection. In *Proceedings of the 13th International World Wide Web Conference on Alternate Track Papers & Posters, WWW Alt. '04, New York, NY, May 19-21, 2004* (pp. 66-73). New York: ACM Press.

Malveau, R., & Mowbray, T. J. (2001). *Software architect bootcamp*. Upper Saddle River, NJ: Addison-Wesley.

Murry, G. (2005). *Asynchronous JavaScript Technology and XML (AJAX) with Java 2 Platform, Enterprise Edition*. Retrieved September 10, 2005, from http://java.sun.com/developer/technicalArticles/J2EE/AJAX

Neville, S (2003). Emerging standards and futures in enterprise integration. *Patterns and Best Practices for Enterprises*. Retrieved September 10, 2005, from http://enterpriseintegrationpatterns.com/Future.html

Nielsen, J. (2000). *Designing Web usability*. Indianapolis, IN: New Riders Publishing.

Pacitti, E., & Simon, E. (2000). Update propagation strategies to improve freshness in lazy master replicated databases. *The VLDB Journal, 8*(3-4) (Feb. 2000), 305-318.

Paulson, L. D. (2005). Building rich Web applications with Ajax. *Computer, 38*(10) (Oct. 2005), 14-17.

Preece, J. (1994). *Human computer interaction.* (pp. 159-163) Reading, MA: Addison Wesley.

Raskin, J. (2000). *The humane interface.* (pp. 178-183) Reading, MA: Addison Wesley.

Reynal, M. (2005). A short introduction to failure detectors for asynchronous distributed systems. *SIGACT News, 36*(1) (Mar. 2005), 53-70.

Rodriguez, P., Spanner, C., & Biersack, E. W. (2001). Analysis of Web caching architectures: Hierarchical and distributed caching. *IEEE/ACM Transactions on Networking*, 9(4) (Aug. 2001) 404-418.

Schmid, H.A., & Rossi, G. (2004). Modeling and designing processes in e-commerce applications. *IEEE Internet Computing, 8*(1), 19- 27.

Stelting, S., & Maassen, O. (2002). *Applied Java patterns.* Palo Alto, CA: Prentice Hall.

Strong, P. (2005). Enterprise grid computing. *ACM Queue, 3*(6), 50-59.

Sun Microsystems (2002). *Designing Enterprise Applications with the J2EE™ Platform* (2ⁿᵈ ed.), *Web-Tier MVC Controller Design.* Retrieved September 10, 2005, from http://java.sun.com/blueprints/guidelines/designing_enterprise_applications_2e/web-tier/web-tier5.html

Tacit (2005). Connect the dots to make the right connections happen. *Tacit.* Retrieved June 7, 2005, from http://www.tacit.com

W3C (2003). *SOAP Version 1.2 Part 1: Messaging Framework: SOAPFault.* Retrieved September 10, 2005, from http://www.w3.org/TR/soap12-part1/#soapfault

Weiss, A. (2005). WebOS: Say goodbye to desktop applications. *netWorker, 9*(4) (Dec. 2005), 18-26.

Whatis.com (2005). General computing terms: Utility computing. *TechTarget.* Retrieved September 8, 2005, from http://whatis.techtarget.com/definition/0,,sid9_gci904539,00.html

Zhang, J., & Buy, U. (2003). A framework for the efficient production of Web applications. In *Proceedings of the Eighth IEEE International Symposium on Computers and Communication*, ISCC, 2003. *30*(1) (pp. 419- 424).

Chapter V

The Demise of a
Business-to-Business
Portal

Arthur Tatnall, Victoria University, Australia

Alex Pliaskin, Victoria University, Australia

Abstract

This chapter describes the development and ultimate demise of the Bizewest portal in the Western Region of Melbourne, Australia. We argue that no matter how good the portal software, the final success or failure of the portal is primarily related to how well it is adopted and used. We begin by discussing the concept and benefits of Web portals, and especially those that are applicable to SMEs, as the Bizewest portal was primarily aimed at SMEs. We describe how the portal was conceived and developed, and the difficulty that its proponents had in persuading regional SMEs to change their business processes to make best use of online trading with each other. The research was socio-technical in nature, and was based on considering this innovation through the lens of innovation translation, informed by actor-network theory. Although Bizewest has ceased operations, the portal project must be considered a success, as it produced substantial benefits.

Introduction

After receiving a government grant under an e-commerce "early movers" scheme, the Western Region Economic Development Organisation in Melbourne, Australia, conceived and developed a business-to-business portal for use by Small to Medium Enterprises (SMEs) in the region. This innovative project was to create a horizontal portal, Bizewest, which would enable the whole range of small to medium enterprises in Melbourne's western region to engage in an increased number of business-to-business e-commerce transactions with each other (Tatnall & Pliaskin, 2005).

This chapter does not describe the Bizewest portal software technology to any degree, but rather investigates the adoption (or perhaps non-adoption) of this technology by SMEs in Melbourne's western region. In regard to technological innovation, we argue that it does not matter how good the technology is if no one makes use of it. If the intended users do not adopt the portal, then it will fail. The chapter investigates reasons for non-adoption of the Bizewest portal and outlines the lessons that might be learned from this. Management decisions to implement new technology, in this case, a business-to-business portal, must take account of the likely adoption and use of this technology, and take necessary steps to ensure that it is adopted and used to full advantage; otherwise, time and money will be wasted.

Web Portals

The term "Web Portal" is rather overused and quite difficult to define precisely, taking on a somewhat different meaning depending on the viewpoint of the stakeholder (Tatnall, 2005). In general terms, unrelated to the World Wide Web, the Macquarie Dictionary defines a portal as "a door, gate, or entrance" (Macquarie Library, 1981). More specifically, a Web portal can be seen as a special Internet (or intranet) site designed to act *primarily* as a *gateway* to give access to other sites containing information or services. An important notion behind the concept of a portal is that it does not provide much content itself, but rather organises content from other providers. Other more restrictive technical definitions of portals are used by some scholars, but we prefer the broader definition that simply equates a portal to a gateway. While some aspects of the Bizewest portal, the subject of this chapter, could be described just as Web pages, as the primary purpose of Bizewest was to provide a gateway to information and services that might be useful to the SMEs, we will describe it as a *portal*.

There is no definitive categorisation of the various types of portal, but Davison, Burgess, and Tatnall (2004) offer the following:

* **General portals:** These portals try to be the "one-stop shops" for all (or at least many) user needs. Many of these have developed from being simple search tools such as Yahoo (http://au.yahoo.com/), Internet service providers such as AOL (www.aol.com.au/), or e-mail services like Hotmail – NineMSN (http://ninemsn.com.au/). Many general portals include services such as: free e-mail, links to search engines and categories of information, membership services, news and sports, business headlines and articles, personalised space with a user's selections, links to chat rooms, links to virtual shopping malls, and Web directories.

- **Regional or community portals** are often set up by community groups in locations such as Canada (webdesign.foundlocally.com/OurPortals.htm) or Launceston in Tasmania (www.elaunceston.com/), or are sometimes set up by people with special or common interests, or based around special interest groups such as older people (www.greypath.com) (Tatnall & Lepa, 2001).

- **Vertical industry portals** are usually tightly focused around specific industry areas, and so tend to be more specialised, offering their services in one particular interest or industry area (Burgess, Bingley, & Tatnall, 2005; Lynch, 1998). Examples of vertical industry portals include the timber industry (http://www.timber.org) and the Bangladesh Garment Manufacturer Exporter Association (www.bangladeshgarments.info). Many vertical portals have services for business partners or "members" only.

- **Horizontal industry portals** are based around a group of businesses in an industry or a local region. A good example of a horizontal portal is the Business to Business(B2B) portal sponsored by the United Overseas Bank in Singapore (http://www.uob.com.sg/). This portal allows small businesses to set up online shopfronts with payments for purchased goods being processed by the bank. Bizewest (Tatnall & Burgess, 2002), the example discussed in this chapter, can be considered to be a horizontal industry portal.

A portal can be described as horizontal when it is utilised by a broad base of users across a horizontal market, or vertical when their focus is primarily attuned to a particular audience such as a specific industry or group of industries (Burgess, Bingley, & Tatnall, 2005; Lynch 1998).

- **Enterprise information portals** serve as the gateway to a corporate intranet. There is a recent trend for larger businesses to set up their own "internal" portals for employee use as part of their intranet services (Searle, 2005). An enterprise information portal offers a single point of entry that brings together the employees, business partners, and (possibly) consumers at one virtual place (Turban, Lee, King, & Chung, 2002).

- **E-marketplace portals:** These extended enterprise portals offer access to a company's extranet services. One example is Covisint (www.covisint.com) developed by the automotive companies, General Motors Corporation, Ford Motor Company, and Daimler-Chrysler. This portal aims to eliminate redundancies and burdens for suppliers through integration and collaboration, with the promise of lower costs, easier business practices, and marked increases in efficiencies for the entire industry (Turban et. al., 2002).

- **Personal/Mobile portals:** Following the trends towards mobile (or pervasive) computing, personal/mobile portals are increasingly being embedded into mobile phones, wireless PDAs, and the like. Some appliances are also being equipped with personal portals aimed at allowing them to communicate with other appliances, or to be used more easily from a distance.

- **Information portals:** Although information portals can, in most cases, also be classified into one of the other categories, they can also be viewed as a category in their own right as portals whose prime aim is to provide a specific type of information.

The sports information portal, ESPN (http://msn.espn.go.com/), is one example of an information portal. Another is Portals Community (http://www.portalscommunity.com/), a portal dedicated to providing information about portals.

- **Specialised/Niche portals** are designed to satisfy specific niche markets. In many cases, these can also be classified as Information portals. For example, ESPN (http://msn.espn.go.com/) is targeted towards 18-34 year-old males, while iVillage (http://www.ivillage.co.uk/) is targeted towards women. Other specialised portals provide detailed industry information, often available only for a fee.

Benefits of Web Portals for SMEs

There are many advantages for business and community groups in using portals, and Burgess, Bingley, and Tatnall (2005) describe a revenue model for horizontal portals in which they examine the role of players, strategies, and content. Although portals have many benefits, they are especially important for small business, offering benefits that make up for some of the problems of being small. These include (Tatnall, Burgess, & Singh, 2004):

- **A secure environment:** Portals provide a secure online environment for small business to set up e- businesses. Portals can include a payment infrastructure that enables SMEs to integrate their accounts receivable and payable to the portal backend systems.

- **Search and directory services:** Search engines that list the portals will automatically enable Web users to find the gateway to small online shops on the Web via these portals, saving substantially on costs.

- **New partnerships:** E-commerce opens up the opportunity for businesses to sell to new buyers, tap into the cyber supply chain and win new business markets, offer complementary products with other businesses, and procure goods electronically.

- **Community building and regional relationships:** Community building features such as chat rooms, message boards, instant-messaging services, online greeting cards, and other Web services are included in the portal infrastructure.

- **Strategy, management, and business trust:** Portals enable businesses to uptake a common structure for e-business that helps them attain management support, or share ideas with other businesses and attain success.

- **Improved customer management:** Portals can make deals with Internet retailers that will also benefit small businesses that are part of the portal.

The Western Region of Melbourne

Australia is a federation of six states and two territories. The states are segmented into smaller regions or communities of interest to deliver base-level services to the people. These services include things like the administration of building standards, the policing of minor by-laws, the provision of garbage collection services and ensuring the welfare of the aged. Much of the revenue of local government comes from the imposition of rates and charges on property owners within the municipality, but a significant part of the income comes in the form of grants from the other two levels of government. Local government is extremely vulnerable in that any administration can be dismissed by a state Local Government Minister. Unlike the two upper levels of government, the parliament or council of local government is composed of politicians who are only part-time and are not paid a salary. However, they are paid allowances to compensate them for expenses incurred while performing their duties (Pliaskin, 2004).

The Western Region of Melbourne contains around 20,000 businesses and is regarded as the manufacturing, transport, and distribution hub of south-eastern Australia (Tatnall, Burgess, & Singh, 2004). Traditionally, this region had encompassed much of the industry in metropolitan Melbourne.

The Western Region Economic Development Organisation Limited, colloquially known as WREDO, is sponsored by the six municipalities (Brimbank, Hobson's Bay, Maribyrnong, Melton, Moonee Valley, & Wyndham) that make up the Western region of Melbourne. Traditionally, these council areas had encompassed much of the industry in metropolitan Melbourne and consequently had been regarded as areas populated by "working class" people, but with the expansion of Melbourne and the desire of professionals to live close to the central business district, much of the demographic of these areas is changing. WREDO is a not-for-profit organisation and is also supported by major business enterprises operating in the western suburbs. WREDO is charged with fostering economic growth and encouraging investment within the Western Region of Melbourne; it is involved in a variety of regular and once off initiatives in order to fulfil its charter. One of its regular activities is a monthly networking breakfast which business leaders in the area attend in order to get to know each other and to listen to a guest speaker (Pliaskin, 2004).

WREDO is also supported by five major business enterprises operating in the western suburbs of Melbourne: Australian Gas and Light Limited, City West Water, McGregor By Road, Powercor Australia Limited, and the Urban and Regional Land Corporation.

The chapter describes the creation of the *Bizewest* Business-to-Business (B2B) Portal, and WREDO's difficulty in persuading local businesses to change their ways sufficiently to adopt and fully utilise the portal. It begins with WREDO applying for a government grant to set up the portal, without much prior discussion on its purpose or value: it just seemed like a good opportunity. Next we discuss the development problems WREDO experienced in setting up the portal, and finally WREDO's attempts to get local SMEs to make use of the portal.

The Creation of the Bizewest Business-to-Business Portal

In February, 2000, the Victorian State Treasurer announced a new government initiative known as the Victorian E-Commerce Early Movers Scheme (VEEM). The scheme was designed to provide assistance to local government to allow it to encourage small to medium enterprises operating within their boundaries to use e-commerce for the purpose of expanding business and to make these trading entities more competitive. VEEM was to provide assistance to local councils in their role as economic development agencies for their municipalities.

A cornerstone of the scheme was the acknowledgement that insufficient numbers of such organisations were using new technology to build business and to enhance competitiveness. This was of concern because international experience with the information economy indicated that significant benefits fall to early movers into e-commerce (Gallaugher & Downing, 2005), and the government decided to empower businesses by providing opportunities to reap the benefits of being online early. The government addressed its vision for growing the information and communications technologies industry and sharing the benefits of these technologies across the community in the "Connecting Victoria" strategy statement of November, 1999, outlining a significant agenda item "Boosting E-Commerce" that set out to "vigorously promote e-commerce" in Victoria (Brumby, 1999).

Assistance under the VEEM scheme could cover up to 75% of all costs associated with projects, and grants were to be made on a case-by-case basis. The maximum funding was to be $45,000 for any discrete e-commerce enabling proposal, or $15,000 per e-commerce workshop project proposal. Councils were able to put in joint submissions in order to obtain a higher level of funding for a project that crossed municipal boundaries. Funding could involve capital, equipment costs, and labour implementation costs, but was *not* to include ongoing maintenance or operating costs of the project. Projects needed to demonstrate that they would provide significant leverage to indirectly improve local economies, and that they would reach a level of self-sustainability within the period of their business plan, as no funding was to be provided for maintenance purposes (VEEM, 2000). They also needed to show that they would provide significant leverage to indirectly improve local economies and that they would improve one or more of the following situations:

- The economic performance of a region;
- The business competitiveness of a region;
- The level of available infrastructure; and
- The ability of councils to perform their economic development role.

The guidelines gave a non-exhaustive list of specific examples of projects that might be eligible for a grant. These included supply chain initiatives, e-commerce business planning workshops, e-commerce vendor and business networking sessions, regional e-commerce expos, regional business portal implementation, enabling local businesses for online fulfilment and procurement, allowing councils and businesses to adopt electronic commerce for procurement, and setting up a Web presence for the facilitation of specific education and awareness requirements. Each participating company within a project must have been operating in Victoria, must show management strengths, must have been committed to exporting or to import replacement, must have been committed to the introduction of e-commerce, and preferably should have trading history of a year or longer.

The notion of interoperability was strongly stressed, and it was noted that the use of electronic commerce was reducing costs and improving the quality of business-to-business transactions. An important requirement of any grant was to maintain the greatest possible measure of interoperability across all forms of government, including local councils. It was stressed

Figure 1: WREDO and Bizewest portals—main entry points

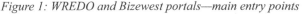
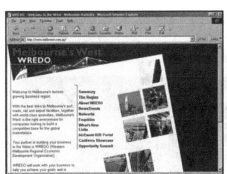

that system interoperability and consistency in an environment that is seamless for buyers and sellers was essential. It was also to be a condition of the grant that recipients operate within the "Framework for National Co-operation on Electronic Commerce in Government Procurement" in their strategic planning for electronic commerce. This framework outlines and explains a number of issues including security, authentication, tender management systems, supplier registration, catalogues, and identification systems (VEEM, 2000).

WREDO thought that this grant was worth pursuing, and after some internal discussions, it decided to apply for funding for the "Western Melbourne Business-to-Business Portal". The proposal aimed at constructing a business-to-business e-business Web portal so as to provide a tangible regional approach to enable organisations in the Western Region of Melbourne to participate in the information economy (Pliaskin, 2004). Because of the short time-frame allowed for the lodgement of proposals, there was little time for discussion with local SMEs or others outside WREDO, and so the WREDO submission was drawn up in haste in the expectation that it would probably not be accepted (Lindley, personal communication, 2003).

In its submission, WREDO argued that this B2B portal was to provide a regional approach to enabling businesses in Melbourne's western region to actively participate in the information economy. It was to be a true B2B portal with trading facilities and a payment gateway linked with a major bank. This was to be *exclusively* regional, and only businesses in Melbourne's Western Region would be permitted to set up trading on the portal. Specifically, the project was to:

- Create a Web portal for business and local government in Melbourne's Western Region to provide a mechanism for businesses to engage in business-to-business e-commerce and to encourage business-to-local-government transactions in the local area.

- Initially target 50 businesses from each of the six western region municipalities making up a total of 300 businesses to participate in the pilot project. These businesses were to come primarily from the key and emerging industries in the region in the transport and distribution, manufacturing, and services sectors.

Figure 2: The Bizewest portal

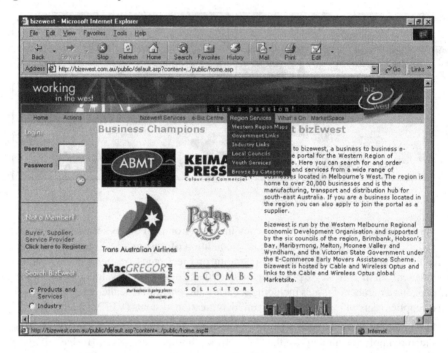

- Develop a regional Web-based registry for the businesses involved. This was to include a Website for each business and the provision of a range of e-commerce enabling tools that would facilitate business-to-business transactions taking place.

- Increase awareness and participation with emerging technologies. The project aimed at encouraging SMEs in Melbourne's western region to be more aggressive in their uptake of e-commerce opportunities. It also aimed at working with these SMEs and operating in growth industry sectors in the region to find and exploit e-commerce solutions.

- Create an ongoing program of regional seminars and training, both informal and formal, for the pilot businesses involved and for new entrants. Training was to focus on effective trading and exporting opportunities in the online environment and was to be provided through existing programs available in the western region.

- Focus on involving the youth of the area in the promotion of new technologies for business. The project team was to work with secondary schools in the region to in-volve senior high school students studying Information Technology or Engineering and Design, in the development of e-business solutions for businesses in the region.

WREDO conducted a SWOT (Strengths, Weaknesses, Opportunities, and Threats) analysis of the project and included the results of this study in its submission.

- The perceived strengths included the regional approach that provided a broad base for recruiting participating enterprises. It was highlighted that the focus on key growth industries ensured that employment outcomes for local people were more likely. With its focus on actual B2B application of e-business technologies, the project aimed to ensure that participating organisations would actually engage in e-commerce rather than just become aware of it. The Western Melbourne B2B portal aimed to complement the individual projects proposed by councils in the area.

- The perceived weaknesses included the notion that the key growth industry areas in the region, transport and manufacturing, are not naturally business-to-consumer operations. Therefore it was thought that e-business applications would need to be tailored to individual businesses. Generic software products might not be a feasible option. It was also felt that it might be difficult to convince some operators of small- and medium-sized enterprises to participate.

- The perceived opportunities included the opportunity for local enterprises to take advantage of e-business solutions in a supported atmosphere. This was an opportunity to have a "team" of new businesses try new technologies and act as "in progress" case studies. The regional focus could act as a catalyst for greater business participation in the project in the short-to-medium term.

- The perceived threats included the thought that the project might be too broad to manage in a short period of time. The notion that rapid changes and advancements in technology may impact on the relevance of e-business solutions proposed for business. There was also an idea that the costs of implementation and ongoing maintenance of the project for individual businesses might prove prohibitive.

In June, 2000, it was announced that WREDO's submission for a B2B portal had been successful, and that government funding of $247,400 for the project was to be provided for a period of twelve months on condition that WREDO provide an additional amount equivalent to one third of this amount from its own funds. WREDO then allocated the further $88,000 towards the project, making a total project budget of $335,400 for the year (Pliaskin, 2004).

Building and Developing the Portal

After receiving a grant for what it thought to be a large amount of money, WREDO originally intended to develop the portal, possibly with the assistance of a software company, and provide training to locals SMEs itself (WREDO staff, 2001), but it did not really anticipate the size or complexity of the task that it was undertaking. The Bizewest project was divided up into four distinct phases, each with identifiable milestones.

1. In the initial phase, it was planned that the project should be scoped, staffed, and equipped. Within the scoping segment, a steering committee would be convened by WREDO. The deliverables in this phase included the establishment of full project

outlines and timelines, the commencement of employment of project staff, the purchase and setup of the equipment, and the determination of the Internet Service Provider for the portal.

2. In Phase Two, it was planned that the participants for the initial stages of the portal would be recruited. A team of students to work on the project was to be recruited by WREDO and, at the same time, WREDO and the Steering Committee were charged with recruiting the first round of 60 businesses to be part of the project. The deliverable here was the recruitment and training of the first 50 students and the first 60 businesses.

3. In Phase Three, it was planned that the Bizewest portal would be established and become operational. During this time, it was planned that educative sessions for participating businesses should be run by WREDO in conjunction with Victoria University. In addition, site pages were to be created and solutions proposed to participating businesses by WREDO, the appointed service providers and the local secondary students recruited for this purpose. At the same time, WREDO and the Steering Committee were to launch the project, to market the project, and consequently, to run a major networking breakfast that was to centre on Bizewest and to plan for the long-term sustainability of the project. The deliverables in this phase were the preparation of case studies on the initial 60 participants, the recruitment and introduction of another 240 businesses from the six council areas, bringing the total to 300, and the promotion of the project within the region and within the state of Victoria.

Figure 3: The Bizewest Portal—services

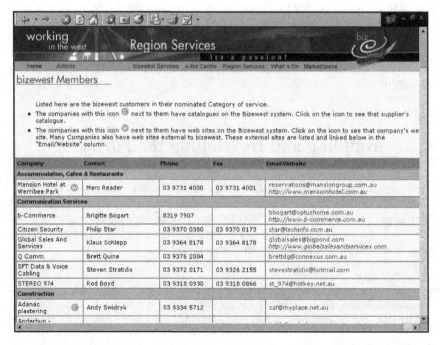

4. The last phase involved the preparation of final case studies and the planning for continuing sustainability for the site. The project commenced and was due to be completed on May 31, 2001. To some degree, each phase overlapped its neighbour, and the Steering Committee was to be responsible for overseeing the project and recommending the progression from one phase to the next. With each phase, the Steering Committee and Project Team were to monitor progress against agreed deliverables and milestones. The deliverables for Phase Four were the establishment and full operation of the whole portal, complete with a sustainability business plan in place.

WREDO issued specifications to both Telstra Australia and Cable and Wireless Optus for hosting the portal, pointing out that they were looking at enabling creation of small business sites of around 10Mb. They requested a price for hosting these sites, but the telecommunications companies did not appear to understand small business requirements; what WREDO received in response had nothing to do with the specifications and little to do with businesses of this size (Pliaskin, 2004). It was clear that more work would also have to be done to identify a software company to assist with building the portal.

Negotiations continued, and an arrangement was finally made with Optus to host the portal and to find a software company to build it. At the WREDO networking breakfast in November, 2000, it was formally announced that the Bizewest Steering Committee would work with Cable and Wireless Optus and Infosentials Limited on the development of the portal. Un-

Figure 4: The Bizewest Portal—payment gateway

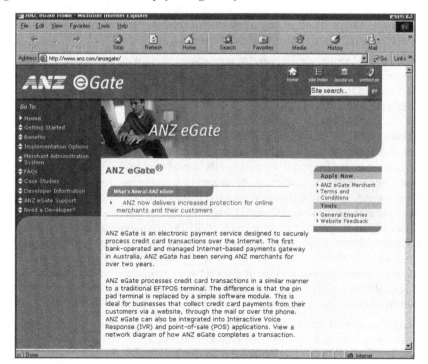

fortunately, in December, 2000, Infosentials was placed in voluntary administration, forcing WREDO to terminate that company's involvement. Cable and Wireless Optus then sought an alternative provider of services for building the portal, and final agreement was reached in January, 2001, with Optus for the supply of services to build and host the Bizewest portal. Building of the portal was subcontracted by Optus to a company called Batteries Included, who used a product called ReadyHub to construct the portal infrastructure (Pliaskin, 2004). The development of the portal infrastructure and services commenced in late January, 2001, with initial testing beginning in late April of the same year.

WREDO soon discovered that what it was doing was anything but straightforward, and that little precedent existed, at the time, for a regional horizontal B2B portal of this type. They also discovered that the money they had available did not go as far as they had thought it might. Some of the difficulties which they experienced in building the portal have subsequently been discussed by other researchers (Gengatharen & Standing, 2003; Lepa & Tatnall, 2002; Pliaskin & Tatnall, 2005). Further, to add to these difficulties, some internal issues associated with Batteries Included meant that this company eventually split into several bits. The part of the company that was building the portal became known as Kitchen Sink Software, and assumed responsibility for the operation and maintenance of the Bizewest portal. Bizewest (www.bizewest.com.au) became operational in May, 2001, but without a payment gateway. This gateway did not become available until February, 2003, after 21 months of further development.

Once the portal was operational, getting local business online was the next step, and this involved two parts: convincing regional SMEs to adopt the portal, and providing them with suitable Websites to link to the portal. Previously, a single enterprise had been identified within each local council area and designated the "business champion" for that locality. These business champions played a pivotal role in ensuring that enterprises within their municipal areas were made aware of the Bizewest portal.

Through a series of initiatives, Bizewest was promoted to industry in the region. WREDO News featured several articles on the site, and the main WREDO website (www.MelbWest. com.au) dedicated space to Bizewest. The media wrote positively on the project after having viewed demonstrations of it, and letters were written to likely prospects. The issue was raised at the monthly WREDO networking breakfasts, and written material was supplied to participants. WREDO also enlisted the help of industry groups and other umbrella bodies in the area. Business breakfasts, workshops, lots of publicity, and no initial costs to the businesses that adopted the portal were part of the considerable effort made by WREDO to convince SMEs that getting onto the portal would be a good idea. To assist businesses to create Web pages to link to the Bizewest portal, WREDO held two "Web-A-Thons" at local shopping centres. At these sessions, year 11 students from local secondary schools assisted local organisations to create their Web pages. WREDO also arranged for some of these students to consult with local businesses on a one-to-one basis on their "work experience" days to set up their Websites. This had the advantage to these businesses of producing a very cheaply-created Website; the cost of using a "work experience" student is only $5 per day. The simple site was, however, one that would serve their initial needs very well. This arrangement continued for some time.

Even though a payment facility for business-to-business e-commerce was not part of the original implementation, the notion was investigated and an understanding was reached that this should become a part of the project. The payment gateway was to become the final crowning achievement of the Bizewest initiative. Ultimately, the ANZ Bank was selected to become the provider of this service (McLure, personal communication, 2004; Shilton, personal communication, February 24, 2004).

Research Methodology: Actor-Network Theory

The discipline of information systems is, by its very nature, a socio-technical one. While researchers in computer science may choose to concentrate on a study of aspects of computer hardware and software alone, the business of information systems is how *people* interact with and use *computer-based* systems. Information systems are complex socio-technical entities involving both human and non-human components: systems analysts, designers, programmers, end-users, managers, PCs, mainframes, software, data and operating systems. These are only some of the many heterogeneous components of an information system. Research into the implementation and operation of information systems needs to take this heterogeneity into account, and find a way to give due regard to both the human and non-human aspects of these systems.

While many approaches to research in technological areas treat the social and the technical in entirely different ways, actor-network theory (ANT) proposes instead a socio-technical account in which neither social nor technical positions are privileged. ANT deals with the social-technical divide by denying that purely technical or purely social relations are possible, and considers the world to be full of hybrid entities (Latour, 1993) containing both human and non-human elements. Actor-network theory developed around problems associated with attempts to handle socio-technical "imbroglios" (Latour, 1993) like electric cars (Callon, 1986a), supersonic aircraft (Law & Callon, 1988), and a new railway system in Paris (Latour, 1996) by regarding the world as heterogeneous (Chagani, 1998). The utilisation of heterogeneous entities (Bijker, Hughes, & Pinch, 1987) then avoids questions of: "Is it social?" or "Is it technical?" as missing the point, which should be: "Is this association stronger or weaker than that one?" (Latour, 1988, p. 27). ANT offers this notion of heterogeneity to describe projects such as the Portal Project discussed in this chapter in which a local semi-government organisation has engaged an Internet Service Provider (ISP) and a computer software company to build a B2B portal for use by SMEs within a regional area. The project involved not just these entities, but also non-human entities such as computers, modems, telephone lines, Web development tools, and human entities including local business proprietors from small- and medium-sized enterprises, customers, programmers, development managers, and local government staff.

As their use necessarily creates change, the implementation of a new information system, or the upgrading of an existing system, should be viewed in terms of technological innovation (Tatnall & Burgess, 2002). The word "innovation" is synonymous with "newness" and "change" (Dutch, 1962), and an innovation can be described as an idea that is perceived to be new to a particular person or group of people (Rogers, 1995). As almost all information systems implementations fit this description, it is quite appropriate to make use of innovation theory when researching these systems. This chapter describes a research approach, based on actor-network theory (Callon & Latour, 1981; Latour, 1986, 1996; Law, 1988), used to investigate a specific innovation: the design and implementation of a business-to-business (B2B) portal for small to medium enterprises (SME) in a regional area of an Australian city.

Adoption of the Bizewest portal must be seen as an innovation and examined accordingly. Information systems researchers using an actor-network approach in this investigation concentrate on issues of network formation, investigating the human and non-human actors and the alliances and networks they build up (Tatnall & Gilding, 1999). They concentrate on the negotiations that allow the network to be configured by the enrolment of both human and non-human allies, and consider any supposed characteristics of the technology only as network effects resulting from association. An actor is seen not just as a "point object" but rather as an association of heterogeneous elements, which constitute a network. Each actor is thus itself also a simplified network (Law, 1992). In actor-network theory, interactions and associations between actors and networks are the important thing, and actors are seen only as the sum of their interactions with other actors and networks.

Some examples of the use of actor-network theory in the information systems field are in investigating the adoption of Visual Basic as a programming language by a major Australian university (Tatnall, 2000), the adoption and use of Internet technologies by older people (Tatnall & Lepa, 2001), the adoption of a particular approach to systems analysis by a lo-cal council in the UK (McMaster, Vidgen, & Wastell, 1997) and to a car parking system (Vidgen & McMaster, 1996). An example of its use in the small business field is given by Tatnall (2002).

Innovation translation, from actor-network theory, offers useful insights on how innovation occurs, and the remainder of this chapter will make use of this approach. It is often the case that an SME which is considering some technological innovation is interested in *only some aspects* of this innovation and not others (Tatnall, 2001). In actor-network terms, it needs to translate (Callon, 1986b) this piece of technology into a form where it can be adopted. This may mean choosing some elements of the technology and leaving out others, resulting in what is finally adopted not being the innovation in its original form, but a translation of it into a form that is suitable for use by the recipient small business (Tatnall, 2002).

Callon (1986b) outlines the process of translation as having four "moments", the first of which he calls *problematisation*, or "how to become indispensable", in which one or more key actors attempts to define the nature of the problem and the roles of other actors to fit the solution proposed. The problem is re-defined in terms of solutions offered by these actors, who then attempt to establish themselves as an "obligatory passage point" (Callon, 1986b) which must be negotiated as part of its solution. The second moment is *interessement*, or "how allies are locked in place", and is a series of processes which attempt to impose the identities and roles defined in the problematisation on the other actors. It means interesting and attracting an actor by coming between it and some other actor (Law, 1986). The third moment, *enrolment* or "how to define and coordinate the roles" will then follow, leading to the establishment of a stable network of alliances. For enrolment to be successful, however, it requires more than just one set of actors imposing their will on others; it also requires these others to yield (Singleton & Michael, 1993). Finally, *mobilisation* or "are the spokespersons representative?" occurs as the proposed solution gains wider acceptance (McMaster et al., 1997) and an even larger network of absent entities is created (Grint & Woolgar, 1997) through some actors acting as spokespersons for others.

While a simplistic view of the adoption of B2B portals would have it that businesses make their adoption decisions primarily because of the portal's characteristics, this would miss other influences due to inter-business interactions and the backgrounds of the people involved. This is the type of approach that would be used if framing the research through innovation diffusion (Rogers, 1995). The theory of Innovation Diffusion is based on the notion that adoption of an innovation involves the spontaneous or planned spread of new ideas, and Rogers defines an innovation as: "... an idea, practice, or object that is perceived as new" (Rogers, 1995, p. 11).

In diffusion theory, the existence of an innovation is seen to cause uncertainty in the minds of potential adopters (Berlyne, 1962), and uncertainty implies a lack of predictability and of information. Uncertainty can be considered as the degree to which a number of alternatives are perceived in relation to the occurrence of some event, along with the relative probabilities of each of these alternatives occurring (Lepa & Tatnall, 2002). Diffusion is considered to be an information exchange process amongst members of a communicating social network, driven by the need to reduce uncertainty. Those involved in considering adoption of the innovation are motivated to seek information to reduce this uncertainty. The new ideas upon which an innovation is based are communicated over time, through various types of communication channels, among the members of a social system. Thus, there are four main elements of innovation diffusion: characteristic of the innovation itself, the nature of the communication channels, the passage of time, and the social system through which the innovation diffuses (Rogers, 1995).

Using an essentialist approach like this to the research, the researcher may begin by outlining all the characteristics of B2B portals and all the advantages and problems associated with their use, and then go on to suggest that the adoption, or rejection, of this technology by the local businesses was due largely to these characteristics. While this is likely to be partially true, it is unlikely to provide a complete explanation.

In this case, the actor-network research began by identifying some of the important actors, starting with WREDO's portal project manager. The interview with the project manager revealed why the project was instigated, and identified some of the other actors. She reiterated how, while WREDO had commissioned and was to oversee the project, the portal software development was to be undertaken by a software company. One line of inquiry resulting from the interview with the project manager was to approach the portal software designer and programmers. It was determined that another set of actors consisted of the proprietors of the local businesses themselves, and the project manager suggested some "business champions" to interview first to find out why they had adopted the portal and what had influenced them in doing so. Some of these business people then pointed to the influence exerted by the computer hardware or software as a significant factor, so identifying some non-human actors.

From this point on, the key was to follow the actors, both human and non-human, searching out interactions, negotiations, alliances, and networks. Negotiations between actors needed to be carefully investigated. Apart from the obvious human-to-human kind of negotiation, there were also human-to-non-human interactions such as the business people trying to work out how the portal operates, and how to adapt this technology to their own business purposes. In ANT terms, they "negotiated" with the portal software to see what it could do for them, and it "negotiated" with them to convince them to adopt its way of doing business.

(Obviously, this is not to suggest any direct agency on the part of the software itself, and is just ANT's way of describing how the human software designers imparted properties to the software that may or may not have made it useful to the SMEs.) The process of adopting and implementing the portal could now be seen as the complex set of interactions that it was, and not just the inevitable result of the innate characteristics of this technology as innovation diffusion theory would suggest.

Persuading Local SMEs to Use the Bizewest Portal

For the project to be successful, the Bizewest portal needed to be seen by the proprietors of the SMEs as a necessary means of undertaking e-commerce and business-to-business transactions. They needed to be convinced that this technology was more worthwhile and offered them better business prospects than the approaches, such as post or fax, which they had previously used. In actor-network terms, the portal needed to set up a problematisation (Callon, 1986b) of B2B trading that brought out the benefits of using a portal for this purpose. There also needed to be an interessement (Callon, 1986b) to interest and convince these SMEs to change from their old business culture and adopt the portal. It was not enough for those promoting the portal to eloquently espouse its benefits: The SMEs would also have to give up at least some of their old methods of business-to-business transactions. After enrolment of these businesses, the portal could be judged to be truly successful when SME proprietors began advocating its advantages to each other (Tatnall & Burgess, 2002). In actor-network theory, Callon (1986b) calls this process "mobilisation".

Interviews with various stakeholders involved in the project, including the project manager, software designers and programmers, and some businesses that were using the portal were conducted in late 2001 and early 2002. One particularly important group were the five companies designated by WREDO as "business champions" for this project. Some of the issues considered important by several of these business champions are discussed below. One of the business champions was a medium-sized Melbourne company, with about 100 employees, that stores frozen food and transports it to supermarkets and other locations around the country. A major reason that this company adopted the portal was the hope that it would provide a better opportunity to deal with people in the local region (Tatnall & Burgess, 2004). The general manager indicated that although he did not really understand much about the portal or what it would do, he thought it was going to provide many benefits for everybody, not just his company. This was important to him. He could see use of the portal changing his business by enabling it to use people in the local region, and that "working together for the benefit of everybody" would be advantageous for the region (Cold Storage[software developer], personal communication, September 3, 2001).

A firm of solicitors had also just started making use of the portal and were trying to work out the best ways to utilise it to advantage. Their primary goal was to use the portal to increase their visibility. "What we want is for people to discover something that they may not have recognised, and that is that there is a top quality legal service in the Western Region that they can come to for most of their legal services." They had few specific expectations of the portal, but hoped later to allow businesses to register interest and gain some access to their legal services using the portal (Footscray Solicitors, personal communication, 2001).

Another business champion was a small printer with 15 employees that had just begun using the portal. They saw the portal as having "fantastic possibilities" but there were currently some problems: "I suppose that people who are on the portal see us and they contact us, but there is something wrong with it at the moment. The problem is that they can't actually send for a quote with us. It has to be fixed up, but once it is fixed it will be good." (Printing Press, personal communication, August 6, 2001). They were, however, not quite sure what use of the portal in their business might eventually lead to.

Finally, a textile company just outside the metropolitan area was using the portal mainly for promoting their image but did intend to move to B2B operations in the future. "I think that it will be inevitable, but not next month, it's still a year or two off. I'm uncertain of what the plan is at this point; there is no plan." One of the problems that this medium-sized business faced was lack of computing expertise. This is a common problem among SMEs (Burgess, 2002). Typically there are one or two people who know something about computers, but do not have much spare time to plan and implement these systems. "I think the way that we will go is like many businesses; we will dip our toe in the water and do some basic ordering: stationery that's a common one. We will choose to start the ball rolling, get our head around a few of the practical issues of that, and then on to bigger things" (Textile Company, personal communication, August 20, 2001).

In summary, these interviews showed that most businesses adopting the portal did so because it seemed to them to be "a good idea" rather than because they had any clear idea of its benefits. Few had looked objectively at the characteristics of portal technology or business-to-business e-commerce. Common reason for adoption included: "If other businesses adopt it and we don't, we will be left behind." "All the talk is about e-commerce and how it is the way of the future." "It doesn't look too hard to make it work, and we have little to lose." and "My kids tell me that everyone will be on the Internet soon and we had better be too" (Tatnall & Burgess, 2002, pp. 179-191).

An interview with the portal software developer was also quite enlightening. When asked whether they thought WREDO knew what they were doing when they commissioned the portal, they replied that WREDO did not really know much about what they were getting into and what was required. "No, we've had this conversation with WREDO many times. When we were first approached to do the development of the portal and the site, neither WREDO nor the Business Champions had any idea of what the solution would be" (Batteries Included [software developer], personal communication, October 12, 2001).

Another very telling interview was with the WREDO staff themselves, including the portal project manager. We were keen to know how it all began and where the idea of a portal had come from. With only four or five weeks' notice to put up the funding submission, how had they decided on a portal? The answer was as follows: "What WREDO does is to promote economic development in the Western region of Melbourne and we do it in three ways: growing businesses in the west, attracting business investment in the west, and marketing the west, so this one fitted very nicely, in *growing business*" (WREDO staff, personal communication, 2001). They indicated that what they had done was refocussed on those three areas, and they wanted something related to these. "We talked about building a business register database. We had a different department coming to do that and it was not as successful as it could have been, but at the time it had been quite difficult. I think that the concept was too hard for people to grasp, so that at the same time we saw that we really needed to get involved in E-Commerce and we had actually been working out with an idea for a while trying to figure out ways to encourage small businesses in particularly to get involved" (WREDO staff, personal communication, 2001). They indicated that they had a history of doing things to assist business, but not really having enough money to put into it. The idea of a portal was thus simply seen as a way of encouraging businesses. "We have a view up here where we want to go, we don't want just to do the things that are nice and safe, we want to do some of the things on the business electronic register that didn't get us any leads at all, but we are going to do that now, and people think that it is terrific, and with very little effort, we have a list of nine thousand businesses and we didn't have to go out and source them by ringing them up: They were there. We just put it all together and one of the things that we have always tried to do at WREDO is to build on what we have done before. We don't pluck something out of left field and hope to create it, we just keep on building. That is actually what we have done" (WREDO staff, personal communication, 2001).

In each case, these interviews indicated that reasons for adoption were not closely related to the characteristics of the technology itself as the theory of innovation diffusion (Rogers, 1995) would suggest. An innovation diffusion approach to investigating these potential adoptions would have looked for explanations for the uptake, or lack of uptake, primarily in the characteristics and properties of the technology itself. It would not have regarded as particularly important the human and non-human interactions described here. Innovation translation, from actor-network theory, would seem to offer a much better explanation in its investigation of the series of interactions, some human-to-human and some human-to-non-human, which led to adoption of the portal by each of these organisations. In our view, the decision to adopt, or not to adopt, has more to do with the interactions and associations of both human and non-human actors involved in the project rather than with the characteristics of the technology itself.

Problems Leading to the Demise of the Portal

Even though the portal infrastructure was in place by mid 2001, there was still a great deal of work to be done to encourage businesses to use the tools now provided. This work was to continue during 2001 and 2002, but by early 2003, WREDO realised that their hopes that things would finally work out well were not being realised, and that something drastic would have to be done. WREDO's experience over the past two-and-a-half years had shown that a one-on-one relationship in taking businesses from non-participation to full participation was highly effective. This was, however, a time- and cost-intensive process requiring additional financial support for it to continue. In early 2003, an internal WREDO report (2003b) outlined several options available to WREDO in relation to the Bizewest portal:

- Pursue additional funding from Multimedia Victoria or another appropriate state government department in order to be able to continue to market and operate the portal for the next 12 months. This funding would need to support the appointment of a part-time marketing/project officer to work with local businesses to encourage them to use the tools already in place.
- Seek a commercial sponsor for the site.

Table 1. Usage of the Bizewest portal—Sessions

Month	Sessions	One Minute Sessions	One Page Sessions
September 2002	2208	68.7%	86.2%
October 2002	3672	77.1%	90.0%
November 2002	2848	74.6%	88.0%
December 2002	2766	71.7%	85.9%
January 2003	2706	82.9%	90.2%
February 2003	2804	86.7%	89.6%
March 2003	2934	88.8%	90.5%
April 2003	2254	87.7%	88.7%
May 2003	2865	86.4%	86.7%
June 2003	2200	84.1%	86.8%
July 2003	78	75.6%	85.9%

Table 2. Usage of the Bizewest portal—Hits

Month	Sessions	Average Hits Per Session	Total Hits
September 2002	2208	8.2	17991
October 2002	3672	5.7	21022
November 2002	2848	7.3	20690
December 2002	2766	9.1	25094
January 2003	2706	6.3	16949
February 2003	2804	4.9	13830
March 2003	2934	5.6	16320
April 2003	2254	6.1	13815
May 2003	2865	7.0	20099
June 2003	2200	7.7	16904
July 2003	78	2.4	189

- Sell the portal.
- Suspend or cease operations as of April, 2003.

Activity on the Bizewest site was always extremely disappointing (Pliaskin, 2004; Pliaskin & Tatnall, 2005), and the proportion of sessions that were one-page hits and/or lasted for one minute or less seems to indicate that a large proportion of sessions were accidental or unintentional.

It should be noted that the tabulated data is typical of the activity on the site for the full period (The activity for July of 2003 is merely a manifestation of an "overhang" effect).

Although a considerable number of SMEs had joined with Bizewest, most baulked when it was suggested that in future they would need to pay an annual fee to cover costs. This was necessary because the grant to set up the portal provided no funds for ongoing mainte-nance and enhancement, and Bizewest was running out of money. When, in early 2003, the WREDO Board began considering options for the Bizewest portal, it was clear that WREDO could not continue to spend money on the hosting and maintenance of the portal at the rate it had been doing. It was also clear that insufficient local businesses would be prepared to pay for the privilege of using the portal. The Bizewest site was intended primarily for busi-ness-to-business trading with an internal regional focus. To use the portal you had to be a business in Melbourne's West. The SMEs in this region, however, seemed to be resistant to embracing the portal.

In April, a confidential report to WREDO (2003a) noted that the portal was approaching its third year of operation. The WREDO Board had been asked to consider the options for the future direction of the Bizewest portal and to reassess the organisation's involvement and financial and resource commitment to the development of an electronic business gateway in the region. It was noted that since the expiration of the grant period on December 31st, 2001, WREDO had continued to develop and support the Bizewest portal without further state government or council financial assistance. It was noted that this further work and improvements since December, 2001, had included:

- Continuation of marketing and promotion for the portal;
- Updating of data, the Websites, and the information accessed via the portal;
- The refinement of portal processes; and
- The development of an online payment gateway to enable credit card transactions to occur; it was noted that this facility went live in February of 2003 after 18 months of development.

The report noted that WREDO had initially allocated a maintenance and site hosting budget of $20,000 per annum for the Bizewest portal, but that since December, 2001, WREDO had incurred additional expenditure on the portal over and above the contractual obligations in the order of $57,705. The report also forecast the best possible income and expenditure scenario for the last nine months of 2003. Even though the portal infrastructure was in place, there was still a great deal of work to be done to encourage businesses to use this tool, and in June, 2003, operation of the Bizewest portal ceased.

The Legacy of the Bizewest Portal

In spite of its apparent failure, the emergence and subsequent demise of Bizewest did leave a worthwhile legacy:

- A multifaceted portal Website, commonly known as Bizewest, was developed.

- The portal allowed for businesses to register online, and this occurred from June of 2001 to December of 2002.

- Because of the existence of the portal, students were able to be trained to work in these businesses from May to November, 2001.

- Initial business participation was 25 registrations in May of 2001, but this had increased to 180 by December, 2001.

- A model was established for the development of regional Web portals for Business-to-Business electronic commerce. This model is capable of being replicated in other regions.

- An e-commerce toolkit for small- to medium-sized businesses was developed.

- In conjunction with the development of the portal, and because of its introduction, WREDO was able to compile a regional register of 11,000 local businesses. This register was incorporated into the Bizewest Website in December, 2001.

Conclusion

The portal concept, although difficult to define and meaning different things to different people, offers many benefits, especially to SMEs. The attempt to establish and maintain an inward-focused Business-to-Business portal to allow SMEs in the Western Region of Melbourne to take advantage of emerging technologies was a brave move. To attempt to change the culture of 300 businesses was, however, a monumental task, and Bizewest was probably doomed to failure right from the outset: It was really too ambitious. Because WREDO has a good reputation in the Western Region, and was well trusted, a lot of the small businesses became involved because WREDO convinced them that this was the way to go. They did not, however, prove willing to contribute money when the portal floundered financially, as they could not see any immediate tangible benefits.

The training needed to make these businesses appreciate the long-term benefits of e-commerce could not be had because of time and resource constraints. Also in hindsight, the establishment of a payment gateway probably was a mistake (Pliaskin, 2004). The Bizewest site, at least for a period, could have remained a catalogue only, and resulted in a good deal less anguish to its managers. In hindsight, it would probably have been better to scale down the size and scope of the portal and to treat it as a pilot project. WREDO was paying much less for maintenance of its main Melbourne West site (www.melbwest.com.au) compared to the cost of the Bizewest portal (www.bizewest.com.au), and it would seem that this excessive cost ultimately precipitated the collapse of Bizewest in its original form. Despite its final demise, however, the emergence and development of the Bizewest portal left a legacy of useful benefits, and its development costs were certainly not wasted. As a postscript to the demise of the Bizewest portal, WREDO itself, unfortunately, also ceased operations in January, 2005, and closed down due to lack of ongoing funds to fulfil its mission.

Regional portals add the benefit of community participation to the list of portal strengths. This is very important to many small businesses. There is, however, another side to portal implementation, especially for those portals initially supported by government funding, for at some stage their operations have to become self-funding. This means that participating small businesses should be aware that a potential sting in the tail involving increased costs of participation may be just around the corner (Burgess, Tatnall, & Pliaskin 2005). There should also be awareness by portal operators, planners, and participant small businesses that just building the portal is not enough, and that there should be a business plan matched with appropriate promotion strategies to encourage businesses to adopt and participate in using the portal. Participating businesses should also be aware that at some stage the portal may fail and should have alternate strategies either in operation or ready to implement at short notice.

There is also an important lesson here for organisations that promote the development of portals based on government grants. While the grant can be extremely useful in getting things going, there must be more than just nominal consideration given to the ongoing operation and maintenance of the portal. If WREDO had had the funds to keep Bizewest going for another year of operation and to educate more small businesses in its benefits, Bizewest might well still be operating today. The SMEs that saw little value in paying a subscription to WREDO for use of the Bizewest portal did so based on their understanding of its value to them in early 2003. As time passed and these business came to understand more about the benefits of e-commerce and the use of a B2B portal, their views may well have changed. This change could have been brought on more quickly if WREDO had access to the funds for better education programs for these SMEs. The lesson for management here is in the need to provide funds and to put into operation longer-term plans for the ongoing maintenance of the project.

References

Berlyne, D. E. (1962). Uncertainty and epistemic curiosity. *British Journal of Psychology, 53*, 27-34.

Bijker, W. E., Hughes, T. P., & Pinch, T. J. (Eds.). (1987). *The social construction of technological systems: New directions in the sociology and history of technology.* Cambridge, MA: MIT Press.

Brumby, J. (1999). *Connecting Victoria.* Retrieved on October 26, 2006 , from http://www.mmv.vic.gov.au/uploads/downloads/Resource_Centre/CVMinisterial.pdf

Burgess, S. (2002). *Information technology in small business: Issues and challenges.* In S. Burgess (Ed.), *Information technology and small business: Issues and challenges,* (pp. 1-17). Hershey, PA: Idea Group Publishing.

Burgess, S., Bingley, S., & Tatnall, A. (2005). Matching the revenue model and content of horizontal portals. In *Proceedings of the Second International Conference on Innovations in Information Technology*, (pp. 1-6), Dubai, UAE University.

Burgess, S., Tatnall, A., & Pliaskin, A. (2005). When government-supported regional portals fall. In *Proceedings of E-Society*, (pp. 170-176) 2005, Qawra, Malta, IADIS.

Callon, M. (1986a). *The sociology of an actor-network: The case of the electric vehicle.* In M. Callon, J. Law, & R. A. London (Eds.), Mapping the dynamics of science and technology (pp. 19-34). Macmillan Press.

Callon, M. (1986b). Some elements of a sociology of translation: Domestication of the scallops and the fishermen of St. Brieuc Bay. In J. Law, R. London, & Kegan Paul (Eds.), *Power, action, and belief. A new sociology of knowledge?* (pp. 196-229). Routledge & Kegan Paul

Callon, M., & Latour, B. (1981). *Unscrewing the big leviathan: How actors macro-structure reality and how sociologists help them to do so.* In K. Knorr-Cetina, A. V. Cicourel, R. London, & P. Kegan (Eds.), Advances in social theory and methodology. Toward an integration of micro and macro-sociologies (pp. 277-303). Routledge & Kegan Paul.

Chagani, F. (1998). Postmodernism: Rearranging the furniture of the universe. *Irreverence, 1*(3), 1-3.

Davison, A., Burgess, S., & Tatnall, A. (2004). *Internet technologies and business.* Melbourne, Australia: Data Publishing.

Dutch, R. A. (Ed.). (1962). *Roget's thesaurus.* London: Longman.

Gallaugher, J. M., & Downing, C. E. (2005). *Portal combat revisited: Success factors and evolution in consumer Web portals.* In A. Tatnall (Ed.), Web portals: The new gateways to Internet information and services, (pp. 40-63). Hershey, PA: Idea Group Publishing.

Gengatharen, D., & Standing, C. (2003). A conceptual framework to support the development of government sponsored community-portal regional electronic marketplaces for SMEs: A stage approach. In *Proceedings of the 14th Australasian Conference on Information Systems* (ACIS-03), (pp. 1-10) Perth, Edith Cowan University.

Grint, K., & Woolgar, S. (1997). *The machine at work—Technology, work, and organisation.* Cambridge: Polity Press.

Latour, B. (1986). The powers of association. In J. Law, R. London, & Kegan Paul (Eds.), *Power, action, and belief. A new sociology of knowledge? Sociological review monograph 32* (pp. 264-280). Routledge & Kegan Paul.

Latour, B. (1988). *The prince for machines as well as for machinations.* In B. Elliott (Ed.), Technology and social process (pp. 20-43). Edinburgh: Edinburgh University Press.

Latour, B. (1993). *We have never been modern.* Hemel Hempstead: Harvester Wheatsheaf.

Latour, B. (1996). *Aramis or the love of technology.* Cambridge, MA: Harvard University Press.

Law, J. (Ed.). (1986). *Power, action, and belief: A new sociology of knowledge.* London, Routledge & Kegan Paul.

Law, J. (1988). *The anatomy of a socio-technical struggle: The design of the TSR2.* In B. Elliott (Ed.), Technology and social process (pp. 44-69). Edinburgh: Edinburgh University Press.

Law, J. (1992). Notes on the theory of the actor-network: Ordering, strategy, and heterogeneity. *Systems Practice, 5*(4), 379-393.

Law, J., & Callon, M. (1988). Engineering and sociology in a military aircraft project: A network analysis of technological change. *Social Problems, 35*(3), 284-297.

Lepa, J., & Tatnall, A. (2002). *The GreyPath Web portal: Reaching out to virtual communities of older people in regional areas*. IT in regional areas (Tech. Rep. No. ITiRA-2002). Rockhampton, Australia: Central Queensland University.

Lynch, J. (1998). Web portals. *PC Magazine*. November 1998, 18-20.

Macquarie Library (1981). *The Macquarie dictionary*. Sydney, Macquarie Library.

McLure, B. (2004). *Personal correspondence*. Melbourne.

McMaster, T., Vidgen, R. T., & Wastell, D. G. (1997). Towards an understanding of technology in transition. Two conflicting theories. In *Proceedings of the IRIS20 Conference, Information Systems Research,* (pp. 1-16) in Scandinavia, Hanko, Norway, University of Oslo.

Pliaskin, A. (2004). The life and times of BIZEWEST. *Information Systems*. Honours thesis. Melbourne, Australia: Victoria University.

Pliaskin, A., & Tatnall, A. (2005). *Developing a portal to build a business community*. In A. Tatnall (Ed.), Web portals: The new gateways to Internet information and services (pp. 335-348). Hershey, PA: Idea Group Publishing.

Rogers, E. M. (1995). *Diffusion of innovations*. New York: The Free Press.

Searle, I. (2005). *Portals in large enterprises*. In A. Tatnall (Ed.), Web portals: The new gateways to Internet information and services (pp. 119-171). Hershey, PA: Idea Group Publishing.

Singleton, V., & Michael, M. (1993). Actor-networks and ambivalence: General practitioners in the UK cervical screening programme. *Social Studies of Science, 23*, 227-264.

Tatnall, A. (2000). *Innovation and change in the information systems curriculum of an Australian university: A socio-technical perspective*. PhD thesis, Central Queensland University, Rockhampton, Australia.

Tatnall, A. (2001). Adoption of information technology by small business—Two different approaches to modelling innovation. In *Proceedings of IRMA 2001: Managing information technology in a global economy,* (pp. 1107-1110). Toronto, Canada: Idea Group Publishing.

Tatnall, A. (2002). *Modelling technological change in small business: Two approaches to theorising innovation*. In S. Burgess (Ed.), Managing information technology in small business: Challenges and solutions (pp. 83-97). Hershey, PA: Idea Group Publishing.

Tatnall, A. (2005). *Portals, portals everywhere ...* In A. Tatnall (Ed.), Web portals: The new gateways to Internet information and services (pp. 1-14). Hershey, PA: Idea Group Publishing.

Tatnall, A., & Burgess, S. (2002). Using actor-network theory to research the implementation of a B-B portal for regional SMEs in Melbourne, Australia. In *Proceedings of the*

15th Bled Electronic Commerce Conference—E-Reality: Constructing the E-Economy, (pp. 179-191),Bled, Slovenia, University of Maribor.

Tatnall, A., & Burgess, S. (2004). *Using actor-network theory to identify factors affecting the adoption of e-commerce in SMEs.* In M. Singh & D. Waddell (Eds.), E-business: innovation and change management (pp. 152-169). Hershey, PA: IRM Press.

Tatnall, A., Burgess, S., & Singh, M. (2004). *Community and regional portals in Australia: A role to play for small businesses?* In N. Al Quirim (Ed.), Electronic commerce in small to medium enterprises: Frameworks, issues, and implications (pp. 307-323). Hershey, PA: Idea Group Publishing.

Tatnall, A., & Gilding, A. (1999). Actor-network theory and information systems research. In *Proceedings of the 10th Australasian Conference on Information Systems (ACIS)*, (pp. 955-966) Wellington, Victoria University of Wellington.

Tatnall, A., & Lepa, J. (2001). Researching the adoption of e-commerce and the Internet by older people. In *Proceedings of the We-B Conference* (pp. 28-36), Perth Australia.

Tatnall, A., & Pliaskin, A. (2005). Technological innovation and the non-adoption of a B-B portal. In *Proceedings of the Second International Conference on Innovations in Information technology* (pp. 1-8), Dubai, UAE University.

Turban, E., Lee, J., King, D., & Chung, H. M. (2002). *Electronic commerce: A managerial perspective.* NJ: Prentice Hall International Inc.

VEEM (2000). *Victorian E-Commerce Early Movers Assistance Scheme.* Melbourne, Victorian Government.

Vidgen, R., T., & McMaster, T. (1996). *Black boxes, non-human stakeholders, and the translation of IT through mediation.* In W. J. Orlikowski (Ed.), Information technology and changes in organizational work (pp. 250-271). London: Chapman & Hall.

WREDO (2003a). *Bizewest—Future Directions—In Confidence.* Melbourne, WREDO.

WREDO (2003b). *Internal WREDO Report—the 'BIZEWEST Portal'.* Melbourne, WREDO.

Chapter VI

A Security Solution for Web-Services Based Grid Application

Yih-Jiun Lee, ChienKuo Technology University, Taiwan

Abstract

This chapter introduces a Web services-based virtual organization solution, which is designed to enhance the security performance of WSGrid. WSGrid is a "Web services" based application for composing computational grids. A WSGrid environment involves WSGrid-enabled nodes as servers. The virtual organizations are formed by the joint of users and nodes. There is no central component in the system, so every node is individual and has equal position. WSGrid releases full access right to the users, so they can manage their resources. In order to prevent the misuse of flexibility, GateService is proposed. Firstly, a user should be able to access his resources if he can prove his identity. Secondly, he is able to access another's resources under owner's permission. Thirdly, long-running processes or crossing-nodes processes should be allowed and executed with only being authenticated at initiation. Finally, Shibboleth no matter cross-domain long-running processes or dynamic delegation should not affect the user's privacy, the host's security, and the system's flexibility. This chapter proposes a security solution for a Web services-based grid application.

Introduction

WSGrid (Henderson, 2004) is a set of Web services for composing simple computational grids (Foster & Kesselman, 2002). It is based on Apache Tomcat as a Web container and Axis as a services container. A machine (also called a server or a host), which has WSGrid installed on it, is called a "node". In the theory of network, a "node" is usually referred to "a processing location, which can be a computer or some other device, such as a printer. Every node has a unique network address" (Webopedia, a). However, this term is used as another similar definition. However, in this article, a node refers to an "individual executable environment", which holds resource(s) and is able to offer services and is also capable to serve one or more clients. The term "clients" (meaning consumers of nodes) might be users, nodes, or services. More specifically, the term "user" might mean groups of users if the members share similar properties, such as same organizations or institutes. Since a node can serve many users and vice versa, a user or a group can register on many nodes. Thus, the relations between users and nodes are many to many. This relationship can form various virtual organizations.

The nodes in the whole WSGrid system have equal privileges and positions. There is no central administrative component in the system. The structure of WSGrid systems is similar to the "Mesh Topology" (Network Dictionary, n.d.). "Mesh topology", which is one of the network Topologies, includes full mesh topology or partial mesh topology (Whatis.com, n.d.). In a full mesh topology system, a node must connect all other nodes in the system. However, in a partial mesh topology environment, a node may or may not connect to all other nodes. It depends on if it can reach the maximum data exchange via limited connection. Since a node can communicate with other nodes, a user is able to access all possible services. This architecture is also similar to peer-to-peer computing (P2P computing), whose detail will be briefed in a later section.

In order to use a WSGrid system to perform a Grid-based task, a user can request a job execution through services invocations within nodes. The services provided by WSGrid are basically File movement and Job submission services. Thus, a job execution may include files (such as job packets, and job descriptions, usually called workflows) transmission from one node to another, and job activation, such as activating other sub-workflows or sub-tasks on different locations. To extend the services, the users are conditionally allowed to deploy self-customized services through WSGrid. Therefore, WSGrid is flexible and scalable.

The aim of this research is to build a secure and suitable security solution for WSGrid. Therefore, this chapter is organized as follows. The second section provides relevant information about distributed computing, including grid computing, and security requirements that a network system should satisfy. Several current security frameworks are also discussed, especially focusing on the point of view of authentication and authorization. WSGrid, the architecture and general information, are provided in the third section. The special security issues from the point of view of WSGrid are also stated in this section. Afterward, in order to form dynamic virtual organizations and enhance the user friendliness, another component, GateService, must be enabled to enhance security and functionality for virtual organizations establishment. Components and functions of GateService are described in the fourth section, followed by a discussion of security fulfillment in the fifth section. In conclusion, future work will be addressed.

Literature Review

WSGrid involves the idea of Node-to-Node Computing (abbreviated to N2N computing). N2N computing derives from Peer-to-Peer Computing (P2P Computing). It is also a new architecture in distributed computing. Therefore, this section firstly briefs the evolution of distributed computing, including grid computing, and then moves to the security requirements that a grid system should fit. Finally, several current security solutions of other grid systems will be provided.

The Evolution of Distributed Computing

The predecessor of distributed computing was the Client-server architecture, first used in the 1980s (Schussel, 1995). Client-server architecture sorted all the participants (computers) in the whole system into two groups, clients or servers. A server in a client-server system is a computer with much higher power, better performance, and connectivity, and can execute over a long period of time. A server can serve more than one client at a time, following their requests. On the other hand, a client (which might be personal computers) has usually a single processor and is less powerful and has fewer resources. Clients can send requests to servers, which process without any further outside assistance (at least from the point of view of the requesters). The job of the client (the requester) is to preprocess and prepare a task and send a request to the server for service. This architecture is very useful for two- or three-tier business applications. However, there is frequently a performance and reliability bottleneck when requests run at a peak.

With the evolution of network infrastructures and the enhancement of the computational power of personal computers, Peer-to-Peer (P2P) computing provides another model of distributed computing, in which the computing devices (computers, servers, or all other devices) can link to each other easily and directly. Each device is called a "peer", and communication or sharing occurs between two peers. A peer can play the role of both client and server, unlike in server-centric computing (Microsoft Glossary, 2004). This is termed an asymmetric client-server system (Foster & Kesselman, 2003). P2P computing is typically used for connecting hosts and sharing resources (particularly, various types of files). The main purpose of P2P is that resources can be provided and consumed by every peer. Compared with a client-server system in which only servers provide resources, P2P is more robust and reliable. However, a P2P computing system cannot differentiate the privileges of different users. Thus, control is lacking.

Traditionally, distributed computing systems might be implemented in the ways of RPC (Remote Procedure Calls) or Java RMI (Remote Method Invocation). Web Services-based technology is another new option based on WWW. The term "Web services" describes "a standardized way of integrating Web-based applications using the Extensible Markup Language (XML), Simple Object Access Protocol (SOAP), Web Service Definition Language (WSDL), and Universal Description, Discovery, and Integration (UDDI) open standards over an Internet protocol backbone" (Webopedia, b). In the traditional Client/Server architecture, the Web application usually uses Web server/Web page system. The main object of Web services is not providing a graphical user interface (GUI) for use, but sharing business logic, data (including structure and format), and processes through a programmatic interface. Then the developer can build a user interface to offer specific functions. A Web services-based application can be built using different programming principles and languages, but the communication between them must be XML formatting messages and via Internet protocol (mostly HTTP).

Grid computing (Foster, Kesselman, & Tuecke, 2001; Foster, Kesselman, Tsudik, & Tuecke, 1998) is a novel and highly-developed environment for distributed computing. The aim of Grid computing is to solve the problems of large-scale computation by allowing resources sharing among every participant. The term "resource" means not only the physical equipment, such as a printer or any device, but also logical resources, such as data sets, file storage, or executable processes. The participants are either resource providers or requesters, or they may play both roles on different occasions. They might belong to different administrative domains in the real world. By "trusting" and "being trusted by" other domains, new virtual organizations (VOs) can be formed, and members of the VO can share resources across networks and boundaries. Grid computing can usually be sorted into two different types of grid, the computational grid and the data grid. The computational grid focuses on how to share computing power by executing operations, and the data grid concentrates on how to manage large and distributed data sharing. Both of them must provide an environment to serve and manage multi-users and multi-resources. Therefore, security is the primary issue.

In the recent released application, grid computing has been merged with Web services technologies. For instance, the Open Grid Services Architecture (OGSA) is a new grid computing architecture (Foster, Kesselman, Nick, & Tuecke, 2002). The Open Grid Services Infrastructure (OGSI), which is included in Global Toolkit Version 3 (GT3), is built on top of Web services. It includes Web services standards, semantics, and service definition mechanisms (Tuecke, Czajkowski, Foster, Frey, Graham & Kesselman et al., 2003 June). OGSA uses a service-oriented architecture. Lorch (2004, p. 58) defines a service as "a software component with a well-defined interface that can be described, published, discovered, and accessed remotely". Therefore, a security policy should be included in the service description, so the process can choose a proper credential to fit the requirement of the service. Moreover, the host is also able to re-route the messages to corresponding components through analysing different configurations.

Security Requirements

Security Requirements of Network-Based Applications

Kall (2003) and Kall and Perkin (2003) have grouped application level security into five categories: authentication, authorization, confidentiality, data integrity, and non-repudiation.

Authentication aims to verify the identity of the user, so the verifier can know who the user really is. The types of identities can be various. For instance, a combination of username and password is the easiest and most popular method, used in most "stand-alone" applications. The Kerberos system, developed by the Massachusetts Institute of Technology (MIT), is another option. Hardware-supported technologies, such as the smart-card card system or the biological verification system, are also available. Since the hardware-supported systems need additional equipment (such as a card reader and a fingerprint scanner), they are not widely used for the network-based environment. The most popular solution in grid computing might be X.509 public-key certificates, which must be issued by trusted certificate authorities (CAs). X.509 certificates include various subtypes of certificates for different usages. The owner of an X.509 public-key certificate can be trusted, authenticated, or verified as a valid member, because the certificate must be issued and signed by a trusted CA. This authentication is impartial.

Once the user is authenticated, the system must decide what he or she is able to do or what access is available. This is also called authorization, and concerns the rights of the user. In the traditional system, authorization is usually achieved by means of access control lists (ACLs). The ACLs itemize the actions that users or groups are able to perform or the roles they are able to play. However, in a network-based system, the number of users or divisions might be too large to be listed. Hence, a more flexible and powerful solution is requested. A modern solution uses X.509 certificates and policy languages. In order to keep the information for authorization, the X.509 certificates need to be modified and enhanced. The types of modification are various. One solution is to keep the user's identity and privilege in the certificate. Thus, the verifier can know who the user is, which group he or she belongs to, and the actions that the user can perform. Another modification keeps some useful attributes of the user in another certificate, so the authorization decision can be made according to the resource's policies. Therefore, authorization decision functions may apply.

The last three items, confidentiality, data integrity, and non-repudiation are similar from the point of view of the message level. Confidentiality states that a message should not be accessed by unauthorized parties, so the privacy of a message can be secured. Data integrity is the same. It checks that messages are not tampered with during transmission. Non-repudiation requires verification that the message sender is who he or she claims to be. These three requirements can be achieved by applying Cryptography. For instance, a user can sign messages with a private key, which should be bound with the X.509 public-key certificate. The receiver, on receipt of the signed message, can verify the digital signature using the public key of the sender. Thus, data integrity and non-repudiation can be applied. However, the signed message can be opened by anyone intercepting messages during transmission. The sender might want to add further protection by encrypting the signed message using the receiver's public key. Therefore, this message can only be decrypted by the receiver, being the only one who knows the decryption key. The latter "encryption" satisfies confidentiality. For a more secure solution, the sender might also perform an agreed message digest function to generate a digested message. The message can be sent along with the original message. The receiver retrieving the plain text from the signed and encrypted cipher can digest the message and compare with the attached digest. Data integrity can then be guaranteed.

Security Solutions in Grid Computing

In the last section, the security that a network application should satisfy was briefly described and classified according to five issues: authentication, authorization, confidentiality, data integrity, and non-repudiation. Since grid computing attempts to enable resource sharing across boundaries, the first two issues (authentication and authorization) must have foremost attention. The current authentication scheme used in most grid systems usually identifies users through verifying their X.509 certificates, which might be X.509 certificates. Different types of certificates may apply in different occasions. The X.509 public-key certificates must be issued (signed) by trusted Certificate Authorities (CAs), and the X.509 proxy certificates (Welch, Foster, Kesselman, & Mulmo, 2004) should be issued by trusted issuers (authenticated user). The proxy certificates (PCs) are usually generated and issued by users or proxies during the time of execution, so the PCs' holders can request services on behalf of the PCs' issuers. The public-key certificate represents the global identity of its owner. A holder of a public-key certificate can use the key associated with his certificate to issue "proxy certificates" (PCs) for further uses. PCs are usually used for long-running processes, so the user is not required to stay online for authentication. This functionality is called "Single Sign-On" (SSO). The authentication of a PC usually needs verification of a chain of certificates, starting from the root, a public-key certificate or identity certificate. The process of generating a PC chain is illustrated in Figure 1.

The above design has been implemented and released in the Grid Security Infrastructure (GSI) (Foster, Kesselman, Tsudik & Tuecke, 1998; Welch, Siebenlista, Foster, Bresnahan, Czajkowski, Gawor, Kesselman, Meder, Pearlman, & Tuecke, 2003, Welch, Siebenlista, Foster, Bresnahan, Czajkowski, Gawor, & et.al, 2003, January). GSI is offered in the Global Toolkit version 2 and a newer version released by the Global Alliance.

Another function achieved by means of proxy certificates is delegation. Delegation can be seen as part of authorization. They are both concerned with ensuring that a user cannot perform an action which he is not supposed to. It mainly deals with the problems when a delegator wishes to delegate a subset of his or her rights to another, a delegatee. Since the grid computing functions in a multi-user, multi-resource environment, in which the participants of one computation system might be dynamically different, pure Access Control Lists (ACLs) are not suitable. Many frameworks have been proposed and implemented for grid computing. In order to reuse the PKI certificates in a multi-domain, some modifications need to be made to enhance the functionality of the certificates. Most solutions use proxy certificates as their basis. For instance, the Community Authorization Service (CAS)

Figure 1. A chain of certificates

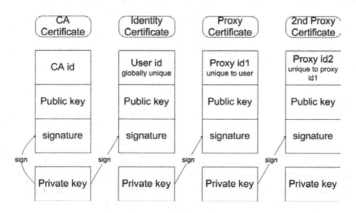

(Canon, Chan, Olson, Tull, & Welch, 2003) returns a restricted proxy certificate, which contains a list of permitted actions using SAML-based authorization decision assertions. The AKENTI authorization service (Thompson, Johnston, Mudumbai, Hoo, & Jackson, August, 1999) has a similar design, but useful user's attributes and privileges are involved in the attribute certificates (ACs) (Farrell & Housley, 2002 April). Thus, a user might need his identity certificate to be authenticated and one or more ACs to pass through the authorization process in an AKENTI system. Virtual Organization Membership Services (VOMS) is one of the components in the European Data Grid (EDG). VOMS is a role-based authorization system that combines user group membership, role(s), and capabilities into certificates as an attribute authority, so the authorization decision functions (ADFs) can comprise grid access control for resources. PRIMA, which is a privilege management and access control system, also uses an X.509 attribute certificate, which contains user capabilities for ad hoc, short-lived communities, so a short-term delegation can be allowed and performed (Lorch, Adams, Kafura, Koneni, Rathi, & Shah, 2002).

WSGrid

According to the earlier section, Peer-to-Peer computing can be used to share resources between sites. Although it is reasonably more robust and reliable, different privileges cannot be configured and given to users using Peer-to-Peer computing. Thus, a new Node-to-Node computing architecture is then proposed.

Node-to-Node Computing

The idea of Node-to-Node computing (N2N) is different from Peer-to-Peer computing, because each client (including users or servers) can be given with distinct privileges. Additionally, different nodes may also have different services and operations. A "node" is denoted as a server and a basic atom in the execution environment. A node is also an individual environment where computation occurs. There are services running on nodes, each of which might serve different tasks. Services can communicate to each other through message passing or service invocations. Therefore, communication occurs between two services or two nodes. In contrast to P2P computing, N2N computing can provide wider usage, more functionality, and different services.

WSGrid

WSGrid uses the idea of Node-to-Node computing and service-oriented architecture. It consists of a set of Web services, built on top of Apache Tomcat and AXIS. It refers to machines as nodes where computation happens. A node in WSGrid is denoted as a server which has WSGrid installed and is a basic component in a WSGrid environment. An environment can include many nodes, and a node can serve many users (clients). The communications and cooperation between nodes are through service invocations. By the use of nodes and users, dynamic virtual organizations can be formed by the dynamic relationship of nodes and users.

Figure 2 shows how to finish a task with the cooperation of nodes by the use of service invocations. A node is represented as a big rectangle. There are services (the small circles inside a node) on nodes, and the arrow lines indicate the entry of services. Each "dotted" line indicates a service invocation and its direction. Every communication or cooperation in Node-to-Node computing happens between two nodes, as with Peer-to-Peer computing (P2P computing), because communication in P2P computing also takes place between two peers. However, P2P computing usually serves specific types of file transfer and all the participants have the same privileges, but N2N computing can be used to "work" transfer, and individual authorization is also allowed.

"Work" transfer represents that a user or a user proxy is allowed to move "tasks" from one node to other nodes. This movement is usually to find the most suitable executive environment. In order to execute a task, some proper resources might be needed. In order to execute the task, the user might need to access logical or physical resources located on different nodes. WSGrid is based on this distributed concept. To remain the maximum freedom and customization for users, there is no central administrative component in WSGrid. The user is free to maintain his/her resources. This is achieved by the idea of personal workspace. Each user holds a personal workspace on each node. This individual workspace is only accessible to a user (owner of space) able to prove his/her identity. The user is able to execute a job, and move files into or out of the workspace.

Because a user might hold workspaces on different nodes, communication between workspaces on nodes has to go through service invocations, in a similar way as in Figure 3. The user on Node A can invoke a service provided by Node B to transfer a file or a work description file to the workspace on Node B. If the transferred file is a task, it might execute another file transfer or work transfer from Node B to Node C via another service invocation. To avoid

Figure 2. WSGrid architecture

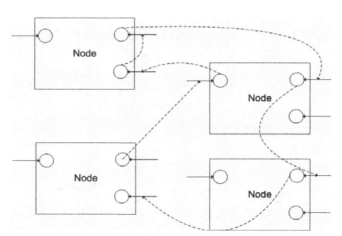

the personal workspace being accessed by another user, each invocation has to include the user's identity information to pass though the "gatekeepers".

Security Consideration for WSGrid

The security requirements that a network application and a grid system should fit have been briefed in the earlier section. This section discusses some additional requirements to assist WSGrid.

Virtual Organizations (VOs) in WSGrid are constructed by "nodes" and valid users. A user or a group of users might be authorized on many nodes. This many-to-many relation forms dynamic virtual organizations. For instance, Alice and Bob are the users on Node1; Bob and Candy are the users on Node2; and Alice, Bob and Candy are all able to access Node3. Thus, (Alice, Candy, Node1, Node3) forms a group. There are more groups formed according to the relationships in this example. Because the user lists on nodes are independent and distinct, the virtual organizations are dynamically changed. Unlike the permanent official membership, short-lived delegation should also be allowed in the system. This will be discussed in a later section. Another issue has been experienced. As discussed in the earlier section, WSGrid gives each user a personal space, so he can GAIN full access to his space without being harmed by another user. This design increases the difficulty of resource sharing. It is possible that Alice wants to perform an action that only Bob can perform in the initial configuration. Bob would like to allow Alice to proceed, so he gives Alice his delegation. In WSGrid, the delegation is global. Therefore, Alice will be able to act in exactly every way that Bob can. It increases the security risks, so a new delegation method must be recovered.

Figure 3. Service invocations from and to workspaces

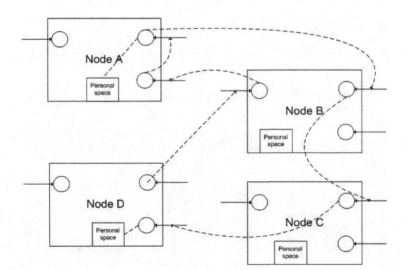

Another issue of concern is "Single Sign-On (SSO)". Single Sign-On provides a solution if one user is legitimate on many nodes or holds multiple identities of different organizations. By means of X.509 certificates, SSO can be achieved. A chain of certificates must be used in the solution, so a user or the proxy of the user can be verified by the service providers. The service request can then access the services on behalf of the user who holds the root certificate of the chain. The authentication is implicit to most of the issuers of PCs and the root. However, a large number of certificates, including identity certificates and proxy certificates, might be generated within the systems. The Liberty Alliance project (Liberty, 2003) provides another possible solution. A Liberty-enabled server can integrate all user identities on behalf of the user. When a user, from a Liberty-compatible organization, firstly accesses a Liberty-related server, he will be asked if he wants to associate his identity on the current server within his other identities on other Liberty-related servers. Once he accepts the offer and is logged-in, he will be automatically accepted (authenticated) by the whole service group. However, it is WWW-based. Shibboleth is another WWW-based solution (Shibboleth, 2002). With every service request, the verifier must trace back to the requester's home authority. The authority can check the user's legality and provide user's attributes on demand. Unfortunately, this kind of centralized control might result in a heavy load on the authority server.

WSGrid allows a user to request a service. If it is a job execution service, the job might be a stand-alone application or a workflow, which control many other tasks. A workflow may split, activate, or affect many other jobs, which might locate on different locations. It is also possible that the whole task will stand for a long time to finish. If all the tasks need user's manual permission (authentication) to start, it is unacceptable. Therefore, "Single Sign-On" is another issue to resolve.

Security Components in GateService

GateService is an extra component in WSGrid to enhance service security and user flexibility. The main aim of GateService is to form dynamic virtual organizations. The security challenges here can be considered in three sections: authentication, authorization, and transmission security. Transmission security is provided by WSGrid. Hence, it is not discussed here. Authentication concerns the users' identity. In WSGrid, it is provided by means of security tokens. However, in order to dynamically delegate access rights, temporary authentication should be given. Another important issue regarding authentication is "Single Sign-On". It is used especially for long-running processes across service boundaries, and in cases where the process submitter does not necessarily have to stay online, authentication is manual. By the use of "Single Sign-On", the user can directly access different resources, even if they are located in different domains (Demchenko, 2004). Authorization addresses the user's privilege of action. Basically, a resource provider is allowed to make an authorization decision referring to the user's capabilities such as The Community Authorization Service (CAS) or relevant information such as attributes of identities, in VOMS on the European Data Grid. It can accept, deny or suspend access requests. In order to make decisions, a decision-making function might be involved and defined, either in an executable module or in an assertion policy such as the PERMIS system (PERMIS, n.d.).

This section introduces the security components in GateService. GateService is the virtual organization solution designed for WSGrid. GateService is composed of four Web services which are implemented in Java and based on WSGrid. Delegation in WSGrid is difficult to achieve because there are nodes and workspaces in the WSGrid environment, with the critical term in WSGrid and GateService being "distributed". It is believed that a free and distributed administrative system can be more flexible and easier to customize. GateService enables adjustment of the workspace by the space owner. Sharing resources between users is the most important concept in grid computing. In order to allow sharing of resources between users, it is important, if somewhat difficult, to allow short-term delegation. GateService is a kind of solution for this specification.

The Delegation Service for Delegators

The problems of delegation in WSGrid are that: (1) It is composed of nodes, and (2) every user owns individual spaces on nodes. With the original design of WSGrid, a user can delegate his access rights to another as a whole. The delegation cannot be partial. This is unacceptable. The problem is solved by the delegation service by allowing delegation of proper actions with the appropriate domain (or effective domain).

Delegation Service is a Web service built on WSGrid. It aims to provide an interface to allow users to transfer a subset of rights to others. Two functionalities exists, "add a delegation" and "withdraw a delegation". The former method creates a new delegation. In order to have a new delegation, the delegator has to create a new security token, which is short-lived and temporarily available. The token associates the information about the identity of the delegator and the identity of the delegatee (as an option). Because each workspace is solo, the information concerning the delegation has to be reposited in the personal space. A record of delegation contains the new token (issued by the delegator), the delegated right, and the effective domain. For instance, "user1" can create a new token "token@1365782" for "user2", which allows right of access to "file2" in "dir2". The delegated right in this case is "file accessing". The effective domain is "dir2/file2".

In order to perform a delegation creation process, the delegator must be authenticated to prove his/her identity, because only a valid member within the virtual organization has the right to delegate. Then, a new temporary token will be generated and signed by the issuer (the delegator). A token used in delegation is only used for one delegation. Hence, before the token generation process, the system has to firstly check for the inexistence of a token issued for the same delegated right and effective domain. If the token does exist, it can be retrieved and sent back to the user. Therefore, the cost of token generation can be reduced.

```
Function addDelegation
        (delegator-id, delegatee-id, delegated-right, effective-domain)
        if delegator-id is not valid
                exit
        if !(delegatee-id, delegated-right, effective-domain) in records
                new a token with (delegator-id, delegatee-id)
```

```
        add (token, delegated-right, effective-domain) into records
        refresh records
else
        retrieve the current token
return token
```

The lifetime of a token is often a concern. If the lifetime is too short, the temporary token has to be renewed or generated frequently. On the other hand, if the token lifetime is too long, the privacy and security of the user might be affected and the token cannot be differentiated from normal official tokens. In GateService, the right of decision is returned to the issuers. They can decide when the delegation should be terminated. Thus, a token can remain valid until the delegator withdraws the delegation. After the execution of a withdrawal process, the token and the delegation it represents is withdrawn from the records.

```
Function delDelegation (delegator-id, token)
        if delegator-id is not valid
                exit
        if (token) in records
          delete (token) from records;
        refresh records
```

Access Service for Delegatees

Access Service is also a Web service. It is designed for the delegatees. In WSGrid, personal workspaces are not accessible to the users apart from the owner. In order to allow cross-space access (such as workspace or data set access), a trusted third party has to be involved to maintain the security for both the delegators and delegatees. Access Service provides this possibility.

The third party mentioned earlier has the permission (delegated by the system and the space owner) to access the destination space on behalf of the owner. This access must be based on the right specified on the token issued in the process of "add a new delegation". In the process of delegation creating, a token containing the delegated right(s) and an effective domain is generated. This procedure is shown in the next Pseudo Code.

```
Function chkPermission (delegator_id, token, request_action, parameters)
        if (delegator-id is not valid) AND (token is not in records)
                exit
        else if (request_action on token)
                get parameters
                execute request_action with parameters
```

> return results or success
>
> else
>
> return permission denied

Two types of delegated rights might be issued: file accessing delegation and space accessing delegation. The file accessing delegation allows the delegatee to access (more specifically, "read only") file (along with its path) shown in the field of the effective domain. With this delegation, a delegatee is allowed to read the file but not change it. Therefore, it is preferable to allow the delegatee to retrieve a duplicate of the file back to his space, so the clone is free to be used.

This file transmission process has to consider the size of the file. It is suitable for small-size files, because the network bandwidth is not a concern. Hence, the delegatee can "read" the file back to his space. However, if the file is quite large, or many files are needed to complete a task, the file transmission might be costly and affect overall performance. Instead, the delegatee might want to send his task file, which is relatively small, to a proper executive environment. This is what is called "workspace delegation". The situation becomes complicated, because the executive environment belongs to another user, and his privacy and security have to be maintained. "Workspace delegation" involves a range of reasons that the delegatee might have for accessing the information or resources in the delegator's workspace ("write", in particular). Thus, the effective domain is usually a subspace in the delegator's space.

In order to protect the user's privacy, a critical assertion "no permanent change can be made by the delegatee (Lee, 2005, pp. 3,5)" has been made. It is achieved by means of a "clone", but it clones the whole delegated space. The clone space can be built either when the delegation is created or when the first access request is made by the delegate, and it copies the whole environment from its incipience. Thus, the delegatee can directly access the clone, upload executable processes, execute tasks, and finally download the result file back to his/her space. Even through the configuration is duplicated, the process and performance is reasonable, because it happens locally. In addition, the network transmission might be reduced if the need for network messages is reduced. The clone space is annullable when the delegation is withdrawn, since the clone still belongs to the domain of the delegator, who still has access to the space.

Figure 4 shows a delegation scenario. Alice and Bob are both members of the virtual organization. Alice would like to allow Bob to execute a job in one of her subspaces ("spaceA" on "NodeB"). A temporary token ("temptoken") is generated and passed to Bob for this delegation and Delegation Service on Node B is also informed via a service invocation. With this token and official credential, Bob is able to put a file (putFile) (probably an executable one) onto a clone of "spaceA" on "NodeB" and execute the uploaded process (runJob). After execution, Bob can retrieve (getFile) the output.

"Single Sign-On" and Identities Federation

"Single Sign-On (SSO)" has been considered as a primary function in grid systems, because an execution of a task might need to involve multi-resources from different owners or virtual organizations, and a user (the task submitter) usually holds many credentials as identities. "Single Sign-On" is the capability to allow the user to be authenticated as a member once, and then retain valid membership for a long time. It is rather important in WSGrid, because the virtual organization is formed by nodes and users, and the relationships are multiple. Therefore, a user might hold different identities and security tokens within different nodes. To invoke services on nodes, the caller needs to be authenticated on behalf of the user, and so needs a proper identity. The users in WSGrid can be authenticated manually. Therefore, the user must stay on line as long as the task is running. Alternatively, he can also manually set up his identities immediately before the service invocation or task submissions, for instance, using:

Change identity to (token@15432)

Submit_task (job1) to Node1

The "Single Sign-On" service of GateService provides another solution to this problem. A preparative function to be done is identities federation. This function associates the proper identities and security tokens with the corresponding node, such as using:

Id_Federation(token@15432, Node1)

After the federation of identities, the service is able to pick up the proper security token for every service invocation. In order to maintain flexibility in the system, three kinds of

Figure 4. Delegation flow in GateService

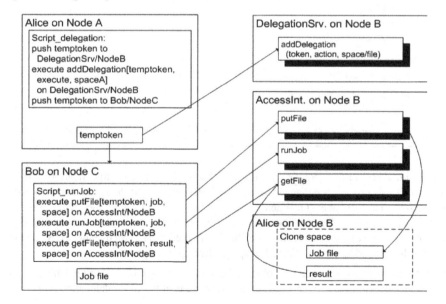

SSO service invocations are provided. The first method is that the user manually sets up identities to use for the next service invocation in the task itself. This is the same method of invocation as in WSGrid. The second method is inheritance, for those whose current identity should remain in use in the following invocation. The last method is to allow the service to automatically pick up a proper token for the specified node used in the next invocation.

By using "Single Sign-On" service, the user is allowed to submit tasks to different nodes at different times of execution without modifying the code.

Adaptable Configuration

Configuration Service is used because of the distributed environment. In the original design of WSGrid, all the spaces/nodes are distinct, even though they might have the same owner. Hence, a difficulty arises when a user wants to set up the same configuration or have the same delegation on different spaces/nodes. The user can "add a new delegation" repeatedly and manually on different nodes, or just create a new delegation and then import those settings to other nodes.

Another usage of Configuration Service is to cooperate with an SSO service. The user can have all identities federated on one node, and then import the identity federation to other nodes to reduce the manual work.

Configure Service provides an easy method for copying the configuration of the user environment between nodes. The precondition of this service is that the performer is authenticated and authorized on the nodes.

```
Alice:     exec getConfiguration on me;
           wait for configFile;
           push configFile to Srv1;
           exec ConfigureService on Srv1;
Srv1/importConfig:
           wait for configFile;
           exec importComfig on me;
```

Summary of GateService

In WSGrid, every service request should come along with identity authentication. Therefore, in order to process a delegated action, both delegatees and delegators have to hold membership in at least one VO. When a new member joins, a token, which represents the user's identity, is created, and all corresponding nodes have to be informed. Additionally, the mapping space of the new identity must be constructed and initiated on nodes. Since the user is only allowed to work in his or her space, the system is protected.

The authorization occurs over two phases. When a user logs in, his official identity is granted the access to his own space. The second phase is optional for delegation work, if a user wants to work on another's behalf, such as by accessing another's space. To perform a delegated process, the delegator must issue a new short-life token, which is unique for this delegation, so the delegatee can request access by showing the token. The delegate-able resources in the system are workspace and computing power. They are directly controlled by the resource owners. Thus, central administration is not necessary. This delegation process executes a "push" model of message sequence, as shown in Figure 5. The steps in the action are defined as follows:

1. The delegator creates a temporary security token, which associates the delegator's identity, the delegatee's identity, the target node, the effective domain, and permission.

2. The delegatee and Delegation Service on the node are informed about the delegation.

3. The delegatee then sends a request, along with the token generated in step 2, to Access Service.

4. WSGrid verifies the user's identity to allow access to services, and Access Service verifies the attached token.

5. An authorization decision function (ADF) included in Access Service then decides if the token states the action that the user is asking for. If permission is granted, the user is redirected.

6. If the action is file reading, the file content is transferred to the delegatee. If he or she is asking for full access, the direction to the clone space will be found and passed. Then, the delegatee can act on behalf of the delegator.

Figure 5. The sequence of delegation in GateService

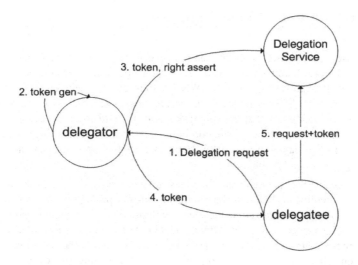

Fulfillment Of Security Requirements

The earlier sections addressed some requirements of general network applications and some special requisites of WSGrid. The security components have also been discussed. This section explains how the design meets the requirements.

Transmission Level Security

Transmission level security is usually concerned with message level security in distributed computing. WSGrid provides elemental transmission security by means of Secure Socket Layer (SSL). It provides an encrypted transmission in communication. In order to find a proper key to encode the messages, every node is expected to recognize others by exchanging machine certificates. Because the authentication has to be mutual, the machine certificates have to be installed before the host (node) joins the virtual organization(s). During transmission, every message has to be encoded by the public key, which can be found on the certificate of the recipient. Thus, the receiver can decode the cipher using a private key.

Because the message is encoded and decoded using the key pair of the recipient, the technology is designed for communication between two participants. However, in WSGrid, every communication and cooperation occurs between two nodes. Hence, SSL can meet the requirement. Unfortunately, the cipher is encoded using the key of the host, so it is open to all the users on the node. To improve security, the user can encrypt the messages personally before sending the messages to the SSL channel. Thus, although other users on the same node can decode the SSL channel, the message is still encrypted. Another benefit of this method is that since the receiver is also a sender, a symmetric encrypting algorithm can be used to enhance performance.

Authentication and Single Sign-On

A WSGrid user must register with the node to access the Web services provided by the WSGrid node before claiming access to services. Authentication in WSGrid is achieved by means of security token verification. The token has to be attached with every service invocation. With access to different nodes or virtual organizations, a user might own different tokens. In order to perform a long-running task requiring multi-resources involved, a user can either set up authentication information in the job description or wait to be manually authenticated. Either way is inconvenient. Hence, GateService provides another solution for this "Single Sign-On" problem.

"Single Sign-On" (SSO) is one of the functions in GateService. To use it, the user must firstly federate identities which must be associated with the proper node or virtual organization. Those associations are kept in the user's configuration. The system can only access them when a SSO service is invoked. After the identity federation, the user or its proxy can access different resources belonging to different nodes without bothering about repeated authentication. This SSO service performs implicitly and has three different methods of invocation to maintain flexibility for the user.

Authorization

Authorization in WSGrid is naturally achieved by means of personal workspaces. One user owns an individual workspace, which is not accessible to other users. A user can fully control his workspace, including the configuration of his environment. The system leaves all privileges to the space owner. In order to access the space, a requester must provide a security token to prove ownership. This ensures security and privacy. Therefore, it is the owner's responsibility to keep malignant codes away from the space. However, this causes another problem. To share resources with another user, delegation must be allowed. In the design of WSGrid, the delegation cannot be partial. This problem is solved by the use of GateService.

Delegation

GateService is designed to allow delegation to happen. Global delegation is inadequate, if a user is requested to share his real, long-term identity with others. Therefore, partial delegation must be enabled. It is what GateService works for. Because of the nature of WSGrid, the delegatable resources are space and computing power. The former allows a delegatee to access to a restricted area owned by the delegator. It usually means "read only". The latter indicates full access to a space, so a delegatee is able to execute processes or modify anything within the promised space. However, user privacy and security being affected by the delegation is not acceptable. Thus, there is an assertion made: "no permanent change can be made by the delegatees". For instance, since file access allows a user to access a file, it is encouraged to copy the file content back to the delegatee's space. Thus, the source will not be tampered with, and the delegatee can still use the file.

However, the delegation of workspace access is more complicated, because workspace access releases the right of full access to the space to the delegatee. In order to keep the completeness of original space, a clone space must be created for full-access delegation. This duplicate has the same configuration to the original space and can be created at any time between the initiation and the first access request of delegation. The space remains its existence until the withdrawl of the delegation. The delegatee can reuse the space as a stateful resource (because the state of this clone is keeping updated). By means of the duplicate space, the delegatee can have full access of the resources without harming the security and privacy of the delegator.

In both situations, the effective domain (including the file or file-store that the delegatee can access to and the space that the delegatee can fully access) must be associated with the token and this delegation.

User Friendliness and Configuration

Configuration in the WSGrid system is for distributed virtual organizations. It is difficult to configure a distributed environment. Configure Server allows users to copy the environment from one node to another. By cooperation with "Single Sign-On" service, a user can also federate his identities on one node and copy the setting to others to reduce the cost of configuration.

Conclusion and Future Works

This Chapter introduced WSGrid and GateService. WSGrid contains a set of Web services in order to enable computational grid on a server. A WSGrid federation can be composed of nodes. Each node in the federation has equal position and privilege. There is no central administrative component in the system. Thus, a WSGrid federation is a fully distributed grid system. A user who is legitimate on one or more WSGrid-enabled nodes can request services to transfer files from one node to another or submit jobs or workflows on a different location. The submitted task can then request other services. However, WSGrid is more than that. Several supportive services are provided in WSGrid. For instance, a user can work on a blank computer (such as a desktop in an Internet Café, without WSGrid-enabled) to access a WSGrid node. Through the WWW-based interface, he can still access the WSGrid services on a WSGrid workstation. As a traveller, he might submit and activate a long-running task, and then leave it from time to time. Once returning online, he can access a Logging Service which records every message to the user. This Logging Service can act as a notification service. Thus, a user does not have to stay online for results, and no message will be missing.

GateService is the security solution of WSGrid. The main aim is to provide convenient delegation and "Single Sign-On" for users, based on existing conditions. This experiment is fully distributed and releases most capabilities to users. The advantages of using GateService are: (1) a user has rights to full control and access space, including partial delegation, so it is flexible; (2) the system administrator only needs to maintain the user list, so it is easy to maintain; (3) two assertions, "no one can access others' workspace" and "no permanent change can be made by the delegatee" ensure the security and privacy for the space owners and the delegators; (4) identity federation and "Single Sign-On" are provided, so the system is user-friendly and easy to control; and (5) the choice of moving a file back to the space of the delegatee or sending a task to access the dataset can be made, depending on which transmission is more efficient, so it provides efficiency for network bandwidth. In order to share resources between users, a user can delegate rights to access of workspace to others. This delegation is hierarchical and also easy to manage. For instance, a node administrator owns one space containing many first-level spaces which are owned by members of the nodes. A member on the node can also delegate a subset of rights (such as a sub-directory) to another.

This security solution is fair, but not perfect yet. The system gives the right to the users to decide which level of security should be applied. The user can choose a proper cryptographic algorithm to encode the important files. He can also apply a digital signature or encrypt his transiting message, before using SSL, to improve security. The system only provides fundamental solutions, which should be necessary to all the users. Additionally, no centralized components exist, which means that each node is isolated. The user has difficulty in finding the location of services. In the future, efforts will be made to provide a grid service broker or indexing service, which should be able to redirect the user to the proper nodes where required services are provided. Even though the broker might have some characteristics of centralized control, the flexibility and scalability of distributed administration will still remain.

References

Alfieri, R., Cecchini, R., Ciaschini, V., dellAgnello, L., Frohner, A., & Gianoli, A., et al. (2003). VOMS, an authorization system for virtual organizations. *The 1st European Across Grids Conference* (pp. 1-8), Santiago de Compostela, February 13-14, 2003.

Canon, S., Chan, S., Olson, D., Tull, C., & Welch, V. (2003, April). Using CAS to manage role-based VO sub-groups. In *Proceeding of Computing in High Energy and Nuclear Physics* (pp. 1-5), *CHEP '03*, April, 2003. Computing in High Energy and Nuclear Physics.

Demchenko, Y. (2004). Virtual organisations in computer grids and identity management. *Information Security Technical Report, 9*(1), 59-76.

Farrell, S., & Housley, R. (2002, April). *An Internet attribute certificate profile for authorization*. Retrieved October 16, 2006, from http://www.ietf.org/rfc/rfc3281.txt

Foster, I., & Kesselman, C. (2003). *The grid 2: Blueprint for a new computing infrastructure*. Morgan Kaufmann.

Foster, I., Kesselman, C., Nick, J., & Tuecke, S. (2002). The physiology of the grid: An open grid services architecture for distributed systems integration. *Open Grid Service Infrastructure WG* (pp. 1-31), *Global Grid Forum June 22, 2002*.

Foster, I., Kesselman, C., Tsudik, G., & Tuecke, S. (1998). A security architecture for computational grids. In *Proceedings of the 5th ACM Conference on Computer and Communications Security* (pp. 83-92).

Foster, I., Kesselman, C., & Tuecke, S., (2001). The anatomy of the grid: Enabling scalable virtual organizations. *Lecture Notes in Computer Science, 2150,* (pp. 1-25).

Henderson, P. (2004). *WSGrid 1.3 Tutorial*. Retrieved on October 16, 2006, from http://www.ecs.soton.ac.uk/~ph/WSGrid/

Johnston, W. E., Gannon, D., & Nitzberg, B. (1999). Grids as production computing environments: The engineering aspects of NASA's information power grid. *The Eighth IEEE International Symposium on High Performance Distributed Computing,* (pp. 1-8), Redondo Beach, CA.

Kall, N. (2003). *Service-Oriented Security Architecture*. Retrieved May, 2006, from http://techupdate.zdnet.com/

Kall, N., & Perkin E. (2003). The intersection of Web services and security management: Service-oriented security architecture. *META Group White Paper,* (pp. 1-18), October, 2003.

Lee, Y. J. (2005). A security solution for Web services-based virtual organizations. *Proceedings of the Information Resources Management Association (IRMA) International Conference,* (pp. 1-5), San Diego, CA, May, 2005.

Liberty (2003, October). *Liberty Alliance & WS-Federation: A Comparative Overview.* *LIBERTY ALLIANCE PROJECT.*

Lorch, M. (2004). *Prima, privilege management, and authorization in grid computing environments.* Unpublished doctoral dissertation, Faculty of the Virginia Polytechnic Institute and State University, VA.

Lorch, M., Adams, D., Kafura, D., Koneni, M., Rathi, A., & Shah, S. (2002, November). The PRIMA system for privilege management, authorization, and enforcement in grid environments. In *Proceeding of the 4th International Workshop on Grid Computing—Grid 2003*, (p. 109) Phoenix, AZ.

Lorch, M., Cowles, B., Baker, R., & Gommans, L. (2004). *Authorization Framework Document.* Retrieved October 16, 2006, from http://www.ggf.org/documents/GWD-I-E/GFD-I.038.pdf

Microsoft Glossary (2004). *.NET glossary of terms—Definition of distributed computing.* Retrieved October 16, 2006, from http://www.microsoft.com/net/basics/glossary.asp

Network Dictionary (n.d.). *Mesh Network Topology and Architecture.* Retrieved May, 2006, from http://www.networkdictionary.com/networking/mesh.php

Pearlman, L., Welch, V., Foster, I., & et.al (2002). A community authorization service for group collaboration. In *Proceedings of the IEEE 3rd International Workshop on Policies for Distributed Systems and Networks,* (pp. 1-10).

PERMIS (n.d.). *Privilege and Role Management Infrastructure Standards Validation.* Retrieved October 16, 2006, from http://www.permis.org/en/index.html

Schussel, G. (1995). *Client/server past, present, and future.* Retrieved May, 2006, from http://www.dciexpo.com/geos/

Shibboleth (2002). *Shibboleth-Architecture Draft Version 05.* Retrieved October 16, 2006, from http://shibboleth.internet2.edu/

Thompson, M., Johnston, W., Mudumbai, S., Hoo, G., & Jackson, K. (1999, August). Certificate-based access control for widely distributed resources. In *Proceedings of the Eighth Usenix Security Symposium,* (pp. 215-228).

Tuecke, S. Czajkowski, K., Foster, I., Frey, J., Graham, S., Kesselman, C., & et al. (2003, June). *Open Grid Services Infrastructure* (OGSI) (pp. 1-86), Version 1.0, Global Grid Forum Recommendation.

Wason, T. (2005). *Liberty ID-FF Architecture Overview.* Retrieved October 16, 2006, from https://https://www.projectliberty.org/liberty/files/specs/draft_liberty_idff_arch_overview_1_2_errata_v1_0_pdf

Wasson, G., & Humphrey, M. (2003). *Policy and enforcement in virtual organizations.* Retrieved October 16, 2006, from http://www.cs.virginia.edu/~gsw2c/research/GRID03.pdf

Webopedia (a). *What is node?* Retrieved October 16, 2006, from http://www.webopedia.com/TERM/N/node.html

Webopedia (b). *What is web services?* Retrieved October 16 2006 from http://www.webopedia.com/TERM/W/Web_services.html

Welch, V., Foster, I., Kesselman, C., Mulmo, O., Pearlman, L., Tuecke, S., & et al. (2004). X.509 proxy certificates for dynamic delegation. In *Proceedings of the 3rd Annual PKI R and D Workshop,* (pp. 1-17).

Welch, V., Siebenlista, F., Foster, I., Bresnahan, J., Czajkowski, K., Gawor, J., Kesselman, C., Meder, S., Pearlman, L., & Tuecke, S. (2003). *GSI3: Security for grid services.* (pp. 1-14). Retrieved October 16, 2006, from http://www-unix.mcs.anl.gov/~welch/pub/GT3%20Security%20HPDC%20Draft.pdf

Welch, V., Siebenlista, F., Foster, I., Bresnahan, J., Czajkowski, K., Gawor, & et.al, (2003 January). Security for grid services. In *Proceedings of the Twelfth International Symposium on High Performance Distributed Computing (HPDC-12).* IEEE Press, Seattle, WA.

Whatis.com (n.d.). *Mesh network.* Retrieved October 26, 2006, from http://searchnetworking.techtarget.com/sDefinition/0,290660,sid7_gci870763,00.html

Chapter VII

Conceptual Model Driven Software Development (CMDSD) as a Catalyst Methodology for Building Sound Semantic Web Frameworks

Thomas Biskup, Carl von Ossietzky University, Oldenburg, Germany

Nils Heyer, Carl von Ossietzky University, Oldenburg, Germany

Jorge Marx Gómez, Carl von Ossietzky University, Oldenburg, Germany

Abstract

This Chapter introduces Hyperservices as a unified application model for Semantic Web frameworks, and proposes Conceptual Model-Driven Software Development as a means of easy adoption to them. Hyperservices are based on agent societies, provided with structured information by the Semantic Web, and using Web services as a collaboration and communication interface. Afterwards, the WASP model is proposed as a framework for implementing

Hyperservices, also adding personalization rules to modify the agents' perception as well as the HIVE Architecture as Semantic Information Server infrastructure within the WASP framework. For easier adoption of these new models, Conceptual Model-Driven Software Development is proposed. It separates the conceptual aspects from the technical details by automatically generating executable code from models while the implementation details are hidden to the end user, the service developer.

Overview

The Semantic Web and its effects are a mainstream catalyst for current Web development. Its influence is felt across many areas of research and business development: Agent systems, knowledge management frameworks, ontology definitions, and other areas are all refined by new ideas from Semantic Web research (and vice versa). Since many complex topics are now combined with the goal of building the "Next Generation Internet", it becomes more and more important to build sound and flexible frameworks to abstract the implementation details of the underlying technologies.

As underlying technologies are still in a state of flux as far as their implementation details are concerned, it seems to be very important to find a simple yet appropriate meta-model for the overall architecture which can be used to follow a kind of model-driven approach: Model the required system in a meta-level and then derive the actual implementation by transforming the model into executable code (or even directly executing the model). This approach allows both the early adoption of Semantic Web technologies and a continuing evolution of the implementation details.

Research shows that the underlying methodology for defining Semantic Web-oriented frameworks can be defined very well. This chapter will explain the main streams which will be integrated towards the Semantic Web and more importantly show, based on a thorough requirements analysis, how Semantic Web-oriented systems might be structured in a simple meta-model, allowing more detailed specification as research progresses. A new software development methodology, named Conceptual Model-Driven Software Development or CMDSD for short, which is currently under development in our research team, is used to provide a notion of the appropriate meta-models which will allow the early adoption of Semantic Web technologies in standard industrial projects.

The following steps in this chapter will lead to an early-stage meta-model which might be used to connect Semantic Web frameworks in an easy and non-intrusive way with standard projects:

- The main research streams and technologies making up the Semantic Web are identified. Their interrelations and resulting requirements for frameworks and systems are shown.

- An in-depth requirements analysis concerning the architecture of Semantic Web systems and the must-have features of such features provides the groundwork for the definition of the cornerstones of future Semantic Web systems. It will be shown that the basic cornerstones are limited in scope, thus making it possible to define a very simple high-level meta-model for a model-driven strategy.

- An approach to build multi-platform Semantic Web frameworks based on the core technologies of Agents, Ontologies, Web Services, and Personalization frameworks is explained. This approach is generic enough to encompass most currently-existing frameworks and lends itself towards the integration of emerging standards. A new type of service, a Hyperservice, is derived from integrating these core technologies into a new type of service infrastructure.

- An overview of Model-Driven Architecture (MDA) and Model-Driven Software Development (MDSD) will be given. It provides the infrastructure for our extension of CMDSD (Conceptual Model-Driven Software Development) which strives to close the gap between technology expertise and conceptual requirements by building meta-models focused on the conceptual task and defining a transformation path to build complex systems from simple meta-models.

Emerging Semantic Web Technologies Reviewed

First we will give an overview of existing Semantic Web research and describe the current underlying problems which need to be solved in the new future to let the Semantic Web become a living reality: The main task will be to narrow or close the gap between the reality of the Web (a disjoined and tangled mass of loosely-coupled information resources) and the vision for the Web: a tightly-integrated and openly-structured information network with machine-readable data that allows autonomous agencies to create new applications empowered by this wealth of information. Currently problems already start in the early stages of developing systems for the Semantic Web: Existing models and theories are relatively complex (compared to established Web standards like XML and HTML), frameworks still have a very dynamic state, and interfaces between frameworks are bound to change more often than not (if they exist at all at this point of time). We propose a framework to allow researchers and developers to choose the level of detail, the type of technologies, and the amount of computing power they want to utilize for their proposed solutions. We will use the building blocks of this framework as the grounding for a flexible yet very simple meta-model that ignores technical complexity and favors the easy integration of existing technologies. We focus for our framework on a flexible abstraction layer, pattern-oriented architecture, and open interfaces to build on the successful foundations of the Web: ease of use, flexibility, and almost unlimited expression power. Agents are the central paradigm for software development using this architecture.

The Evolution of the Web

The Semantic Web is pushed by the World Wide Web Consortium (W3C) as the foundation for a true information society (Berners-Lee, 1998; Berners-Lee, Hendler, & Lassila, 2001).

The efforts of the W3C are supported by a wide range of multi-national research efforts combining theoretical and practical experiences from information technology.

Nonetheless progress is slow, and even if research would yield results at much greater speed, the results still need to be implemented. Current research hints at much more expressive and thus also more powerful means to represent data and information, but the price is added complexity required to build the representations. We therefore focus on trying to provide simple models which completely hide the underlying complexity of Semantic Web technologies. The World Wide Web was successful because people basically overnight were enabled to share information, with simple technology. This allowed for the enormous growth in information resources which we now face. We strive to reproduce this pattern to guarantee the further growth of the Web (Berners-Lee, 2000) by providing an early example for a simple meta-model (with ample extension points) at the end of this chapter.

The Web of Systems

The World Wide Web in its current form is the largest information system ever built by humans. At the same time, it probably is also one of the least structured information systems ever built. There are billions of Web pages (not counting other resources like images, videos, sounds, CGI interfaces to large databases, and more), and almost none of them are structured in a standardized way. The "Deep Web" is even larger (Bergman, n.d.). Most pages are built with HTML and coupled in a very loose manner; links lead into oblivion as often as they do not. Most existing links do not provide much semantic information (e.g., what is the meaning of a specific link except "someone thought that two information resources should be connected in some way"). Most information is presented in a way that allows humans to use it, although access to this information usually is a problem because it becomes harder and harder to find the few tidbits of information in the existing mess of data. Studies by search engine companies show that current problems are to be found at a more basic level: Even the simple requirements of HTML are rarely correctly fulfilled and semantic information provision is not a topic high on the list of most interest groups present on the World Wide Web (Web Authoring Statistics, n.d.).

Thus we argue that we need to find ways to evolve from the current World Wide Web (a Web of Systems, so named because there are many individual systems that usually are only connected by the simplest means, namely hyperlinks) to something more.

It would be foolish and dangerous to try too much at once. At the same time, it would be as foolish and dangerous to create artificial boundaries and introduce building blocks that limit our power of expressiveness. Thus we propose to search for architectures and frameworks that support gradual evolution without limiting the final goal. We find practical examples that support the viability of this approach: Modular programming has spawned object-oriented programming to be able to control complexity with more natural concepts. For certain problem areas, agent-oriented systems have been discovered to be an immensely powerful and very natural concept for defining solutions (Ciancarini & Wooldridge, 2001). Now the industry momentum offers a huge chance to solve one of the basic problems of agent societies: Communication by Web services promises to do away with the artificial system boundaries currently inhibiting large-scale distributed autonomous agent systems. And finally, model-driven approaches (either MDA or MDSD) (Stahl & Völter, 2005) seem to be highly appropriate to serve as the glue between the evolving and varying technologies.

The Web of Services

Web Services currently are the preferred integration technology for business software companies. Web Services (Christensen, Curbera, Meredith, & Weerawarana, 2001; Gottschalk, Graham, Kreger, & Snell, 2002) in theory offer a standard means to communicate between disparate systems and applications with absolute disregard for programming languages, computer hardware, and system-specific communication protocols. Based on XML (eXtensible Mark-up Language) (Biskup & Marx Gómez, 2005), this new and exciting standard promises a new way of defining interfaces, without sticking to implementation details and basic technical questions. Together with HTTP (Hypertext Transfer Protocol) (Gourley & Totty, 2002) and SOAP (Simple Object Access Protocol) (Mitra, 2001) as protocols, we face an enormous opportunity to bring together previously-separated building blocks for the next generation Internet. XML is the unifying data representation standard that could be used to basically encode any kind of information. HTTP and SOAP are simple yet flexible protocols that allow a system-independent communication between heterogeneous systems. More generally, the basic notion of application-level protocols is very important to be able to conceptualize a working architecture for a true Web of Services. While it currently is very difficult to connect different Web-based systems, future interfaces could greatly benefit from these standards (e.g., when trying to combine a flight information system and a hotel booking system).

While theoretically already very strong in practice, many Web Services standards are not yet available. The specifications currently evolve at a much faster pace than the implementations, and many of the core technologies (e.g., distributed transactions and security) are still in a state of continuing change. These movements will stabilize eventually, but in the meantime the permanent flux of changes creates investment risks which cause many commercial endeavors to use as little as possible of the new technologies. In turn, this causes specifications to be created with a certain lack of practical experience, which in turn shows in the quality of early specification versions and again hampers adoption.

If models can be provided that collect the basic ideas of the standard and completely hide the implementation details, companies could start today with integrating the existing standards. A model-driven approach seems to be the most appropriate way for this task: The conceptual tasks could be modeled on a meta-level by using a simple and abstracted modeling technology, and some kind of transformation engine would take these models and either directly execute them or transform them into executable code. In this way systems could be easily upgraded to new versions of specific Web Service technologies, as the meta-models will probably only change in minor ways or not at all.

A Web of Services thus could become a tangible possibility. This could be the next important step for Web technologies—because Web services possess many powerful features ideally suited for industrial use and commercial success stories. This also could build the momentum to ensure the wide-spread use of, in our point of view, a very important technology. Current developments support this theory; most new API versions and programming systems supply some sort of Web Services integration (from ancient languages like COBOL to the most recent developments like .NET).

The Web of Semantics

All afore-mentioned efforts target one underlying and ever present goal: the Semantic Web, an information network of machine-readable data that allows autonomous agencies to gather data, turn it into information, reason about it, and come to conclusions. This information network will be traversed by intelligent agents to fuel new and exciting services (Joy, 2000; McIlraith, Son, & Zeng, 2001; Metcalfe, 2000). Humans will never be able to fully utilize the mass of data collected in the World Wide Web; thus we need to find new ways to turn all the data into something more than a loosely connected set of HTML pages. The basic building blocks for the Semantic Web are made up by:

- **Semi-structured data:** XML has been accepted as the means of choice to represent platform-independent data in a semi-structured way that allows for an open-ended way of describing data (Bray, Paoli, Maler, Sperberg-McQueen, & Paoli, 2000). Based on plain text (but powered by Unicode), XML enriches pure data with metadata to allow machines to use the data more effectively and in ways not initially coded into the data format.

- **Machine-readable data:** The current proposal for this building block relies on XML as a means of expression and has been named RDF (Resource Description Framework) (Brickley & Guha, 2000; Lassila, 2000). It should be noted that RDF has various means of representation, but XML seems to be the most natural for the World Wide Web and the most widely used right now. RDF allows describing resources, properties of resources, and relations between resources. RDF can be extended to create more complicated languages and at the same time provides powerful foundations for reasoning (being based on first-order logic). Interestingly, RDF takes a very pragmatic approach to provide a viable solution for information representation: Right away, it allows for inconsistence, incorrectness, and incompleteness in the represented information and takes it as given that data can lead to situations where agents will not be able to come to a decisive or correct conclusion. This pragmatism adheres to the concepts that established the current Web, ease of use with an allowance for mistakes.

- **Ontologies** as a means to describe the relations between objects and to define standard hierarchies as descriptions of "the world": A lot of research is concerned with the question of what should be in an ontology language in order to once more find the best way of combining computing and expression power with ease of use. Ontology languages like SHOE (Heflin, Hendler, & Luke, 1999), DAML (Hendler & McGuiness, 2000), and DAML+OIL (DAML+OIL, 2000) hint at the power of future metadata structures.

So far major concerns in the World Wide Web community were to standardize the encoding of data and information. Retrieval, automated reasoning about information, connection of services, and basically all other means of exploiting this information pool were only moderately successful. The Web spawned a variety of search engines and meta-search engines, but these, together with shop systems and Web directories, cover the efficient means of access to the World Wide Web for humans. There were some experiments with agents and agent societies (Brickley & Guha, 2000), but so far these attempts failed to become wide-spread successes due to the lack of a unified information infrastructure and lack of standardized interfaces; CGI (the Common Gateway Interface) is hardly sufficient to build even semi-complex applications in an abstract and elegant way. Other experiments (De Bruijn, Fensel, Keller, & Lara, 2005; Harper & Bechhofer, 2005) hint at different exciting possibilities to enhance the knowledge acquisition process for users, but still lack the unified foundation required to build a whole generation of such service enhancements. The need for such a foundation is proven by some extensive first-generation systems (Lin, Harding, & Teoh, 2005)), which show the basic building blocks that will be required again and again, and thus are the primary target for standardization attempts.

To cope with this situation we propose a new model of regarding future applications building on the foundations mentioned so far, a unit of abstraction we have named Hyperservices.

Proposing Hyperservices as a Unified Application Model

We believe that the next important step will be to find a unifying, language- and system-independent architecture that allows for a convergence in current research areas surrounding the Semantic Web. When we talk about Web-based applications, we mean "based on Web technologies". Web technologies have been widely accepted and have managed to bring together disparate system structures. While this goal in the first moment might be very ambitious, we will present a very simple (one might think trivial) way of allowing all these technologies to be integrated into current run-time environments. Ample extension points will be provided, and we refrain from requiring any specific implementation technologies.

Looking at the components currently available, a unified application model based on agent societies seems to be in reach: The Semantic Web allows us to reason about information by structuring information appropriately. This provides the basis for "intelligent" agents (with "intelligence" on a pragmatic hands-on level). Web services introduce the interface for collaboration among systems. Agents are the natural extension to achieve autonomous systems (Benjamins, 2003). Currently we face a multitude of ontology languages (Benjamins, Fensel, & Asunción, 1998) and many models and theories to map information to efficient data models and retrieval algorithms, but these means will only see wide-spread use if they become easy to communicate to future users (e.g., programmers), based on standard architectures and easy to integrate into existing systems. Integration still is one of the main problems faced by current computer science (from the business perspective), but the Web can only remain successful if it manages to stay commercially interesting (whether by drawing enough people to it to supply Internet Providers with customers, or by introducing truly successful e-business models is not that important). Thus the integration of these new models into existing structures will be the most important task from a business point of view.

Topics under current discussion (e.g., agent societies and the Semantic Web) will not be able to replace classic information systems (e.g., tax accounting, enterprise resource planning, and logistics). But if built in the right way, they will be able to enrich classic systems by providing added value. They will open up a new venue of information systems, built around the necessity to decide between precision and speed. The sheer size of the Web and its constant flux will make it impossible to store nearly enough data in local systems to allow for efficient information systems (in the classic sense). Thus it seems much more likely that future information systems will be build around the idea of semi-autonomous agents wandering across the Web, collecting information, reasoning about it, and yielding results, either continuously or until specified resource limits (e.g., time, bandwidth, or a financial budget) have been exhausted (Hendler, 2001).

The WASP Model

We propose a unified framework that is founded on four building blocks which, in our point of view, will be absolute necessities to populate the future Web with more powerful applications:

- *W*eb Services as a means of providing a unified communication interfaces between applications and agencies (Christensen et al., 2001; Dale, 2002; UDDI, 2001);
- *A*gents as a natural and central means to represent typical tasks and solutions for a distributed and constantly changing information environment;
- *S*emantic Web technologies as a means to provide data and information in a consistent manner that allows retrieval and reasoning; and
- *P*ersonalization technologies to customize processes to the needs of the individual user, an absolute necessary concerning the current (and future) size of the World Wide Web, lest it becomes impossible to separate useless from useful information.

(The initials of these core technologies also provide the acronym for our framework: WASP)

Agents will be the central building block of this architecture, because they implement the actual business logic. Web Services are the natural means of communication and collaboration for agents working under the described model; the Semantic Web is the environment (world) for these agents, and the personalization rules basically can be used to make up or modify the beliefs of the agents. Thus the described components integrate very nicely and in a very natural manner into the underlying agent paradigm.

The WASP framework will account for a variety of necessities explained in the next sections. In contrast to existing major endeavors in this area (Finin, Labrou, & Mayfield, 1997; Object Management Group, n.d.; O'Brien & Nicol, 1998), we plan to provide an architecture that focuses on:

- proactive information agents that collect information and provide results by using inference mechanism to reason about the existing information;
- high-level technical support for the application developer (e.g., communication, distribution, data storage);
- tight integration of Web technologies (RDF, Web Services, DAML, SOAP, etc.);

- independence from specific kinds of implementations (e.g., no specific communication language will be enforced); and
- focus on agents relying on the Semantic Web as the dominant information source.

Thus the following central paradigms will be of greatest importance:

Open Interfaces

Since it is impossible to enforce one true operating system, one true programming language, or one true CPU architecture for the network underlying the World Wide Web, it is of paramount importance to provide a powerful means of communication between the interacting agencies. SOAP and HTTP (as the underlying protocols), together with Web Services (as a means of interface specification), seem to be natural choices. The framework will provide a layer of abstraction to be able to disconnect from these particular technologies, should, for example, other protocols become more important.

Service Agencies

Agents seem to be a very natural way for describing typical scenarios of Web usage. They are the machine representation of human beings who right now have to do most of the work manually. Thus the WASP framework will provide means to define a variety of agents: mobile, autonomous, reactive, and so forth. To enhance the usefulness of the framework, it is set up to allow agents to be self-describing, thus automatically turning agents into services that can be used by others and integrated via standard interfaces. This allows for wide-spread service dissemination and easy integration with other systems.

It will be especially important to integrate current agent research into this framework layer; efforts like DAML (DARPA Agent Mark-up Language) allow for powerful modeling means to devise agents and agencies.

Data and Information Gathering

The framework must provide for means to accumulate data, compare it, and reason about it. Data might be persistent (to allow for agents with increasing reasoning power) or transient (to model short-effect tasks), and data should be interchangeable between different agents. It must be possible to integrate ontologies to allow for a solidified view of the "world" (in regards to the agent or agents).

Personalization Integration

It must be easy to integrate personalization technologies. At the most basic level, it should be possible to specify user preferences and dislikes, and to integrate them in the reasoning and retrieval process to improve the quality of the returned information.

The HIVE: Semantic Web Brokering Simplified for WASP Agents

Web servers have been the technical foundation for the success of the World Wide Web. Applications servers have been a successful model in abstracting from the everyday chores of building complex applications and thus form the basis for modern large-scale business applications. Thus it seems natural to evolve to Semantic Information Servers that provide a corresponding environment for Semantic Web agents specialized on utilizing the Semantic Web resources to provide information services to the end user.

Application servers offer persistence, transactions, distributed processing, and scalability if the software complies with a predefined component model (e.g., Java 2 Enterprise Edition / J2EE). This allows developers to focus on the actual task at hand, for example, implementing the business logic for a complex transaction portal. In our view, a similar model is required for Semantic Web applications based on agent societies. Different layers of abstractions will allow concentrating on functional requirements and help to abstract from the details of the implementation. In the same way that a J2EE application server takes away the details of persistence from the developer, a Semantic Information Server can abstract from the details of, for example, storing semantic information, retrieving it, and reasoning about it. This holds true for other areas as well (e.g., information recovery from the Web, resource management for agents, and communication between members of local and remote agencies). Within the WASP framework, we intend to call the Semantic Information Servers a HIVE (not an acronym but rather a play of words continuing the WASP idea).

These ideas result in the infrastructure diagram in Figure 1.

Figure 1. HIVE architecture

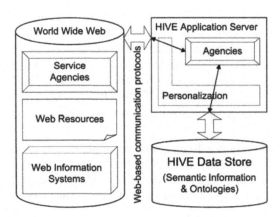

Important Semantic Web Research Areas

In this section we intend to describe a few of the more important current research topics needing to be solved to further the development of Semantic Web services:

- Ontology integration and translation is a major problem for interconnecting distributed services and systems (Gruber, 1993; Heflin & Hendler, 2000; Heflin et al., 1999): How can differing ontologies for related topics be mapped on each other?

- Web Service orchestration, interoperation, and transaction handling needs to be standardized (UDDI, 2001; Web Services Choreography Requirements, 2003; Web Services Transaction, 2002).

- Standards to allow for personalization need to find wide acceptance (PICS, n.d.; Stahl & Völter, 2005; for discussions on currently-available, yet still rarely-used standards).

Remaining Challenges

Besides the technical questions which currently enjoy most attention, a multitude of additional topics needs to be investigated before distributed agent systems and the Semantic Web become truly viable. A few of them are:

- **Modeling challenges:** In which way can Semantic Web systems be modeled so that a broad user base will be able to understand and utilize these technologies? We make an early attempt to answer this question in the last major part of this chapter.

- **Cost challenges:** Who is going to pay for the resources being used in distributed agent networks? It is safe to assume that such agent services will be a lot more cost-intensive than the "simple Web information platforms of today" (e.g., Web servers).

- **Pricing challenges:** Already now there is a tendency to commercialize high-quality services. How will future information systems be rated in terms of usage fees if the component services of some complex service (e.g., the logistics service, the currency conversion service, and the mapping service for a complex online order service) each incur fees, but the user of the complex service might not necessarily add to the income of the complex service provider (e.g., because the user decides against buying something after getting the shipment information)?

- **Business challenges:** What are viable business models for Semantic Web agencies and services?

- **Quality challenges:** How will services be able to guarantee a certain level of quality if they rely on the data collected in the Semantic Web, an information storage that will be as inaccurate as the currently-available World Wide Web (mostly because everyone will be able to put up whatever he or she deems correct and appropriate)?

- **Trust challenges:** How can I be sure that not only the quality of results gained by Semantic Web analysis is sufficient for me but also correct at all?

- **Workflow challenges:** How can complex workflows (like booking a complete holiday trip) be orchestrated when dynamic service directories, user preferences, potentially faulty information, and other factors need to be considered?

- **Performance challenges:** How must services be constructed to be able to retrieve useful data in a timely manner from the Semantic Web, a Web that is infinitely more complex to search compared to current search engines and technologies due to the far more involved complexity created by allowing inferences, conclusions, and reasoning about information?

- **Security challenges:** How can personal and private information be protected from prying eyes? What new security challenges arise from the architectural decisions made for the WASP framework?

- **Legal challenges:** Who will be held responsible for incorrect, imprecise, or faulty information derived from or modified by Semantic Web content?

- **Architectural challenges:** What are the best-of-breed software infrastructures/ application architectures to allow for a rapid dissemination of the technologies involved? How can user and developer acceptance be increased?

Requirements Analysis Concerning Semantic Web Architectures

As explained in our example Semantic Web architecture, different technology layers usually will be found in a Semantic Web-based system. In this section, we will continue the example by analyzing the essential requirements to be fulfilled both by our similar architectures in order to be Semantic Web-ready. We will start at the bottom-most layer (the database tier) and work upwards from there. Differences compared to standard enterprise architectures will be explained in the individual sections.

Requirements for the HIVE Data Store

The HIVE Data Store will store and evaluate data gained by analyzing Semantic Web resources. To provide a useful and extensible model, the following functional and technical requirements must be taken into account:

- The HIVE Data Store should be independent from the specific type of storage (DBMS, RDF store, flat file, some kind of network service). Thus it will be possible to choose the best type of storage for a given situation. Additionally this is a basic requirement to be able to exchange data store implementations as technology and research continue to evolve.

- The HIVE Data Store must not assume that data is correct, complete, or unambiguous. The Internet by design is a place where data is provided in a spontaneous and improvised manner. Thus the Data Store must be able to cope with such data. This is also a major difference from classical enterprise systems, where usually the utmost care is taken to insert only verified, correct, and unambiguous data into databases.

- The HIVE Data Store must provide inference support. The true value of the Semantic Web can be used only by analyzing the gathered data and drawing conclusions. Thus inference support is paramount. Nonetheless there must not be any assumptions about the specific inference approaches being used, again to allow flexibility and configurability.

- The HIVE Data Store must be able to access data from a variety of sources. This is absolutely necessary due to the size and varied nature of the underlying information sources. The Internet itself is just too large to be kept on one server or a whole farm of servers; while in most cases an application will not need to access all the information available on the whole of the Internet, for some of the more exciting Semantic Web applications it will be a necessity to be at least potentially able to access all available information.

- The HIVE Data Store must be able to integrate ontologies into its repository. Ontologies are the basic mechanism to define the meaning of concepts modeled in, for example, RDF structures. An important add-on functionality will be the ability to compare ontologies and map them onto each other to be able to integrate differing ontologies designed for the same problem area.

- The HIVE Data Store must include a facility to manage the credibility of sensitive information. Mission-critical data must only be accepted from sources that are able to authenticate themselves and prove their credibility (e.g., with certificates or similar mechanisms).

- The HIVE Data Store should be able to organize itself physically, to manage its resources, and to restructure information based on dynamic changes of the environment. This is an optional but highly recommended functionality, as it is to be expected that the Data Store of a widely-used system will grow with leaps and bounds. To remain efficient and to conserve resources, the Data Store itself has to take responsibility for this.

- The HIVE Data Store must explicitly consider data retention periods, along with models and algorithms for purging; otherwise, the data cached there will rapidly become stale and will overload the database.

- The HIVE Data Store must provide a management facility so that external users can examine the state of the server, the data, and the rules accumulated in the store. Additionally, typical functionality must be provided to configure the data sources and control resource allocation of the store. It should be noted that the management facility might have a very different outlook depending on the underlying storage mechanism being used for the specific server.

To be able to incorporate these widely varying requirements, an abstraction layer will be required through which all HIVE Data Store access operations will be routed. This will add functionality as required (e.g., by defining a HIVE Data Store proxy that collects requests, runs through a caching layer to increase performance, and then delegates unanswered requests to the actual physical or distributed Data Store).

Requirements for the HIVE Agent Server

The HIVE Application Server is responsible for running the various agents that implement the business logic side of the framework and access all other components to achieve their goals. The following functional and technical requirements need to be taken into account:

- The HIVE Agent Server must provide a run-time environment for varying agents that share a common interface, as defined by the WASP framework. There must be support for both mobile and static agents to allow for a wide range of application scenarios.

- The HIVE Agent Server must provide a security layer that controls resource access for all agents operating on the server. This is an absolute necessity for servers incorporating mobile agents and allowing mobile agents to migrate from one server to another.

- The HIVE Agent Server must provide access to the HIVE Data Store in an abstracted and generalized manner. Agents must not be required to know about the details of data storage or inference.

- The HIVE Agent Server must provide access to the "outside world" so that the sensors of the agents involved can operate. The HIVE Agent Server may modify perceived data based on personalization and security rules.

- The HIVE Agent Server must allow for communication using a variety of agent communication languages (ACLs) to be able to integrate a variety of agent systems. This probably will include the necessity to provide translation services between different agent communication languages in order to allow communication between agents of different breeds.

- The HIVE Agent Server must provide a management facility so that external users can examine the state of the server and the agents running on it. The management facility must include all kinds of standard management functionality to allocate resources, control permission, direct agents and so on.

- The WASP Agent Interface must be structured so that existing agent frameworks can be easily integrated into the system while there also must be enough room to develop new concepts and architectures. Additionally, the interface must be extensible, so that incremental extensions may be made both forward and backward compatibly, allowing upgrades to clients or servers in either order.

Interestingly, the requirements concerning the actual agents are very small; when examining, for example, the proposed scope of software agents in Gilbert, Aparicio, Atkinson, Brady, Ciccarino, Grosof, et al. (1995), the only functional requirements that must be provided by the HIVE Agent Server is mobility. Everything related to the intelligence aspects of agents can be modeled in the HIVE Data Store and the agent implementation. All other aspects are determined by the actual agent implementation.

Figure 2. Scope of intelligent agents (Adapted from Gilbert, et al., 1995)

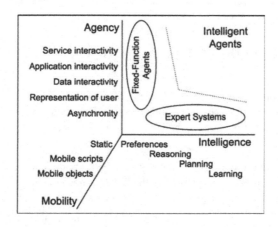

Requirements for the HIVE Personalization Layer

The HIVE Personalization layer modifies both the perceived external environment (e.g., the Internet and other servers) and the perceived internal environment (especially the information gathered in the HIVE Data Stores). To provide a meaningful level of personalization, the following functionalities are of utmost importance:

- The HIVE Personalization Layer must provide permission-based personalization so that the perceived environment adjusts based upon the permissions of each individual agent. Permissions will have to be modeled on per-server-, per-agent- and per-user-base in order to be fully effective.

- The HIVE Personalization Layer must be able to handle agent-specific inference rules in order to modify and control the inference process based on agent preferences.

- The HIVE Personalization Layer must be able to handle user-specific inference rules in order to modify and control the inference process based on agent preferences.

Requirements for the HIVE Communication Layer

The HIVE Communication Layer connects the HIVE Agents with external systems (e.g., the Internet, other servers, and so on).

The argumentation in the sections above shows that the HIVE Communication Layer also should serve another important purpose: The various components of the WASP Framework need to be connected in a system-independent and flexible way; by using the HIVE Communication Layer not only for inter-system but also for intra-system communication, several powerful synergy effects can be utilized:

- Communication uses but one protocol layer. This makes it much simpler to distribute agents, objects, and servers since no separate protocols are required for communication and information exchange. The implementation of the HIVE server itself is simplified, too.

- Intra-system services (e.g., resource management, process supervision, and more) can, if wanted, be modeled as agents to use the infrastructure provided by the WASP framework to implement the WASP framework itself. This is analogous to database systems that store database meta-information in their own database structures or compilers used to compile themselves, and serve as a good proof of concept for the simplicity and validity of the architecture, once implemented.

- The communication layer must integrate mechanisms to transparently handle both scalability of the system as a whole and to increase the fault tolerance when concerned with individual requests.

To be able to fulfill these expectations, a number of functional requirements must be considered:

- The HIVE Communication Layer must be implemented with a system-independent protocol and communication API. It must be possible to exchange atomic and complex information objects. Web Services and the associated communication protocols (e.g., SOAP) will serve nicely as a basis for the HIVE Communication Layer.

- The HIVE Communication Layer must be able to communicate with external systems through a standard protocol. Otherwise communication would be too limited for a reasonable system trying to support Semantic Web applications.

- The HIVE Communication Layer must provide some means to execute a lookup for external services and resources. Services like UDDI (Heflin & Hendler, 2000) and maybe also LDAP are typical candidates to be integrated. Although this might seem like a rather minor and trivial point at first (especially given the fact that more or less established technologies like LDAP and UDDI already exist), it must be stressed that the integration of a powerful lookup service for other services and resources is of major importance, especially so when considering the stress on "fault tolerance" and "scalability".

Scalability is rather easy to achieve in some respects if a lookup mechanism exists: Requests for services, on one hand, can be dispatched to service endpoints based on a variety of load-balancing strategies and algorithms; only imagination limits the possible scenarios ranging from simple round-robin algorithms to elaborate agent-based schemes where agents monitor the CPU load on connected systems and use that information to control the dispatching of further incoming requests. Hardware-based load-balancing mechanisms can also be easily integrated as the endpoint of a service, and can represent a façade for a server cluster with a hardware load balancer handling the incoming requests. Naturally these techniques can also be combined.

To be able to effectively handle faults, several approaches can be implemented; the important concern is whether service faults on the actual service level (e.g., complete service failures due to unavailable servers, etc.) or on the logical level (e.g., service errors, etc.) are examined. The communication layer can easily enhance the fault tolerance of a Hyperservice-based system on the service level: A simple protocol handler extension can be integrated in order to allow the resubmission of service requests if a service endpoint fails to respond. This behavior can be enhanced by integrating a regular availability check into the service/resource registry to be able to filter out or deactivate temporarily-unavailable endpoints and thus reduce the overall network load. Errors on the logical level cannot be handled in a transparent level in the HIVE communication layer without extensive semantic descriptions of the services themselves. Since the idea of the HIVE architecture is to provide a simple and extensible architecture. For now, no logic fault handling at all will be integrated into the communication layer. Future research will have to show whether such extensions can be integrated in a simple yet effective manner.

Finally it is important to note that, as the internal HIVE services also can and should make use of the service and resource registries, the HIVE system itself transparently benefits from the integration of the features concerning fault handling and scalability as described above.

- The HIVE Communication Layer must be system- and programming language-independent. Again, Web Services and the associated protocols nicely fit this requirement.
- The HIVE Communication Layer must use standardized protocols to be able to connect to as many systems as possible.

Common Requirements

Finally there are some common requirements that are shared by all frameworks like, for example, compositionality, reusability and extensibility, that must be taken into account. Of special importance for the WASP framework is language independence (even if the reference implementation might use a specific language like Java or C#), in order to be able to connect as many systems as possible. Since these requirements are not unique or special to the presented topic, we will not elaborate them any further within the bounds of this chapter.

The Requirements Analysis in Review

In order to make the Semantic Web as accessible as possible, a highly-abstracted framework with open interfaces and simple overall concepts is very important, especially since the underlying technologies mentioned above individually already require a high level of expertise to be able to use them effectively. We have shown that such an infrastructure framework is defined by a manageable amount of requirements, and that available standards (ready or just evolving) already cover a lot of ground. The next challenge is to provide a means of integration that is simple yet powerful and extensible at the same time. This will be the focus of the rest of this chapter.

Model-driven Software Development for the Semantic Web

In this final section, we will try to give an answer on how to increase the acceptance of Semantic Web technologies by leveraging recent developments in the area of model-driven software development (MDSD). So far we have talked about how to simplify the development of Semantic Web-based systems, and this is the classical perspective of most approaches available today.

Now we would like to concentrate on a new way of approaching software development. Model-Driven Architecture (MDA) and Model-Driven Software Development (MDSD) both strive to simplify software development by automatically generating executable code from models (Stahl & Völter, 2005). These approaches seem to be well-suited for Semantic Web development considering the implied semantic definitions of models, agents, and ontologies, for example, provided by DAML. Nonetheless, one inherent weakness is left unconsidered by these approaches: Both MDA and MDSD require a sound understanding of the underlying technological and theoretical foundations, combined with a good amount of experience about how to model systems in the best way. This does not really help in transferring the conceptual knowledge that software customers possess into software systems as the developers still concentrate on building sound technological models and keep all the minute details under control.

We thus propose the next step in model-driven technologies, which we have named "Conceptual Model-Driven Software Development (CMDSD)".

The Notion of Conceptual Model-Driven Software Development (CMDSD)

The basic idea of our methodology of Conceptual Model-Driven Software Development (CMDSD) is to model systems through intuitive models on the conceptual level. These models must not be based on one global theory (like MDA with the Meta-Object Facility (MOF)), but rather utilize the most pragmatic theoretical foundation possible for the problem at hand. Additionally, the model should abstract as much as possible from the technological details of the system and focus on the conceptual facets which are possible. Models are aggregated into more complex models while great care is taken to provide a simple transformation from the individual model to the run-time system representation of the model. This allows software developers and architects to work together with customers and concentrate on the business side of the system; a simple and effective transformation from business problem to system representation is assumed. Existing design patterns support this notion.

Of greatest importance is the way in which CMDSD-based models are made available to the conceptual experts at hand: We require that models use a language (in the formal meaning) that comes as close as possible to the tools and ways used by the target audience to express their concepts. Thus the way of modeling will differ between areas of expertise. While this might feel like a disadvantage at first because software engineers will have to learn many differing modeling languages, we regard this as an advantage for a simple reason: The rules for transforming/executing these models need only be understood by a very small number of persons, namely those persons who build the actual transformers or interpreters. In contrast the user base for the concepts modeled typically will be very large in comparison. Thus it seems more reasonable to build models which are intuitive for the end user base and not the (intermediate) developers. Additionally it benefits the developers by forcing them to concentrate on the conceptual aspects of development and to hide the technical details.

One might argue that this is just a step back to the "model wars" in the years from 1990 to 2000 before the advent of UML. We argue that UML and similar OMG approaches did not really solve those problems as far as the actual specification of conceptual tasks goes. UML provides very effective models in order to specify technical details, but those technical details, most of the time, are of no interest at all to the conceptual experts who require a solution for their non-technical problems. The gap between available means to specify technical aspects and the lack of means to formally specify the purely conceptual parts of a problem leads to a high number of failing software projects (failing software projects are those that fail to meet their goals in time, money, or quality).

Current studies concerning success and failure of software projects seem to prove this point (Standish Group, n.d.): More than 75% of all failed software projects failed due to problems with requirements analysis and errors in the resulting specifications. We thus argue that more problem-oriented models are a must-have in order to facilitate the communication between technical and non-technical experts which work together on a complex project.

Additionally, our CMDSD methodology requires Rapid Prototyping (Reilly, 1996) as a means to be easily able to verify specifications.

Using CMDSD to Build Semantic Web Servers

How does all this help with Semantic Web development? Many of the underlying technologies for the Semantic Web are highly complicated and very involved. Rare is the architect or developer who understands agent technologies, Web service specifications (in their ever-growing numbers), and the details of building efficient application servers all at once. If architects and developers trained in more than one of these topics are already rare, how can we then assume that the end users for Semantic Web technologies (e.g., the people building Websites today) will be able to grasp the varying concepts and details of implementation?

As explained in the sections above, one of the research directions currently being actively investigated is the research in semantically-rich descriptions for Web services. Now imagine a development system that can understand existing semantic descriptions of services, load them, and generate definition and aggregation interfaces for such services. Suddenly developers and customers can work together in a semantically-rich environment to model the business side of systems and, by using a framework like the WASP framework, can mostly ignore the technological side as the underlying framework handles configuration and assembly.

While we still need to work on the actual implementation of a server that can handle arbitrary agent frameworks and expose them as Web Services, a specialized server for one type of agent system is within reach. Additionally, many projects will be able to be handled today by using but one technology, as the integration of differing agent systems requires quite a bit of research in the future. The next section will show how such a system can be integrated into existing application and Web servers with CMDSD methods.

A CMDSD-Based Approach for Agent and Service Integration

First of all, we specify the most important requirements that must be fulfilled in order to make it simple to use Semantic Web technologies. Please note that these definitions are flexible and based on our point of view; different focuses will yield different definitions. We intend to base our initial CMDSD-based model on the following requirements:

1. The model must be formulated in such a way that current Web developers will feel immediately comfortable using its syntax.

2. The model must hide the complexities of both the underlying technology and the integration questions popping up as soon as actual integration into an application or Web server comes to mind.

3. The model must allow for flexible data structures to both be sent to the agents and be received from the agents.

4. It must be possible to modify the data in both directions.

5. Standards should be used to implement the model transformation/executions.

To fulfill these requirements, we make the following decisions:

1. The model will be formulated in "an XML-like syntax similar to HTML" (see below). This will allow current Web developers to easily grasp the concepts. As a side effect, the model definitions for now will be included in the definitions for HTML pages. The special tags defined to describe WASP models will be shown below.

2. The model for now will only fulfill the most basic requirements of a basic IO system. Complex logic will be hidden in the underlying agents and processes. The model is thus only concerned with retrieving data from some source and sending (other) data to a sink (which provides the results as a response).

3. Technically we will assume that some kind of extension of the underlying server that analyzes the HTML code before it is sent to the client, extracts the WASP-specific definitions, processes them, and re-integrates the results of those definitions. Possible technical solutions could be Apache Plug-Ins (Bloom, 2002), Java Servlet Filters or

Java Servlets (Bell, Loton, Allamaraju, Dalton, Brown, Harbourne-Thomas, et al., 2002) or ISAPI extensions for the Microsoft Internet Information Server (Genusa, Addison, & Clark, 1999).

4.   XML will be used to represent data (Bray et al., 2000).

5.   Simple transformations will be handled by XSL transformations (Cagle, Cornig, & Diamond, 2001). Complex data transformations will require specialized agents or Web services.

6.   Services and agents will be represented by URNs (Uniform Resource Names) (URI Planning Interest Group, n.d.) in the models. The interpretation of those models will, for now, be server-specific, although future systems should strive to standardize URNs in the same way as XML namespaces.

Based on these requirements and definitions, we now will provide a simple example for a Hyperservice call. Note that in the HTML snippet in Figure 3, all WASP- (and model-) specific elements use the "wasp:" namespace.

The interpretation of the given code snippet is intuitive if you are even slightly versed in HTML; and now about the meaning of XSLT:

•   The tag "<wasp:hyper service="urn:wasp:service:GetStockQuotes">" defines a hyperservice call. The service itself is identified by the given URN. The specifics of connecting to the service are completely hidden from the user (e.g., the Web page author) and must be configured in the server environment. A definition of the interface of that service also exists separately and is fulfilled implicitly by the next two lines of code (see below).

•   Two parameters are defined:

   o   The parameter "verbosity" is set to the value "detailed" which (intuitively) means that a detailed list of stock quotes is requested.

   o   The parameter "stockMarketLocation" is defined dynamically (as indicated by

Figure 3

```
...
<table width="100%">
<wasp:transform xslt="/xslt/
CreateRowsFromStockQuotes.xslt">
  <wasp:hyper service="urn:wasp:service:GetStockQuotes">
    <wasp:parameter name="verbosity" value="detailed"/>
    <wasp:parameter uses="stockMarketLocation"/>
  </wasp:hyper>
</wasp:transform>
</table>
...
```

Figure 4

```
...
<table width="100%">

<wasp:hyper
service="urn:wasp:service:CreateRowsFromStockQuotes">

  <wasp:parameter name="list">

    <wasp:hyper service="urn:wasp:service:GetStockQuotes">

      <wasp:parameter name="verbosity" value="detailed"/>

      <wasp:parameter uses="stockMarketLocation"/>

    </wasp:hyper>

  </wasp:parameter>

</wasp:hyper>

</table>
...
```

the attribute "uses" instead of "value" as in the previous example); "uses" implies that the parameter value is taken from the request parameters. This allows
defining parameters dynamically by, for example, building dynamic URLs or
submitting parameters with a form.

- The result of the service request is transformed using XSLT as defined in the enclosing
  tag "<wasp:transform xslt="/xslt/CreateRowsFromStockQuotes.xslt">>". This special
  tag applies an XSL transformation to the body of the tag (which in turn is produced by
  dynamically executing the service call explained above). Again an implicit knowledge
  about the result structure is assumed. Given a meaningful XSL transformation, the
  stock quote list (in XML format) will be transformed into a user-friendly and nicely
  formatted HTML representation of the data.

In order to allow for more complex structures, we will allow extended parameter definitions
so that the results of calls can be, in turn, reused as parameters for other calls. Assuming the
existence of a service to transform stock quote lists from XML format to HTML, we could
rewrite the code above in the way Figure 4 shows.

In this revised example, the parameter named "list" is derived by calling the above-mentioned stock quote service and using the result of that service as the input for the second
service. In a certain way, we pipe inputs and outputs in a comparable way to UNIX shell
commands. The true power of these rather simple models becomes obvious when chaining
several services (Figure 5).

In this example, three input parameters are processed: For a given user ("userID"), a destination ("destination"), and an indicated price limit ("maxPrice"), first the list of preferred
airports is determined by calling one service, and then the available flights are searched by
calling a second service, and combining both dynamic parameters and results from user
interaction. In this way complex scenarios can be based on a very simple model.

Also the level of abstraction is very high: Assume, for example, that all XML data structures
are connected to an ontology. If service A requires input conforming to ontology o_A and re-

Figure 5

```
...
<table width="100%">
<wasp:hyper service="urn:wasp:service:FindFlights">
  <wasp:parameter name="airportList">
    <wasp:hyper
service="urn:wasp:service:FindPreferredAirports">
      <wasp:parameter uses="userID"/>
    </wasp:hyper>
  </wasp:parameter>
  <wasp:parameter name="benefits">
    <wasp:hyper
service="urn:wasp:service:FindPersonalBenefits">
      <wasp:parameter uses="userID"/>
    </wasp:hyper>
  </wasp:parameter>
  <wasp:parameter uses="destination"/>
  <wasp:parameter uses="maxPrice"/>
</wasp:hyper>
</table>
...
```

Figure 6

```
...
<table width="100%">
<wasp:hyper>
  <wasp:parameter name="service">
    <wasp:hyper service="urn:wasp:service:ServiceLookup">
      <wasp:parameter name="serviceName"
value="FindFlights"/>
      <wasp:parameter name="typeSpecialization"
value="lastMinute"/>
    </wasp:hyper>
  </wasp:parameter>
  <wasp:parameter name="airportList">
    <wasp:hyper
service="urn:wasp:service:FindPreferredAirports">
      <wasp:parameter uses="userID"/>
    </wasp:hyper>
  </wasp:parameter>
  <wasp:parameter name="benefits">
    <wasp:hyper
service="urn:wasp:service:FindPersonalBenefits">
      <wasp:parameter uses="userID"/>
    </wasp:hyper>
  </wasp:parameter>
  <wasp:parameter uses="destination"/>
  <wasp:parameter uses="maxPrice"/>
</wasp:hyper>
</table>
...
```

ceives its input from a service B which in turn is only able to produce results conforming to ontology o_B the runtime environment can (transparently for the model builder!) search for a transformation rule $o_A \rightarrow o_B$ and apply it, all this without requiring any in-depth knowledge of the "end user" (the HTML modeler/designer). Additionally, it will be possible to optimize the system by changing the configuration and not the model; the interpreter for the model will automatically take into account the new settings. Finally a change of technologies also is transparent for the "end user" (e.g., the page designer) as the special tags introduced above are independent of the implementation.

The final aspect of flexibility to be introduced within the context of this chapter is a way to an actual service lookup. To allow for this, we now also allow the service URN to be provided dynamically (Figure 6).

Another simple extension of the model focuses on the "hyperlinked" nature of the Web: By not only accepting special URNs but generic URIs, it easily becomes possible to link separate systems into a more complex system. The following example illustrates this by using external URIs for some services from the previous example (Figure 7).

Figure 7

```
...
<table width="100%">
<wasp:hyper>
  <wasp:parameter name="service">
    <wasp:hyper service="http://www.quinscape.de/services/
ServiceLookup">
      <wasp:parameter name="serviceName"
value="FindFlights"/>
      <wasp:parameter name="typeSpecialization"
value="lastMinute"/>
    </wasp:hyper>
  </wasp:parameter>
  <wasp:parameter name="airportList">
    <wasp:hyper service="https://www.foo.bar/
FindPreferredAirports">
      <wasp:parameter uses="userID"/>
    </wasp:hyper>
  </wasp:parameter>
  <wasp:parameter name="benefits">
    <wasp:hyper
service="urn:wasp:service:FindPersonalBenefits">
      <wasp:parameter uses="userID"/>
    </wasp:hyper>
  </wasp:parameter>
  <wasp:parameter uses="destination"/>
  <wasp:parameter uses="maxPrice"/>
</wasp:hyper>
</table>
...
```

Again most of the underlying complexity is moved to the run-time environment which has to determine the actual service descriptions, match it against the expected interfaces, call the remote service with an appropriate protocol, accept the results, and so forth. Even details like session-based authentication might be handled transparently for the page designer by the underlying framework.

The formal semantics of the model are beyond the scope of this chapter but should be intuitive enough to derive for the interested reader.

Implementing the Proposed CMDSD Model

The most basic component required to implement the model proposed in the previous sections is the actual tag parser component. If, for example, a J2EE application server were used as the run-time environment, it would be a natural fit to implement the special WASP tags as a Tag Library (Brown, 2003) because tag libraries integrate in a very natural way into the run-time environment. The more complicated components concern the actual integration of services and agents. A way needs to be found to describe service descriptions from agent specifications/implementations. An efficient system needs to be implemented to allow for ontology comparisons and transformations. Finally, a performance analysis of the implementation is a necessity in order to estimate how well the implementation scales under real-world conditions. Current research projects work on answering these questions.

Summary and Conclusion

In this chapter, we have shown how viable Semantic Web Frameworks can be developed with currently-existing technologies. We have underlined the importance of providing ways to allow for an easy adoption of Semantic Web technologies lest all efforts are moot due to not being accepted by the public. We have defined our notion of Hyperservices and presented the WASP architecture which facilitates the creation of extendable Semantic Web systems. We have analyzed the requirements for general Semantic Web frameworks and used the results thus gained in order to describe a conceptual model for our WASP framework. In order to facilitate these endeavors we have described our "Conceptual Model-Driven Software Development (CMDSD)" approach and given examples to illustrate how easy a model for accessing Hyperservices can be defined.

By providing such a foundation, we have disconnected undergoing research in the Semantic Web area from the need to start making these technologies available for a wider audience.

Background Information

This chapter is based on published and well-accepted papers by the authors as well as their continuing research in the areas of Semantic Web, Agent Systems, and Conceptual Model-Driven Software Development, among them Biskup, Marx Gómez, and Rautenstrauch (2005), Biskup and Marx Gómez (2004a, 2004b), and Biskup and Marx Gómez (2005).

References

Bell, J., Loton, T., Allamaraju, S., Dalton, S., Brown, S., Harbourne-Thomas, A. et al. (2002). *Professional Java Servlets 2.3*. Birmingham, UK: Wrox Press Ltd.

Benjamins, R. (2003). *Agents and the semantic Web: A business perspective*. Paper presented at Agent Technology Conference (ATC, 2003), Barcelona, Spain.

Benjamins, V. R., Fensel, D., & Asunción, G. P. (1998). Knowledge management through ontologies. In *Proceedings of the second international conference on practical aspects of knowledge management (PAKM-98)* (pp. 5.1-5.12).

Bergman, M. K. (n.d.). *The deep Web: Surfacing hidden value*. Retrieved February 12, 2006, from http://citeseer.ist.psu.edu/bergman00deep.html

Berners-Lee, T. (1998). *Semantic Web Roadmap*. Retrieved February 12, 2006, from http://www.w3c.org/DesignIssues/Semantic.html

Berners-Lee, T. (2000). *Weaving the Web*. London: TEXERE Publishing ltd.

Berners-Lee, T., Hendler, J., & Lassila, O. (2001). The semantic Web. *Scientific American, May 2001 issue*. Retrieved February 20, 2006, from http://www.sciam.com/article.cfm?articleID=00048144-10D2-1C70-84A9809EC588EF21

Biskup, T., & Marx Gómez, J. (2004a). Building blocks of a semantic Web framework—Requirements analysis and architectural implications. In *Proceedings of 3rd International Workshop on Web Semantics—WebS'04, in conjunction with the 14th International Conference on Database and Expert Systems Applications DEXA 2004—Zaragoza, Spain* (pp. 214-218).

Biskup, T., & Marx Gómez, J. (2004b). Component requirements for a universal semantic Web framework. *Semantic Web and Information Systems, AIS SIGSEMIS Bulletin, 1*(3) (October Issue), 25-28.

Biskup, T., & Marx Gómez, J. (2005). *Building a semantic Web framework with reusable and configurable core technologies*. Paper presented at IRMA 2005, San Diego, CA.

Biskup, T., Marx Gómez, J., & Rautenstrauch, C. (2005). The WASP framework—Bridging the gap between the Web of systems, the Web of services, and the Web of semantics with agent technology. *International Journal of Intelligent Information Technologies (IJIIT) 1*(2), 68-82.

Bloom, R. B. (2002). *Apache Server 2.0. The complete reference*. Berkeley, CA: Osborne McGraw-Hill.

Bray, T., Paoli, J., Maler, E., Sperberg-McQueen, C. M., & Paoli, J. (Ed.). (2000). *Extensible Markup Language (XML) 1.0. W3C Recommendation.* Retrieved February 12, 2006, from http://www.w3c.org/TR/REC-xml

Brickley, D., & Guha, R. V. (Ed.). (2000). *Resource Description Framework (RDF) Schema Specification 1.0. W3C Candidate Recommendation.* Retrieved February 12, 2006, from http://www.w3c.org/TR/RDF-schema

Brown, S. (2003). *Professional JSP tag libraries.* Birmingham, UK: Wrox Press Ltd.

Cagle, K., Cornig, M., & Diamond, J. (2001). *Professional XSL.* Birmingham, UK: Wrox Press Ltd.

Christensen, E., Curbera, F., Meredith, G., & Weerawarana, S. (2001). *Web Services Description Language (WSDL) 1.1. W3C Note.* Retrieved February 12, 2006, from http://www.w3c.org/TR/wsdl

Ciancarini, P., & Wooldridge, M. J. (Ed.). (2001). First International Workshop on Agent-Oriented Software Engineering. *Lecture Notes in Computer Science, Vol. 1957.* Berlin, Germany: Springer.

Dale, J. (2002). *Exposing Web services.* Paper presented at Agentcities.NET iD2, Lisbon, Portugal.

DAML+OIL (2000). Retrieved February 12, 2006, from http://www.daml.org/language/

De Bruijn, J., Fensel, D., Keller, U., & Lara, R. (2005). Using the Web service modelling ontology to enable semantic e-business. *Communications of the ACM, 48*(12), 43-47.

Finin, T., Labrou, Y., & Mayfield, J. (1997). KQML as an agent communication language. In J. M. Bradshaw (Ed.), *Software agents* (pp. 291-316). Cambridge, MA: AAAI/MIT Press.

Genusa, S., Addison, B., & Clark, A. (1999). *Special edition using ISAPI.* Indianapolis, IN: Que Publishing.

Gilbert, D., Aparicio, M., Atkinson, B., Brady, S., Ciccarino, J., Grosof, B., et al. (1995). *IBM intelligent agent strategy.* IBM Corporation.

Gottschalk, K., Graham, S., Kreger, H., & Snell, J. (2002). Introduction to Web services architecture. *IBM Systems Journal, 41*(2).

Gourley, D., & Totty, B. (2002). *HTTP: The definitive guide.* O'Reilly.

Gruber, T. R. (1993). A translation approach to portable ontologies. *Knowledge Acquisition, 5*(2), 199-220.

Harper, S., & Bechhofer, S. (2005). Semantic triage for increased Web accessibility. *IBM Systems Journal, 44*(3), 637-648.

Heflin, J., & Hendler, J. (2000). Dynamic ontologies on the Web. In *Proceedings of the Seventeenth National Conference on Artificial Intelligence (AAAI-2000),* (pp. 443-449) Menlo Park, CA. Cambridge, MA: AAAI/MIT Press.

Heflin, J., Hendler, J., & Luke, S. (1999). *SHOE: A knowledge representation language for Internet applications* (Tech. Rep. No. CS-TR-4078 / UMIACS TR-99-71). College Park, Maryland: University of Maryland, Department of Computer Science.

Hendler, J. (2001). Agents and the semantic Web. *IEEE Intelligent Systems, 16*(2), 67-73.

Hendler, J., & McGuiness, D. L. (2000). The DARPA agent markup language. *IEEE Intelligent Systems, 15*(6).

Joy, B. (2000). Shift from protocols to agents. *IEEE Internet Computing, 4*(1), 63-64.

Lassila, O. (2000). The resource description framework. *IEEE Intelligent Systems, 15*(6), 67-9.

Lin, H. K., Harding, J. A., & Teoh, P. C. (2005). An inter-enterprise semantic Web system to support information autonomy and conflict moderation. In *Proceedings of IMechE 2005: Vol. 219, Part B* (pp. 903-911).

McIlraith, S. A., Son, T. C., & Zeng, H. (2001). Semantic Web services. *IEEE Intelligent Systems, 16*(2), 46-53.

Metcalfe, B. (2000). The next-generation Internet. *IEEE Internet Computing, 4*(1), 58-59.

Mitra, N. (Ed.) (2001). *SOAP Version 1.2, Part 0: Primer, Part 1: Messaging Framework, Part 2: Adjuncts. W3C Working Draft.* Retrieved February 12, 2006, from http://www.w3c.org/TR/soap-part0, http://www.w3c.org/TR/soap-part1, http://www.w3c.org/TR/soap-part2

Object Management Group (n.d.). Retrieved February 12, 2006, from http://www.omg.org

O'Brien, P. D., & Nicol, R. C. (1998). FIPA—Towards a standard for software agents. *BT Technology Journal, 16*(3), 51.

Platform for Internet Content Selection (PICS) (n.d.). Retrieved February 12, 2006, from http://www.w3.org/PICS

Reilly, J. P. (1996). *Rapid prototyping: Moving to business-centric development.* Coriolis Group (Sd). Boston/London: International Thomson Computer Press

Stahl, T., & Völter, M. (2005). *Modellgetriebene Softwareentwicklung. Techniken, Engineering, Management.* Heidelberg, Germany: dpunkt.verlag.

The Standish Group (n.d.). *Chaos Chronicles Version 3.* Retrieved February 12, 2006, from http://www.standishgroup.com/chaos/index.php

UDDI Technical White Paper (2001). Retrieved February 12, 2006, from http://www.uddi.org

URI Planning Interest Group, W3C/IETF (n.d.). *URIs, URLs, and URNs: Clarifications and Recommendations 1.0.* Retrieved February 12, 2006, from http://www.w3.org/TR/uri-clarification/

Web Authoring Statistics (n.d.). Retrieved February 12, 2006, from http://code.google.com/webstats/index.html

Web Services Choreography Requirements 1.0 (2003). *W3C Working Draft.* Retrieved February 12, 2006, from http://www.w3.org/TR/ws-chor-reqs

Web Services Transaction (WS-Transaction) (2002). Retrieved February 12, 2006, from http://www-106.ibm.com/developerworks/library/ws-transpec/

Chapter VIII

Automatic Replication for Web Applications

Pablo Galdámez, Instituto Technológico de Informática, Spain

Abstract

This chapter proposes a software architecture to enhance the availability of Web-based applications at a reasonable cost. The architecture is pluggable to existing Web-applications, so that no modifications are required to existing code. There are no specific hardware or server software requirements. Availability is achieved by replication, and strong replica consistency is automatically guaranteed by using off-the-shelf group communication components. The proposed architecture is explained in detail, and it is compared against some of the most relevant highly-available solutions used nowadays. The most distinctive feature of the proposed architecture is that it explicitly addresses replica consistency, providing automatic strong replica consistency. Besides automatic consistency, attention is given to simplicity and pluggability.

Introduction

Since the invention of the World Wide Web, we have seen an explosive increase in the number of running Websites and a continuous increase in the importance of Websites as fundamental parts of business strategies. Today, more and more companies and organizations rely on Websites to offer their products and services, up to the extent that Website unavailability means, in many cases, profit losses. As Website availability is increasingly seen as a must, Website owners need to invest resources to reduce down time to a minimum. To that end, several technologies have been developed over the past years and probably some others will appear soon.

Big companies usually solve the availability problem with large investments in hardware, software, and personnel that can be prohibitive for medium and small businesses. That is one of the reasons why small companies usually lack a real highly-available solution. Most of them just blindly rely on their Internet providers. Internet providers host Websites on shared or dedicated servers running, in the best case, on high-end computers with replicated disks and uninterruptible power supplies. Availability is "guaranteed" by the hardware quality they provide for the Website, by the quality of their Internet connection, and by manual intervention in case of crashes. Even though this common solution may seem enough for a wide range of Websites, there are many others that cannot afford the potential downtime. These increasingly greater numbers of small companies do need an affordable true highly-available solution. Unfortunately, high-availability concerns are only perceived when unavailability appears. In this sense, high availability is similar to other computer system threats, such as those related to computer security, that disrupt computer-based businesses. The solution, as in those cases, is a combination of awareness, prevention, and a balance between cost and risk. Risk should be measured in potential profit losses, and cost should include hardware, software, personnel, and technical support.

This chapter focuses on affordable highly-available solutions for small Websites, where reduced cost implies low hardware cost, no significant code development or recoding, and little proprietary software dependencies. In particular, this chapter is specifically devoted to explain mechanisms for automatic replication applicable to existing Web applications. To do so, the chapter shows a quite simple architecture that may cover a gap among the currently-existing highly-available solutions, providing an affordable true highly-available solution. The architecture is basically made by integrating a set of inexpensive off-the-self components, it does not require specialized hardware or software, and it does not need the Website to be recoded (if it fits a specific class of Websites). However, it is a true highly-available solution that could be installed over a cluster or span a set of physically-separated servers. It guarantees full consistency among the server replicas, and recovery time after failures is negligible from the user perspective.

The central core of the architecture is a simple piece of software that should be implemented. In this sense the proposed architecture could be interesting for Website owners and Internet providers that look for cheap highly-available solutions for their current Websites, but it could be even more interesting for system programmers and highly-available solution providers looking for new ideas for their products.

The chapter covers the subject in depth, explaining technical details required to understand and develop the proposed architecture. Readers will benefit if they have some computer science background, basic knowledge about distributed systems concepts, and general terms related to fault tolerance, high availability, and maintainability. However, many fundamental concepts are introduced and explained, so most readers can follow the chapter contents.

To introduce the topic, the second section makes an overall overview to generic high-availability techniques, explaining concepts related to replication, scalability issues, and failure detection. After the main concepts behind high availability are covered, the third section discusses existing highly-available solutions for Websites. Once the pros and cons of those existing solutions are mentioned, section four will explain the proposed architecture that provides automatic replication for Web applications at low cost. Limitations and advantages of the model are detailed, and a set of common scenarios highlight the range of situations where the architecture would do its best. Following the architecture overview, section five explains each component, giving enough details to allow an expert reader to experiment with them. Finally, section six concludes the chapter with some remarks about automatic replication.

High-Availability Concepts

High availability is usually pursued by server replication. The same piece of server software is placed into different computers, so that in case failures occur in one server, the other servers can take over its tasks. Clients access the replicated service by sending invocations to the servers. When invocations reach the server set, they coordinate themselves to perform the requested actions and send the corresponding replies to the clients. As there can be a number of concurrent clients requesting services, server coordination has to be designed carefully to show an acceptable performance. Performance is threatened by the required

Figure 1. Single server compared to a replicated service

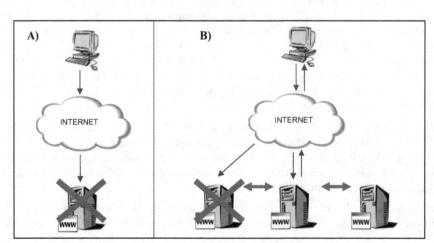

coordination tasks that the server set has to perform before replying to each client. Such coordination has to do mainly with data consistency.

For instance, let us consider a very simple service that just stores a number in a database. Clients retrieve or update that number invoking such a remote service through a network. Without replication, the system would just be formed by a set of clients, the network, and a single server. In this case, server software can easily be designed to serve requests sequentially, storing and returning the number as requests arrive. Naturally, in case the server crashes, the service would become unavailable. To enhance its availability, let us suppose that two servers cooperate to serve such requests. In this scenario, if one client sends a request to store one value, the servers have to cooperate to store the same value. Doing so, any of them will be able to reply to subsequent client requests, even if the other server crashes.

There are different replication models to structure the set of server replicas, a number of optimizations can be considered to increase performance and scalability under particular circumstances, and systems may be prepared to cope with a range of different failure types with distinct semantics.

Replication Models

There are two basic replication models: active replication and passive replication. With *active replication* (Schneider, 1990), client requests are multicast to all servers. When each server receives the request, it processes it as if the service was not replicated and replies to the client. The client has just to select one of the server replies as the service reply, discarding the others. As long as each server receives the same client requests in the same order, it is easy to realize that all of them will end up with the same state. In this situation, if one server crashes, no special action is required: All the surviving servers will have the same state, and all of them can continue serving requests. The key concept behind active replication is message ordering. Messages sent by clients to the group of servers are multicast using a group communication protocol (Hadzilacos & Toueg, 1993), which ensures the proper message ordering.

Whereas active replication servers are active, in that all of them receive, process, and reply to requests, *passive replication* (Budhiraja, Marzullo, Schneider, & Toueg, 1993) is an asymmetric scheme. With passive replication, only one server processes requests and replies to the client. This special server is called the primary replica, and the other replicas are called the secondaries or backup replicas. Client requests are sent to the primary, which processes them. After the primary has processed each request, it checkpoints its state to the secondaries, and after the checkpoints terminate, it replies to the client. This checkpointing ensures that all replicas will have the same state after each client request. In case any secondary fails, no special action needs to be taken, but if the primary replica fails, some extra recovery actions need to be performed before resuming the service activity: At least one of the secondaries has to be promoted to the primary role, and clients have to locate it and bind to it.

The main advantage of active replication over passive replication is that active replication does not require any recovery action when failures occur. On the other hand, its main disadvantage is the need of a group communication protocol that sometimes can be quite expensive. Additionally, with the active replication model, all the servers are active, implying that all of them consume resources to perform exactly the same tasks. In contrast, passive replication needs recovery after failures occur, but some resources are saved since possibly only one replica does the actual job.

A number of intermediate models exist. One of the best known is the so-called coordinator-cohort model (Birman, Joseph, Raeuchle, & El~Abbadi, 1985). This model tries to benefit from the advantages of both active and passive replication models, without their disadvantages. In a service structured with this replication model, all the servers are active and passive at the same time. The primary role is assigned for each client request, resulting in that each server can be selected as the primary for each different request. For a particular client request, the server selected as the primary is called the request coordinator, whereas the rest of the replicas are called the request cohorts. Given that each request is just processed by a single server, compared to the active replication model, computational resources are saved. On the other hand, as each server is prepared to serve client requests at each time, recovery is kept as efficient as the active replication recovery.

The main subtle but important disadvantage of the coordinator-cohort model is that server coordination becomes more complex, and that the model usually requires the servers to be modified. As each server receives both client requests and server checkpoints, servers need two concurrent distinct mechanisms to update their state. For client requests, the actual service code is executed, whereas for server updates, just the updates have to be processed. Notice that if servers would execute the requested service for the server updates too, the model would be the active one. On the other hand, if server checkpoint processing was deferred, servers would not be able to attend any further client requests, so the model would become the passive one.

State Machine Servers

If server code is deterministic, high availability can be enormously simplified. A state machine server is a server that behaves exactly the same when it processes the same sequence of client requests. In this case, a replicated service can be easily implemented out of a set of identical servers that could have been designed without replication in mind. As long as the replication support delivers the same sequence of requests to the server set, servers will reach the same final state, so that data consistency among servers is automatically guaranteed.

Interestingly, both active and passive replication models can benefit from state machine servers. In the active case, the group communication protocol delivers the same sequence of requests to all servers, so that this model actually implies that servers fulfill the state machine assumption. On the other hand, if servers are state machines, passive replication checkpoints could simply consist of the client requests themselves. This way, the primary server would process client requests, and it would checkpoint them to the secondaries. Secondaries would lazily process those client requests in the same order as the primary did; enforcing a complete request log processing only when promoting to the primary role when failures occur.

However, not every server is a state machine server. There are many sources of randomization that should be taken into account when planning a highly-available setting for a particular service. Local computer time, randomly-generated numbers, non-deterministic hardware, or concurrency within servers and system software may lead to servers that do not behave exactly the same way under the same sequence of requests.

If servers are non-deterministic, active replication cannot be used. The passive replication model or the coordinator-cohort model should then be considered. The bad news is that non-deterministic servers require replication support code at each server, so that server code has to be modified to send and process checkpoints. In this case, client requests will not suffice as checkpoint data. Secondaries will need to receive the state modifications using application-dependent checkpoint messages, so that they can update their state as the primary did.

Replicable Actions

Besides determinism, active replication implies that every action executed by the service can be executed as many times as there are active servers. Let us suppose, for instance, that one of the actions executed by the service is to send an email; then, if every server executes the same action, a number of emails would be sent, which is not probably the desired behavior.

Naturally, most non-replicable actions can be converted into replicable actions, but this conversion usually implies server code modifications or proxy software developments. For instance, the example above could be modified so that emails were sent through a local proxy that would discard duplicates. Notice that software gets more complex since the proxy itself should be made highly available.

Replicable actions should not be confused with idempotent actions. With replicable actions, we mean actions that can be executed by each replica, whereas idempotent actions should be understood as actions that can be executed by a single replica as many times as needed, with the same results. For instance, if each replica holds a database replica, writing a record into the database is a replicable action, and it is idempotent; however, increasing the value of a record is a replicable action, but it is not idempotent.

Scalability and Performance Issues

One of the biggest challenges when designing highly-available services is keeping performance under acceptable limits as the system grows. Scalability problems may appear as the number of replicas grows, as the number of clients grows, or as the number of concurrent requests grows.

The second fundamental factor that affects performance when scaling up is the ratio between read and write operations. If the number of read operation is orders of magnitude higher than the number of write operations, efficient and scalable systems can be developed. Consider, for instance, Internet DNS. It shows Internet-wide scalability because the number of domain name modifications is very much lower than the number of lookups. Another interesting example are peer-to-peer networks that provide highly-available data storage just because basic operations are upload and download files, but there is little support to modify files.

Finally, possibly the most important factor that constrains scalability is consistency. If data among servers has to be consistent, systems will not scale as much as if some inconsistencies could be tolerated. Let us consider again Internet DNS. In order to allow a huge amount of concurrent lookup operations, write operations are not applied synchronously to every domain server. This implies that data provided by different servers to the same lookup request could be different at the same time. A detailed analysis of each particular application domain is essential to determine whether consistencies could be tolerated. Interestingly, most applications do tolerate certain levels of inconsistencies in some data.

Failure Types and Failure Detection

Highly-available systems have to cope with failures. More precisely, they mask failures from the user as they occur. There are many interesting results in distributed systems about failures. One of the most significant, known as the FLP impossibility (Fischer, Lynch, & Paterson, 1985), states the impossibility to solve consensus (Guerraoui & Schiper, 2001) problems in asynchronous distributed systems where nodes may crash. To circumvent this limitation, the most used artifacts are failure detectors (Chandra & Toueg, 1996). Failure detectors are usually based on time-outs to make suspects of possible faulty nodes, so that crashed nodes and nodes that are too slow are removed from the system. Failure detectors make suspects of faulty nodes that could be erroneous since slow nodes have not actually failed. These erroneous suspects may lead to distributed systems that do not agree on which nodes are "alive".

Consider for instance, nodes A, B, and C. Let us suppose that node A considers that B has failed, but C perceives B as alive. In this scenario, how does one design distributed protocols? Should nodes A and C start a recovery protocol to take over B's job? The most common solution to overcome this situation is to implement a membership protocol (Cristian, 1991a). Membership protocols' goal is to agree on the set of correct nodes. This agreement allows highly-available systems to be easily designed since agreed correct nodes can safely execute consensus protocols.

Besides crashes, there are some other failure types (Cristian, 1991b) that could appear in a system. Temporization failures, omission failures, and Byzantine failures are well-known examples. Fortunately, several mechanisms allow most kinds of failures to be converted to fail-stop (Schlichting & Schneider, 1983) behavior. The only extra failure type not considered is the Byzantine one. Nodes subject to Byzantine failures may fail exhibiting arbitrary behavior, including behavior similar to correct computations. These failures are usually masked by voting protocols and n-versioning (Avizienis, 1985), where a set of active servers process the same request, and where the final result is what the majority of servers produced.

Finally, another significant problem appears when a combination of network failures produces a partition in the system, resulting in sets of nodes that cannot reach each other. In this case, consistency can be seriously compromised if each partition is allowed to proceed separately. The safest solution consists of blocking minority partitions, so that only the majority one makes progress. As it can be noticed, partitions are indistinguishable from combinations of node failures, so that we should conclude that if we are designing a system where partitions can physically occur, consistency could be compromised if only a minority of nodes are seen as working. Whichever the case, to architect a highly-available system, it is highly recommended to integrate a partitionable membership protocol (Fekete, Lynch,

& Shvartsman, 2001) into our system, so that system components are informed about the majority/minority situations and about partition mergings.

Virtual Synchrony

One of the soundest concepts to design correct highly-available systems is virtual synchrony (Birman & Joseph, 1987; Moser, Amir, Melliar-Smith, & Agarwal, 1994). It takes its name from the computational model provided, which resembles that of synchronous systems, where computations are made by rounds. At each round, every node takes a computation step. Virtual synchrony achieves this model by ordered messages that are delivered to every node. Upon reception, nodes take a step. When failures occur, every node delivers a special event called a view change which includes the set of correct nodes. Those events are delivered with the proper order with respect to ordinary messages so every surviving node takes its computation step. In this chapter, we will further explore this concept to build our replication architecture for Web-based applications.

High-Availability Solutions for Web Sites

Some of the most outstanding technologies used nowadays to enhance the availability and performance of large-scale and heavily-used Websites can be found within the so-called large-scale Web replica hosting systems (Sivasubramanian, Szymaniak, Pierre, & Van Steen, 2004). Widely-known examples of such systems are *Akamai, Globule,* or *Radar,* among others. Those systems, also called *Content Delivery Networks,* are specifically designed for the large scale, and they try to solve many significant problems such as performance, adaptation, replica placement, request routing, and consistency enforcement. However, given their focus on the large scale, they seldom provide strong consistency among the service replicas. As explained by Saito and Shapiro (2005), a wide range of optimistic strategies do exist to build relaxed consistency replicated systems. Those techniques are used for scalability and flexibility but are inappropriate if replicas are not allowed to diverge.

If replica consistency must be strong, large-scale replication cannot be generally used. In those cases, the most usual solution consists of replicating services over a cluster (Cardellini, Casalicchio, Colajanni, & Yu, 2002). Cluster-based solutions for Websites generally make use of a front-end node (see Figure 2), which receives HTTP requests and delivers them to the cluster machines.

Cluster machines are generally conventional Web servers that run over general-purpose hardware, executing operating systems like Unix or Windows. The front-end node is usually a device that integrates proprietary hardware and software from a particular vendor.

Front-end nodes are generally divided into two broad categories: level-4 and level-7 front-ends. The level number refers to the ISO/OSI protocol stack layering number. Therefore, level-4 front-ends analyze TCP traffic (ISO/OSI level 4 in TCP/IP networks) to make distribution decisions among the cluster machines.

Figure 2. Cluster replication

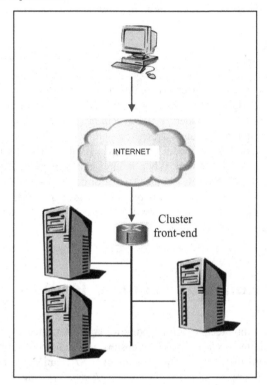

On the other hand, level-7 front-ends analyze application level protocol information. Specifically, they analyze the HTTP protocol information and they make distribution decisions depending on details such as the file type being requested, the request type, or any other significant information included in the protocol.

There are many examples of level-4 front-ends. Research projects such as *ONE-IP* (Damani, Chung, Huang, Kintala, & Wang, 1997) from the Bell Laboratories, *LSMAC* (Gan, Schroeder, Goddard, & Ramamurthy, 1999) from the University of Nebraska, or *MagicRouter* (Anderson, Patterson, & Brewer, 1996) from Berkeley are relevant examples. Of course, there are commercial and open-source solutions too. Some examples include *LocalDirector* from Cisco, *ServerIron Web* from Foundry Networks, Nortel's *Alteon ACEdirector* series, or the open-source project *HA Linux* (Zhang, 2000). As level-7 examples, we can mention the *Alteon ContentDirector* from Nortel, the *CCS 11000* routers from Cisco, or the *ServerIron Web* family of products that can work as level-4 front-ends or as level-7 front-ends.

In either case, clustering solutions are far from being generic, scalable, and usable without modifications. They usually include proprietary hardware and software, and in most cases they do not integrate well with existing Web servers and applications. Actually, most times they can be considered as load-balancing solutions more than highly-available solutions.

They do not usually include any specific mechanism to ensure consistency among the replicas that could be installed into the cluster, leaving all the consistency concerns to be solved with ad hoc solutions. This lack of consistency management is usually argued in that Web-based applications generally follow a common n-tier architecture, where the Web application is a stateless component and consistency management should only be considered at the database tier. This way, Web clusters can safely focus on load balancing, assuming that databases cope with consistency by their own mechanisms.

On the other hand, there exist complete highly-available solutions for Websites. However, they assume that some specific Web server is to be used within the cluster and that applications will be developed using some specific set of highly-available mechanisms. In this sense, this kind of solution is similar to that of some application servers that could be used to develop highly-available software, *JBoss*, for instance (Fleury & Reverbel, 2003). In those cases, only those applications completely developed under those environments can benefit from their highly-available support.

Both with cluster solutions and with application servers with highly-available support, we can conclude that they demand significant resources to provide high-availability support for existing Web applications if strong replica consistency is required. Development effort and software/hardware investments could be prohibitive, and future developments could remain constrained by the chosen environment.

In order to enhance Website availability, several Internet providers offer simple, yet usable solutions, based on the DNS support for multiple IP addresses (Brisco, 1995; Gulbrandsen & Vixie, 1996). They usually provide modified DNS servers that simply return the set of IP addresses corresponding to the servers that are working correctly. To limit the caching problem that DNS clients may impose, they provide DNS records with very small TTLs (time-to-live). These solutions, as it happened with cluster-based solutions, are just concerned about routing client requests to the proper servers, but again without actual support to make the servers cooperate.

As a result, we have shown that there are many solutions for high availability in the market, some of them for the large scale and some others for local area networks. Some of them are intended to run on clusters and some of them are to be used as run-time support to build applications. Interestingly, most of those solutions lack support for automatic strong replica consistency enforcement.

Automatic Replication Architecture Overview

The main goal of the architecture that we detail in this chapter is to enhance the availability of existing Web-based applications, without the need of specific hardware or proprietary software, without requiring the source code to be modified, allowing the combination of the architecture with other highly-available solutions such as clusters and round-robin DNS, and providing automatic strong replica consistency.

The full architecture can be thought of as a software module that distributes HTTP requests to the set of pre-configured replicas. In this sense, its role is somehow similar to that of cluster front-ends. However, instead of having just one front-end for the whole cluster, every replica will be equipped with the proposed software module.

This software module, that we will call *HA-module,* will distribute HTTP requests made by the service clients (Web navigators) to the set of replicas, so that, in case one of them fails, the rest of the replicas will take over the failed one. All this highly-available setting will be achieved without any specific software requirements for clients and without clients perceiving significant downtime intervals.

As shown in Figure 1, a Web server without replication is unavailable as soon as the server fails. At the right part of the Figure, a replicated Web server, as it will be the case using the HA-module, continues processing client requests using the set of working servers.

As we have mentioned, nowadays there are many highly-available solutions, some of them actually quite successful; however, the architecture which we propose offers five advantages that altogether could be important for many Web applications:

1. **General-purpose hardware:** The proposed solution does not imply to use any particular cluster or expensive hardware. It can be deployed over general-purpose hardware, much cheaper, and powerful enough for most applications.

2. **No software recoding:** Many highly-available solutions require a particular Web server, or there is a need to implement the software using some specific programming language, or there is a need to make substantial modifications to the running software. In all those cases, cost due to the highly-available support increases. The solution proposed in this chapter allows some applications to be plugged to the highly-available solution, without any of those requirements.

3. **Unconstrained replica placement:** Most current solutions for Web applications use clusters placed in local area networks. Even though the availability level achieved that way may be sufficient, local area networks should be considered themselves as points of failures. The Internet provider's network connection may fail, or it may suffer disasters such as flooding, fire, or long power outages. The architecture explained in the next pages will allow system administrators to place replicas at distinct administrative domains, so that unavailability risks can be reduced.

4. **Composable solution:** The architecture can be combined with existing clusters and with existing round-robin DNS installations, so that investments already made in system settings can be used while availability increases.

5. **Strong replica consistency:** Most highly-available solutions focus on efficiency rather than in replica consistency. In fact, strong replica consistency is many times considered prohibitive or something to be addressed by the database layer. However, strong replica consistency is what makes high-availability support a pluggable concept in the architecture we propose.

These properties make the architecture usable by itself as a low-cost, highly-available solution, or it can be used to enhance availability and simplify software of already existing systems.

Replication Model and System Assumptions

To enhance availability, Web applications will be replicated over a set of computers that could be interconnected by a local area network (or by a wide area network). Replication will ensure that service availability will be preserved when some of the replicas fail. It is important to realize that computers may fail because of many causes; among them, we could highlight hardware failures, cluster front-end failures, network failures, including failures that occur in network routers, software faults, or human mistakes. Moreover, systems can become unavailable just because of maintenance tasks needed for the hardware or the software.

One of the key aspects of every replicated solution consists of which element is to be replicated (the replication granularity) and how consistency is going to be preserved. In this sense, the replication granularity we chose is the complete *Web application*. As it is shown in Figure 3, we define Web application as the aggregation of the Web server itself, those databases used by the application, and any other software module and data needed to serve requests.

About consistency, roughly speaking, we adopt a strict consistency model, where every replica will contain the same data between two client requests. Consistency will be provided by the highly-available support, so that existing current Web applications can benefit from availability enhancements without requiring software modifications. This approach is quite advantageous and is one of the key distinctive properties of the system we propose.

As disadvantages of the proposed solution, we should mention that it will not be usable for every Web application. Particularly, only those applications designed with replicable actions (see section *Replicable Actions*) could benefit from this high-availability support. Moreover, Web applications should exhibit deterministic behavior (they should be state machine servers).

Figure 3. Web application

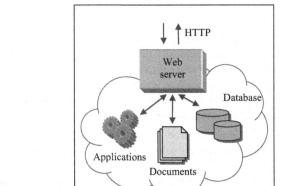

For instance, the proposed architecture could not be used to enhance availability of corporate systems that access non-replicated systems, components which are difficult to replicate such as complex legacy systems or remote systems managed by different organizations.

As a rule of thumb, automatic replication will only work for complete and self-contained systems which behave deterministically.

However, if systems to be replicated access remote systems, but interfaces to access them are clear, it should be interesting to assess whether simple proxy software modules could suffice to convert the system into a self-contained one.

Whichever the case, in this chapter we are mostly interested in automatic replication, so that we explain the architecture as a highly-available solution that is not fully generic for every Web application, but applicable to a large enough number of cases. Those many cases may benefit from its simplicity and availability enhancements.

On the other hand, to ensure that the system support which we propose manages replica consistency, we assume that the only way to access the service is through the Web server. This way, replicas cannot update their state through requests out of the system control, preventing potential inconsistencies.

Given that the replication granularity is the complete Web application, each replica will be constituted of the set of computers, software, and data needed to provide the service. In this sense we also assume that the complete Web application is a unit of failure. This prevents replicas to behave erratically because of the lack of some component that they may need to work. Naturally, the simplest scenario would be that of having just one computer with the Web server, the application, and its data.

In the rest of this chapter, we will use the term *replica* to refer to a replica of the complete Web application, and we will use the term *client* to refer to a conventional Web navigator that uses conventional Internet domain resolution mechanisms to locate Websites and that uses HTTP requests to access them.

General Operation

Figure 4 shows the general interaction between clients and the replicated service. This Figure represents three replicas placed on geographically-distant sites interconnected by a WAN, which cooperate to serve client requests. Each replica is composed of a complete copy of the Web application and a *HA-module*. This module is the software component that enhances availability. The HA-module intercepts client requests and coordinates itself with the rest of the HA-modules to ensure that all replicas are mutually consistent.

An important factor about this general operation is the mechanism that clients use to locate replicas to request services. The most common solution is shown in the Figure itself and uses the Internet DNS support for multiple IP addresses (Brisco, 1995). With this support, when a client requests a name such as http://dot.com, the navigator sends a lookup request to the DNS server. The server will then reply with just one IP among the configured IP addresses. Once the navigator has the chosen IP address, it connects to that address to request the service. Subsequent requests done by this client or by other clients will work the same way, but the DNS server will return a different configured IP addresses in a round-robin fashion.

Figure 4. General operation over a WAN

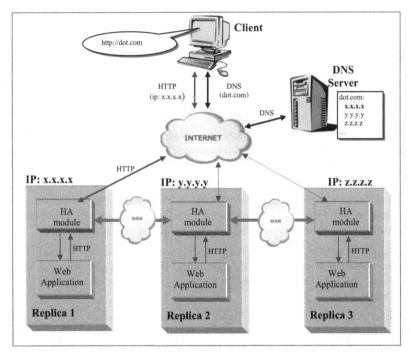

Using this mechanism, it is highly probable that different clients will receive distinct IP addresses, so that in our case, different HA-modules will be processing different requests from different clients at the same time.

Using multiple IP addresses as they are provided by Internet servers has the problem that DNS servers keeps providing IP addresses even if their corresponding nodes have failed. To overcome this problem, a possible solution is to reduce the TTL (time-to-live) of domain name records, combined with automatic management of DNS records in case of failures. The goal is to dynamically delete (insert) DNS records as nodes fail (recover). This solution is far from being perfect, since clients may use caching to resolve names, and DNS servers may take some time to update their records, even if very low TTLs are used. Nevertheless, this solution has proven its usability in a wide variety of settings, ranging from highly-available environments, to dynamic DNS services. Moreover, some variations of this scheme exist (Cardellini, Colajanni, & Yu, 2003; Delgadillo, 1999; Szymaniac, Pierre, & Van Steen, 2003) which solve most of the mentioned limitations.

Complementary solutions include sending scripts to the navigator intended to ping the chosen server, reverting to another one in case of timeouts. Additionally, IP takeover techniques (Damani et al., 1997), as will be mentioned later on, may enhance responsiveness to higher levels.

Whichever the mechanism is used to route requests, and following the general operation scheme depicted in Figure 4, a thick blue arrow represents the interaction between a particular client and Replica 1, chosen as the service entry point. The client will interact with that replica as if the service was not replicated. However, the HA-module at that node, when it receives the client request, instead of giving it to its attached Web application, will multicast the request to the other HA-modules. Once that multicast terminates, all HA-modules, including that of Replica 1, will send the client request to their respective Web application replicas. Each Web application copy will process the same client request, sending its reply to its corresponding HA-module. When all replicas terminate the request processing, all of them will share the same final state.

Once the HA-modules receive the request reply from the Web application, they will reply the returned result to the client. In a failure-free scenario, just the replica that received the client request in the first place, in our Figure Replica 1, will reply to the client. The other HA-modules will retain the reply, so that they can send it to the client in case Replica 1 fails.

The replication scheme that we have depicted corresponds to the active replication model explained in the section named *Replication Models*. The HA-modules will ensure that all Web applications will receive all requests in the same order. This way, all Web applications will constantly execute the same sequence of client requests in the same order.

The replication model can be easily changed to the passive one, just by removing the passive replica addresses from the DNS server, so that client requests do not reach them. In those replicas, request processing could be deferred until failures occur or they could be executed lazily.

Another issue relevant to the automatic replication scheme consists of the HTTP analysis which the HA-module makes. Its operation is similar, to some extent, to level-7 cluster front-ends. It also provides replication transparency to the service clients. Analogously, Web applications interact with the HA-module as it if was the actual client, so that the Web application is also unaware about replication.

Additionally, HTTP analysis allows several optimizations to be included into the HA-module. For instance, it will be possible to detect several read-only operations, so that they are not multicast to the replica set, but only processed by one replica. Examples of read-only operations would be, for instance, image downloads, or any URL that could be configured into the HA-module as a read operation.

Replication Examples and Replication Scenarios

As an example of Web-based application, let us consider an online personals contact service. Write operations that need high-availability support could be, besides online payment, profile editing, and person-to-person contact messages. Additionally, a set of cumulative statistics could be recorded. However, the most used action is probably profile search and browsing.

Let's suppose that the Web application is already implemented. The way we propose to enhance its availability could be summarized with the following actions:

1.   **Integrate the HA-module:** Install the replicas with copies of the Web application and install a copy of the HA-module in front of them.

2. **Ensure that the Web application is self-contained:** The most problematic action is probably online payment. If the application is already implemented, it will probably contact a remote Web service to order payments. To convert this action into a replicable one, a simple approach could be to implement a little proxy that intercepts online payments produced by the Web application, so that the committed payment is simply recorded into a database. This way, if every replica processes payment requests, all of them will end up simply updating their database. To finally process payments, a Web service could be implemented and configured to be executed automatically, so that it selects committed payments from any replica and uses the remote payment service to order the real payment, updating afterwards the related information stored at every replica.

3. **Optimize the HA-module:** Configure the HA-module so that only write operations are multicast with strict ordering to whole replica set. These actions would be limited to profile updates and personal messages. With this simple configuration, read operations, which are clearly dominant in this example, will show a performance similar to the non-replicated Web application.

4. **Enhance availability of consistency-relaxable actions:** In our example, a set of statistics such as pages viewed, preferred profiles, or visits received could be examples of data that do not need strict consistency, and most cases allow some amount of data loses. A simple way to enhance their availability without the need of synchronous ordered multicasts could be to create a Web service to be requested automatically, let us say, at night, to read each replica data, updating all of them with cumulative data. To this end, ordinary page requests would be fast, and just those URLs requested during the global updating phase would be configured as write operations into the HA-module.

With these quite simple steps, a fairly complex Web application could be made highly available. Finally, one additional step that should be analyzed is replica distribution.

In every case, a detailed balance between performance and availability needs should be done. If replicas are installed within a cluster, performance is guaranteed, since ordered multicasts within a fast local area network exhibit very reasonable numbers, mainly if just a few replicas are installed (two to four). If performance of the whole system tolerates placing replicas at different Internet sites, an important gain in availability would be achieved. Performance would basically be constrained by ordered multicasts made for write operations. However, it should be clearly highlighted that most times, having just two or three Internet-wide replicas enhances availability up to extraordinary levels, and that most times, ordered multicasts can be efficient enough (Anker, Dolev, Greenman, & Shnayderman, 2003) for write operations.

One of the most important problems to analyze when planning an Internet-wide setting is network partitioning. If partitions within a cluster can be avoided, in wide area networks they are real threats. Therefore, if strict consistency needs to be guaranteed, only those partitions with the majority of replicas should be allowed to make progress. This means, for instance, that if we install three replicas for the service, and one of them finds itself disconnected from the rest, it should stop accepting client requests. Just those settings consisting of two or three replicas should accept client requests.

Figure 5. HA module architecture components

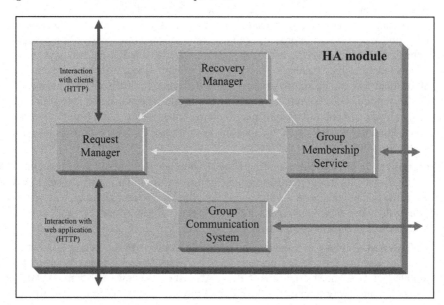

Automatic Replication Architecture Components

This last section concentrates on the different components that build up an infrastructure for automatic replication. Figure 5 shows the four components we propose: a request manager, a group communication system, a group membership system, and a recovery manager.

The most important interactions between components are illustrated with yellow arrows, whereas red arrows represent the HA-module interaction with the HA-modules placed at the other replicas. Finally, blue arrows represent interactions between the module with both clients and the Web application itself.

The Group Membership System

Every software replication-based system that executes on a distributed environment needs mechanisms to allow its operation when failures occur. One of the best-known and commonly-accepted techniques consists of integrating some kind of failure detector, which will inform when one replica is down. When the goal is not just to detect failures, but to reach agreement on which replicas are working and which of them have failed, the problem is usually solved using a group membership system (Cristian, 1991a).

The main mission of this service is to monitor the rest of the replicas, so that replica failures are detected. Analogously, this supervision will also allow for detecting when previously-failed replicas recover and start working again. In this context, it is commonly said that a given replica *has failed* or has crashed, when the membership service decides so. Recall the discussion about failure detectors and membership services made in the section named *Failure Types and Failure Detection*. Similarly, it is commonly said that a given replica *has recovered* when the membership service reaches agreement on that point. Notice that from the point of view of the membership service, it is irrelevant in the distinction between the several possible causes that may lead a given replica to be inoperative. Therefore, we will state that a given replica has failed, somehow abusing the term "failed", when the membership service agrees that it is not operative.

As mentioned before, the main contribution of membership services over mere failure detectors consists on agreement: Given some suspect about some replica operation, the rest of the replicas have to coordinate to agree whether the given replica has failed or whether it was erroneously suspected. Thanks to this distributed agreement, all membership service components placed at each replica will continuously keep consensus about the working and the failed replica sets. This distributed consensus stacks over two concepts: *view* and *view changes*. A view is nothing but a "snapshot" of the operating replica set. When some replica recovers and joins the group or when it fails and is removed from the group, it is said that a view change happens. Therefore, the distributed consensus reached by membership services consists on the operating replica set installing the same view changes.

There are many variations, implementations, and results related to the membership problem (Chockler, Keidar, & Vitenberg, 2001). Variations come from multiple factors, such as the number of nodes that may join the group, the network speed, reliability or topology, the symmetry among the different nodes, the failures types that may occur, the ensured guarantees about view changes delivery order at each node.

For the HA-module proposed in this chapter, we should opt for a membership service that ensures view synchrony (Birman & Joseph, 1987; Moser et al., 1994), a service that is optimized for a small number and pre-configured set of nodes, where partition support would be required (at least for WAN installations), and where networks should be considered as unreliable.

Fortunately, there are many stable implementations of such a service. The best known are possibly *JGroups* (Ban, 1998), *Appia* (Miranda, Pinto, & Rodrigues, 2001) or *Spread* (Amir & Stanton, 1998). They provide implementations of membership services altogether with implementations of group communication systems, which will be mentioned in the next subsection.

Inside the HA-module architecture, the group membership system interacts with the rest of the components as shown in Figure 5. It is clearly shown that every other component receives notifications from this service. Particularly, all of them will be interested in receiving the view changes events as they are installed by the group membership system. This way, the request manager, the group communication system, and the recovery manager will be able to execute "code" to react on each view change so that they will be able to reconfigure their state to reflect the new replica set, removing data related to failed nodes, and including data to manage the newly-joined replicas.

The Group Communication System

This component is present in many systems and projects (Amir & Stanton, 1998; Dolev & Malki, 1996; Landis & Maffeis, 1997; Moser, Melliar-Smith, Agarwal, Budhia, & Lingley-Papadopoulos, 1996; Renesse, Birman, & Maffeis, 1996) focused on high-availability guarantees. Its primary goal consists on providing communication mechanisms to multicast messages to a group of recipients ensuring some specific properties (Hadzilacos & Toueg, 1993). Properties to be ensured are related to the message delivery reliability and with the order in which messages are delivered at each node. Additionally to these properties, there are many variations of group communication protocols depending on the particular system parameters. Factors such as the system size, the channels reliability, the possible hardware and support for multicasts, greatly influence the kind of protocol to use.

The HA-module will require a group communication protocol that ensures reliable non-uniform message delivery, virtual synchrony, and FIFO and total order message delivery guarantees. Reliability means that a message sent will be delivered by every working node. Uniformity means that messages delivered by failed nodes have to be also delivered by operating nodes. As we do not require uniformity, the HA-module group communication protocol will not require support to find out whether failed nodes have delivered some particular message. Virtual synchrony (Birman & Joseph, 1987) means that messages delivered by different nodes have to complete delivery into the same view, so that view changes are completely ordered with respect to message deliveries. Finally, total order (Défago, Schiper, & Urbán, 2004) means that messages have to be delivered in the same order by every node, and FIFO means that messages sent from one node must be delivered in the same order as they were sent by every recipient.

It is remarkable that total order delivery will only be required if we choose the active replication model, whereas if the passive model is chosen, FIFO order would suffice.

The common system setting parameters would be a reduced number of nodes (two to four), an unreliable network, no system support for multicasts, and a fully-connected network.

The group communication system will basically interact with the request manager and with the membership service. From the first one, it will receive those requests that should be multicast to the rest of the replicas with reliability guarantees, total and FIFO order, and virtual synchrony. Conversely, the group communication system will deliver to the request manager those client requests multicast by the other replicas.

Relationship between the group communication system and the group membership system is so tight that many actual implementations provide both of them in the same module. The most basic relationship between them is related to virtual synchrony. As *view changes* and message deliveries need to be mutually ordered, the group communication system needs to receive notifications of *view changes* so that it can implement flush protocols to enforce message delivery when failures occur.

As mentioned in the previous subsection, there are some stable implementations of group communication protocols, which are stable enough to be used in production environments. Some of the best examples are *Spread* (Amir & Stanton, 1998), *Appia* (Miranda, Pinto, & Rodrigues, 2001) and *JGroups* (Ban, 1998). We would also refer the interested reader to a recent performance comparison between them (Baldoni, Cimmino, Marchetti, & Termini,

2002). As shown there, performance is quite reasonable when protocols are executed over a reduced set of nodes, which is the most typical situation for a highly-available Web application setting.

The Request Manager

This component is possibly the most visible component of the highly-available architecture we propose. Visibility is important because this is the component that directly interacts with both clients and Web applications, and it will be the component that should be configured for optimizations.

Its goal is to ensure that client requests are processed, and that service replies reach clients even if failures occur. To ensure it, besides parsing and analyzing HTTP requests, it implements a reliable invocation protocol.

Reliable invocation protocols (Rodrigues, Siegel, & Veríssimo, 1994) are required by every replicated system when replicas have distinct addresses. In these scenarios, clients contact one particular replica to request a service, and in case that replica fails, clients have to reconnect to another replica to retry the service request. This scheme is different to the replication scheme that results when all replicas share the same address (Damani et al., 1997). In this second case, when a particular replica fails, a working replica takes over the client connection reusing the same address that was using the failed replica, without needing the client to reconnect.

The single address approach is mainly used in cluster environments (see Figure 2), and provides a great failure transparency. However, the cluster front-end becomes a single point of failure. Moreover, since replicas will have to be placed into the same physical location, and will be sharing the same local area network, the local area network itself also becomes a single point of failure. The HA-module we propose could be deployed over cluster installations. In this case, since just one replica would be interacting with clients, the most convenient replication model would be the passive one, and with this setting, reliable invocation protocols are not strictly required. However, if the Web application is replicated over the Internet, a reliable invocation protocol must be implemented.

Reliable invocation protocols depend on the chosen replication model: active (Schneider, 1990), passive (Budhiraja et al., 1993), semi-active (Powell, 1991), or semi-passive (Defago, Schiper, & Sergent, 1998). Additionally, the protocol should ensure some particular semantics about the service execution (Spector, 1982): exactly once semantics, at least once semantics, or at most once semantics.

The HA-module architecture could work by adopting either the active or the passive replication models. If the active model is chosen, since clients do not belong to the groups, they should be considered as open. Using this model, the reliable invocation protocol should ensure that client requests reach the replica set even if the selected replica at first fails. In the passive model case, the invocation protocol should retry requests on the secondary replica which has been promoted to the primary role. To reduce complexity, clients could just retry connections over any known replica, so that the selected replica could return the address of the actual primary if the contacted one was a secondary.

Execution semantics should be the exactly-once semantics, the one best suited for highly-available environments. To ensure it, two considerations should be fulfilled:

1.   Clients should reconnect to a new replica when connections fail (for both the active and the passive models)
2.   Client connections should be identified, so that retried connections can be identified as such by the replica selected for the reconnection.

The second requirement can be easily achieved using cookies created by the HA-module. Each new client request could be associated to a cookie to uniquely identify it. Using these cookies, when a client retries a request, its cookie will allow the receiving HA-module to identify it as a retrial. Once it has been identified, the HA-module will be able to know whether the requested action was already completed or if it should be executed.

The first requirement is more difficult. To fulfill it, there are two basic solutions whose combination would be probably the best choice:

1.   **Do nothing:** Current Web navigators, in case connections fail, just show an error message, but they do not retry them. Therefore, if we chose to do nothing when connections fail, the user should manually retry its request. In this case, we should rely on that user behavior, and we should rely on the DNS service to provide a new IP address on client retrials. This approach is quite simple and it actually provides an exactly-once semantics if users do manually retry failed actions. Its clear disadvantage is the lack of failure transparency at the client side.
2.   **Install software at the client side:** This approach consists of installing a little software module at the client side to track and retry connections. Several techniques could be employed to this end: a small applet to track the service activity, a script to ping the replica status, or a small proxy to intercept navigator requests, so that they are retried in case of failures. This approach shows the failure transparency advantage, but needs the client side to cooperate since it should be enabled to execute scripts or applets that could be forbidden in some cases.

The best approach could be a combination of the two solutions overviewed here. If clients agree to execute the reconnecting software, failure transparency will be ensured and if they do not, highly-available behavior would still be provided. Whichever the case, all replicas will share the same state, and client reconnections, whether manually ordered by users or automatically executed by client software, will be identified as such and resumed from the point of failure.

Finally, this component has some interesting interactions with the other components that should be highlighted. The group communication system will be invoked to multicast those requests that are configured as write operations with consistency demands. Those actions should also be uniquely identified with cookies, so that retrials are detected. To that end, the HA-module should be designed to load the set of URLs and URL patterns that should be considered as write operations with unique identifiers. Conversely, the request manager will receive client requests from both the client side and the group communication system, and it should queue and process them in the proper order. Those requests received from the group communication system, will be executed by the local Web application and their results temporarily retained to return them in case of retrials. Those retained results could be discarded on subsequent actions requested by the same client, or after the replica, which interacts with that request, confirms that it has replied to the client.

Finally, the request manager interacts with the group membership system to react on view changes, and with the recovery manager to block and resume client activity when replicas recover. This last but important relationship will be explained in the next subsection.

The Recovery Manager

An additional problem that appears in fault tolerant systems is that replicas may recover after they have failed. When this occurs, the recovered replica has a possibly outdated state because the other replicas have been updating their state as they have been serving client requests. A similar situation appears when a completely new replica has to be added to the replica set that has been working for some time. In both cases, some mechanism is needed to provide the new replica with an updated copy of the service state before it can safely interact with clients.

This problem can be generally faced by two approaches which are commonly complementary: some mechanism that stores into the working replica set those updates as they are being applied, so that those updates could be provided to new replicas, and mechanisms to provide the complete service state to the joining replica. With this latter mechanism, the joining replica should just discard all its previous state and install the received state.

In general, both approaches should be provided. The first one would be used when transient failures occur on replicas, so that they leave and join the replica set just after shorts periods of disconnection. The second method would be used when replica disconnections last longer than a certain time threshold and when completely new replicas join the service. Moreover, since complete state transfers could last quite a long time, most times it should be required to combine both mechanisms when fresh replicas join the group. Therefore, usual state transfers for new replica additions are performed in two phases. The first one starts the whole state transfer. During the time it takes the transfer to complete, new state updates are being recorded. When the full state transfer terminates, the second phase starts. In this second phase, those recoded updates stored during the first phase will be applied to the joining replica.

To recover transient failures, the recovery manager could store, in a log file, all client connections. If the joining replica had a previous state and if it rejoins within a given threshold, the connection log will be provided. This replica will provide the connection log to its Web application so that it can execute them in the same order as the other replicas did.

To implement full state transfers, an external application should be executed. This external application should ensure that all the state is transferred. An external application for state transfers is required given the diverse Web application contents that need support. In order to provide a generic full-state transfer mechanism, it would be required to restrict the variety of components that could constitute Web applications. Moreover, even if only simple components were allowed, generality would be constrained by product- and vendor-specific differences. However, it should be noticed that for many existing Web applications, the external state transfer application could be as simple as a script that transfers state using off-the-shelf state transfer programs such as *rsync* (Tridgell & Macherras, 1996) or that simply execute remote file copy commands.

Besides the state transfer mechanisms, update logging, and full-state transfer commands, the recovery manager should include a blocking/resuming mechanism. This mechanism should be used by those replicas that run the state transfer protocol, to prevent race conditions between state transfers and new client requests.

Regarding the relationship among components, the most important one related to the recovery manager appears in the implementation of the blocking/resume mechanism. The recovery manager should direct the request manager to block new client requests until the connection log file had been processed. Besides that relation, the recovery manager will also be interested in view changes. When it receives failure notifications, it will start logging client activity, and when it receives join notifications, it will start the state transfer protocol.

Conclusion

Automatic replication of existing applications is one of the most interesting challenges in high availability. Since a huge amount of applications do currently exist that were not designed to explicitly face failures and recovery, a pluggable highly-available solution has an enormous role to play. This chapter has detailed a fairly simple software architecture as the instrument to explain the basic problems and solutions that appear in automatic replication for Web applications.

We have shown that the most discouraging problem is the set of assumptions that Web applications should fulfill to benefit from this approach. Replicable actions, or in other words, self-containment of the full application, could be problematic. However, it can usually be solved by implementing some extra proxy software modules; but in this case, the solution cost may rise due to extra development effort. Additionally, determinism may also become a problem, especially in complex systems where internal server concurrency may lead to unpredicted behavior. In those cases, a simple approach could be to execute client requests sequentially, but then performance might decrease notably. Another performance problem appears on write operations, which need to be multicast with strict ordering, a communication mechanism much less efficient than conventional multicast. Additionally, recovery has to be complemented with application-specific state transfer code if simple copy commands do not suffice, and finally, application-specific configurations should be provided to optimize read operations, which in some cases could be complex to analyze.

The key element in the architecture is the request manager. It is responsible of selecting which actions should be multicast; it has to build the bridge between clients and Web applications, and many points of inefficiency could appear in simple designs. Some effort should be placed into its configurability and its relation with recovery actions, but significant effort should be placed to design the component to allow most operations to proceed concurrently without ordered multicasts.

Despite the many problems and limitations of automatic replication, its goal is encouraging. Many existing Web applications may benefit from its support. Its performance losses may be acceptable in many real-world applications. Existing cluster solutions that do not provide consistency support and round-robin DNS services could be easily extended with an automatic replication support, and total cost would be clearly lower than highly-available environments that require application redesign and coding. In most cases, the required application specific tasks would simply consist of simple state transfer scripts and simple configuration files. Moreover, fairly general proxies could be implemented to be applicable to a wide range of common non-replicable actions. Examples of those proxies could be proxies for online payments and email deliveries.

The set of real-world examples that could benefit from automatic replication support is as large and as diverse as the Web. Some examples would be online stores, where products are updated by restricted access through specific interfaces, and clients usually browse more than buy. Online services such as the contact service example detailed in the section named *Replication Examples and Replication Scenarios*, discussion forums, online gameing and betting, online newspapers, magazines, libraries, etc.

In general, candidates to benefit from automatic replication infrastructures are all those small- to medium-sized Web applications that provide some sort of information that is mostly browsed and where updates are identifiable and occur not so frequently.

References

Amir, Y., & Stanton, J. (1998). *The spread wide area group communication system* (Tech. Rep. No. CNDS 98-4). Johns Hopkins University, Baltimore.

Anderson, E., Patterson, D., & Brewer, E. (1996). *The Magicrouter, An application of fast packet interposing.* Unpublished technical report. Berkeley, California: Computer Science Department, University of Berkeley.

Anker, T., Dolev, D., Greenman, G., & Shnayderman, I. (2003). Evaluating total order algorithms in WAN. In *Proceedings of the International Workshop on Large-Scale Group Communication* (pp. 1-4).

Avizienis, A. (1985). The N-version approach to fault-tolerance software. *IEEE Transactions on Software Engineering, 12*(11), 1491-1501.

Baldoni, R., Cimmino, S., Marchetti, C., & Termini, A. (2002). Performance analysis of Java group toolkits: A case study. In *Proceedings of the International Workshop on Scientific Engineering of Distributed Java Applications, LNCS: Vol. 2604* (pp. 49-60).

Ban, B. (1998). *Design and implementation of a reliable group communication toolkit for Java* (Unpublished Technical Report). Cornell University.

Birman, K. P., & Joseph, T. A. (1987). Exploiting virtual synchrony in distributed systems. In *Proceedings of the ACM Symposium on OS Principles* (pp. 123-138).

Birman, K. P., Joseph, T. A., Raeuchle, T., & El~Abbadi, A. (1985). Implementing fault-tolerant distributed objects. *IEEE Transactions on Software Engineering,* 502-528.

Brisco, T. (1995). *DNS support for load balancing*. RFC 1794. Technical report. Internet Engineering Task Force.

Budhiraja, N., Marzullo, K., Schneider, F. B., & Toueg, S. (1993). The primary-backup approach. In S. Mullender (Ed.), *Distributed systems (2nd ed.)* (pp. 199-216). Addison-Wesley.

Cardellini, V., Casalicchio, E., Colajanni, M., & Yu, P. S. (2002). The state of the art in locally distributed Web-server systems. *ACM Computing Surveys, 34*(2), 263–311.

Cardellini, V., Colajanni, M., & Yu, P. S. (2003). Request redirection algorithms for distributed Web systems. *IEEE Transactions on Parallel and Distributed Systems, 14*(4), 355–368.

Chandra, T. D., & Toueg, S. (1996). Unreliable failure detectors for reliable distributed systems. *Journal of the ACM, 43*(2), 225-267.

Chockler, G. V., Keidar, I., & Vitenberg, R. (2001). Group communication specifications: A comprehensive study. *ACM Computer Surveys, 33*(4), 1-43.

Cristian, F. (1991a). Reaching agreement on processor group membership in synchronous distributed systems. *Distributed Computing, 4*, 175-187.

Cristian, F. (1991b). Understanding fault-tolerant distributed systems. *Communications of the ACM, 34*(2), 56-78.

Damani, O. P., Chung, P. E., Huang, Y., Kintala, C., & Wang, Y. M. (1997). ONE-IP: Techniques for hosting a service on a cluster of machines. *Computer Networks and ISDN Systems, 29*, 1019-1027.

Défago, X., Schiper, A., & Sergent, N. (1998). Semi-passive replication. In *Proceedings of the Symposium on Reliable Distributed Systems* (pp. 43-50).

Défago, X., Schiper, A., & Urbán, P. (2004). Total order broadcast and multicast algorithms: Taxonomy and survey. *ACM Computing Surveys, 36*(4), 372-421.

Delgadillo, K. (1999). *Cisco DistributedDirector.* Technical report. Cisco Systems, Inc.

Dolev, D., & Malki, D. (1996). The Transis approach to high availability cluster communication. *Communications of the ACM, 39*(4), 63-70.

Fekete, A., Lynch, N., & Shvartsman, A. (2001). Specifying and using a partitionable group communication service. *ACM Transactions on Computer Systems, 19*(2), 171-216.

Fischer, M. J., Lynch, N. A., & Paterson, M. S. (1985). Impossibility of distributed consensus with one faulty process. *Journal of the ACM, 32*(2), 374-382.

Fleury, M., & Reverbel, F. (2003). The JBoss extensible server. In *Proceedings of the International Middleware Conference* (pp. 344-373).

Gan, X., Schroeder, T., Goddard, S., & Ramamurthy, B. (2000). LSMAC and LSNAT: Two approaches for cluster-based scalable web servers. In *Proceedings of the 2000 IEEE International Conference on Communications, 2* (pp. 1164-1168).

Guerraoui, R., & Schiper, A. (2001). The generic consensus service. *IEEE Transactions on Software Engineering, 27*(1), 2941.

Gulbrandsen, A., & Vixie, P. (1996). *A DNS RR for specifying the location of services* (DNS SRV), RFC 2052. Technical Report. Internet Engineering Task Force

Hadzilacos, V., & Toueg, S. (1993). Fault-tolerant broadcasts and related problems. In S. J. Mullender (Ed.), *Distributed systems* (pp. 97-145). ACM Press & Addison-Wesley.

Landis, S., & Maffeis, S. (1997). Building reliable distributed systems with CORBA. *Theory and Practice of Object System, 3*(1), 31-43.

Miranda, H., Pinto, A., & Rodrigues, L. (2001). Appia: Flexible protocol kernel supporting multiple coordinated channels. In *Proceedings of the 21ˢᵗ International Conference on Distributed Computing Systems* (pp. 707-710).

Moser, L. E., Amir, Y., Melliar-Smith, P. M., & Agarwal, D. A. (1994). Extended virtual synchrony. In *Proceedings of the 14ᵗʰ IEEE International Conference on Distributed Computing Systems* (pp. 56-65).

Moser, L. E., Melliar-Smith, P. M., Agarwal, D. A., Budhia, R. K., & Lingley-Papadopoulos, C. A. (1996). Totem: A fault-tolerant multicast group communication system. *Communications of the ACM, 39*(4), 54-63.

Powell, D. (Ed.). (1991). Delta-4—*A generic architecture for dependable distributed computing*. ESPRIT Research Reports series. Springer-Verlag.

Renesse, R., Birman, K. P., & Maffeis, S. (1996). Horus: A flexible group communication system. *Communications of the ACM, 39*(4), 76-83.

Rodrigues, L., Siegel, E., & Veríssimo, P. (1994). A replication-transparent remote invocation protocol. In *Proceedings of the 13ᵗʰ Symposium on Reliable Distributed Systems* (pp. 160-169).

Saito, Y., & Shapiro, M. (2005). Optimistic replication. *ACM Computing Surveys, 37*(1), 42-81.

Schlichting, R. D., & Schneider, F. B. (1983). Fail-stop processors: An approach to designing fault-tolerant computing systems. *ACM Transactions on Computer Systems, 1*(3), 222-238.

Schneider, F. B. (1990). Implementing fault-tolerant services using the state machine approach: A tutorial. *ACM Computing Surveys, 22*(4), 299-319.

Sivasubramanian, S., Szymaniak, M., Pierre, G., & Van Steen, M. (2004). Replication for Web hosting systems. *ACM Computing Surveys, 36*(3), 291-334.

Spector, A. (1982). Performing remote operations efficiently on a local computer network. *Communications of the ACM, 25*, 246-260.

Szymaniac, M., Pierre, G., & Van Steen, M. (2003). Netairt: A DNS-based redirection system for Apache. In *Proceedings of the International Conference WWW/Internet,* (pp. 435-442).

Tridgell, A., & Macherras, P. (1996). *The rsync algorithm* (Tech. Rep. No. TR-CS-96-05). Australian National University.

Zhang, W. (2000). Linux virtual servers for scalable network services. In *Proceedings of the Ottawa Linux Symposium* (pp. 212-221).

Chapter IX

A Scalable QoS-Aware Web Services Management Architecture (QoSMA)

M. Adel Serhani, United Arab Emirates University, United Arab Emirates

Elarbi Badidi, United Arab Emirates University, United Arab Emirates

Mohamed Vall O. Mohamed-Salem, University of Wollongong in Dubai, United Arab Emirates

Abstract

As Web services are growing rapidly and as their adoption by a large number of business organizations is increasing, scalability and performance management of Web services environments are of paramount importance. This chapter proposes a scalable QoS-aware architecture, called QoSMA, for the management of QoS-aware Web services. The aim of this architecture is to provide QoS management support for both Web services' providers and consumers. The proposed architecture is based on the commonly-used notion of QoS brokerage service. The QoS broker mediates between service requestors and service providers. Its responsibilities include performance monitoring of Web services, supporting users in Web services selection based on their QoS requirements, and the negotiation of QoS issues between requestors and providers. The QoSMA architecture provides the following benefits: First, it allows the automation of QoS management and QoS monitoring for both provid-

ers and clients. Second, the scalability of the architecture allows for better handling of the increasing demand while maintaining the pre-agreed-on QoS between service requestors and providers.

Introduction

Web services are increasingly used as a new technology for providing and/or consuming services artifacts via the Internet. Web services approach presents fundamental changes in the way systems are required, designed, developed, deployed and managed. Due to this rapid growth, quality of service (QoS) is becoming a key feature in Web services competition. End-to-end quality management of Web services is a critical issue that is highly related to the changing and dynamic environment of Web services. In fact, the QoS delivered to a client is highly affected by factors such as the performance of the Web service itself, the hosting platform, and the underlying network.

Web services paradigm is a recent concept of emerging Web applications. It connects a set of technologies, protocols, and languages to allow automatic communication between Web applications through the Internet. A Web Service is an application that exposes its functionality through an interface description and makes it publicly available for use by other programs. Web services can be accessed using different protocols, different component models, running on different operating systems. Web services make use of eXtensible Markup Language (XML)-based messaging as a fundamental means of data communication, and often use the standard Hypertext Transfer Protocol (HTTP) to exchange messages between service consumers (clients) and service providers (services).

As Web services are a new emerging technology, most existing work focuses more on their development and their interfacing practices. Research on Web services has focused more on functional and interfacing issues, that is, Simple Object Protocol (SOAP), Web services Description Language (WSDL), and Universal Description, Discovery, and Integration (UDDI). QoS support in Web services is still at the earlier stages of maturity as a research area where most of the efforts are focused on the enumeration of QoS requirements and mechanisms for QoS management. Also, considerable research efforts have been conducted to address the issues of QoS, manageability, and security in service-oriented architectures (SOA) in general.

Our aim, in this chapter, is to provide QoS management support for both service provider and consumers. Web services providers need support to publish and guarantee (enforce) the QoS of their Web services, while users need support to be able to express service-specific requirements while selecting Web services. The quality of service management process is automatically conducted through a set of phases ranging from specification of QoS parameters, selection of QoS-aware Web services, contract negotiation between providers and users, QoS monitoring, and guarantee.

The success of QoS support for Web services depends largely on the scalability of the proposed mechanisms as the number of clients and servers is expected to be very high in a SOA. This issue was not considered in SOA standard, and until very recently the issue was only highlighted without any real solution to tackle the problem. The need for performance and scalability has been recognized since the early stage of Web development. For example, in single server architecture, techniques to improve performance include the use of faster and/or multiple processors and the various forms of content caching. Further scaling is accomplished by means of replication. This has led to the development of distributed architectures integrating clusters of servers. The objective behind these architectures is to provide solutions that have the ability to grow gradually as the demand for resources grows.

With the proliferation of Web services in business and as the number of users is increasing, it is anticipated that the capacity of single Web services architectures will become insufficient to handle the load. Hence, server replication might be used to improve scalability. Load distribution among servers may be achieved by taking into account performance data gathered from each server, and clients' requests assigned to servers according to a load distribution strategy.

To deal with this issue, we have built a scalable QoS management architecture capable of supporting at run-time the QoS management phases (QoS specification, monitoring, and guarantee), QoS provisioning, and assurance in delivering Web services. The scientific benefits of our approach are twofold. First, it allows the automation of the QoS management, and QoS monitoring for both providers and users of Web services. Second, the scalability of our proposed architecture allows for a better handling of the increasing demand while maintaining pre-agreed-on QoS between service requestors and providers.

The proposed solution challenges the following questions: How scalable is the Web services architecture? Does the Web services architecture leads to a better scalability than the traditional existing Web architectures? How could a scalable Web services architecture be built in such a dynamic and unpredictable environment, and how could it support QoS provision and management? To what extent is the level of advertised QoS is maintained in such a scalable architecture?

The proposed architecture is based on the commonly-used notion of QoS brokerage service. The QoS Broker mediates between service requestors and service providers. Its responsibilities include performance monitoring of Web services, implementation of Web service selection policies, supporting users in Web services selection based on their QoS requirements, and the negotiation of QoS issues between requestors and providers.

Web Services Overview

Definition

Web services is an emerging technology that has attracted a lot of attention over the last few years as a new way of building and deploying software to simplify development and integration of IT systems. They represent a new approach for application integration of domestic IT systems and for connecting software over the Internet. The objective is to reduce the complexity and expense of traditional business-to-business (B2B) connectivity. Web services technologies are based on open standards recommended by the World Wide Web Consortium (W3C). The standards enjoy unprecedented industry support from major

IT suppliers such as IBM, Microsoft, and Sun Microsystems, together with the foremost CORBA vendors, such as BEA, Borland, and IONA Technologies.

Before Web services and these standards (i.e., SOAP, WSDL, UDDI) came to the scene, connecting applications over a network such as the Internet was not an easy task, because each application needed to have knowledge regarding the conditions under which the other applications were running such as hardware, operating system, language, as well as the transport protocol to convey data between applications.

Now a common interface description, communication method, and message transport allows businesses to realize the benefits of connecting over the Internet. Any application can autonomously connect to other applications over the Web, independent of software, platform, or hardware, by using Web services protocols and leveraging a ubiquitous transport.

Many definitions of Web services were introduced in the literature. Some of them are incomplete and others are more detailed, more expressive, and clearly explain the main characteristics of Web services. A more formal definition of a Web service may be borrowed from IBM's tutorial on the topic (Tidwell, 2000).

Web services are a new breed of Web application. They are self-contained, self-describing, modular applications that can be published, located, and invoked across the Web. Web services perform functions, which can be anything from simple requests to complicated business processes. Once a Web service is deployed, other applications (and other Web services) can discover and invoke the deployed service.

Web Services Architecture

As depicted in Figure 1, this architecture is based on three roles and three operations. The three roles are the service provider, the service requester, and the service registry. The objects involved in the interactions between these roles are the service and the service description, and the operations performed by the actors on these objects are publish, find, and bind.

Figure 1. The SOA model (taken from Gottschalk, Graham, Kreger, & Snell, 2002)

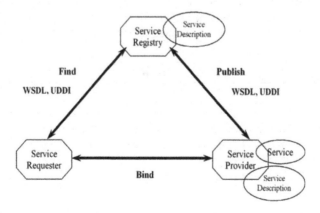

A service provider creates a Web service and its service description, using a standard called the Web services Description Language (WSDL), and then publishes the service (Publish operation) with a service registry based on a standard called the Universal Description, Discovery, and Integration (UDDI) specification. The service registry is a server that acts as a repository, or "yellow pages", for software interfaces that are published by service providers.

Once a Web service is published, a service requester may find the service via the UDDI interface (find operation). The UDDI registry provides the service requester with a WSDL service description and a URL (uniform resource locator) pointing to the service itself. The service requester may then use this information to directly bind at run-time to the service and invoke it (bind operation).

Web Services Development Life Cycle

The Web services development life cycle may be summarized into four phases for each role described above. These phases are: design and implementation, deployment, run-time execution, and management. Each role has particular requirements for each phase of the development life cycle.

1. **Design and implementation:** This phase includes the design, the specification of the service interface description, and the development and testing of the Web service implementation. Web service implementations can be provided by creating new Web services, transforming existing applications into Web services, and composing new Web services from other Web services and applications.

2. **Deployment:** This phase includes the publication of the service interface to a service requestor or service registry and the deployment of the executables of the Web service into an execution environment such as a Web application server.

3. **Execution:** During this phase, the Web service is available for invocation. At this point, the Web service is fully deployed, operational, and network-accessible from the service provider. At this time, the service requestor can perform the find and bind operations.

4. **Management:** This phase deals with continuing management and administration of the Web service application. Security, quality of service in terms of availability and performance, and business processes must all be addressed.

Web Services Programming Stack

The Web service protocol stack is the collection of standardized computer networking protocols and application programming interfaces (APIs) that are used to define, locate, implement, and make Web services interact with each other. The Web service protocol stack is mainly composed of four areas:

1. **Service Transport:** This area is responsible for transporting messages between network applications and includes protocols such as HTTP, SMTP, FTP, as well as the more recent Blocks Extensible Exchange Protocol (BEEP). Other kinds of network protocols, such as the Internet Inter-ORB** Protocol (IIOP) or the IBM MQSeries, are also used.

2. **XML Messaging:** This area is responsible for encoding messages in a common XML format in order that messages can be understood at each end of the network connection. Presently, this area includes such protocols as XML-RPC, SOAP, and REST, that facilitates publish, find, bind, and invoke operations described previously.

3. **Service Description:** This area is used for describing to clients the public interface to a specific Web service. The Web services Description Language (WSDL) is typically used for this purpose. WSDL is often used in combination with SOAP and XML-Schema to provide Web services over the Internet. A client connecting to a Web service can read the WSDL to find out what functions are available on the server. Any special datatypes used are embedded in the WSDL file in the form of XML-Schema. The client can then use SOAP to actually call one of the functions listed in the WSDL.

4. **Service Discovery:** It centralizes services into a common registry such that network Web services can publish their location and description, and makes it easy to discover what services are available on the network. At present, the UDDI protocol is normally used for service discovery.

Web service protocol stack also includes a whole range of recently set-up protocols: WSFL, and SOAP-DSIG.

In order to meet the rigorous demands and requirements of today's e-business applications, an enterprise Web services infrastructure must be provided. This infrastructure should include, in addition to the above areas, security, management, and quality-of-service management. These infrastructure components, represented on the right side of Figure 2, have to be ad-

Figure 2. Web services programming stack (Gottschalk et al., 2002)

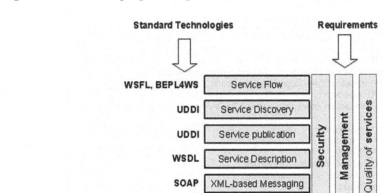

dressed at each layer of the stack. As the Web services paradigm is increasingly adopted throughout the industry, these issues are already undergoing standardization (Della-Libera ,Hallam-Baker, Hondo, Janczuk, Kaler, & Maruyama, 2002; OASIS, 2005).

Simple Object Access Protocol (SOAP)

SOAP is an extensible, text-based framework for exchanging structured and typed information between peers, without prior knowledge of each other or of each other's platforms, in a decentralized, distributed environment using XML. SOAP does not itself define any application semantics such as a programming model or implementation specific semantics, that is, distributed garbage collection. It rather defines a simple mechanism for expressing application semantics by providing a modular packaging model and encoding mechanisms for encoding data within modules (World Wide Web Consortium, 2003). This allows SOAP to be used in a large variety of systems and software application environments. SOAP consists of three parts:

- An extensible envelope (mandatory) expressing what features and services are represented in a message, who should deal with them, and whether they are optional or mandatory. The envelope contains two elements: an optional header and a body;

- A set of encoding rules (optional), which define a serialization mechanism that can be used to exchange instances of application-defined data types; and

- An RPC representation (optional), which defines a convention that can be used to represent the remote procedure calls and responses.

Box 1. Sample of a SOAP message using HTTP

```
POST /Accounts/xxxxx HTTP/1.1
Host: www.webservicebank.com
Content-Length: nnnn
Content-Type: text/xml; charset="utf-8"
SOAPAction: "Some-URI"

<SOAP:Envelope
xmlns:SOAP="http://schemas.xmlsoap.org/soap/envelope/"
  SOAP:encodingStyle="http://schemas.xmlsoap.org/soap/encoding/">
   <SOAP:Header>
      <t:Transaction xmlns:t="some-URI" SOAP:mustUnderstand="1">
         5
      </t:Transaction>
   </SOAP:Header>
   <SOAP:Body>
      <m:Deposit xmlns:m="Some-URI">
         <m:amount>200</m:amount>
      </m:Deposit>
   </SOAP:Body>
</SOAP:Envelope>
```

Web Services Description Language (WSDL)

WSDL is the Web Services Description Language. It describes where the Web service is located, what it can do, and how these services can be invoked. The operations and messages are described abstractly, and then bound to a concrete network protocol and message format to define an endpoint. Related concrete endpoints are combined into abstract endpoints. WSDL defines services as a collection of network endpoints (ports) (World Wide Web Consortium, 2004). The abstract definition of the endpoints and messages enables reuse of these definitions. A WSDL document uses the following elements when defining a Web service:

- **Types:** a container for data-type definitions using some type system;
- **Message:** an abstract typed definition of the data being communicated;
- **Operation:** an abstract description of an action supported by the service;
- **Port type:** an abstract set of operations supported by one or more endpoints;
- **Bindings:** a concrete protocol and data format specification for a particular port type;
- **Port:** a single endpoint defined as a combination of binding and a network address; and
- **Service:** a collection of related endpoints.

While theoretically independent of SOAP and HTTP, WSDL is generally used with SOAP/HTTP/MIME as its remote invocation mechanism.

Universal Description, Discovery, and Integration (UDDI)

UDDI is the Universal Description, Discovery and Integration Service. It provides a mechanism for clients to dynamically find Web services. The UDDI registry is similar to the CORBA trader service (OASIS, 2004). Clients of the UDDI registry can publish services, or search for service and bind programmatically to the service. The UDDI registry is composed of three sections:

- the white pages that contains data on a business including address, contact, and known identifiers;
- the yellow pages that describes groups of related Web services; and
- the green pages that provide technical data about a given Web service, mainly to do with how to connect to the Web service after it has been found. They include references to specifications for Web services, as well as support for pointers to various file and URL-based discovery mechanisms if required.

UDDI is layered on top of SOAP and assumes that requests and responses to UDDI objects are sent as SOAP messages.

Web Services Flow Language (WSFL)

Web Service Flow Language (WSFL) is an XML language for the description of Web services Composition. Web services may be produced by composing existing Web services. Intra-enterprise Web services might collaborate to present a single Web Service Interface to the public, whereas Web services from different enterprises might collaborate to perform business-to-business transactions. A service flow describes how service-to-service communications, collaborations, and flows are performed (Leymann, 2001).

QoS Issues

Background

Quality was early recognized in industry and academia, and then many definitions were proposed in the literature. A commonly-used definition comes from the international quality standard ISO 8402 (ISO 8402, 2000, p. 39): "*The totality of features and characteristics of a product or service that bear on its ability to satisfy stated or implied needs*". Quality of service as a related quality concern is defined in CCITT Recommendation E.800 (1988, p. 191) as "*The collective effect of service performances which determine the degree of satisfaction of a user of the service*". QoS comprises a number of factors or attributes, which are enumerated and defined in Recommendation E.800 (CCITT Recommendation E.800, 1988). Web services QoS concerns the non-functional aspects of the service being provided to the Web service users. In Service Oriented Architectures (SOA), both service providers and service users should be able to define QoS-related statements to enable QoS-aware service publication, service discovery, and service usage.

Many software products and Web site quality model were proposed in the literature and have different goals. They can be classified as: mathematical-based models or Artificial Intelligence-based models (Gray & MacDonell, 1997; Martin-Albo, Bertoa, Calero, Vallecillo, Cechich, & Piattini, 2003; Norman, Fenton, & Pfleeger, 1997). In the context of Web services, considerable attention was brought to the QoS support by Web services. Therefore, a number of works were proposed to categorize, specify, measure, and evaluate QoS for Web services (Li, Ding, Chen, Liu, & Li, 2003; Mani & Nagarajan, 2002; Menascé, 2002; Shuping, 2003).

Modeling QoS for Web services is in general similar to modeling quality for software products. According to Salamon and Wallace (1994), there are two approaches to model product quality: fixed model and define-your-own model. The existing fixed model for software or component quality evaluation, such as the approaches referred to in Trendowicz and Punter (2003), provides a fixed set of quality characteristics. In the second approach, the model reflects the organization context and the QoS perceived by the quality model developers. The Quality view (goals, requirements) may differ from one organization to another and among users.

QoS from the networking point of view refers to the capability of a network to provide better service to selected network traffic over one or heterogeneous networks (e.g., IP-based, ATM, VoIP, etc.). Supporting end-to-end QoS through the network was widely covered in literature and industry. Hence, diverse solutions were developed to implement QoS support at the network infrastructure. Integrated Services (IntServ) (Braden, Clark, & Shenker, 1994), Differentiated Services (DiffServ) (Blake, Black, Carlson, Davies, Wang, & Weiss, 1998), Multiprotocol Label Switching (MPLS) (Rosen, Viswanathan, & Callon, 1999), and Bandwidth Broker for DiffServ Networks (Stattenberger & Braun, 2003) are all technologies used to guarantee the QoS at the network level.

Clients are using Internet to invoke Web services; currently, the Internet treats all traffic equally as "Best Effort" and provides no support for QoS. Supporting QoS between Web services and their clients cannot be delivered while neglecting the QoS at the underlying network connecting both parties. QoS of Web services have to include network properties according to the public network (i.e., Internet). Specific QoS attributes for networks are bandwidth, delay, jitter, latency, and loss characteristics.

QoS Issues in Web Services

To evaluate quality of Web services, it is necessary to define quality attributes. These attributes are used as criteria for discriminating high-level Web service quality. Many quality attributes have been proposed in the software engineering literature (Zeng, Benatallah, Dumas, Kalagnanam, & Sheng, 2003; Martin-Albo, Bertoa, Calero, Vallecillo, Cechich, & Piattini, 2003; Norman, Fenton, & Pfleeger, 1997; Salamon & Wallace, 1994; Trendowicz & Punter, 2003); however, they are insufficient to cover all the important aspects of Web services. Common quality attributes are efficiency, functionality, portability, reliability, usability, maintainability, expandability, interoperability, reusability, integrity, survivability, correctness, verifiability, flexibility, performance, dependability, security, and safety (Hailpern & Tarr, 2001). A few works on Web services QoS classification are presented in Mani & Nagarajan (2002) and in Shuping (2003). Their focus is on the classification of QoS-supported attributes.

Differentiated Classes of QoS for Web Services

Selecting suitable Web services regarding the QoS provision is a determinant factor to ensure customer satisfaction. Different users may have different requirements and preferences regarding QoS. For example, a user may require minimizing the response time (RT) while satisfying certain constraints in terms of price and reputation, while another user may give more importance to the price than to the response time (Badidi, Esmahi, & Serhani, 2005). A QoS classification is needed to provide different requirements for different user profiles. We defined classes of QoS so each class of service corresponds to a specific level of quality

Table 1. Differentiated classes of services

Class of web services QoS Parameters	Class 1	Class 2	Class 3	...	Class n
Response Time	N/A	0.7 ms	0.5 ms		0.1ms
Latency	N/A	N/A	0.1 ms		0.01 ms
Availability	N/A	N/A	0.8		1 (100%)
Reputation	N/A	N/A	N/A		5/5
Service charge	0.10 $	0.2 $	0.25$		0.35$

N/A: not applicable

of service delivered to customers. The same WSDL interface is able to provide multiple classes of service to their customers.

In the context of Web services, different classes of service may be considered, either depending on a classification of users in occasional buyers, regular clients, and VIP clients, or depending on a service charge which the user is willing to pay. It is therefore appropriate to provide different classes of services, not only in terms of available options, but also in terms of QoS, especially services availability and response time. Table 1 describes examples of Web services classes implementing different QoS properties.

QoS Measurement in Web Services

Measurement is fundamental for dealing with quality. Indeed, quality should be measured prior to its evaluation and management. A metric defines a qualitative or quantitative property of the elements that users want to evaluate. It is characterized by: its name, data type, type of element to be measured, and computation logic. Operational metrics characterize the QoS that Web services exhibit when they are invoked. Paradoxically, when Web services users need to identify metrics that exhibit operational properties at run-time, the autonomy characteristic of Web services prohibits that exhibition. Nevertheless, when composing a process, it is indispensable to inquire the Web services operational metrics. In Web services environments, metrics and reports (log files) are not "static", and they should always be modified to handle the changes. In spite of this, it is difficult to manage the computational resources (metrics values) of Web services when the workload is unpredictable.

Quality metrics (e.g., service time, cost, reliability, fidelity of results) are useful in many regards. A Web service can be selected based on the supported quality metrics. Is it highly available? Does it answer a client's requests in an acceptable time? Furthermore, quality metrics will serve as the basis for adaptation of QoS. During process execution, the QoS needs to be monitored and checked against predefined and expected values, and when deviations are identified, dynamic adaptation mechanisms may be triggered.

QoS Management

Overview

Since network architectures (protocols) and the distributed applications deployed on those networks are continuously evolving, a configurable, realizable, manageable and maintainable QoS support is needed.

QoS management in distributed systems is among the hot topics that have received a great deal of interest in recent years. Many architectures have been proposed to manage the QoS for distributed applications (Benerjea, Ferrari, Mah, Oran, Verma, & Zhang, 1996; Braden, Clark, & Shenker, 1994; Aurrecoechea, Campell & Hauw, 1998; Campbell, Coulson, & Hutchison, 1994; Fischer, Hafid, Bochmann, & de Meer, 1997). The main objective of these architectures is to define a set of configurable quality of service interfaces to formalize QoS in end-system and networks. This is achieved by providing frameworks that integrate QoS control and management mechanisms.

The main approaches for QoS management are listed in Aurrecoechea, Campbell, and Hauw (1998) and in Campbell, Coulson, and Hutchison (1994) as follows:

- **Extended Integrated Reference Model (XRM)**, which is being developed at Columbia University;
- **Quality of Service Architecture (QoS-A)**, which is being developed at Lancaster University;
- **OSI QoS Framework**, which is being developed by the ISO SC21 QoS Working Group;
- **Heidelberg QoS Model**, which is being developed at IBM's European Networking Center;
- **TINA QoS Framework**, which is being developed by the TINA Consortium;
- **IETF QoS Manager (QM)**, which is being developed by the IETF Integrated Services Working Group;
- **Tenet Architecture**, which is being developed at the University of California at Berkley;
- **OMEGA Architecture**, which is being developed at the University of Pennsylvania; and
- **End System QoS Framework**, which is being developed at Washington University.

These architectures and frameworks may be classified into two classes according to the scope of the components considered (e.g., network component, end-system component). For example, the Tenet architecture (Fischer, Hafid, Bochmann, & de Meer, 1997), consider the QoS at the communication system level, while other architectures, like for instance the QOS-A architecture from Lancaster University (Campbell, Coulson, & Hutchison, 1994), include end-system components. A detailed survey of existing QoS architecture is given in Campbell, Aurrecoechea, and Hauw (1997).

There is still more work to be done in order to come up with comprehensive QoS architectures for distributed systems that will incorporate QoS interface, control, adaptation, and management across all architectural layers.

As Web services are recent paradigm, most works in the area focus on the development and deployment of Web services. Management of Web services, and in particular QoS management, is not a mature area. Proposals are still emerging, and architectures (approaches) for Web services and QoS management are still under experiments.

Approaches for QoS management of Web services can be divided into two categories. The first category extends existing approaches for network management to support the management of Web services. The second category of approaches has been developed specially for the management of Web services.

The approaches from network management such as Simple Network Management Protocol (SNMP) and Common Management Information Protocol (CMIP) are not totally appropriate for Web services. This is due to the nature of network services (components) that are tightly coupled to the standardized network protocols with specific QoS attributes. These network QoS attributes are typically different from those for Web services.

In the second category, some management tools have been developed to be integrated into Web services environments. For example, the HP Web services Management Engine (HP Open View, 2005) allows management operations for Web services as well as the definition and the enforcement of Service Level Agreement (SLA). The Parasoft platform (Parasoft, 2005) offers a set of tools (SOAPTest, TEST, Webking) to support management during the Web services development process. The IBM Tivoli management framework (IBM Tivoli, 2006) includes a business systems manager component to carry out management operations.

These management frameworks differ in terms of the QoS parameters considered and in the way the management tasks are performed. Now, most of the management infrastructures for Web services are moving towards the integration of the QoS management within the service-oriented architecture. An example of these infrastructures are the OASIS Web Services Distributed Management (WSDM) (OASIS, 2005), and the WS-Management from Microsoft (WS-Management, 2005). Some issues such as scalability, QoS guarantee, and high availability of Web services are still less considered in the above frameworks. These features will add value to the emerging architectures for QoS management in Web services.

QoS Management Functionalities

Most works on QoS management have been done in the context of multimedia distributed systems (e.g., delivery of video documents). QoS issues were also considered in Web-based applications, such as electronic commerce, where users access online catalogues, which may contain multimedia information. Traditionally, QoS provisioning is achieved through a number of phases such as the following: QoS specification, publication, discovery, negotiation, binding, adaptation, termination, and billing. Subsections explain in more detail each of these phases.

QoS-Aware Web Services Specification

Many efforts have been conducted to specify QoS constraints in Web services description. DARPA presents DAML-S which works on the semantic description of Web services, including the specification of functionalities and QoS constraints (DAML-S Coalition, 2002). IBM also works on WSLA (Web Service Level Agreements), which is an XML specification of SLAs for Web Services, focusing on QoS constraints (Keller & Ludwing, 2002). Another group from Carleton University developed the Web Service Offerings Language (WSOL) for the formal specification of various constraints, management statements, and classes of service for Web Services (Tosic, Pagurek, & Patel, 2003). Table 2 illustrates an example of a WSDL document, which describes QoS properties of a Web service.

QoS-Enabled Web Services Publication

A research group from Cardiff University has developed the Universal Description, Discovery, and Integration extension (UDDIe) registry (Ali, Rana, Al-Ali, & Walker, 2003) as an extension to the well-known UDDI standard. UDDIe supports the notion of "blue pages" to record user-defined properties associated with a service, and to enable discovery of services based on these. Searching on other attributes of a Web service are achieved by extending the

Table 2. WSDL description of video Web service within its QoS

```
<?xml version="1.0" encoding="UTF-8"?>
1.   <wsdl:definitions

.....
<wsdl:message name="getVideoResponse">
  <wsdl:part name="return" type="SOAP-ENC:string"/>
</wsdl:message>
....
<wsdl:portType name="VideoService">
  <wsdl:operation name=" getVideoClasses "
                  parameterOrder="symbol">
    <wsdl:input message="intf:getVideoClassRequest"/>
    <wsdl:output message="intf:getVideoClassResponse"/>
  </wsdl:operation>
</wsdl:portType>

<wsdl:binding name=" VideoWSSoap"
type="intf:VideoService">
  <wsdlsoap:binding style="rpc"
....
</wsdl:binding>
```

Differentiated class of QoWS

```
<wsdl:QoS serviceClass="1">
        <cpu_count>100</cpu_count>
        <disk_storage>150</disk_storage>
        <Capacity>1000 <Capacity/>
</wsdl:QoS>
```

Guaranteed QoS per service resources

```
<wsdl:QoS serviceClass="2">
<Service operationName="getLastPrice" ResponseTime="5"/>
<Service operationName="getPeriod" ResponseTime="10"/>
 </wsdl:QoS>
</wsdl:definitions>
```

Guaranteed QoS per operation

businessService class in UDDI with *propertyBag*, and extending the find method to enable queries addressed to UDDI to be based on numeric and logical (AND/OR) ranges. UDDIe can co-exist with the existing UDDI and enables a query to be issued to both simultaneously. It has been implemented as open-source software. Table 3 describes an example of client requests to find Web services based on its desired proprieties.

Web Services QoS Discovery

Once the UDDIe registry receives and analyzes a request obtained from a client, it sends a response to the client. Table 4 provides a scenario for request handling using the UDDIe.

Web Services QoS Negotiation

The QoS negotiation is the process of settling the level of QoS that the client is looking for, and that the provider is able to deliver. This process can be conducted using a negotiation protocol or/and with the involvement of a third party negotiator. The negotiation is ended by an agreement or a disagreement on the QoS that the Web services might support. If an agreement is reached, a QoS contract is signed between concerned parties. The contract specifies what the provider should deliver, the guaranteed QoS, and the cost.

Web Services QoS Binding

After the negotiation is finished and the QoS contract is signed between the user and the provider of Web services, the user can invoke the requested Web services with the QoS agreed upon. The invocation operation is achieved using binding information described in WSDL.

Table 3. Client request to UDDIe within specified QoS (Ali, Rana, Al-Ali,& Walker, 2003)

```
<find_service generic="2.0" xmlns="urn:uddi-org:api_v2">
    <name>MathService</name>
    <propertyBag>
        <property>
            <propertyFindQualifier>equal_to</propertyFindQualifier>
            <propertyName>cpu_count</propertyName>
            <propertyType>number</propertyType>
            <propertyValue>100</propertyValue>
        </property>
        <property>
            <propertyFindQualifier>equal_to</propertyFindQualifier>
            <propertyName>disk_storage</propertyName>
            <propertyType>number</propertyType>
            <propertyValue>150</propertyValue>
        </property>
    </propertyBag>
</find_service>
```

Table 4. UDDIe, a SOAP response to a client request described in Table.3 (Ali, Rana, Al-Ali, & Walker, 2003)

```
<save_service generic="2.0" xmlns="urn:uddie-org:api_v2">
  <name xml:lang="en">MathService</name>
    <bindingTemplates>
      <bindingTemplate bindingKey="">
<accessPoint URLType="http">http://localhost/MathService/services/mathService</accessPoint>
        <tModelInstanceDetails>
          <tModelInstanceInfo tModelKey="*****">
            <instanceDetails>
             <overviewDoc>
               <overviewURL>http://localhost/MathService_interface.wsdl</overviewURL>
             </overviewDoc>
            </instanceDetails>
          </tModelInstanceInfo>
        </tModelInstanceDetails>
      </bindingTemplate>
    </bindingTemplates>
  <propertyBag>
    <property>
      <propertyName>cpu_count</propertyName>
      <propertyType>number</propertyType>
      <propertyValue>100</propertyValue>
    </property>
    <property>
      <propertyName>disk_storage</propertyName>
      <propertyType>number</propertyType>
      <propertyValue>150</propertyValue>
    </property>
  </propertyBag>
  </businessService> </save_service>
```

Web Services QoS Monitoring

QoS monitoring for Web services is an important management activity which is required to sustain the contracted QoS and to support other management activities such as QoS adaptation, QoS policing, and QoS renegotiation. QoS monitoring is the continuous observation of the QoS that is actually provided. When the measured value of a QoS parameter does not meet the agreed one, violation is detected and a notification is issued to indicate the violation and, if possible, the cause.

QoS monitoring had been previously used in distributed multimedia applications, network services, and Web-based applications such as electronic commerce (Bochmann, Kerherve, Hafid, Dini, & Pons, 1996; Bolot, Turletti, & Wakeman, 1994; Campbell, Coulson, Garcia, Hutchison, & Leopold 1993; Lu, Abdelzaher, Lu, & Tao 2002; Nait-Abdesselam & Agoulmine, 1999). It is typically performed using techniques such as measurement (Nait-Abdesselam & Agoulmine, 1999) or by deploying mobile agent observers (Benharref, Glitho, & Dssouli, 2005).

Web Services QoS Adaptation

When QoS is violated, adaptation mechanisms are invoked. The role of QoS adaptation is to maintain, as much as possible, the continuity of a service when the initially-contracted QoS is no longer supported. Adaptation takes various forms, and can affect one or more QoS parameters. The adaptation process is initiated based on a set of feedbacks (violation detection) generated from the monitoring procedures. The provider adapts violated QoS to a level agreed or acceptable by the client.

Web Services QoS Termination and Billing

Once the Web services provision is terminated, the reserved resources are released and a bill is prepared for the client. Messages must be exchanged between the two intervening roles in QoS management (Web services provider client) to terminate the QoS processes.

Scalability Issues

Scalability is the capacity of the system to accommodate an increasing number of users without a degradation of the performance parameters. Scalability was widely addressed in earlier decentralized architectures. Therefore, many scalable solutions (architectures, tools, and environments) were proposed and implemented. Unfortunately, scaling systems may introduce some problems to the management of distributed services, such as the extra load generated from the execution of management and monitoring operations. The following section overviews some traditional scalable distributed architectures.

Background

Scalability in distributed systems was studied in Kartz, Butler, and McGrath (1995); Dias, Kish, Mukherjee, and Tawari (1996); Baentsch, Baum, and Molter (1997); Obraczka (1994); and Ould Mohamed-Salem (2002), and is mostly related to the scaling up of the capacity of a system to support more users with more requests. Many solutions have been proposed and implemented to enhance the capacity of systems. The proposed solutions diverge according to their adopted approaches, and their applicability depends on the type of service and architecture. Several approaches have been investigated in this context to provide scalable solutions. Caching and prefetching are standard techniques used in distributed systems to reduce the user response time. Caching documents close to clients that need them reduces the number of server requests and the traffic associated with them. The basic idea of prefetching stems from the fact that after retrieving a page from a server, a user usually spends some time viewing the page and, during this period, the generally idle network link can be used to fetch some files in anticipation. Other approaches are based on anycast services (Bhattacharjee, Ammar, Zegura, Shah, & Fei, 1997; Patridge, Mendez, & Milliken, 1993), pushing and multicasting, and DNS-based approach (Dias, Kish, Mukherjee, & Tawari, 1996; Kartz, Butler, & McGrath, 1995). Replication is a well-known and natural way to distribute load and improve system performance (Baentsch, Baum, & Molter 1997; Obraczka, 1994). The primary aim of replication is to increase data availability and to reduce the load on a server by balancing the service accesses among the replicated servers.

Scalability in SOA

The SOA architecture enhances the interoperability of distributed systems through the integration of languages and independent protocols that make easier the publication, the discovery, and the binding of distributed components. According to scalability, SOA do not address this issue and do not lead to better scalability than the traditional existing architectures. However, SOA can scale using the same approaches described above.

Nowadays, the trend in Web services management is to integrate scalability within the service-oriented architecture. However, scalability in SOA is highly related to the scalability of the Web server on which the services are deployed, the transport protocols (SOAP), the public registry in which services are published and discovered, and the description language used to define the service interface (WSDL).

Little has been done for the scalability in SOA architecture; until now, most of the works are still under the definition of requirements. Scaling SOA can be done by integrating the approaches used before to scale distributed systems such as those described above. It also can be done by extending the programming language and protocols stack involved in SOA to support increasing numbers of clients with different requirements.

Scalable QoS-aware Web Services Management Architecture (QoSMA)

Objectives

With the growing interest in QoS support in Web services and the limited number of QoS-aware management architectures for Web services, we set out to develop an architecture that meets the following requirements:

1. Provide a QoS model for the specification of the quality of services in Web services. The model should provide an integrated view for both service providers and requestors, which do not have the same view, and should allow providers to specify the classes of services which they can provide to their customers;

2. Allow description, publication, and discovery of Web services based on their QoS attributes;

3. Provide support for QoS management operations such as selection, negotiation, and monitoring;

4. Enables monitoring the provision of QoS agreed between provider and clients, and the adaptation of QoS once the latest is violated;

5. Be scalable by providing support for a large number of clients with QoS requirements; and

6. Allow the implementation of various policies for the selection of QoS-aware Web services.

Architecture Overview

To meet the above requirements, we chose a broker-based architecture for our framework, an architecture that has been successfully used in many distributed systems. It usually consists of clients requiring services, a front-end broker component or service, and a set of service providers. The broker allows clients to find suitable providers that are able to deliver their required Web services. Figure 3 depicts the main components of the QoSMA architecture.

- **Clients** are any applications that can select a Web service and bind to it. We distinguish between different types of clients with different QoS requirements. We may find some clients more interested in the service availability, while other clients search for the

Figure 3. QoSMA architecture

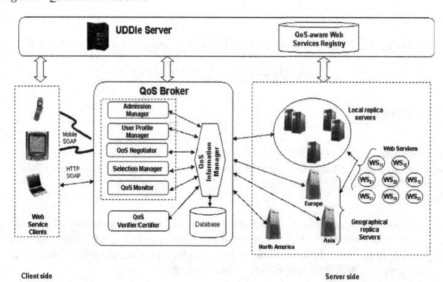

cheapest Web services, and they do not care about the performance features of Web services.

- **Providers** are those who develop, test, and deploy Web services, then publish them on the registries. The providers can implements different interfaces of the same Web services according to the QoS it supports. They also can deploy services on different replicas' servers to insure high availability and scalability of their architectures.

- **QoS broker** is a service or set of services, that (1) accepts incoming requests from clients, (2) maintains information about the resources and services rendered by Web services provider, and monitor their QoS, and (3) finds, through the UDDIe registry, the set of QoS-aware Web services able to deliver the client's required service. Details about the broker design are given in *Web Service QoS Broker*.

- **UDDIe registry** is a registry that allows clients to discover Web services based on the QoS specification. It also allows providers to publish their Web services which hold a description of QoS parameters that they support.

As a first step in our architecture, the provider specifies their Web services-enabled QoS in WSDL and publishes them through UDDIe registry, an extended registry for Web services, which enables publication and discovery of Web services with range-based QoS attributes. Once Web services are published in UDDIe, clients may search through the UDDIe registry for Web services which are able to deliver their required services with QoS constraints.

Web services providers and clients typically do not have the required capabilities to negotiate, manage, and monitor QoS; they delegate tasks such as Web services selection, QoS negotiation, and QoS monitoring to an independent QoS Web Service Broker (WSB). WSB is developed as Web service is deployed, and then published through the UDDIe.

The broker selects Web services based on the service and the QoS required by clients. The common operations carried out in a SOA are performed in QoSMA as follows:

1. **Publish:** The provider specifies a QoS-enabled Web service in WSDL and publishes it in the UDDIe registry. Afterward, the clients can find the description in the registry. Among the Web services description is the description of the WSB.

2. **Find:** Clients searching for services are able to satisfy their desired QoS. This operation returns the WSDL description document of suitable Web services. The WSDL description includes all QoS classes the service is providing (e.g., Class1: [Best Effort], Class2: [Guaranteed: RT < 12ns, Cost = 50$, NQ/day = 100], Class3: [.....]).

3. **Invoke:** The invocation operation is achieved using binding information described in WSDL. Clients may invoke first the WSB in order to negotiate the QoS of a Web service.

4. **Bind:** After a negotiation phase is finished, the client is redirected by WSB to the available service that provides the required QoS. Selection of the target service by WSB is based as well on the load distribution among duplicated Web services. To achieve this task, WSB continually requests performance information from the server side and uses it to make the selection decision (Web services availability, Web services capacity, server location, load information, etc.).

Web Service QoS Broker

The QoS broker consists of the following components: Admission manager, User profile manager, QoS negotiator, Selection manager, QoS monitor, QoS verifier/certifier, QoS information manager, and a database. The components of the broker presented in Figure 3, which are enclosed by a dashed line, concern both provider and client, while the verifier/certifier component concerns only the provider of Web services.

- **QoS Information Manager:** The *QoS Information Manager* is in charge of specifying the QoS parameters of interests according to the user-required QoS, and collecting actual values for these parameters from the Web services providers. QoS information as well as information regarding QoS violations is maintained in the broker's database. The other components of the broker get QoS information from the QoS Information manager to achieve their objectives. These might be useful for services providers to enhance their QoS-aware Web services.

- **Admission Manager:** The *Admission Manager* classifies incoming requests and verifies the provisioned classes of QoS. The goal of the admission control algorithm implemented by the admission manager is to determine whether the received requests are allowed to use the services. This means that Web services access is denied to requests from users who did not negotiate the level of QoS with the selected Web services providers.

- **User Profile Manager:** The *User Profile Manager* is responsible for managing users' preferences and their required QoS. This allows the user to update its preferences and required QoS after receiving, for example, a certain level of QoS.

- **QoS Negotiator:** The *QoS Negotiator* is in charge of conducting and managing the negotiation process through a negotiation protocol. At the end of negotiation and after an agreement is reached, the QoS negotiator defines and issues the clauses of the QoS contract, which specifies what the provider should deliver, the guaranteed QoS, and the cost. The contract is stored in the broker's database, and a copy of it is sent to both the user and the provider.

- **Selection Manager:** The *Selection Manager* is in charge of implementing different selection policies in order to provide an acceptable quality of service to the users. These policies can range from simple policies, as random and round-robin, to complex ones taking account of the current state of servers in terms of availability, load, and level of quality of service which they can deliver.

- **QoS Monitor:** The *QoS Monitor* is responsible for monitoring the QoS that is being delivered by Web services providers to clients. The monitoring process is based on the information described in the contract stored in the broker's database. A detailed description of this process is described in *QoS Monitoring*.

- **QoS Verifier and Certifier:** The *QoS Verifier* is responsible for verifying Web services and their QoS. The verification is performed based on information received from providers and the results of the tests performed by the broker. This information concerns Web services location (URL), and QoS information description. The QoS verifier performs the following tasks:

- • It asks for information about the provider and its Web services (servers resources capacity, connections used, network information, etc.);
- • It checks the WSDL files of the Web services under consideration (location, interface, and implementation description);
- • It checks the correctness of the information provided by the services supplier;
- • It makes sure that all published operations are available;
- • It verifies the QoS of Web services described in WSDL. The QoS verifier can initiate, if necessary, additional tests to validate other information provided in the WSDL document. This information concerns QoS attributes classification (definition, computation logic, upper and lower bound); and
- • It stores the verification report in the broker database.

- • **Databases:** The broker's *database* stores information generated by the broker's components: user profile manager, QoS verifier/certifier, QoS negotiator, QoS monitor, and QoS information manager. It also supplies information to these components. Information stored in the database comprises certificates, verification and confirmation reports, monitoring information, and so forth.

Management Operations in QoSMA

The management operations in QoSMA concern essentially QoS negotiation between provider and customer, and QoS monitoring and adaptation when there is a violation of the agreed QoS.

QoS Negotiation

The negotiation process is carried out by the broker in order to reach an agreement, regarding QoS to be delivered, between Web service providers and customers. The client first informs the broker about its required service and the class of QoS that it is willing to accept. Based upon the QoS information maintained by the Information Manager component, the Selection Manager Component selects a suitable server which may be able to satisfy the required QoS. Then, this server is approached to determine whether it will be able to satisfy the required class of QoS given its current conditions. In the positive, a contract is signed by the client and the provider. The contract specifies the service to be provided by the provider to the client, the guaranteed QoS, the cost of the service, and the actions to be taken when there is a violation of the agreed QoS.

If the selected server is not able to deliver the required QoS because of its current conditions, the broker selects another server and repeats the negotiation process. If no server is available to satisfy the required QoS, the client is informed so that it may reduce its QoS expectations or wait until the conditions of the system may allow obtaining the required level of service.

QoS Monitoring

As we have explained before, QoS monitoring of QoS-aware Web services in QoSMA is carried out by the QoS Monitor component of the broker to assure their compliance with the contracted QoS and to take appropriate actions when a violation of the contract is detected. The QoS monitor continually observes the level of QoS level rendered to clients. It gets information about the QoS parameters to be evaluated, prior to the observation, from both the client and the Web service provider. Observation is achieved through periodic measurement and computation of these QoS parameters at some observation points (locations) between the client and the Web service provider. Measurement of QoS parameters, such as response time, availability, and latency, requires the definition of: the observation points (provider or requester side), the frequency of measurement, the length of the interval over which the QoS parameters are to be measured, and a set of procedures for computing, at run-time, these QoS attributes.

The QoS monitor detects QoS violation when the measured value of a QoS parameter does not meet the requirements of the agreed one. In this case, it notifies both the client and the provider about the violation, and sends them a report including the cause of the violation. The QoS monitor stores information about violations in the broker database for future use, and it includes: the type of violation, the name of violated parameters, the time of violation, and the cause of violation. The stored information can be used to perform dynamic adaptation of QoS and/or to generate some statistics, such as the number of violations of a given parameter, the last violation of a given parameter, the mean time between two violations, time spent to recover from violations, the most frequent cause of violations, and so forth.

QoS attributes can be measured at different observation points: client side, provider side, or between the two sides as depicted by Figure 4. Nevertheless, the location of the observation point should be carefully chosen depending on the nature of the QoS attribute to be measured. For example, the *response time* parameter, when it is measured at the provider side (P2), the delay and latency of the underlying network are not considered. However, when it

Figure 4. Measurement-based QoS monitoring

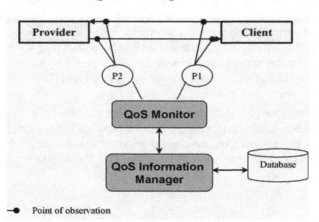

is measured at the client side (P1), it is affected by the delay introduced by the underlying network infrastructure as it will be perceived by the client.

To monitor the QoS attributes, the QoS monitor instantiates observers at the observation points (P1 and P2 in Figure 4). To measure the *response time,* for example, the observer at P1 captures the time stamp when the request leaves the client and the time stamp when the response is received by the client. The QoS monitor calculates, then, the response time by performing the difference between the two time stamps, and reports the measured value to the QoS information manager. A violation is detected by the QoS monitor if the measured value is below a threshold value agreed with the provider.

QoS Adaptation

When the agreed QoS is violated, adaptation mechanisms should be employed in order to adapt the violated QoS to a level agreed or acceptable by the client. The role of QoS adaptation is to maintain, as much as possible, the continuity of a service when the initially-contracted QoS is not preserved. In distributed systems, it is often very hard to sustain QoS over a long period of time. Adaptive methods could be used as alternatives and enhancements to resource reservation-based QoS provisioning. Adaptation takes various forms, and could affect one or more QoS parameters of the Web services.

Scalability in QoSMA

The scalability in QoSMA architecture is achieved via replication. Web services are deployed on various servers, which could be local replica servers and/or deployed on separate geographical servers. The QoSMA architecture supports the addition and removal of Web services according to demand variation. This will allow each server to implement its replication policies that suit its objectives and the particularities of each type of Web services. The QoSMA architecture can also be extended to a federation of brokers where a QoS broker is deployed, for example, within an organizational domain. These brokers may exchange QoS information about servers within their domains and cooperate to achieve the management operations we describe in Management operations in QoSMA.

Evaluation and Discussions

To develop components of QoSMA architecture, we are using WebLogic platform 8.1 with service pack 2, which includes the application server and the development environment (workshop) (BEA WebLogic platform, 2003). We store data generated from the execution of operations performed by the QoSMA components in Oracle Database version 9i (Oracle Database, 2004). The Weblogic platform supports, in addition to other functions, the scalability function since it allows dynamic instantiation and management of more than one instance of servers. Components of the QoSMA which have been completely implemented and tested on real environment involving clients, providers, and the broker are: the QoS selection manager, the QoS verifier and certifier, and the QoS monitor. Other components are partially implemented, such as the QoS negotiator where the negotiation algorithm is defined and still to be implemented and tested. We are working on the implementation of the admission manager and the QoS information manager. Work is also in progress to implements the interaction and the collaboration between components of the QoS brokers.

We are also working to build a simulation model to evaluate our QoS monitoring-based measurement approach with scenarios involving providers, clients, and service monitor. By monitoring QoS properties, mainly the response time, latency, and the service availability; we will verify whether each client selects the right service provider, which guarantee the client's QoS requirements. This work will be reported in future publications.

We are convinced that the proposed architecture is a good starting point for QoS management of Web services. The service provider does not have to design and develop her/his own broker but just invokes one from the published brokers. The client will also find a good support during its Web services selection using the broker services. Additionally, the broker insures the provision of QoS via the continuous monitoring of QoS.

In addition to the technical aspects of the architecture that we have described in the previous sections, the economic aspect of the QoSMA architecture has to be considered. This aspect is critical for its adoption by organizations. Hence, the ongoing cost associated with the adoption of QoSMA has to be determined. This aspect includes the requirements in terms of software and hardware, architecture components integration, deployment, and implementation. The weight of each of these requirements may differ from one organization to the other depending on the type of Web services that will be deployed, integrated, or used by the organization.

Hardware and Software Requirements

The requirements in terms of hardware and software vary from the provider to the consumer of Web services. At the provider side, powerful machines are typically recommended. Each machine should have at least 1GO of RAM, Pentium-3 processor and above, and a considerable capacity of storage. At the client side, the hardware requirement is highly dependent on the type of applications used by the client to access Web services. In terms of software, a Web application server environment supporting Web services technologies is required. Examples of such environments are: AXIS, WebSphere from IBM, and Weblogic from BEA Systems. Also, a Web services development platform is required to test Web services and to integrate them within QoSMA. Examples of such platforms are: Weblogic Workshop from BEA Systems and WebSphere Studio from IBM.

Integration Requirements

The operations provided by the architecture have to be understood by both the clients and the providers of Web services. In addition, the broker and the monitor components of the architecture should be fully operational, and their interfaces have to be known in advance by both the providers and clients. The integration phase requires a minor configuration and adjustment of the provider's and/or the client's application.

Monitoring Automation Requirements

The monitoring requirements are especially related to the management of the communications between the monitor component and the Web service providers and clients. They are also related to the integration of SOAP handlers at the provider and/or the client environment. These handlers are used for intercepting messages circulating between the Web services provider and clients for the sake of monitoring.

Implementation and Deployment Requirements

These requirements are mainly related to the installation of the hardware and software infrastructure, the setting up of the development environment, the configuration of servers, the testing of the architecture components as well as the organization's Web services, and the deployment of the organization's Web services within the architecture.

The main limitations of the architecture are the requirement of its adoption. The architecture is centralized around one single broker; however, it will suffer from the same weakness of centralized architectures such as the failure of the broker (one point of failure) and the degree of trustfulness to the broker component. However, these limitations are weighted against the benefits in terms of QoS management, monitoring, and scalability.

We are working to enhance the proposed architecture to support a proliferation of distributed and independent set of brokers from different vendors. These QoS brokers will cooperate collectively in delivering QoS management for providers and clients of Web services. Each broker will be deployed in an organizational domain. The new additions to the architecture will improve its reliability and will enable a more flexible and trustable environment with multiple participants. Results of this work will be reported in future publications.

Conclusion

QoS management is among the hot issues in the Web services community. As Web services are becoming a new trend in Internet technologies. As they spread to large numbers of organizations, managing their QoS becomes an urgent need for both clients and providers of these very demanding applications. We have presented a new architecture for scalable management of QoS based on a broker component. The QoSMA architecture presents a framework for Web services QoS-aware specification, publication, negotiation, monitoring, and discovery; as well as achieving Web services scalability by means of replicating Web services and performing services selection and QoS management through an independent brokerage Web services.

In this chapter, we presented scalable broker-based architecture for QoS management of Web services. The QoSMA architecture has the following features:

- QoSMA's broker is only involved in the Web services selection and QoS negotiation conducted at the beginning of a session. The clients then interact directly with the assigned Web services. With respect to scalability, this approach is superior to those where a server is selected for each request.

- QoSMA provides architectural support for the provision of similar Web services with different categories of QoS.

- QoSMA completes the selection of Web services based on their QoS and support QoS negotiation and monitoring.

- QoSMA's server replication increases Web services availability and reduces the load on the Web services.

- QoSMA provides architectural support for performance information gathering for reliability and load-balancing purposes.

- QoSMA provides scalable mechanisms by which users may locate suitable Web servers without any prior knowledge of the organization of resources or their physical locations.

- QoSMA Manages QoS provision for a diverse population of users that may not have the same requirements.

- QoSMA has the ability to provide different levels of Web services to different classes of clients.

- QoSMA has the ability to grow gradually as the demand for resources grows.

In the future, we are going to explore extensions to the QoSMA to support a distributed broker. We are also going to add more features to our management components and make it available for both clients and providers.

References

Ali, S. A., Rana, O. F., Al-Ali, A., & Walker, D. W. (2003). UDDIe: An extended registry for Web services. In *Proceedings of the Workshop on Service-Oriented Computing: Models, Architectures, and Applications at SAINT Conference* (pp. 85-89). Florida. IEEE Computer Society Press.

Aurrecoechea, C., Campbell, A. T., & Hauw, L. (1998). A Survey of QoS Architectures. *ACM/Springer Verlag Multimedia Systems Journal.* Special Issue on QoS Architecture, 6(3), 138-151.

Badidi, E., Esmahi, L., & Serhani, M. A. (2005). A queuing model for service selection of multi-classes QoS-aware Web services. In *Proceedings of the 3rd IEEE European Conference on Web Services (ECOWS'05),* Sweden, November, 2005 (pp. 204-212).

Baentsch, M., Baum, L., & Molter, G. (1997). Enhancing the Web's infrastructure: From caching to replication. *IEEE Internet Computing, 1*(2), 18-27.

BEA WebLogic platform. Retrieved October 17, 2006 from http://e-docs.bea.com/platform/docs81/

Benerjea, A., Ferrari, D., Mah, B. A., Oran, M., Verma, D. C., & Zhang, H. (1996). The tenet real-time protocol suite: Design, implementation, and experiences. *IEEE/ACM Transactions on Networking* (pp. 1-10).

Benharref, A., Glitho, R., & Dssouli, R. (2005). Mobile agents for testing Web services in next generation networks. In *Proceedings of the International Conference on Mobile Agents for Telecommunication Applications* (pp. 182-191), Montreal, Canada.

Bhattacharjee, S., Ammar, M. H., Zegura, E. W., Shah, V., & Fei, Z. (1997). Application layer anycasting. In *Proceedings of INFOCOM '97* (vol. 3, pp. 1388-1396).

Blake, S., Black, D., Carlson, M., Davies, E., Wang, Z., & Weiss, W. (1998). *An Architecture for differentiated services.* RFC 2475, IETF, December 1998.

Bochmann, G. V., Kerherve, B., Hafid, A., Dini, P., & Pons, A. (1996). Architectural design of adaptive distributed multimedia systems. In *Proceedings of the IEEE International Workshop in Distributed Multimedia Systems Design* (pp. 31-40), Berlin, Germany.

Bolot, J.C., Turletti, T., & Wakeman, I., (1994). Scalable feedback control for multicast video distribution in the Internet. *ACM SIGCOMM '94.*

Braden, R., Clark, D., & Shenker, S. (1994). *Integrated services in the Internet architecture: An overview.* RFC 1633. Internet Engineering Task Force, June 1994.

Campbell, A., Coulson, G., Garcia, F., Hutchison, D., & Leopold, H. (1993). Integrated quality of service for multimedia communications. In *Proceedings of IEEE INFOCOM '93,* San Francisco, CA (vol. 2, pp. 732-739).

Campbell, A., Coulson, G., & Hutchison, D. (1994). A quality of service architecture. *ACM SIGCOMM Computer Communication Review 24*(2).

CCITT Recommendation E.800 (1988). *Quality of service and dependability vocabulary,* Vol. II Rec. E.800. pp. 191 (ITU-T Rec. E. 800)

DAML-S Coalition (2002). Web service description for the semantic Web. In *Proceedings of the International Semantic Web Conference,* (pp. 348-363).

Della-Libera, G., Hallam-Baker, P., Hondo, M., Janczuk, T., Kaler, C., & Maruyama, H., (2002). *Web services security policy (WS-securitypolicy).* Retrieved from http://www-106.ibm.com/developerworks/library/ws-secpol/

Dias, D. M., Kish, W., Mukherjee, R., & Tawari, R. (1996). A scalable and highly available Web server. In *Proceedings of the 41st IEEE Computer Society International Conference* (pp. 85-92).

Fischer, S., Hafid, A., Bochmann, G., &. de Meer, H. (1997). Cooperative QoS management in multimedia applications. In *Proceedings of the IEEE International Conference on Multimedia Computing and Systems (ICMCSO '97),*(pp 303-310) Ottawa, Canada. IEEE Computer Society Press.

Gottschalk, K., Graham, S., Kreger, H., & Snell, J. (2002). Introduction to Web services architecture. *IBM Systems Journal, 41*(2), 170-177.

Gray, A. R., & MacDonell, S. G. (1997). A comparison of techniques for developing predictive models of software metrics. *Entrainment and Software Technology, 39*, 425-437.

Hailpern, B., & Tarr, P. L. (2001). *Software engineering for Web services: A focus on separation of concerns* (IBM Research Report).

HP Open View (2005). Retrieved October 17, 2006 from http://www.managementsoftware.hp.com

IBM Tivoli (2006). Retrieved October 17, 2006 from http://www.tivoli.com/

ISO 8402 (2000). Quality management and quality assurance. *International Organization for Standardization* (technical comittee QSAE/TC 1/SC 5) (ed. 1, pp. 39).

Kartz, E. D., Butler, M., & McGrath, R. A. A. (1995). Scalable HTTP server: The NCSA prototype, computer networks, and ISDN systems. In *Proceedings of the First International Conference on the World Wide Web, Elvister Science BV,* (pp. 155-164).

Keller, A., & Ludwing, H. (2002). *The WSLA framework: Specifying and monitoring service level agreements for Web services* (IBM Research Report).

Leymann, F. (2001). Web Services Flow Language (WSFL 1.0). *IBM Corporation.* Retrieved May, 2001 from http://www-306.ibm.com/software/solutions/webservices/pdf/WSFL.pdf

Li, Y., Ding, X., Chen, Y., Liu, D., & Li, T. (2003). The framework supporting QoS-enabled Web services. In *Proceedings of the International Conference on Web Services.*(pp. 156-159), Las Vegas, NV.

Zeng, L., Benatallah, B., Dumas, M., Kalagnanam, J., & Sheng, Q.Z. (2003). Quality driven Web services composition. In *Proceedings of WWW2003.* Budapest, Hungary. ACM 1-58113-680-3/03/0005.

Lu, Y., Abdelzaher, T. F., Lu, C., & Tao, G. (2002). An adaptive control framework for QoS guarantees and its application to differentiated caching services. In *Proceedings of IWQoS* (pp. 23-32), Miami Beach, Florida.

Mani, A., & Nagarajan, A. (2002). Understanding quality of service for Web services. *IBM Corporation.* Retrieved October 17, 2006 from http://www-106.ibm.com/developer-works/library/ws-quality.html

Martin-Albo, J., Bertoa, M. F., Calero, C., Vallecillo, A., Cechich, A., & Piattini, M. (2003). CQM: A software component metric classification model. In *Proceedings of the 7th ECOOP Workshop on Quantitative Approaches in Object-Oriented Software Engineering,* (pp. 1-10). Darmstadt, Germany.

Menascé, D. A. (2002). QoS issues in Web services. *IEEE Internet Computing, 6*(6), 72-75.

Nait-Abdesselam, F., & Agoulmine, N. (1999). QoS control and adaptation in distributed multimedia systems. In *Proceedings of the IPPS/SDP Workshops,* (pp. 75-383), San Juan, Puerto Rico.

Norman, E., Fenton, E. N., & Pfleeger, S. L. (1997). *Software metrics, A rigorous & practical approach* (2nd ed.). International Thomson Computer Press.

OASIS (2004). *Universal Description, Discovery and Integration (UDDI) Version 3.0.2 (UDDI Spec Technical Committee Draft)*. Retrieved October 17, 2006 from http://uddi. org/pubs/uddi-v3.0.2-20041019.htm

OASIS (2005). *Web Services Distributed Management: Management of Web Services (WSDM-MOWS) 1.0.* Retrieved October 17, 2006 from http://docs.oasis-open.org/ wsdm/2004/12/wsdm-mows-1.0.pdf

Obraczka, K. (1994). *Massively replicating services in wide-area inter-networks.* PhD. thesis, University of Southern California.

Oracle Database (2004). Retrieved October 17, 2006 from http://www.oracle.com

Ould Mohamed-Salem, M. V. (2002). *Scalable server selection for Web applications using a broker node.* PhD thesis, University of Montreal.

Parasoft (2005). Retrieved October 17, 2006 from http://www.parasoft.com

Patridge, C., Mendez, T., & Milliken, W. (1993). *Host anycasting service.* IETF RFC 1546. Nov 1993.

Rosen, E., Viswanathan, A., & Callon, R. (1999). *Multi-protocol label switching architecture.* Internet Draft <draft-ietf-mpls-arch-05.txt> IETF April 1999

Salamon, W. J., & Wallace, D. R. (1994). *Quality characteristics and metrics for reusable software.* National Institute of Standards and Technology. Computer Systems Laboratory. Gaithersburg MD.

Shuping, R. (2003). A framework for discovering Web services with desired quality of services attributes. In *Proceedings of the International Conference on Web Services,* (pp. 208-213) Las Vegas, NV.

Stattenberger, G., & Braun, T. (2003). *Performance of a bandwidth broker for DiffServ networks.* No.557212. TR. Bern, Switzerland: Institute of Computer Science and Applied Mathematics, University of Bern.

Tidwell, D. (2000). Web services—The Web's next revolution. *IBM Corporation.* Retrieved November, 2000 from http://www6.software.ibm.com/developerworks/education/ws-basics/wsbasics-ltr.pdf

Tosic, V., Pagurek, B., & Patel, K. (2003). WSOL, A language for the formal specification of classes of service for Web services. In *Proceedings of the International Conference on Web Services* (pp. 375-381), Las Vegas, NV.

Trendowicz, A., & Punter, T. (2003). Quality modeling for software product lines. *Proceedings of the 7th ECOOP Workshop on Quantitative Approaches in Object-Oriented Software Engineering,* Darmstadt, Germany. Retrieved October 16, 2006 from http://ctp.di.fct. unl.pt/QUASAR/QAOOSE2003

World Wide Web Consortium (2003). *SOAP (Simple Object Access Protocol) Version 1.2. W3C Recommendation.* Retrieved on October 17, 2006 from http://www.w3.org/TR/ soap/

World Wide Web Consortium (2004). *Web Services Description Language 2.0. W3C Working Draft 3.* Retrieved October 17, 2006 from http://www.w3.org/tr/wsdl20

WS-Management (2005). Retrieved October 17, 2006 from http://msdn.microsoft.com/ ws/2005/02/ws-management/

Chapter X

Information System Development Failure and Complexity:
A Case Study

Abou Bakar Nauman, COMSATS Institute of Information Technology, Pakistan

Romana Aziz, COMSATS Institute of Information Technology, Pakistan

A.F.M. Ishaq, COMSATS Institute of Information Technology, Pakistan

Abstract

This chapter examines the causes of failure in a Web-based information system development project and finds out how complexity can lead a project towards failure. Learning from an Information System Development Project (ISDP) failure plays a key role in the long-term success of any organization desirous of continuous improvement via evaluation and monitoring of its information systems (IS) development efforts. This study reports on a seemingly simple (but only deceptively so) failed ISDP to inform the reader about the various complexities involved in ISDPs in general, and in developing countries in particular. An existing framework from contemporary research is adopted to map the complexities found in the project under study and the critical areas, which lead to the decreased reliability and failure in Web-based information system development, are highlighted.

Introduction

Information and Communication Technologies (ICTs) are globally recognized as an enabler of economic and social growth, and Information Systems (IS) can play a key role in accelerated growth and development if applied properly. In the developing countries, there is much talk of "development leapfrogging" by deployment of Information and Communication Technologies (ICT). Developing countries are making direct deployment of the latest technologies, techniques, and methodologies for the use of information systems without the step-by-step use of previous technologies already abandoned in the Western-developed countries. In this scenario, most development efforts in the field of Information Systems are overshadowed by organizational dissatisfaction and schedule and cost overruns resulting in project abandonment and failure. The following quote from a UN report (Gilhooly, 2005, p. 25), mentioning Least Developed Countries (LDC), sums up the severity of the situation:

Failure to urgently and meaningfully exploit the available means to bridge the digital divide may consign many developing countries, particularly LDCs, to harmful and even permanent exclusion from the network revolution.

In this chapter, our focus is Information System Development Project (ISDP) failure from the perspective of a developing country. Learning from an ISDP failure plays a key role in the long-term success of any organization desirous of continuous improvement via evaluation and monitoring of its information systems development efforts. The "learning from failure" factor assumes a higher level of significance in the context of developing countries. In developing countries it is very important that the scarce resources are optimally utilized in such a way that the probability of failure is minimized. This study reports on a seemingly simple (but only deceptively so) failed ISDP to inform the reader about the various complexities involved in information systems development projects in general and in developing countries in particular.

This chapter is organized in five sections. In section two we describe the general information system development process and the associated rate of failure in this industry. Section three discusses the relationship between failure and complexity. A case study is presented in section four, followed by conclusions in section five.

Background

Most of the IS research reported in the literature falls in three main categories, that is, positivist, interpretive, and critical, and there is widespread consensus that interpretive style with a critical stance is most suited for researching the IS-related issues in developing countries. The research is interpretive in nature, and an interview approach is used for investigations. The research is of significance to a wide audience in the IS community who are interested in understanding the impact and influence of various factors on failure of an ISDP in the peculiar environment of a developing country.

An organization may have one or many business processes (work processes) producing products, services, or information. In order to run properly, these processes need support from:

- **External environment,** including regulatory policies, supplier, and competitor behavior; and
- **Internal environment,** in the form of resources and managerial and organizational commitment.

Information systems support or automate the business or work processes by processing the information which is usually limited to capturing, transmitting, storing, retrieving, manipulating, and displaying information. An innovative information system usually changes the existing business/work processes in order to make them more suitable for automation.

A typical organization is created, established, and eventually evolved through a mix of indigenous factors like social, cultural, technical, and political mechanisms and interventions. IS are tools that contribute to the effectiveness and efficiency of the certain processes of an organization; therefore, IS development efforts in the organizations of a developing country have to be oriented towards local innovation needs and prevalent professional techniques and methods. These techniques and methods bear a strong influence of the above-mentioned indigenous factors. In order to understand and analyze information systems in organizational context, it is useful to first review the issues that cast a strong influence on the implementation and success or failure of an IS. The theory of information systems has discussed these issues in different pedagogical forms. For example, Alter's theory (Alter, 1999) defines an information system as a particular type of work system that "processes information by performing various combinations of six types of operations: capturing, transmitting, storing, retrieving, manipulating, and displaying information". The fourteen statements characterizing a work system in general and an information system in particular, as described by Alter (Alter, 1999, p. 8) are given below:

1. **Definition of work system:** A work system is a system in which human participants and/or machines perform a business process using information, technology, and other resources to produce products and/or services for internal or external customers. Organizations typically contain multiple work systems and operate through them.

2. **Elements of a work system:** Understanding a work system requires at least cursory understanding of six elements: the business process, participants, information, technology, products, and customers.

3. **Environment of a work system:** Understanding a work system usually requires an understanding of its environment, including the external infrastructure that it relies upon in order to operate and the managerial, organizational, regulatory, and competitive context that affect its operation.

4. **Fit between elements of a work system:** The smooth and painless operation of a work system depends on the mutual balance and alignment between the various elements of the system plus adequate support from the external environment.

5.   **Definition of an information system as a work system:** An information system is a work system whose internal functions are limited to processing information by performing six types of operations: capturing, transmitting, storing, retrieving, manipulating, and displaying information.

6.   **Roles of information systems in work systems they serve:** An information system exists to produce information and/or to support or automate the work performed by other work systems.

7.   **Degree of integration between an information system and a work system it serves:** The information system may serve as an external source of information; it may be an interactive tool; it may be an integral component of the work system; the information system and work system may overlap so much that they are virtually indistinguishable. The information system may also serve as shared infrastructure used in many diverse work systems.

8.   **Content vs. plumbing in information systems:** An information system can be viewed as consisting of content and plumbing. Its content is the information it provides and the way that information affects the business process within the work system. Its plumbing is the details that concern information technology rather than the way information affects the business process.

9.   **Impact of an information system:** An information system's direct impact on work system performance is determined primarily by how well it performs its role in the work systems it supports.

10.   **Definition of a project as a work system:** A project is a time-limited work system designed to produce a particular product and then go out of existence.

11.   **Phases of a project that creates or significantly changes a work system:** A project that creates or significantly changes a work system goes through four idealized phases: initiation, development, implementation, and operation and maintenance.

12.   **Impact of the balance of content and plumbing in a project:** For projects of any particular size, those in which both content and plumbing change significantly have more conceptual and managerial complexity than projects in which the changes are mostly about content or mostly about plumbing.

13.   **Work system success:** The success of a work system depends on the relative strength of internal and external forces supporting the system versus internal and external forces and obstacles opposing the system.

14.   **Inheritance of generalizations, truisms, and success factors:** Generalizations, truisms, and success factors related to work systems also apply to information systems and to projects (because these are work systems).

Information System Development Project

According to Alter, an Information System Development Project is also a work system, though a time-limited one. The development process of an information system incorporates a high level of innovation, and therefore inherently possesses uncertainty of results. Chris Sauer (1993) divides this process into four stages as shown in Table 1. These stages are identified

Table 1. Phases of information system development

Phase	Activities
Initiation	• Detection of performance gap • Formation of attitudes • Development of proposal • Strategic decision-making
Description: The efficiency of certain work/business processes and tasks can be improved with an information system. These candidate processes and tasks are identified in the initiation phase, and an analysis is carried out about the extent and nature of changes that are necessary for improved efficiency; also, the people likely to be affected by these changes are also considered. A cost benefit analysis is carried out to ensure that the benefits of the proposed information system outweigh its costs, and then necessary resources are allocated for the project.	
Development	• Development of abstract system • Development of concrete system • Establishment of project infrastructure
Description : In this phase, the information system and supporting documents are produced and the related procedures are defined.	
Implementation	Introduction of concrete system to operational and organizational context
Description: In this phase, the new system is introduced in the workplace and users are trained to use it.	
Operation	Operation, maintenance, and enhancement
Description: In this phase, the new system is accepted and is running smoothly in the work environment. In case a major change is required by the users, a new iteration of the four phases will start.	

by the objectives and problems they posses, and at each of the four stages there are some influences from supporters, users, and developers on this innovation process.

ISDP Failure, Definitions, and Classification

All human endeavors, scientific, technological, or other result in success or failure. This success or failure outcome is also related with technological and organizational efforts regarding development of information systems. Generally success is praised at every level, and itself defends its characteristics and long-term effects; however, it is considered better to disown a failure. In a particular project, both success and failure can be companions, that is, when the project is facing a status of partial failure. Richard Heeks (2000) describes these three statuses of an information system as:

- **Total failure:** In this type of failure, a system is either not implemented or it is discarded soon after the implementation.

- **Partial failure:** In some cases a system is implemented and used for some period of time; however, the system fails to meet some of its primary objectives. This type of failure can also result in producing some undesirable byproducts or features in that system. In other words, the system only covers a subset of its objectives. Partially-failed projects are also referred to as challenged projects in literature.

- **Success:** The success is straightforward, a status of project where all the objectives of all the stakeholders are fulfilled by the resulting system.

Many researchers have believed that the study of failed information system projects can enrich information systems' body of knowledge by making us aware of the dynamic and cross-cutting reasons that lead to partial or full failure. An information systems development project can fail due to any number of reasons and the possible list can easily stretch to triple figures. Therefore, in order to understand the reasons that lead to failure in information systems development it is important to first understand the different categories of failure. One classification of failures is proposed by Chris Sauer (1993) and it defines the following five categories of failure:

- **Correspondence failure:** When a particular ISDP is not able to achieve its predefined objectives, it is categorized as correspondence failure, for example, the selected project was not able to meet the objectives defined in the contract.

- **Process failure:** When a development process is not able to produce the desired system or could not meet the resource limitations, it is categorized as process failure.

- **Interaction failure:** Sometimes, it happens that the users are not satisfied with the delivered system or some portion of the delivered system, which leads the users to lose interest in that system, and hence the level of system use is decreased subsequently. This situation is referred to as interaction failure.

- **Expectation failure:** A project always starts with some tough and high expectations of its stakeholders; however, the resultant product may not be able to fulfill the expectations of any or all stakeholders, thus resulting in expectation failure.

- **Terminal failure:** This is the case when a project is abandoned or cancelled before the final delivery. Termination of a project is the last thing that can happen to a failing project, that is, when there are no hopes of meeting any of the objectives of the project, it is terminated.

ISDP Failure Statistics

Many researchers have attempted to study the extent of failure in the IS industry. A milestone study in this area is the Chaos Report of 1994 by the Standish Group (1994). They surveyed 365 companies and conducted a number of focus groups and interviews in order to determine:

- The scope of software project failures
- The major factors that cause software projects to fail

The Chaos Report stated that 16.2% of projects were successful, that is, these projects completed on-time and on-budget, with all features and functions as initially specified. 52.7% of projects were partial failures, that is, these projects were completed and they became operational, but were over-budget, over the time estimate, and offered fewer features and functions than originally specified. 31.1% of projects failed, that is, they were canceled at some point during the development cycle. This research survey also tried to determine the most important success, partial failure, and failure criteria. Table 2 lists the three criteria in descending order of importance.

To emphasize the gravity of the prevailing problem of failure in IS projects, some more reports are examined and a summary of findings is presented in Table 3 (IT Cortex, 2005).

Table 2. Criteria of success and failure

	Success	Partial Failure	Failure
1.	User Involvement	Lack of User Input	Incomplete Requirements and Specifications
2.	Executive Management Support	Incomplete Requirements and Specifications	Lack of User Involvement
3.	Clear Statement of Requirements	Changing Requirements and Specifications	Lack of Resources
4.	Proper Planning	Lack of Executive Support	Unrealistic Expectations
5.	Realistic Expectations	Technology Incompetence	Lack of Executive Support
6.	Smaller Project Milestones	Lack of Resources	Changing Requirements and Specifications
7.	Competent Staff	Unrealistic Expectations	Lack of Planning
8.	Ownership	Unclear Objectives	Did Not Need It Any Longer
9.	Clear Vision and Objectives	Unrealistic Time Frames	Lack of IT Management
10.	Hard-Working, Focused Staff	Use of New Technology	Technology Illiteracy

Table 3. Failure statistics

	The Robbins-Gioia Survey	The Conference Board Survey	The KPMG Canada Survey	The OASIG Survey
Year	2001	2001	1997	1995
Country	USA	USA	Canada	UK
Survey Size	232	117	176	45
Survey Method	Not Mentioned	Interview	Questionnaire	Interview
IS Type	ERP	ERP	Multiple	Multiple
Failure Rate	51%	40%	61%	70%

- The Robbins-Gioia Survey was primarily focused on studying the implementation of Enterprise Resource Planning Systems in 232 companies. Out of these 232 companies, only 36% had experience of ERP implementation. The success or failure of the ERP implementation was measured based on perception instead of some objective criteria. Fifty-one percent of the companies perceived their ERP implementation as unsuccessful.

- The Conference Board Survey also studied ERP implementation. The most important finding of this survey was that 40% of the projects failed to achieve the business case within one year of going live. Projects covered in this survey were 25% over budget.

- The KPMG Canada survey was focused on identifying the reasons that lead to failure of IT projects. The survey reported that 61% of the analyzed projects were judged as failure. In this survey, more than 75% of projects were late and more than 50% of projects were over budget.

- The OASIG Survey reported that 7 out of 10 IT projects fail in some respect.

These statistics show the edge of the iceberg in the ocean of information system developments. The above-mentioned reports are concluded in these statements:

- An IT project is more likely to be unsuccessful than successful;
- About one out of five IT projects is likely to bring full satisfaction; and
- The larger the project, the more likely the failure.

These surveys are from the developed economies of the world. The financial costs of these failed projects no doubt present a constant threat for the companies in these countries; however, these countries have a solid financial base. This solid financial base lets them absorb the losses incurred by the failed projects. Now let us see some of the statistics of developed countries where the financial base is not strong enough, and the impact of a single project failure can do a lot of damage.

ISDP Failure Statistics for Developing Countries

Information Technology (IT) innovation is now considered necessary for development; during the last two decades, an understanding has emerged that IT can effectively be used to narrow the gap between the industrialized and developing countries. Information systems are now an important part of the diffusion and implementation of IT. In developing countries, information system development efforts are most widespread in areas of governance, health care, education, finance, and poverty alleviation. The main thrust of these initiatives has been to apply technology appropriately in such a manner that its adoption brings the perceived socio-economic benefits. There have been cases where imported information system solutions have been used as a starting point for adaptation, but mostly developing countries and donors have focused on developing appropriate and sustainable local information systems. The emerging trend is that most of the information system initiatives have not been appropriately conceived or developed, and therefore they have failed to fulfill the desired outcomes. There is not much empirical evidence available on whether information systems failure rate is very similar or widely different in developing countries as compared with developed countries. Very little research has been conducted in general IS failure in developing countries, and in the particular area of information systems for e-government there are some statistics available.

In developing countries, e-government is a representative area of IS development as it involves sufficient financial and technical resources. Richard Heeks (2003) presents a generic situation in his report about success and failure rates of e-government projects in developing countries. This report presents findings of multiple surveys and studies which help to draw a wider picture. The estimates from past surveys present a situation that encourages Heeks to conclude that the failure rate in developing countries is higher than in the developed countries. The success and failure rates estimated in the Richard Heeks (2003) report from past surveys are in Table 4.

Results of some more existing studies from developing countries are summarized as:

- Braa and Hedberg (2000) have reported wide-spread partial failure of high-cost health information systems in South Africa;

- Kitiyadisai (2000) has concluded that in the public sector, IS initiatives failure cases seem to be the norm in Thailand;

- Baark and Heeks (1999) found that all donor-funded projects in China were partial failures; and

Table 4. Success and failure rates in developing countries

Classification	Literature	Poll	Survey
Success	15%-	20 %	15%
Partial Failure	60%+	30 %	50%
Total Failure	25%+	50 %	35%

- Moussa and Schware (1992) concluded that almost all World Bank-funded projects in Africa were partial failures.

These findings tell us that at least one quarter of the projects in the developing countries tend to fail, and this rate may be as high as 50%. The success rate range is 15% to 20%. A majority of the projects tend to end in what is termed as partial failure where major goals of the project were not achieved or there were significant undesirable results. These statistics of success and failure in developing countries become even graver when other factors pertaining particularly to the under-developed world are also taken into consideration. For example, as a general rule the investments involved in big IS projects are always high from a developing country's perspective, and if the project fails, the resultant losses incur long-term negative effects on the progress of a developing country. Also, IS development companies in developing economies are small and do not have sufficiently deep pockets to survive the impact of a failed project. As a result, a high failure rate in the IS industry indirectly impedes the growth of the IS industry.

ISDP Failure and its Effects on Developing Countries

Information systems projects are initiated in developing countries typically in institutions like governance, management, healthcare, and education, and usually the general aims are to increase efficiency, introduce transparency in working, and improve accountability. The above-mentioned institutions in developing countries are very local in context and have deep historical roots. The evolution of these institutions has been different from that of the similar institutions in the developed countries. Information system projects in developing countries are usually perceived as pure technical initiatives aimed at making the functioning of an organization or institution more efficient and effective. The current prevalent IS strategies have matured in the developed countries and thus have a strong association with a particular way of management and administration style. It is difficult to embed these IS strategies in local institutions of developing countries without regarding social and organizational aspects.

The main objectives of an information system are to enhance capabilities of an organization and to help the organization save monetary resources by reducing workforce, travel, communication costs, and so forth (Mirani & Lederer, 1994). A good information system is expected to help an organization meet its information requirements at all levels and produce the appropriate information results. The information systems of e-government projects are meant to provide access to information at all levels of society with faster retrieval or delivery of information, with features like concise and better format, flexibility, and reliability. The aim is to improve the responsiveness of public organizations. These benefits are expected to fulfill the needs of a developing country, save its resources and provide better living standards to its society at minimum cost. This particular goal is an attempt to bridge the gaps of digital divide in the world and to compete in the race of progress. A typical IS project requires a high level of investment in terms of resources and efforts. Once a project is started, expected results are projected at all levels of society and stakeholders. Unfortunately, if a project fails, it generates much more relative damage in a developing country than in developed countries. With the failure, not only all the prestigious and scarce resources involved in that project are lost, but it is considered as a setback to the progress and development of the country. In the long run, this failure is considered as a bad example for future investments in that type of IS project. This scenario discourages further attempts to develop information systems projects in the developing country. Hence a developing economy takes a long time to fully recover from the effects of failure in a large-scale IS project.

Web-Based Information System and Reliability

The failure in Web-based information systems is an area which is being studied with great interest. The case study presented in this chapter provides us an in-depth analysis of the causes of deficiency in reliability of a Web-based application. This lack of reliability not only decreased the use of the application, but also made the higher management reluctant to enforce its use on a regular basis.

Web-based applications, like the academic records management portal in our case study, are a unique type of information systems which interconnect a large number of users with the organization and cater to variable access rates. As the pool of users is big, the variation of influences is also wide ranging, which makes the user preferences a significant factor in the development of such applications.

With the increasing use of Web interfaces across organizations, for example, corporate and supporting applications, comes a dramatic increase in the number of users of the resulting systems. Due to this trend of connecting more and more of an organization's staff and clients together via Web interfaces, the system design models are becoming more user-centric, and place user requirements higher on the priorities list. Moreover, user satisfaction is also a major performance and quality indicator. This trend is also evident in our case study. As we report, the development team tended to focus totally on the user satisfaction and kept on incorporating the new and changing user requirements in the project design even to the last stages of development. This factor brought the Web application closer to failure due to a decrease in reliability.

Learning Lessons from a Failure

The IS failure in developing countries carries more importance for learning and investigation of failure causes, as it not only wastes the scarce and precious allocated resources but also discourages further investment. The opportunity costs are certainly higher in developing countries because of the more limited availability of resources such as capital and skilled manpower. This situation is best described (Heeks, 2000, p. 4) in the following words:

The failures keep developing countries on the wrong side of the digital divide, turning ICTs into a technology of global inequality.

For these types of reasons, a failure in development of IS in developing country poses a significantly important area of study. In countries like Pakistan, where domestic market and domestic IS demand has traditionally been very low, ISDP failures discourage further demands and growth in IS industry. This scenario has established the need for studying ISDP in Pakistan, especially the failed ones. We believe that there are more opportunities and lessons for learning from failed IS projects, than there are from the successful IS projects. We are not aware of an existing study that has reported on the extent of failed IS projects in Pakistan. This chapter is a first step to fill this gap. We have chosen one small and simple IS project to study ISDP failure in Pakistan. We would also like to point out that a single case study can provide no basis for estimation of overall failure/success rates in Pakistan, and further work needs to done in this direction.

ISDP Failure And Complexity

In this section we discuss the type of factors that can participate in an information system development failure and the associated role of project complexity in failure.

ISDP Factors and Dependencies

In this section we discuss what type of factors can participate in an information system development failure. During the four stages of the information system development process (initiation, development, implementation and operation), the development process is influenced by various factors; however, the degree of influence of these factors varies at different stages. There is no definite list of factors and no definite degree of influence which they make on the process. In order to understand the different possible factors, it is useful to discuss them from different perspectives. One perspective is that of the user factors (Havelka, 2002); these include:

- Biasness of users towards system performance;
- Commitment of users towards providing support to project;
- Communication skills of the users: whether or not the users can elaborate the needs and shortcomings of delivered system;
- Computer literacy levels of the users: whether or not the users can understand barriers and bottlenecks of common systems;
- Extent of users' participation in requirement gathering phase to the training phase;
- Users' know-how about the organizational processes and work flows; and
- Users' understanding of the requirements of the new information system.

Ananth Srinivasan (1987) has discussed organizational factors and the type of effects that these make on the IS development process. These include:

- Available resources (both human and financial): The human resources affect the development process positively, but increased financial resources are related to team disagreement;

- External influences on the development process: The degree of external influence on the system development effort needs to be carefully monitored and controlled; and

- Project team's exposure to information systems: Systems exposure in the firm allows an increase in the degree of awareness among project group members about the different problems encountered by users and systems staff.

There are also some exogenous factors involved in influencing the development process as discussed by Chris Sauer (1993). These factors are cognitive limits, technical process environment, organizational politics, structure, and history. The environment is a collection of some other factors such as suppliers, technology, customers, competitors, interests, regulators, and culture.

All of these factors exist in their respective contexts and influence the information system development project. This is not a definite list; however, it helps to understand that there exist different factors when the system is studied with different perspectives. To examine the roles and dependencies of these factors in an integrated environment of information system development project, Chris Sauer presented Triangle of Dependencies (Sauer, 1993). The triangle of dependencies presents a cycle of interaction between supporters/users, the project development organization, and the system (under development) itself.

Model of IS Project: Triangle of Dependencies

The project organization (ALPHA in this case study) is defined as a group of people who, at a particular point in time, are occupied with the development, operation, or maintenance of a given information system (project GAMMA in this case). The information system must serve some organizational stakeholders and thereby function as a resource for the project organization in gathering support. Supporters (BETA and its employees in this case) provide support in terms of monetary resources, material resources, information, and so forth. This triangle is depicted in Figure 1, and it is not a closed triangle. Each relationship is subject to a variety of exogenous factors which influence how it will affect the rest of the triangle. It was obvious that some resources were given to ALPHA development team by BETA management and the development of project GAMMA started. ALPHA delivered documentations and presentations on the working and status of the project to BETA at different milestones, to win the support from them by satisfying their needs.

It is important to keep in mind that information systems are developed and exists to fulfill the needs of stakeholders, and it is important for stakeholders to support the system in return. As the project organization plays the creator role for the system development, it is not possible to do it without any support from the users. Thus this situation exists like a triangle where the user organization supports the developers so that they can develop a system which fulfills their needs. If the system satisfies the users, they support the developer's organization in the development process, which enhances the system for further needs.

Dependencies of the Factors

This triangle clearly presents three sides of the software development process. It starts with the flow of support from supporters to project organization, the second side is the relation of system to supporters and the third side is the relationship of project organization to the information system. In the next paragraphs, the sides and corners of this triangle are discussed in detail.

The project organization is the group of people who are involved in the development of the system. Different people play different roles in the complete information system process, for example, development, implementation, and maintenance. The team leader plays an important role; he guides the whole team towards a particular goal. The competency of the team in understanding the problem and scope of the problem, as well as the development model they follow, are two of the major factors beside many others which influence the project.

The supporters are the people who support the project organization by providing them with resources as well as problem scope and definition. The resources, including monetary resources, material resources, information, social legitimacy, and control of strategic contingencies, are provided by the supporters to the project development organization. The supporters can also be categorized as funders (because they provide financial resources), power brokers (because they exert influence on project organization), and fixers (because they provide information and control decisions) (Sauer, 1993). Users of the system are an important part of the supporters as they not only provide basic information and requirements but also provide feedback to the funders and power brokers to make long-term decisions. It is important to note that the factors like organizational politics, nature and sources of power, history, and environment of the organization are the factors which make direct influences on the triangle.

The relationships among the system, project organization, and supporters are also interesting to examine. Each relationship contains different types of characteristics and factors which also influence the whole system. For the supporters-project organization relationship, the most significant thing is the flow of support. If the system satisfies the supporters, then the support for the system is there; if the system does not meet the goals, as perceived by the

Figure 1. Triangle of dependencies

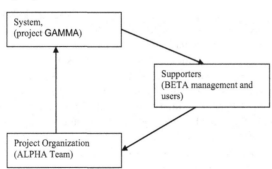

supporters, then the flow of support becomes problematic. The supporters-project organization relationship is based on human cognitive behaviors and is directly affected by organizational structure and politics. The second relationship is the system-supporters relationship, which also depends on the organizational factors. The needs of the organization for the system may change with time, due to which the system may become unacceptable. There can be some political changes due to which the degree of satisfaction may diminish. Factors related to users (biasness, skills, commitment, and understanding of needs) as well as the technical process by which the system is being evaluated directly influence this relationship. The relationship between project organization and system has a technical orientation, as it mainly consists of a technical process of information system development. This process consists of designing, creating, implementing, and making changes as required by the supporters. In this relationship, factors like communication and cooperation among team members, tools for development, requirement specification, the team's exposure to information systems, development process, and skills have influences. There are also some factors which come from the other sides of triangle to affect this relationship, for example, structural changes in the user organization can cause changes in requirements, and the system may need to be modified accordingly. The project organization might be at a stage where it cannot afford any shortage of support from the supporters, and the system may also be at a stage where it needs major changes and as a result may overshoot schedule. These types of problems demand a great skill set from the team leader.

Flaw

As discussed in the previous section, there are many factors which influence an information system development project, and these factors have different dependencies among each other. Every factor influences the project, and its effect is important for the success or failure of the project. Thus one cannot say that a particular factor should be ignored or its influence should be negated. These influences create a state of balance between different stakeholders and can make a project successful. However, at some stage the effect of these influences makes some aspects of the process uncontrollable, but at the same time, helps other factors to render positive influences. These unbalanced influences create flaws in the process, and the result is a flawed system/project (Sauer, 1993). The factors which highly influence a system and then tend to create flaws and make hurdles in the success of an IS project are termed as risks (Ward, 1995).

Information systems development process is open to flaws, and every information system is flawed in some way. However flaws are different from failure. Flaws are a characteristic of the system itself and also of the innovation process. Flaws are never desired by any stakeholder, for example, project organization, users, or supporters. Flaws are corrected at a cost or are accepted at some other cost. One technical type of flaw is a bug, which either stops a running program or destroys the results. Another type of flaw is any system characteristic which the users find inconvenient or otherwise undesirable, for example, a particular data entry form. This kind of flaw can also be corrected or accepted at a cost. There may also be flaws in the development process that are introduced by a decision about how to proceed in a particular step in the process. A particular decision may give the desired result with perhaps a greater cost, or may produce some other flaws.

Thus flaws are problems which occur as a consequence of events in the development process. Unless there is support available to cope with them, they will have the effect of reducing the system's capacity to serve its supporters or of resulting in further flaws. As this capacity to serve the supporters decreases and cost of managing the flaws increases, the project becomes more prone to failure. No stakeholder can continue to support the costs of flaws forever. In the long run, they will start to take notice of rising costs and undesirable results and reduce their support. When the support dries up, the system lacks the necessary resources and tends towards failure.

Complexity

We have discussed flaws in information systems and their negative effects on information system development, and one may reach the logical argument that flaws of a system should be removed. However, as these flaws are caused by interconnected factors, removing a flaw can generate negative effects on other parts of system. This situation renders complexity into the information system development process, where removing one flaw can develop other flaws. The definition of complexity varies in different contexts. Baccarini (1996, p 202) defines complexity as:

The complexity can be defined as an interaction of several parts which can be made operational differently and in interdependent ways.

Suppose we have a particular system in which there are many components. All these components have some intra-component dependencies. Each component may be independent and may have a particular behavior and influence in the whole system. Every component is not only dependent on its internal dependencies but is also affected by other components. These inter-component dependencies help the components to make a complete system for a particular purpose. All these components interact with each other to fulfill requirements and dependencies of other components. As all the components are independent, and have their own intra-component structure, they can work and behave differently if some changes occur in their internal composition. When these components work in a system, they can operate in different ways, and can have different effects on the system at different times. One or more than one independent component can lead to a situation where it has different effects on the system, and these influences can create an imbalance in the system's working. Now the problem solving can produce a complex situation, that is, which factors of a component should be negated to let the system keep working?

A similar situation arises in an information system development project, where the project is a collection of many different sub-processes and components. Each sub-process is not only separate but also dependent on the other components of project. In this type of system, the complexity is a situation where we have to leave a negative effect of a component on the system to let the system not be destroyed due to negative effects of other components. Thus the complexity of most information systems means that:

Cost of leaving a flaw uncorrected may be significant because of consequential effects it might have on other parts of system. (Sauer, 1993, pp. 63-64).

Suppose in a particular project a new requirement is made by the user and the project is delayed because of this particular requirement. Now if the requirement is not provided in the system, the user is not willing to accept the project, and if the requirement is fulfilled the project is delayed. This is a complex situation where we need to leave one flaw to avoid consequential cascading effects on the project. The factors involved in creating imperfection lead toward increasing the complexity of an ISDP and subsequently decrease its probability of success.

Complexity and Failure Relationship

Although flaws are in every system, they are not the cause of every failure; however, flaws lead a system towards failure. The relationship between flaws and complexity has been discussed in the previous section, and we saw that complexity also leads an information system towards failure. The complexity which is caused by the flaws is one of the major risk factors involved in the failure of information system development projects. Presence of complexity is considered one of the biggest risk factors involved in project failure (Barki, Rivard, & Talbot, 1993). Level of complexity and time duration of project are directly related to failure. As the complexity of the project increases, the time duration needed to solve the problems also increases, and on the other hand the sense of urgency also creeps up and wrong decisions are made. One way to reduce the level of project risk and failure is to reduce the level of complexity (Murray, 1993). British Computer Society (2003) found that the most common attribute underlying the failed projects was the high level of inherent complexity in the failed projects. Thus it is obvious that to improve ISDP success rate and the rate of return on IS investment, organizations must address the problem of complexity in ISDP and reduce it within manageable limits (Xia & Lee, 2004).

Virtually every IS project will increase in complexity once it has been initiated. Sense of urgency in announcing the end date and addition of post-initiation components/technology are two major causes of complexity for an IS system (Murray, 1993). Size is also a source of increasing complexity, because to solve a bigger problem the project is decomposed in smaller components, and thus complexity of interaction between the components increases (AlSharif, Walter, & Turky, 2004). This implies that complexity is one of the major causes of failure of information systems, thus studying the complexity of an information system can reveal the causes of failure. Dissecting a particular failure in the light of complexity will help us to understand the areas and flaws which should be provided more careful analysis in the development process.

Classification of Complexity

Complexity is one of the major reasons for information system development project failure, which encourages one to study an information system development project and analyze dif-

Figure 2. Taxonomy of ISD projects complexity

	Structural	Dynamic
Organizational	Structural Organizational Complexity	Dynamic Organizational Complexity
vs. Technology	Structural IT Complexity	Dynamic IT Complexity

Structural vs. Dynamic

ferent complexities related to it. For this purpose we select a framework for ISDP complexity to classify different complexities. In this classification the ISDP complexity is divided into four different categories including technological and organizational factors. Xia and Lee (2004) classifies complexity in two major dimensions, organizational and technological, and then plots it against a third dimension called uncertainty for both the organizational and technological dimensions. As a result, four classifications emerge which are depicted in Figure 2.

Structural Organizational Complexity

A project always gets maximum influences from the organizational environment for which the project is being developed. The current organizational environment and the business processes present their own influences and complexities. This category of complexity presents the nature and strength of the relationships among project elements in the organizational environment, including project resources, support from top management and users, project staffing, and skill proficiency levels of project personnel.

Structural IT Complexity

The technology is itself a factor which causes many complex situations in the development project. Information technology not only includes the hardware, but also represents the software engineering and project development factors. This category represents the complexity of the relationships among the IT elements, reflecting the diversity of user units, software environments, nature of data processing, variety of technology, need for integration, and diversity of external vendors and contractors.

Dynamic Organizational Complexity

As the time passes in the stages of development of an information system project, there come many changes in organizational environment and its business processes. The dynamic organizational complexity covers the pattern and rate of change in ISDP organizational environments, including changes in user information needs, business processes, and organizational structures; it also reflects the dynamic nature of the project's effect on the organizational environment.

Dynamic IT Complexity

Information technology is rapidly growing and changing. In the life span of an information system development project, there come many changes in the underlying information technology platform and tools for software engineering. This dimension of complexity measures the pattern and rate of changes in the ISDP's IT environment, including changes in IT infrastructure, architecture, and software development tools.

Now let us discuss some of the factors from each of the categories and understand their effect on increasing the complexities. In a particular project, the users may not provide the type of support needed by the project organization. In this situation, the requirements may not be provided correctly to the development team, which in turn may produce a faulty system which may not satisfy the needs of users or supporters. This situation can be worse if the top management does not give sufficient support, as the financial support is directly under the control of top management. The formation of the development team also plays a crucial role, as lack of team staffing or their skills can delay the time lines and lose further support. Then there are also some organizational factors from both of the users' and developers' organizations. As time progresses, there are some changes in the organizational environments and some new factors emerge from this situation. There may be some changes occurring in the organization itself, for example, the business processes of the organization are changed by the management. The management structure of the organization can also change; and this can cause changes in the organizational needs and rules. These changes can also be due to the new information system, and in this case the developer has to face an opposition from different sectors of the user organization. Some organizations do not have a defined set of business processes or have flexibilities in them; due to adoption of information systems, these flexibilities are limited and this scenario can also cause opposition from the users.

The nature of the project also poses its own complexities, for example, if the project involves multiple user units or involves different vendors and contractors. This type of project is open to different stakeholders to impose their decisions, and prone to different influences and flaws in return. These factors are summarized in Table 5.

Table 5. Factors of ISDP complexity (Xia & Lee, 2004)

Complexity Factor
Structural Organizational Complexity - The project manager did not have direct control over project resources. - Users provided insufficient support. - The project had insufficient staffing. - Project personnel did not have required knowledge/skills. - Top management offered insufficient support.
Structural IT Complexity - The project involved multiple user units. - The project team was cross-functional. - The project involved multiple software environments. - The system involved real-time data processing. - The project involved multiple technology platforms. - The project involved significant integration with other systems. - The project involved multiple contractors and vendors.
Dynamic Organizational Complexity - The project caused changes in business processes. - Users' information needs changed rapidly. - Users' business processes changed rapidly. - The project caused changes in organizational structure. - Organizational structure changed rapidly.
Dynamic IT Complexity - IT infrastructure changed rapidly. - IT architecture changed rapidly. - Software development tools changed rapidly.

The Case Study

In our case study, the developer is referred to as ALPHA and the client is referred to as BETA. ALPHA was one of the leading software houses in Pakistan operating as an independent business unit of a large and reputed international company. BETA was a top bracket public sector university. The ISDP was a Web-based portal for academic records management referred to as project GAMMA in this case study.

Research Methodology

In order to understand the factors which led the project GAMMA to failure, we conducted several in-depth qualitative interviews. These interviews were flexible and exploratory in nature. In these interviews our later questions were adjusted according to the response of the interviewee in answering the earlier questions. Our aim was to clarify the earlier responses, to follow new lines of inquiry, and to probe for more detail. The overall interview style was unstructured and conversational, and the questions were open-ended and designed to elicit detailed, concrete information.

The persons interviewed included the ALPHA Project manager and the ALPHA technical team lead, and the BETA team lead, BETA coordinator, and a few users at BETA. The answers that warranted more clarification or were, to some extent, conflicting to the views expressed by the other side were further probed in the second round of discussions. ALPHA and BETA interviews were segregated from each other. Interview settings included individual and collective participation of the interviewees. The information collected was mapped on contemporary theoretical frameworks discussed in Sauer (1993) and Xia and Lee (2004) to analyze the responses and understand the role of different factors that led to the failure of our specific case under study. The information was then examined with the help of Taxonomy of ISDP complexities, and factors of each category were identified.

In the sections bellow, the process of different phases of information system development is discussed.

The Team from ALPHA

ALPHA had a team of skilled software engineers, and the average experience of team members was three-and-a-half years. The manager of the ALPHA team had software project management experience of six-and-a-half years. The ALPHA team comprised of a blend of analysts, designers, coders, and testers. ALPHA followed the incremental development approach for projects with a time period of more than eight weeks, and hence the same approach was followed in this case.

The Team from BETA

BETA made a focal team comprising of senior faculty members from different departments led by one Head of the Department. The focal team at BETA was mandated to collaborate with the ALPHA team. The responsibilities of the focal team were to help the ALPHA team to capture the information about policies and procedures of the academic and administrative departments and units of BETA. Its main role was also to help ALPHA understand the processes and verify the requirements against specific processes. The focal team acted as the client representative and in the later stages also tested the portal and gave feedback to ALPHA team.

The Complete Process

At the start of the project, a preliminary set of requirements was agreed upon between the BETA focal team and the ALPHA team. A total of eleven modules were identified, out of which eight modules were deemed to be more critical than others. The technological requirements were not rigid, and it was generally agreed to encourage the platform-independent technologies including Java and Linux. Regarding the choice of database, BETA preferred to use Oracle as it already had the license. Next the ALPHA team analyzed the preliminary requirements by collecting the data and observing the business processes and procedures. Both of the teams visited different academic departments and held meetings with the heads of the departments and different other employees. The same was done in the administrative units to record the data and procedures of different business processes. After analyzing the collected information and additional requirements, a standard requirement specification document was developed and agreed upon.

In the meanwhile, some significant changes occurred at BETA. Due to some routine and policy decisions, some of the members of the focal team from BETA were transferred, and newly-appointed persons took their place. As the people changed, the mindset changed and the vision about the project also changed. Changes at the organizational level of BETA led to some new requirements emerging from nowhere and caused frequent changes in the old requirements.

Surprisingly, ALPHA team had to face many objections on the already-settled requirements, which were conveyed from the user departments and the end users themselves. The new members of the BETA focal team were not clear about the scope and objectives of the project GAMMA, and they also did not agree with the version of the requirements provided by the former members of the BETA focal team. Due to this kind of divisive environment, a huge time was lost in the advancement of the project. ALPHA team was willing to work according to the satisfaction of the client organization and hence wanted to listen to the client's focal team members. As there was no consensus on requirements within the client organization, ALPHA decided to conduct some presentations and meetings with the representatives of all departments and the focal team.

After some presentation and discussion sessions, the analysis of the requirements with a conclusive set of requirements was presented, and the software requirements specification document was once again finalized after incorporating the revised requirements.

At this stage, in order to minimize the impact of organizational changes on the project, the management of BETA appointed a software engineer to lead the BETA focal team with the mandate that the newly-appointed lead person will work continuously in the next phases until the completion of project GAMMA. The new lead person coordinated with the ALPHA team and helped them to complete the trial version of the project. ALPHA finalized the trial version of the project and deployed it at BETA. In April, 2004, the first version of the project was deployed at BETA, and testing was done by ALPHA's testers using real data.

At this stage, training sessions were held by the ALPHA team members to guide the key potential users at BETA, with the objective that these people will use this portal and identify errors, bugs, and changes. As per the evaluation and trial report of the project, the users complained about a number of deficiencies. They reported variances in the expected and actual implementation of different functionalities. There were errors in data processing which caused the potential users at BETA to lose their interest. They also complained that the training was of very basic level and was not properly designed and executed. The ALPHA team was of the opinion that people attending the training sessions were mostly used to using an older existing IS system and thus were reluctant to shift to the new system. Their association and familiarity with the older system created hesitancy and an attitude of disinterest which prevented them from appreciating and exploring the full functionality of the new portal.

It was observed that for some particular processes there were no standard operating procedures, and different departments followed different procedures. This situation demanded flexibility in different data structures and functionalities of the GAMMA system. As an example, the pattern of student registration numbers varied in different departments. Such anomalies caused some requirements changes, even at the later phases, and delayed the implementation.

At this stage, the person who was hired earlier and was leading the BETA focal team through the development phase left BETA for another job. This particular development compelled BETA to restore the old structure of the focal team of BETA. Now the Head of the Department of Computer Sciences was assigned the role of team lead by the client organization. The project at this stage required transferring the existing data from the old system to the new system, and new data entry as well as testing the real-time application behavior. The developers from ALPHA provided scripts to convert data from the old system based on SQL server to the new system. However, according to BETA, the scripts did not work as per requirements which had to be modified time and again. BETA formed another team referred to as "Testing Analysis Team", to test the portal, and the team members were provided training by ALPHA. Moreover a person was selected from each faculty as master trainer, who was entrusted the task to further train the end users within his faculty. This task took another six months of time and further delayed the successful implementation.

The project started in September, 2002, with the planned completion date of December, 2003. A formal audit was conducted by the external auditors, engaged by ALPHA, in December, 2003, who found that the delay was justified as the requirement engineering phase took a much longer time as discussed above. The project took off a little in September, 2004, when the Head of the Department of Computer Sciences started to lead the team to implement the project. However, the project implementation came to a standstill in December, 2004, when the client organization desired deputation of full-time experts by the ALPHA organization to supervise the implementation, which included training of the end users to use the system and subsequently adopt it. ALPHA expressed their inability to depute an expert without charging further expenditure to BETA.

At present the status of the new portal is that it is being used as a passive repository of data. The new system has not been adopted by the end users, and the system that earlier existed is in use at the organizational level. ALPHA has received part of the agreed payment amount and has an outstanding claim for the balance payment from BETA. Both organizations consider it a failed project. BETA considers it a failure as it has not been implemented and adopted at the organizational level. ALPHA considers it as a failed project because, besides the financial loss, the product is termed unsatisfactory by the end users and has not been successfully deployed and adopted at organizational level.

The main reasons for the failure of this simple IS project can be summarized as follows:

- Adaptation and modification of underlying organizational processes in such a way that they become conducive for automation is an issue deeply intertwined with project definition and has to be tackled in the very beginning. Once the processes have been reengineered, only then the scope of an automation project can be fully visualized by all the stakeholders. This factor was initially ignored in the project GAMMA when the first version of project requirements was specified. Halfway through the development process of project GAMMA, the inadequacy of the organizational processes of BETA, in terms of their capacity to lend themselves to automation, was realized.

- The existing organizational processes of BETA were not fully mature. Introduction of a new organization-wide IS system for records management and decision-making implied a number of changes in the way things were done at BETA. Alignment of organizational processes and the IS systems was very important for successful implementation of GAMMA. The end users at BETA were not ready to adopt the changed organizational processes necessitated by the introduction of new technology.

The various complexity factors (Xia & Lee, 2004) and their impact on project GAMMA is summarized in Table 6 and Table 7.

Conclusion

The main aim of the GAMMA project was to implement a Web portal for the academic and administrative records management of BETA. Hence system GAMMA was required to capture, store, and process data for a number of departments within BETA. Each department had its own perspective regarding the policies and procedures of data and records management. Being in the same organization, these processes were interlinked and processed similar data.

Table 6. Structural complexity categories and their impact on GAMMA

Complexity Factor	Effect in this case	Level of Risk
Structural Organizational Complexity	Yes/ No	
- The project manager did not have direct control over project resources.	No	
- Users provided insufficient support.	Yes	High
- The project had insufficient staffing.	No	
- Project personnel did not have required knowledge/skills.	No	
- Top management offered insufficient support.	No	
Structural IT Complexity		
- The project involved multiple user units.	Yes	High
- The project team was cross-functional.	Yes	Medium
- The project involved multiple software environments.	No	
- The system involved real-time data processing.	No	
- The project involved multiple technology platforms.	No	
- The project involved significant integration with other systems.	Yes	Low
- The project involved multiple contractors and vendors.	No	

Table 7. Dynamic complexity categories and their impact on GAMMA

Complexity Factor	Effect in this case	Level of Risk
Dynamic Organizational Complexity		
- The project caused changes in business processes.	Yes	High
- Users' information needs changed rapidly.	Yes	High
- Users' business processes changed rapidly.	Yes	Medium
- The project caused changes in organizational structure.	No	
- Organizational structure changed rapidly.	Yes	Medium
Dynamic IT Complexity		
- IT infrastructure changed rapidly.	No	
- IT architecture changed rapidly.	Yes	Low
- Software development tools changed rapidly.	Yes	Low

The different departments of BETA created complexity for the requirement analysis team to decide on a particular set of requirement specifications. On the other hand, the users also did not provide sufficient support, and their behavior was critical. The users from the lower management just pointed out the flaws in the system, even if they were because of flaws in the organizational processes of BETA. They did not accept the changes in business/organizational processes which were caused by the new information system. On the other hand, the business processes kept on changing due to their own needs as the people were also changing in the BETA organization. The changes in business processes caused the rapid change in information needs. At the technological dimension, there were also some changes in IT architecture and software development tools, which caused more complexity in managing the project on target. The analysis shows that Dynamic Organizational Complexity, Figure 3, contributed most to the project failure in this case.

One of the important objectives of IS in developing countries is to bring about improvement in organizational and business processes. The information systems support the current processes to enhance the operations and improve information processing, which is helpful to the organization for making its business processes more efficient. These improvements are not without incurring any risk, as modifications or improvements are prone to introduce complexities (Heeks, 2000). However, this case study shows that the changes towards improvements in the processes caused by IS were not accepted by the supporters, which in turn increased the weight of various risk factors. On the other hand, the change in processes, due to the organization itself, caused delays and led the requirements to change significantly, which in the end proved fatal for the project. The inability of the development team to freeze the requirements and stick to the standard requirement specification is a major cause of the failure. However, the business scenarios, in developing countries like Pakistan, demand this type of flexibility in business agreements and job specifications.

With the help of this case study, we are able to identify a major problem area in the development of information systems in general and Web-based applications in particular. The lack

Figure 3. Crucial area in ISDP complexity with respect to case study

Organizational vs. Technology	Structural Organizational Complexity	Dynamic Organizational Complexity
	Structural IT Complexity	Dynamic IT Complexity

Structural vs. Dynamic

of standard operating procedures in business processes and the evolution of new knowledge of business processes and technology encourage the managers of an organization to demand more features as well as the flexibility in them. The managers want to include many processes in the Web-based information system while these processes are either immature or are in phase of standardization; consequently, this demands extra flexibility from the developers and consumes more time. On the other hand, these immature processes are prone to changes as a result of political or structural changes. These business processes become the first target of new management to show that they are making changes in the organization. A weak legal environment in the developing countries like Pakistan does not allow the development team to challenge the client on the basis of service level agreement. This leaves only one choice for the developer's organization to adjust the demands (which look small as they come in pieces at a time) of the client, so that the support can be won from the client in the shape of financial resources. After some time it is realized by the developers that the small changes have combined, and there is a big requirement change demanding huge amounts of extra effort and time. The developers try to make these efforts and invest time in the project; however, at a certain moment it is realized that the complexities have been increased beyond control, and the project is heading towards failure.

The dynamic organizational complexities demand that a project should cover the business processes which have been standardized, or the information system should be allowed to standardize these processes. It is also the responsibility of the organization to show respect to the agreements and demand minimum changes in the requirements. In case of political and structural changes, a project should be owned by the organization, and the changes should not affect the project scope.

The responsibility of the developers is also high, as they should be aware of these complexities and adopt a strategy to cope with them. They should be able to take strong business and technical decisions to restrict the changes in requirements to a minimum level. On the technical end, they should be able to provide maximum flexibility in a minimum time frame. It can be concluded that responsibility of these types of failures cannot be given to one stakeholder; rather it is the responsibility of both the developers as well as the client organization to facilitate a project towards success.

References

Alter, S. (1999, March). A general, yet useful theory of information systems. *Communications of AIS, 1*(13), 1-70.

AlSharif, M., Walter, P. B., & Turky, A., (2004, April). Assessing the complexity of software architecture. In *Proceedings of the 42nd Annual Southeast Regional Conference* (pp. 98-103).

Baark, E., & Heeks, R. (1999). Donor-funded information technology transfer projects. *Information Technology for Development, 8*(4), 185-197.

Baccarini, D. (1996, August). The concept of project complexity: A review. *International Journal of Project Management, 14*(4), 201-204.

Barki, H., Rivard, S., & Talbot, J. (1993). Toward an assessment of software development risk. *Journal of Management Information Systems, 10*(2), 203-225.

Braa, J. & Hedberg, C. (2000). Developing district-based health care information systems. In *Proceedings of the IFIP WG9.4 Conference 2000, Cape Town, South Africa. Information flows, local improvisations, and work practices*(pp. 113-128).

British Computer Society (2003, April). *The challenges of complex IT projects* (Report). The Royal Academy of Engineering.

Gilhooly, D. (2005, April). Innovation and investment: Information and communication technologies and the millennium development goals. *United Nations Information and Communication Technologies Task Force Millennium Project.* Retrieved September 16, 2005, from http://www.unicttaskforce.org/perl/documents.pl?id=1519

Havelka, D. (2002). User personnel factors that influence information system development success. *Issues in Information Systems, 3*, 229-235.

Heeks, R. (2000). Failure, success, and improvisation of information systems projects in developing countries (Development Informatics Working Paper Series, Paper No. 11). *Institute for Development Policy and Management, University of Manchester, UK.* Retrieved April 1, 2005, from http://www.sed.manchester.ac.uk/idpm/publications/wp/di/di_wp11.htm

Heeks, R. (2003). E-government for development success and failure rates of e-government in developing/transitional countries: Overview. *E-Government for Development Information Exchange IDPM, University of Manchester, UK.* Retrieved April 8, 2005, from http://www.egov4dev.org/sfoverview.htm

IT Cortex (2005). Failure rate, Statistics over IT projects failure rate. Retrieved April 10, 2005, from http://www.it-cortex.com/Stat_Failure_Rate.htm

Kitiyadisai, K. (2000). The implementation of IT in reengineering the Thai revenue department. In *Proceedings of the IFIP WG9.4 Conference 2000, Cape Town, South Africa. Information flows, local improvisations, and work practices.*

Mirani, R., & Lederer, A. L. (1994, April). Anticipated benefits of new jnformation systems: The role of the prosper. In *Proceedings of the 1994 Computer Personnel Research Conference on Reinventing IS. Managing information technology in changing organizations* (pp. 155-164).

Moussa, A., & Schware, R. (1992). Informatics in Africa. *World Development, 20*(12), 1737-1752.

Murray, J. (1993). Reducing IT project complexity. *Information Strategy, 16*(3) (Spring, 2000), 30-38.

Sauer, C. (1993). *Why information systems fail: A case study approach.* Oxfordshire, UK: Alfred Waller Ltd., Publishers.

Srinivasan, A., & Kaiser, K. M. (1987, June). Relationships between selected organizational factors and systems development. *Communications of the ACM, 30*(6) (June, 1987), 556-562.

The Standish Group (1994). The CHAOS report. Retrieved September 15, 2005, from http://www.standishgroup.com/sample_research/chaos_1994_2.php

Ward, J. (1995). *Principles of information system management*. Routledge Publications.

Xia, W., & Lee, G. (2004, May). Grasping the complexity of IS development projects. *Communications of the ACM, 47*(5), 69-74.

Chapter XI

SLA Monitoring of Presence-Enable Services:
A New Approach Using Data Envelopment Analysis (DEA)

Tapati Bandopadhyay, ICFAI Business School, India

Pradeep Kumar, ICFAI Business School, India

Abstract

The concept of presence was initially associated with an instant messaging service, allowing an end user to recognize the presence of a peer online to send or receive messages. Now the technology has grown up to include various services like monitoring performance of any type of end user device, and services are accessible from anywhere, any time. The need for enhanced value remains the driving force behind these services, for example, Voice over Internet Protocol (VoIP) services, which is drawing tremendous research interest in services performance evaluation, measurement, benchmarking, and monitoring. Monitoring service level parameters happens to be one of the most interesting application-oriented research issues because various service consumers at the customer companies/end users' level are finding it very difficult to design and monitor an effective SLA (Service Level Agreement) with the presence-enabled service providers. This chapter focuses on to these specific issues and presents a new approach of SLA monitoring through Data Envelopment Analysis (DEA). This extreme point approach actually can work much better in the context of SLA monitoring than general central-tendency-based statistical tools, a fact which has been corroborated by similar application examples of DEA presented in this chapter and has therefore it acts as the primary motivation to propose this new approach. Towards this end, this chapter first builds up the context of presence-enabled services (Day, Rosenburg, & Sugano, 2000), its SLA and SLA parameters, and the monitoring requirements. Then it explains the basics of DEA and its application in various other engineering and services context. Ultimately, a DEA application framework for monitoring an SLA of presence-enabled services is proposed which can serve as a clear guideline for the customers of presence-enabled services, not only for SLA monitoring but also at various other stages of implementing presence-enabled services frameworks. This approach exploits the definitive suitability of the application of DEA methods to presence-enabled service monitoring problems, and can be easily implemented by the industry practitioners.

Introduction

Presence-Enabled Services

Presence technology allows end users and network elements to know the status and availability of other end users in order to improve communications efficiency. Today, presence has expanded to include monitoring the registration and the busy or idle status of any type of end user device, including wireless phones, VoIP clients, traditional POTS phones, push-to-talk clients, multimedia clients, and more. In addition, the concept of presence has been extended to include various other dimensions. For example: Availability: It allows an end user to explicitly share their availability to communicate with their colleagues (Gurbani, Faynberg, Lu, Brusilovsky, Gato, & Unmehopta, 2003). Typical availability states include out of office, in a meeting with a client, in a conference call, on vacation, and so forth. An end user can provide this information, or it can be inferred from the end user's online calendar. Other dimensions include Location: geographical location of an end user's device. Wireless networks can triangulate signal strength measurements to provide the location of wireless handsets and PDAs. Instant messaging clients is another dimension where the concept of location was extended to laptop-based, instant messaging clients, or IP softphones that might connect to wireline access networks at work, home, or remote locations (Sun, 2002). Presence server and presence policies are important dimensions which determine the ability of the end user to control access to their presence and location information, using the presence server in conjunction with their presence policy. The presence server, in accordance with the end user's policy, provides the presence and location information to various presence applications.

By collecting and disseminating presence information (status of end user devices, availability of the individual, and location), the most effective and appropriate means of communicating to a person or a device can be identified. Network applications (for example, find me/follow me service) can use presence information to efficiently and appropriately route or block incoming communication requests (Roach, 2002).

Presence-Enabled Services Architecture

Presence service architecture (Day, Rosenberg, & Sugano, 2000) includes a wide variety of end user communication clients, integration of multiple real-time communication services into an integrated communications suite, and new end user services that can be developed for spanning and combining wireline telephony, wireless telephony, messaging services, and so forth. Types of information and protocol elements include presence information from a wide variety of end user clients and network elements that can be accessed through a central presence server, plus standard presence protocols and standard event packages that allows presence-enabled services to be developed separately from the end user clients and presence server vendors. These all support the basic requirement of seamlessly integrating or enhancing existing services through the inclusion of presence information.

Presence-enabled services may be classified broadly as:

- **Information sharing services:** These help to determine the most appropriate means of contacting another end user/device. For example, if end users do not have their instant messaging client active, their colleagues might send an e-mail. In more complex scenarios, the presence server can collect and forward presence information across a variety of end user devices. Another instance may be where an employee may have multiple presence clients such as a wireless phone, a VoIP soft-client, an instant messaging client, and so forth, and the most appropriate means to contact him/her can be found given the nature of the communication, priority, time schedules, and work/availability status.
- **Service-enabling:** Presence information allows service providers to automatically re-route high priority incoming communication sessions.

Various Types of Presence-Enabled Services

Examples of presence-enabled services include: call services like Presence-Enabled Call Pick Up, which is a wire-line call pick-up service that allows multiple employees/groups or remote workers to answer each others' phones, and Presence-Enabled Call Distribution, which is a centralized call distribution system that subscribes to the presence and availability status of the devices across multiple switching systems and PBXs. Consequently, devices can be geographically distributed and served by a multiple switching system or PBXs, or they can be served by a combination of PBXs and switching systems. This includes devices served by wireless switching systems.

Then there are facilities like Presence-Enabled Conferencing where existing conference services can be augmented to provide presence information to all participants, and Presence-Enabled Find Me/Follow Me Service where the application server queries the presence status of the wireless phone before forwarding the call and routes it to the appropriate communication device accordingly. Other services include Presence-Sensitive Voice Mail Greeting service to automatically switch between multiple prerecorded messages. Location-based services cater to requirements regarding information like Location Information to simplify the interaction if the agent or IVR system knew the location of the calling party, Location-Based Call Routing where incoming calls are forwarded to the nearest, idle wireless phone or VoIP soft-client, and Location Proximity Alerting.

Implementation of Presence-Enabled Services

The key network/service delivery elements (Day, Rosenberg, & Sugano, 2000) for providing presence-enabled service are as follows.

From Figure 1, the following basic service elements can be identified from the viewpoint of a customer company for setting up the SLA performance parameters:

1.   Presence user agents
2.   Presence network agents
   a.   IP MS (IP multimedia subsystems)
   b.   MSC (Mobile switching centers)
   c.   IMSA (Instant messaging service agents)

In the next section, we discuss SLA and the SLA components of presence-enabled services.

Main Thrust of the Chapter

Service Level Agreement (SLA) For Presence-Enabled Services

Typical SLAs identify and define the service offering itself, plus the supported products, evaluation criteria, and QoS (Quality of Service) that customers should expect. It includes the responsibilities of an IT services provider (such as an ISP or ASP), reflects the rights of the service provider's users, and also includes the penalties assessed when the service provider violates any element of the SLA.

SLAs are the key to ensuring consistent QoS, performance, and uptime in business-critical computing environments, and they complement other contractual agreements that cover a variety of details, including corrective actions, penalties and incentives, dispute-resolution procedures, nonconformance, acceptable service violations, reporting policies, and rules for terminating a contract. These contracts generally fit under what some analysts call Service Level Management (SLM), which provides managing and service contract capabilities. Four areas that require detailed SLAs are the network itself, hosting services, applications, and customer care, including help desk services. Each area contains its own set of elements, metrics, typical industry ranges, and criteria for calculating these metrics. For instance, the

Figure 1. A basic presence-enabled services framework (Based on RFC 2778, IETF, Feb., 2000) (Day, Rosenberg, & Sugano, 2000)

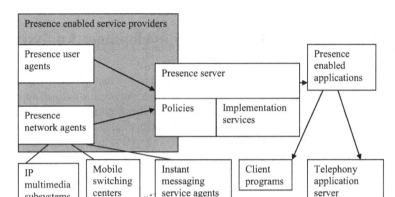

network SLA would include details on bandwidth, performance, and QoS. Well-designed SLAs also detail the nature and types of tools required for users and service providers to monitor and manage them.

Some enterprises accept a "best effort" delivery standard for the service providers (which are best suited for the approach elaborated in this chapter using DEA for such SLA monitoring), while others demand that their providers offer service with specific guarantees for application availability on a customer-by-customer basis (in these cases, traditional statistical approaches still work).

The SLA parameter value-range varies accordingly to the type of services; for example, real-time applications such as presence-enabled technologies such as Voice over IP (VoIP) or interactive media cannot operate effectively at a loss rate of 5% which is acceptable for typical Web browsing (Gurbani, Faynberg, Lu, Brusilovsky, Gato, & Unmehopta, 2003). Data latency, as with data loss, is another critical parameter in VoIP and multimedia environments where delays must not impact end-user performance; real-time interactive applications require response times of 100 milliseconds (ms) or less.

SLA Parameters for Presence-Enabled Services

Considering the parameters that a network SLA should include, and the typical elements of presence-enabled services, SLA parameters for presence-enabled services will include service hours and availability, downtime and so forth, customer support levels, throughputs, responsiveness, restrictions, functionalities, multi-platform communication domains support (synchronous/asynchronous), multiple device support, multiple protocol support, data loss acceptability, data security, real-time application suitability, and many other characteristics depending upon the specific implementation scenario of the presence-enabled service.

DEA Approach for the SLA Monitoring of Presence-Enabled Services

Basic Introduction to DEA (Data Envelopment Analysis)

DEA or Data Envelopment Analysis is commonly used to evaluate the relative efficiency of a number of producers/providers of any goods/services. A typical statistical approach is characterized as a central tendency approach, and it evaluates producers relative to an average producer. In contrast, DEA is an extreme point method and compares each producer with only the "best" producers. A producer is usually referred to as a decision-making unit or DMU. The DEA approach is essentially to find a set of criteria weights which present each entity in the best possible light.

A fundamental assumption behind an extreme point method is that if a given producer, A, is capable of producing Y(A) units of output with X(A) inputs, then other producers should also be able to do the same if they were to operate efficiently. Similarly, if producer B is capable of producing Y(B) units of output with X(B) inputs, then other producers should also be capable of the same production schedule. Producers A, B, and others can then be combined to form a composite producer with composite inputs and composite outputs. Since this composite producer may not necessarily exist, it is typically called a virtual producer.

The analysis primarily focuses on finding the "best" virtual producer for each real producer. If the virtual producer is better than the original producer by either making more output with the same input or making the same output with less input, then the original producer is *inefficient*. The procedure of finding the best virtual producer can be formulated as a linear program. Analyzing the efficiency of n producers is then a set of n linear programming problems.

DEA has got some features which make it an interesting and effective tool for comparing various decision-making units in a real-life situation. For example, in the DEA method, multiple input/output models are handled, where no assumption of a functional form relating inputs to outputs is a must. DMUs are directly compared against a peer or combination of peers. Inputs and outputs can have very different units. These features make DEA an effective option for estimating "relative" efficiency of a DMU; it converges very slowly to "absolute" efficiency or "theoretical maximum". The limitation is that since DEA is a non-parametric technique, statistical hypothesis tests are difficult and are the focus of ongoing research.

Examples of DEA Applications in Various Engineering and Services Sectors

DEA applications have generally focused on evaluation of alternative design configurations, performance improvement interventions, assessment of process/system performance and benchmarking. Example application domains range from design evaluation of turbofan jet engines (Bulla, Cooper, Wilson, & Park, 2000), circuit-board manufacturing processes (Triantis, 2003), to process improvement intervention (Hoopes, Triantis, & Partangel, 2000) with a need for the input/output variables of the empirical function to effectively represent the underlying processes (Sun, 2002); example applications of DEA in this context had been well-documented by Hoopes and Triantis (2001).

The key application issues have been, for example, how well-established engineering design methodologies, such as design of experiments (DOE), could effectively interface with the DEA methodology; how to explore these methodological interfaces (Kabnurkar, 2001), and how to continue to pursue innovative engineering DEA applications.

One DEA modeling approach: The network model has been proposed to measure and improve disaggregated process performance, by *open the input/output transformation box* (Cooper, Park, & Yu, 2001). This application of DEA is useful where efficiency performance of the specific production stages (represented by nodes) (Cooper, Park, & Yu, 2001) or modules are evaluated, for example, the basic service elements of presence-enabled services architecture (Day, Rosenberg, & Sugano, 2000). Goal Programming and Data Envelopment Analysis (GODEA) (Triantis, 2003) provided another application domain for DEA with an approach that combined conflicting objectives of efficiency, effectiveness, and equity in resource allocation for service organizations, for example, banks or financial services institutions.

Consequently, Data Envelopment Analysis (DEA) has been a popular technique for bank efficiency studies; however, DEA requires that units operate in consistent "cultures" to produce fair and comparable results .DEA has been appropriately applied to measure performance in the service sector, as a means of measuring performance and possibly as a monitoring tool for use in the longer term. In software processes also, DEA has been well applied. Data Envelopment Analysis (DEA) methods are ideal for measuring the efficiency of software production processes. DEA methods have proven to be very valuable, in practice, as a management tool appropriate for both planning and control activities, and as new tools for forecasting and trade-off analysis.

Another most interesting application of DEA has been in the context of dynamical systems, be it historical, causal or closed (Vaneman & Triantis, 2003), which exhibit a high degree of correlation between the variables at the initial time $t0$ with the variables at the final time t. Here, DEA techniques have been defined and developed as the dynamic data envelopment analysis (DDEA) by adding the element of time to the DEA model. This application of DEA can be directly connected to the real-time data handling aspects of SLA monitoring of services like VoIP, and so forth.

Characteristics of Problems Suitable for DEA Applications

The basic strength of DEA as a tool or method, as is apparent from the basic introduction, is that DEA generates an efficiency frontier by defining a "best producer" which does not necessarily have to be real, and is most often virtual, that is, combinations of the most desirable values across all real producers making the best virtual producer profile which gets reflected in the efficiency frontier. Consequently, problems which can be better solved by DEA other than statistical/operations research approaches have some typical characteristics which actually can be directly mapped onto DEA characteristics; for example:

- Problems with multiple inputs and outputs with different units of measurement;

- Unstructured, not well-defined problems where no or minimally-stable functional forms are available or can be assumed to relate inputs to outputs;

- Problems dealing with similar level payer comparisons;

- Problem domains which have no/minimal/extremely dynamic or changing/evolving benchmarking standards (extreme point techniques can actually be useful to derive the benchmarks in such situations);

- Problems/systems where "relative" efficiency is more important than "absolute" efficiency; and

- Problem domains where the parameters are not clearly defined so it cannot be modeled around parameters as is possible with many traditional operations research techniques.

DEA Model Orientation Options

An input-oriented measure quantifies the input reduction which is necessary to become efficient holding the outputs constant. Symmetrically, an output-oriented measure quantifies the necessary output expansion holding the inputs constant. A non-oriented measure quantifies necessary improvements when both inputs and outputs can be improved simultaneously. In applications, the choice of a certain measure mostly depends on three criteria:

- the "primal" interpretation, that is, the meaning of the efficiency score with respect to input and output quantities;

- the "dual" interpretation, that is, the meaning of the efficiency score with respect to input and output prices; and

- the axiomatic properties of the efficiency measure (e.g., monotonicity, units invariance, indication of efficiency, continuity).

Most of the measures are similar with respect to these criteria. T denotes the technology and (X^k, Y^k) denotes the input output data of the DMU under evaluation.

Distance

- **Radial**: This measure (Debreu-Farrell-measure) indicates the necessary improvements when all relevant factors are improved by the same factor equi-proportionally. This can also be thought of as the "radial part" of the CCR (Charnes, Cooper, & Rhodes, 1978) / BCC (Banker, Charnes, & Cooper, 1984) measure.

non-oriented: $\max\{\theta \mid ((1 - \theta)X^k, (1 + \theta)Y^k) \in T\}$

input: $\min\{\theta \mid (\theta X^k, Y^k) \in T\}$

output: $\max\{\varphi \mid (X^k, \varphi Y^k) \in T\}$

- **Additive**: This measure quantifies the maximal sum of absolute improvements (input reduction/output increase measured in "slacks"). It has a price interpretation (as the difference between actual and maximal profit) and indicates Koopmans efficiency, but it is not invariant with respect to units of measurement.

non-oriented: $\max\{\sum_i s_i + \sum_j t_j \mid (X^k - s, Y^k + t) \in T, (s, t) >= 0\}$

input: $\max\{\sum_i s_i \mid (X^k - s, Y^k) \in T, s >= 0\}$

output: $\max\{\sum_j t_j \mid (X^k, Y^k + t) \in T, t >= 0\}$

- **maxAverage:** This measure (Färel-Lovell or Russell or SBM (School-Based Management) measure) quantifies the maximal average of relative improvements (input reduction/output increase measured in percentages of the current level). It has no straightforward price interpretation, but it is both an indicator for Koopmans efficiency (for positive data) and units invariant.

- **minAverage**: This measure quantifies the minimal average of relative improvements which is necessary to become weakly efficient. Weak efficiency means there does not exist a point in the technology set which is better in every input and output. For a weakly efficient point, an arbitrary small improvement suffices to become Koopmans-efficient, whence the minAverage measure also quantifies the infimum average of improvements which is necessary to become Koopmans efficient. It has neither a straightforward price interpretation nor is it an indicator for Koopmans efficiency, but it is units invariant.

Which model option will be applicable to which parameter depends primarily upon the following:

1. the purpose of analysis, for example, for benchmarking, the output-oriented model will be suited, whereas for cost monitoring, the input-oriented cost minimization model can be more applicable; and

2. the availability of criterion data, for example, if there is no coinciding point in the data spectrum where both input and output are getting better (a very likely scenario with conflicting objective criteria as is the case of SLA parameters, e.g., QoS vs. cost), then the minAverage model can be chosen.

Presence-Enabled Services SLA and DEA: Applicability

Problems with presence-enabled services are typically different from traditional engineering context in various aspects. For example, they have multi-platform, non-standardized communication domains. For monitoring these services thereof, we need an approach to efficiently, and even more desirably, automatically handle real-time service-oriented performance data. Other problems related to these sets of services are the facts that they are still non-stabilized, ever-evolving, or developing procedures and policies, which is the reason why there is a lack of benchmarking data availability for the SLA parameters themselves. The basic operational elements will therefore include efficient and, preferably, automated recording, processing, and monitoring SLA data elements.

The DEA Application Framework for Monitoring the SLA Parameters of Presence-Enabled Services

In the following section, we are presenting a simple algorithm to implement the DEA approach for automated monitoring of the SLA parameters in a generic implementation scenario of presence-enabled services. Consequently, we have taken the following assumptions:

1.   In this implementation scenario, we are concerned primarily with getting the best possible efficiency from the service providers with the minimum possible cost, which is reflected in the first consideration of the algorithm.

2.   This being a generic and simplified scenario, we have not specified the variables in designing the DEA input/output variables formulation. The variables will have to be defined in the specific implementation contexts of presence-enabled services. As we have seen in the previous sections, there are various types of presence-enabled services, each of which need a set of inputs, some of which are common and some which are unique to their specific implementation requirements. And consequently, the output requirements also vary. For example, location information service performance requirements will primarily be the real-time accuracy of the data, whereas for call services, the availability of QoS parameters will be the most important output variables for monitoring and control. So, depending on the implementation-specific requirements, the input-output variables can be defined.

Using these assumptions, now we can formulate the algorithm.

In this algorithm, the number of suppliers/providers (called as **Decision-Making Units or DMUs** in context of DEA) of presence-enabled services about which adequate SLA parameter values/historical data is available $= n$. Number of output decision variables $Y =$ SLA parameter values + cost $= s$. Number of input variables X i.e. SLA parameter values $= r$. Weights on input variables $= w_j$ and Weights on output variables $= v_i$

The Algorithm

- **Step 1:** Minimum cost/maximum efficiency ratio-wise best producer: Basic LP form -:

$$\text{MIN} \, e_0' = \frac{\sum_{i=1}^{r} v_i x_{i0}}{\sum_{j=1}^{s} w_j y_{j0}}$$

  e_0' reflects the reciprocal measure of input minimization model.
- **Step 2:** Calculate e_0' for all DMUs.
- **Step 3:** Choose the DMU with minimum value-set (as we are calculating the reciprocal measure) of the parameters. This can be represented as the best virtual producer.
- **Step 4:** Calculate the SLA parameter value-variances for each parameter from this best virtual producer against each real producer. The value-variances can be calculated in real-time automatically and can be identified during the monitoring process.
- **Step 5:** Invoke the appropriate SLA management action consequently when required.

The implementation framework as described in the algorithm above, for monitoring presence-enabled services SLAs with DEA is shown in Figure 2.

Figure 2 does not show the SLA parameters exclusively emanating from each service delivery unit/element because in that case the Figure will become very complex and hence not highly readable and practically applicable. Moreover, the algorithm, being generic, will have to be qualified with implementation-specific variables which will in turn depend on the types of service delivery units/elements involved to produce a particular type of presence-enabled service. Also, many parameters will emanate from more than one service element so there exists an m:n relationship between the SLA parameters and service delivery elements, which actually makes it a best-suited application for DEA.

Implementing the Framework

Explanation on how to implement the framework as shown in Figure 2 is given below, with the help of two example cases on two SLA parameters. We have used the EMS software in these examples. Efficiency Measurement System (EMS) is software for Windows 9x/NT which computes Data Envelopment Analysis (DEA) efficiency measures. EMS uses the LP Solver DLL BPMPD 2.11 for the computation of the scores. It is an interior point solver.

Preparing the Input Output Data

The first and probably most difficult step in an efficiency evaluation is to decide which input and output data should be included. EMS accepts data in MS Excel or in text format. Additionally to "standard" inputs and outputs, EMS can also handle "nondiscretionary" inputs and outputs (i.e., data which are not controlled by the DMUs).

The size of analysis is limited by the memory of the machine used. There is theoretically no limitation of the number of DMUs, inputs, and outputs in EMS. Although the code is not optimized for large-scale data, EMS has successfully solved problems with over 5,000 DMUs and about 40 inputs and outputs.

When EMS computes an efficiency score (which is a distance to the efficient frontier), it does not alter the values of non-discretionary data, that is, the distance will only be computed in the directions of the "normal" (discretionary) inputs and outputs while the non-discretionary are fixed.

Weights restrictions can be specified in the form W(p, q) >= 0, where p is the vector of input weights and q is the vector of output weights (or shadow prices). Both "Cone Ratio" constraints and "Assurance Region" constraints can be incorporated.

Figure 2. Role of DEA in monitoring of SLAs of presence-enabled services

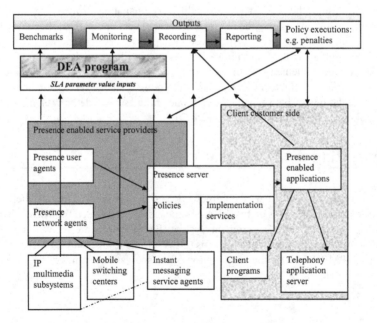

Example Case I

Suppose we have three input parameters for SLA monitoring, for example, cost, bandwidth, and availability, and two outputs, for example, throughput and reliability, and we want to have the restriction $p1 > p2$ then the corresponding row in the weights restriction matrix W is $(1;-1; 0; 0; 0)$. If we incorporate bounds on the marginal rates of substitutions like $0.5 <= q1 / q2 <= 5$, then it can be transformed into two constraints, $q1 - 0.5q2 >= 0$ and $-q1 + 5q2 >= 0$, yielding the rows $(0; 0; 0; 1;-0.5)$ and $(0; 0; 0;-1; 5)$ in the matrix W. Thus in this example one has W =

1	−1	0	0	0
0	0	0	1	−0.5
0	0	0	−1	5

This form of input can be now loaded onto the specific DEA model to be chosen in the next few steps. Input-output data can be loaded by pressing Ctrl+O (Menu File ! Load data). Ctrl+M (Menu DEA ! Run model) will display a dialog where the model can be specified.

•   returns to Scale,

•   convex and nonconvex envelopment, and

•   constant, variable, no increasing or no decreasing returns to scale.

Example Case II: Choosing an Efficiency Measure and Super-Efficiency

An efficiency measure quantifies, in one way or another, a "distance" to the efficient frontier of the technology, that is, the service delivery mechanism in this context. EMS allows computation of various distances in input-, output-, and non-oriented versions. Detailed discussions on orientation are in the previous section.

Super-Efficiency

If we choose a radial distance, then EMS allows us to compute so-called "super-efficiency" scores by checking the box. For inefficient DMUs, the super-efficiency score coincides with the standard score. For efficient DMUs, a score is computed which indicates the maximal radial change which is feasible such that the DMU remains efficient. Formally, it is defined like the standard score, but the DMU under evaluation is excluded from the constraints (i.e., the definition of the technology set).

So, if we want to find out the actually-available best producer based on the SLA parameters values they had promised to deliver and they actually deliver, then we can choose the super-efficiency model. If we choose the super-efficiency model, then in the results table a big score may appear. This means that the DMU remains efficient under arbitrary large increased inputs (input-oriented) or decreased outputs (output-oriented), respectively.

We can specify selections of DMUs which should be computed (Evaluation) and which should be used for building the envelopment (Technology), for example, producers of world-standard services but which are not available as options. This allows us to compute producer efficiency, that is, for each DMU selected in Evaluation, a score is computed.

If computations are finished, EMS will display the results in a table. The window caption tells which model was computed, that is, whether with constant returns to scale, radial distance, input orientation, or weights restrictions with restriction matrix. The result table contains:

- **DMU name:** An additional {X} indicates that this DMU was excluded from building the technology as specified in Technology. A DMU name without score indicates that this DMU built the technology but was not evaluated as specified in Evaluation.
- **Benchmarks:**
  o **for inefficient DMU:** the reference DMUs with corresponding intensities (the "lambdas") in brackets;
  o **for efficient DMU:** the number of inefficient DMUs which have chosen the DMU as Benchmark, slacks {S} or factors {F}. Depending of the chosen distance, for radial and additive measures the slacks are displayed;
- For the minAverage and maxAverage measures the factors are displayed. In addition, for the minAverage measure, slacks are displayed for those inputs and outputs with factors = 1 (or 0 for non-oriented measure); and
- For Nonconvex (FDH) models, instead of the weights for each DMU, the number of dominated and dominating DMUs and lists of these DMUs are displayed.

From the results table, the benchmark values for the input parameters (if input-oriented model is chosen) or the output parameters (if output-oriented model is chosen) are chosen and this set of values can now be used for variance analysis with the actual parameter values delivered during the SLA monitoring process.

The two examples show how DEA can be used for SLA monitoring and benchmarking based on:

1. how the parameter values can be input as constraints into the system; and
2. how a benchmark can be obtained, using the EMS software as the example tool.

Implementing the framework as shown in Figure 2 can be done using other LP-supporting tools with further programming extension abilities to develop the DEA models.

Conclusion

The primary contribution of this chapter has been into the exploration of applicability of DEA as a new approach to benchmark, assess, and monitor SLAs and the service providers for presence-enabled services. It serves this purpose finally with two simple and specific examples addressing two basic application issues of DEA models, that is, the input and the model selection process.

The concept that has been developed and explained in this chapter can be extended further:

- to incorporate the SLA parameters values being generated/monitored from each of the service delivery elements;

- to incorporate other aspects of DEA models to suit specific company needs; for example, in this chapter, the example is primarily concerned with the virtual best producer with minimum cost/maximum efficiency ratio. But a company for which cost is not a critical factor but efficiency is, can go for a different DEA model; based on other parameters too; and

- to incorporate the tools for implementing the DEA programs that can also be integrated into the framework as shown in Figure 2.

The potential of application of this concept is even more significant in the current context where presence-enabled services like VoIP are emerging as the primary services in ITeS based on which many businesses/organizations are evolving and progressing. This will also enable industrial practitioners who are actively involved in designing and managing service level agreements. This is seen as a very crucial component of the overall business processes of many organizations of today which are showing a proliferating trend towards outsourcing basic support/infra-structural services, the need emanating primarily from these organizations' priorities to focus on developing core competencies to gain and retain sustainable competitive advantage. Being the backbone of the basic process-running and services required by these organizations, the support/infra-structural services like presence-enabled services quite often determine the quality of services that are produced as part of these organizations' core competencies. Consequently, the effective and efficient benchmarking, monitoring, and controlling of these services becomes crucial for organizational success. Therefore, not only from an academic or research point of view, but also from the hard-core industry practitioners' view, it is a crucial challenge for managing the service level agreements with various service producers/providers, a challenge which needs to be addressed with innovative, new ideas and approaches aiming towards a cost-effective, sustainable method which utilizes IT resources optimally for managing SLAs. This chapter suggests one such method, and opens up possibilities of using various other methods and approaches for handling the challenges of service-level management.

References

Banker, R. D., Charnes, A., & Cooper, W.W. (1984), Some models for estimating technical and scale inefficiencies in data envelopment analysis. *Management Science, 30*(9), 1078-1092.

Bulla, S., Cooper, W. W., Wilson, D., & Park, K. S. (2000). Evaluating efficiencies of turbofan jet engines: A data envelopment analysis approach. *Journal of Propulsion and Power, 16*(3), 431-439.

Charnes, A., Cooper, W., & Rhodes, E. (1978), Measuring the efficiency of decision making units, *European Journal of Operational Research, 2*(6), 429-444

Cooper, W. W., Park, K. S., & Yu, G. (2001). An illustrative application of IDEA (Imprecise Data Envelopment Analysis) to a Korean mobile telecommunication company. *Operations Research, 49*(6), 807-820.

Day, M., Rosenberg, J., & Sugano, H. (2000). *A Model for Presence and Instant Messaging* (RFC 2778). Internet Engineering Task Force.

Gurbani, V. K., Faynberg I., Lu H. L., Brusilovsky A., Gato J., & Unmehopta, M. (2003). *The SPIRITS (Services in PSTN Requesting Internet Services) Protocol,* Internet Engineering Task Force, RFC 3910.

Hoopes, B., & Triantis, K. (2001). Efficiency performance, control charts, and process improvement: Complementary measurement and evaluation. *IEEE Transactions on Engineering Management, 48*(2), 239-253.

Hoopes, B., Triantis, K., & Partangel, N. (2000). The relationship between process and manufacturing plant performance: A goal programming approach. *International Journal of Operations and Quantitative Management, 6*(4), 287-310.

Kabnurkar, A. (2001). *Math modeling for data envelopment analysis with fuzzy restrictions on weights.* M.S. thesis, Virginia Tech, Department of Industrial and Systems Engineering, Falls Church, VA.

Kao, C., & Liu, S. T. (2000). Fuzzy efficiency measures in data envelopment analysis. *Fuzzy Sets and Systems, 113*(3), 427-437.

Roach, A. B. (2002). *Session Initiation Protocol (SIP)—Specific Event Notification* (RFC 3265), Internet Engineering Task Force.

Rosenberg, J. (2003). A Presence Event Package for the Session Initiation Protocol (SIP), Internet Engineering Task Force.

Sun, S. (2002). Assessing computer numerical control machines using data envelopment analysis. *International Journal of Production Research, 40*(9), 2011-2039.

Triantis, K. (2003). Engineering applications of DEA: Issues and opportunities. In W. W. Cooper, L. M. Seiford, & J. Zhu (Eds.), *Handbook of DEA* (pp. 401-442). Kluwer Publishers.

Vaneman, W., & Triantis, K. (2003). The dynamic production axioms and system dynamics behaviors: The foundation for future integration. *Journal of Productivity Analysis, 19*(1), 93-113.

Chapter XII

All-Optical Internet:
Next-Generation Network Infrastructure for E-Service Applications

Abid Abdelouahab, Multimedia University, Malaysia

Fouad Mohammed Abbou, Alcatel Network Systems, Malaysia

Ewe Hong Tat, Multimedia University, Malaysia

Toufik Taibi, United Arab Emirates University, United Arab Emirates

Abstract

To exploit the unprecedented opportunities offered by the E-Service Applications, businesses and users alike would need a highly-available, reliable, and efficient telecommunication infrastructure. This chapter provides an insight into building the next-generation network infrastructure, that is, the All-Optical Internet. It also reveals the factors driving the convergence of the Internet Protocol (IP) and the Wavelength-Division Multiplexing (WDM) technology. The chapter discusses the dominant optical networks architectures in an attempt to show the evolution towards the ultimate all-optical packet-switching network. A special focus is given to the Optical Burst Switching (OBS) as a new emerging switching paradigm and a highly promising technology. OBS network architecture, burst assembly, signaling and reservation protocols, QoS support, and contention resolution techniques are presented. Furthermore, realistic suggestions and strategies to efficiently deploy OBS are given.

Introduction

The Internet is a technology with many properties that has the potential to influence, and even transform established ways of conducting business, especially Electronic Services, while at the same time creating entirely new industries and businesses. The Internet has a profound impact on the competitive landscape, since it is affecting the way that firms' activities are coordinated, how commerce is conducted, how business communities are created, and how communications are defined and performed.

As we are moving towards the Web-dependent era, the 99 percent or even the 99.99 percent network reliability would be inadequate for the mission-critical applications that have genuine requirements that exceed the typical application needs.

The e-service applications are typically reliant on IP data networks that construct the Internet, which has become a ubiquitous success. Furthermore, the capacity of optical fibers is doubling annually toward a terabit per second per fiber, providing strong incentives to exploit the huge bandwidth of fiber-optic networks, which has increased considerably with the introduction of Wavelength-Division Multiplexing (WDM) technology.

The rapid advancement of optical technologies and the growing effort to enhance the Internet Protocol (IP) makes it possible to move from the current network architecture to an all-optical Internet, where the network traffic is optically transmitted, buffered, amplified, and switched through high performance Internet switches and routers directly connected using WDM optical links.

All-Optical Internet

The Internet is an interconnection of computer networks that are a combination of hardware and software, controlled by a set of protocols to transmit and communicate data. The Internet uses the TCP/IP protocol suite, where the Transmission Control Protocol (TCP) is a connection-oriented end-to-end protocol. TCP is used to create logical connections between various applications running on different hosts, prior to executing protocols that exchange information. TCP relies on the Internet Protocol (IP) to route the packets (data units that are routed between an origin and a destination) through the network. Therefore, the Internet is simply a massive network of networks.

Depending on the deployed physical technology, three network generations can be distinguished. The first-generation networks are based on copper wire or radio; subsequently; the copper wire (around 10 gigabits per second) was replaced by a more sophisticated transmission medium, the optical fiber, which offers an immense bandwidth (theoretically, 50 terabits per second), low error rate, high reliability, availability, and maintainability. Additionally, optical fibers feature many other advantages, for example, lightweight and small space requirements, resistance to corrosive materials, less signal attenuation, and high immunity to tapping. Having optical fiber as the transmission medium in the second-generation networks enhanced the network performance and throughput; however, this improvement was restricted by the so-called Electronic Bottleneck. Electronic bottleneck phenomenon is caused by the limited processing speed of electronic components (a few gigabits per second) deployed in switches/routers, multiplexers, and end-nodes in the network. As the electronic processing speed is at its peak, the solution is to transfer the switching and routing functions from the electronic domain to the optical domain. Therefore, the third-generation networks will be designed as all-optical networks, where the data are transmitted all-optically through the network from source to destination.

IP and WDM Convergence

The success of the Internet and its omnipresence has made the Internet Protocol (IP) a de facto standard, and the demand for IP network solutions has increased exponentially. With the Internet protocol, voice and video as well as real-time multimedia traffic could be integrated and transmitted with the data traffic over a single network infrastructure, providing unprecedented opportunity for businesses to improve their services, reduce expenses, and increase their revenues. With the technological evolution, IP diminished the boundaries between the computing, entertainment, and the telecom industries, which led to more customer centric business models. Being an intermediate layer between an immense variety of IP-based services and almost all the layer-2 technologies, IP is more than a revenue-generating integration layer. IP convergence is not merely an option; it is inevitably becoming a business necessity in the Internet-dependent era and the new customer-centric economy. Such convergence is best supported by the WDM technology. WDM, which is conceptually similar to Frequency Division Multiplexing (FDM), is a method of transmitting many light beams of different wavelengths simultaneously down the core of a single optical fiber. Therefore, with WDM the available bandwidth can be increased without deploying additional optical fibers. Furthermore, WDM relieves the effect of electronic bottleneck by dividing the optical transmission spectrum into a number of non-overlapping channels; thus, the electronic components would only work at their own speed (few gigabits per second) and not at the aggregated transmission rate. IP/WDM convergence will eventually be translated to an efficient, robust, reliable, and feasible all-optical Internet.

Optical Switching Paradigms

Several different switching paradigms have been devised to transfer data over WDM, such as Optical Circuit Switching (OCS), a wavelength-routed network (Mukherjee, 1997), Optical Packet Switching (OPS) (Xu, Perros, & Rouskas, 2001; Yao, Dixit, & Mukherjee, 2000), and Optical Burst Switching (OBS) (Qiao & Yoo, 1999). Wavelength-routed optical networks (currently deployed) represent a promising technology for optical networks. However, wavelength-routed optical networks, which employ circuit switching, may not be the optimal choice and the most appropriate switching paradigm to support the various requirements of the Internet traffic. Alternatively, optical packet switching paradigm appears to be the optimum option. Unfortunately, OPS is not mature enough to provide a viable solution. Therefore, a switching technique that provides granularity in between wavelengths and packets was shaped, thus occupying the middle of the spectrum between circuit switching and packet switching paradigms. Optical burst switching is a switching technique where the benefits of both packet-switching networks and circuit-switching networks are combined; OBS borrows ideas from both to deliver a completely new functionality.

Optical Circuit Switching

In circuit switching, each sender and receiver are connected with a dedicated communication path (circuit), established through one or more intermediate switching nodes. The communication path must be set up between the two end-nodes before they could communicate. Although circuit switching is the most familiar technique used to build communication networks, and even though wavelength-routed optical networks have already been deployed, circuit switching may not be the most appropriate switching technique for the emerging optical Internet. Circuit-switched networks lack flexibility and convergence capabilities, which lead to poor wavelength utilization, especially if the connection holding time (i.e., the time of data exchange) is very short; the situation is worsened by the bursty nature of the data traffic. Therefore, in order to fully utilize the WDM wavelengths, a sophisticated traffic grooming mechanism is needed to statistically multiplex the data coming from different sources.

Optical Packet Switching

Optical packet switching is an alternative optical switching paradigm that appears to be the optimum choice. However, with the immature current optical technology, it is impossible (at least in short-medium term) to deploy OPS networks viably. Packet switches usually work synchronously, where the arriving packets at different input ports must be aligned before being switched using the switching fabrics. This process is difficult and expensive to be implemented fully in the optical domain. Another operation concern is the relatively long time in which the optical-switching fabrics are configured compared to the data transmission speed. This is clearly demonstrated using the following example based on the current developments in the optical technology, considering an optical packet switch, with a switching fabric that takes 1 ms to be configured (i.e., set up a connection from an input port to an output port). At a data rate of 2.5 Gbps, it takes about 5 μs to transmit a 12,500-bit packet. Therefore, if a switch operates at the packet level, then less than 0.5% of the time is used for switching data, while the rest is wasted in setting up the switching fabric.

A more prevailing OPS's deployment issue, is the realization of the "Store and Forward" concept that is the requisite idea in packet switching networks. To store packets in switches, a buffering strategy is needed to resolve contentions in the output ports. Optical switches currently use optical fibers as Fiber Delay Lines (FDL) to emulate buffers by delaying packets for a fixed time (Xu et al., 2001). The FDLs are far away behind the random access electronic buffers, in term of cost, performance, and deployment simplicity.

Optical Burst Switching

The concept of burst switching first emerged in the context of voice communications. OBS is an adaptation of a stander known as ATM Block Transfer (ABT) developed by the telecommunication standardization sector of the International Telecommunication Union (ITU-T) for burst switching in Asynchronous Transfer Mode (ATM) networks. OBS consists of core nodes, built from optical and electronic components, and edge (Ingress/ Egress) nodes connected by WDM links. OBS differs from optical packet switching and the original burst-switching concept introduced in the 1980's (Amstutz, 1989; Kulzer & Montgomery, 1984) in a main aspect, that is, the separation of the control and the data payloads, both in time (i.e., the control information is transmitted at an offset time prior to its corresponding data payload) and physical space (i.e., the control packets and the data propagate on different designated channels). In conventional OBS, there is no need for buffering and electronic processing of data. Furthermore, OBS insures efficient bandwidth utilization, since the bandwidth is reserved only when the data is to be transferred through the link.

Optical Components

In order to build an all-optical Internet, different functional optical elements are required. These elements could be classified either as "switching" or "non-switching" components; "switching" components enable networking, while "non-switching" components are primarily used on optical links. However, a simple classification could be determined by the placement of the optical elements in the system. They can be placed either on the transmitting-end, on the link, or on the receiving-end. In this section, the key optical communications elements are briefly described.

- **Optical fibers:** Optical fibers are made of glass or plastic, and they transmit signals in the form of light at about two-thirds the speed of light in a vacuum. In the optical fibers, the lightwaves (signals) are guided with a minimum attenuation.

- **Light sources and light detectors:** At both ends of an optical transmission system, light sources and light detectors are found. At the transmitting-end, the light source (light emitter) modulates electrical signals into light pulses. The opposite process, that is, to modulate light pulses into electrical signals, is performed by the light detectors at the receiving-end.

- **Optical Amplifiers:** To amplify an attenuated optical signal, unlike the conventional repeaters that perform respectively optical-electrical conversion, electrical amplification, and then electrical-optical conversion, the optical amplifiers operate completely in the optical domain. The optical amplifiers can boost the power levels of the optical signals. Amplifiers can be classified to two fundamental amplifier types: Semiconductor Optical Amplifiers (SOAs) and Doped-Fiber Amplifiers (DFAs).

- **Multiplexers and De-multiplexers:** Multiplexers and De-multiplexers are essential components in the optical transmission systems. Multiplexers converge and combine multiple incoming signals into one beam. The de-multiplexers have the ability to separate out the combined components of the beam and discreetly detect the different signals.

- **Optical Add/Drop Multiplexers:** Optical Add/Drop Multiplexers (OADMs) are key elements on the progress toward the ultimate goal of all-optical networks. Unlike the multiplexers and de-multiplexers, the OADMs are capable of adding or removing one or more wavelengths without the need for combining or separating all wavelengths.

- **Wavelength converters:** An optical wavelength converter is a device capable of directly translating (converting) data contained on an incoming wavelength to another wavelength without optical-electrical-optical conversion. Therefore, wavelength converters are very important elements in the deployment of all-optical networks. Two classes of wavelength converters can be identified: Optical-Gating Wavelength Converters and Wave-Mixing Wavelength Converters.

Optical Burst Switching

In this chapter, a comprehensive discussion of Optical Burst Switching (OBS) is presented. The OBS networks variants, reservation protocols, node architecture and switching technology, Quality of Service provisioning, and contention resolution techniques are discussed.

OBS Network Functionality

Optical Burst Switching is a relatively new switching technique and is still at the definition phase, which is clearly indicated by the number of research groups and their publications, specifically, on new OBS architectures (Callegate, Cankaya, Xiong, & Vandenhoute, 1999; Dolzer, 2002; Verma, Chaskar, & Ravikanth, 2000; Xu et al., 2001; Yoo, Qiao, & Dixit, 2001), prototypes (Baldine, Rouskas, Perros, & Stevenson, 2002), reservation mechanisms (Detti & Listanti, 2001; Dolzer, Gauger, Spath, & Bodamer, 2001; Qiao & Yoo, 2000; Tancevski, Yegnanarayanam, Castanon, Tamil, Masetti, & McDermott, 2000; Turner, 1999; Wei, Pastor, Ramamurthy, & Tsal, 1999; Xiong, Vanderhoute, & Cankaya, 2000; Yoo, Jeong, & Qiao, 1997) and assembly mechanisms (Ge, Callegati, & Tamil, 2000; Hu, Dolzer, & Gauger, 2003; Vokkarane, Haridoss, & Jue, 2002). However, despite the fact that there is no standard architecture or a universal definition of optical burst switching, OBS networks assume the following general characteristics:

- **Granularity:** The transmission units (called bursts) are macro-packets, each of which should have a duration that is as short as possible, as it does not require a dedicated channel, but long enough to be efficiently switched optically; that is, between the optical circuit switching and optical packet switching granularity.

- **Separation of control and data:** Control information and data payload propagate on separate channels (wavelengths).

- **One-way reservation:** Network resources are generally allocated in one-way reservation fashion. That is, bursts (data) are transmitted at an offset time after their control information without receiving or waiting for any acknowledgements, to confirm the switching resources reservation, back from the destination nodes.

- **Variable burst length:** The duration (size) of the data burst may be variable. However, the burst duration should be long enough to be efficiently switched in the optical domain, and short enough to be statistically multiplexed.

- **Optical Buffering/Wavelength conversion:** In the conventional implementation of OBS networks, optical buffers/wavelength converters are not mandatory in the intermediate nodes. Thus, the data bursts would be switched optically from source to destination, without any delay (buffering), and using the same wavelength.

Not all of these characteristics need be satisfied at once and without variation in all OBS implementations, thus, allowing for design flexibility and a possible smooth evolution towards the packet switching technique, when the development on the optical switching technology matures.

As mentioned before, the model of burst switching is not new as a concept. Burst-switching has been already known since the 1980's. However, the concept has never been implemented widely and successfully in conventional electrical networks. Due to its complexity and high cost, burst switching could not compete with established, flexible, and relatively cheap electronic packet switching techniques (e.g., Asynchronous Transfer Mode (ATM)). However, with the introduction of very high-speed optical transmission techniques, this has changed. It has been agreed that it is more advantageous, cost effective, and efficient to keep data in the optical domain and to avoid optical-electrical-optical conversions. In view of the fact that all-optical packet switching techniques are still too complex to be widely deployed, a hybrid approach is desirable. In this approach, the data payload (that does not need to be processed at the core nodes) is kept in the optical domain, whereas the control information can go through optical-electrical-optical conversions to be efficiently processed in the electrical domain. OBS offers exactly that, by separating the control and the data in the physical space, that is, the control information and the data propagate discretely in different designated channels, and maybe with different data rates. OBS also separates the control and the data in time, that is, the control packet is transmitted at an offset time prior to its corresponding data. In the buffer-less core nodes, the offset time is to compensate for both processing and configuration time, needed respectively by the control unit to process the control information and the switching-fabric to be configured.

Figure 1 shows some of the main components of an OBS network. There are two types of nodes, edge (ingress/egress) nodes and core nodes. In the edge nodes, network traffic is collected from access networks and assembled into macro data units called data bursts (DBs). Core nodes serve as transit nodes at the core network. Their main task is to switch bursts (data) all-optically without any conversion or processing. The switching fabrics are configured according to the control information contained in the Burst Control Packets (BCPs), which are transmitted as reservation requests at an offset time ahead of their corresponding data bursts.

Figure 1. Illustration of optical burst-switched network components

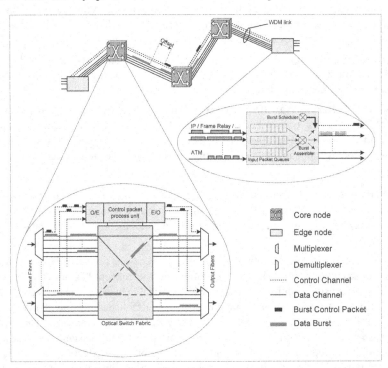

In the literature, various OBS switching protocols with different tradeoffs can be found. The OBS switching protocols differ in the choice of the offset time that can be zero or more, and the bandwidth reservation and release techniques (bandwidth holding time).

Three main OBS implementations can be identified, based on the offset time which is defined as the interval of time between the transmission of the first bit of the BCP and the transmission of the first bit of the data burst. The offset time can be nil, round-trip dependent, or source-routing dependent.

- **Nil offset time:** This OBS implementation is the closest to optical packet switching, and it is similar to ATM Block Transfer and Immediate Transmission (ABT-IT). The DBs and their corresponding BCPs are transmitted on different wavelengths and separated by a zero or a negligible offset time. The BCPs reserve the network resources (wavelength and buffer) upon arrival to the core nodes. The DBs are buffered until the BCPs are processed and the switching fabrics are configured. Currently the buffers are hard-to-implement expensive FDLs that can buffer the data optically only for a short fixed time. Therefore, this implementation is feasible only when the switch configuration time (including the BCPs processing time) is very short.

- **Round-trip-dependent offset time:** The offset time is equivalent to the round-trip time, that is, the time between the sending of a BCP and the receiving of its corresponding acknowledgment. In this implementation, a DB is transmitted only after receiving a positive response (acknowledgment) to its resource reservation request sent via the BCP, therefore, guaranteeing an uninterrupted all-optical transmission path for the DB from source to destination. Suffering from lengthy offset time due to the two-way propagation delay needed to set up an end-to-end lightpath before transmitting the user data, this scheme is the closest to optical circuit switching.

- **Source-routing-dependent offset time:** This implementation is similar to the ATM Block Transfer and Delayed Transmission (ABT-DT). The ingress node sends each control packet, followed by its corresponding data burst after an offset time. Thus, data bursts are sent without waiting for any acknowledgment or feedback on the reservation requests. This one-way reservation scheme avoids the two-way-reservation propagation delay in order to reduce the data waiting time at the ingress nodes. In this scheme, to efficiently calculate the offset time, some sort of source routing is used to determine the number of intermediate nodes from source to destination.

Channel Reservation Schemes

Under the *source-routing-dependent offset time* implementation, four channel reservation schemes can be identified. Depending on when the channel reservation starts and ends, the reservation schemes differ in their burst-dropping performance and their complexity. Accompanied by the illustration in Figure 2, the schemes are briefly explained as follows:

- **Scheme 1:** Each BCP contains the offset time that separates it from its corresponding DB, but not the duration of the DB. Thus, the core nodes reserve a channel as soon as they receive the BCP (reservation request). The channel remains reserved until the core nodes receive a release message that follows the transmitted DB. Therefore, for each channel, only an on/off ($1_2/0_2$) flag should be kept in each core node to indicate whether the channel is busy (reserved) or free (available). This scheme is usually referred to as Explicit Setup and Explicit Release scheme.

- **Scheme 2:** Each BCP contains the offset time that separates it from its corresponding DB and the duration of that DB. Thus, the core nodes reserve the channels as soon as they receive the BCP. Since the end of each DB is known (calculated using the duration of the DB), the channels are reserved only until the end of the DB. This scheme is more complex than the previous scheme, as each channel should be associated with a timer, which indicates when the channel will become available. This scheme is referred to as Explicit Setup and Estimated Release scheme.

- **Scheme 3:** Similarly to "scheme 1", each BCP contains the offset time that separates it from its corresponding DB, but not the duration of the DB, and the reserved channels are released only when the core nodes receive the corresponding release messages. However, the reservation of the channels starts approximately at the time of the DBs arrivals. This scheme is referred to as Estimated Setup and Explicit Release scheme.

- **Scheme 4:** Similarly to "scheme 2", each BCP contains both the offset time that separates it from its corresponding DB and the duration of that DB as well. Since both the

Figure 2. One-way-based channel reservation schemes

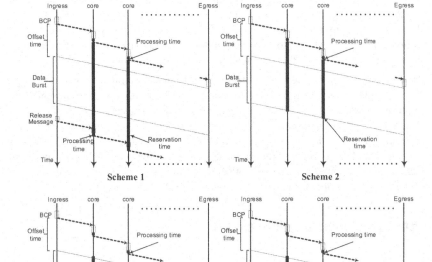

beginning and the end of each DB is known (calculated respectively using the offset and the duration of the data burst), the reservation starts at the beginning of the burst and ends at its end. The reservation process is controlled using a two-element array that its elements correspondingly refer to the arrival and departure time of the burst to/from the core node. This scheme is referred to as Estimated Setup and Estimated Release scheme.

Several signaling protocols were developed for OBS networks, with different tradeoffs. For example, Just-In-Time (JIT) was developed by Wei and McFarland (2000) under Scheme 1. The Horizon protocol was proposed by Turner (1999) under Scheme 2; under Scheme 4, Just-Enough-Time (JET) was developed by Qiao and Yoo (1999). JET was further extended by Gauger, Dolzer, and Scharf (2002) to be deployed in switches with optical buffers. For the complete operation of these signaling protocols, a variety of Channel Scheduling algorithms were proposed in the literature. Channel scheduling algorithms are used by the schedulers in the core nodes to determine the status of each channel (or possibly the optical buffer), on which the channel reservation decision is based. A channel is said to be scheduled, if it is occupied/reserved by a data burst. The time that a channel is unscheduled is known as "void", that is, the time that the channel is not occupied between two successive bursts. Schedulers use the information associated with the BCPs, for example, offset time (burst arrival time), and burst length (burst exit time). In certain Scheduling algorithms, the schedulers need to keep track of the voids between scheduled burst. Three main channel scheduling algorithms can be found in the literature: (1) First Fit Unscheduled Channel (FFUC) algorithm, (2) Latest Available Unscheduled Channel (LAUC) algorithm, and (3) Latest Available Void Filling (LAVF) algorithm. The implementation and the working of these algorithms are beyond the scope of this chapter.

Node Architecture and Switching Technology

The switching technology is a very critical architectural aspect in the design of OBS networks. In order to effectively operate an OBS network with efficient bandwidth utilization, the switching time should be negligible compared to the mean transmission time of the data bursts. Therefore, both the deployed switching technology and the mean burst length have to be chosen appropriately. For example, an OBS network using fiber links at the rate of 10 Gbps to transmit a burst of about 1 Mbyte cannot adopt Micro Electro-Mechanical Systems (MEMS) (Suzuki, Otani, & Hayashi, 2003), since they require switching times between 1-10 ms, which is greater than the transmission time of an entire burst. However, if the mean burst duration is selected properly, both the Acousto-Optic Tunable Filters (AOTFs) (Sadot & Boimovich, 1998) and Semiconductor Optical Amplifiers (SOAs) (Renaud, Bachmann, & Erman, 1998) could be used as switching technology for OBS networks, as their switching time is respectively below 10 μs and 10 ns.

The OBS nodes are classified as edge nodes or core nodes. Edge nodes (Ingress/Egress) provide an interface between the OBS network (optical domain) and legacy access networks. Besides serving as an interface point between access networks and OBS, an ingress node should be capable of performing bursts assembly, BCPs generation, burst/channel scheduling, and routing. The ingress architecture is illustrated in Figure 3(a). Generally an ingress node will contain input interface cards to legacy networks, BCPs generator, bursts assembler, scheduler, and optical transmitters. In addition to the output interface cards, the Egress node contains bursts disassembler, BCPs processor/terminator, and optical receivers. Note that a generic edge node should have the functionalities of both the ingress and the egress nodes. As intermediate nodes between the edge nodes, the core nodes are located inside the OBS network. A general architecture of OBS core node is shown in Figure 3(b). The OBS core node (switch) should be equipped with the capabilities of routing, bursts switching (optically), and BCPs processing (electronically). The capabilities of a core node may be farther extended to provide optical data buffering and wavelengths conversion.

A generic core node contains the following:

- **Optical receivers/transmitters:** Reception/Transmission of the control information and data bursts; *Optical multiplexer and de-multiplexers:* Responsible for optical channels multiplexing and de-multiplexing;

- **Input/Output interface for BCP:** Control reception/transmission and O/E/O conversions;

Figure 3. (a) Architecture of OBS egress node, (b) Architecture of OBS core node

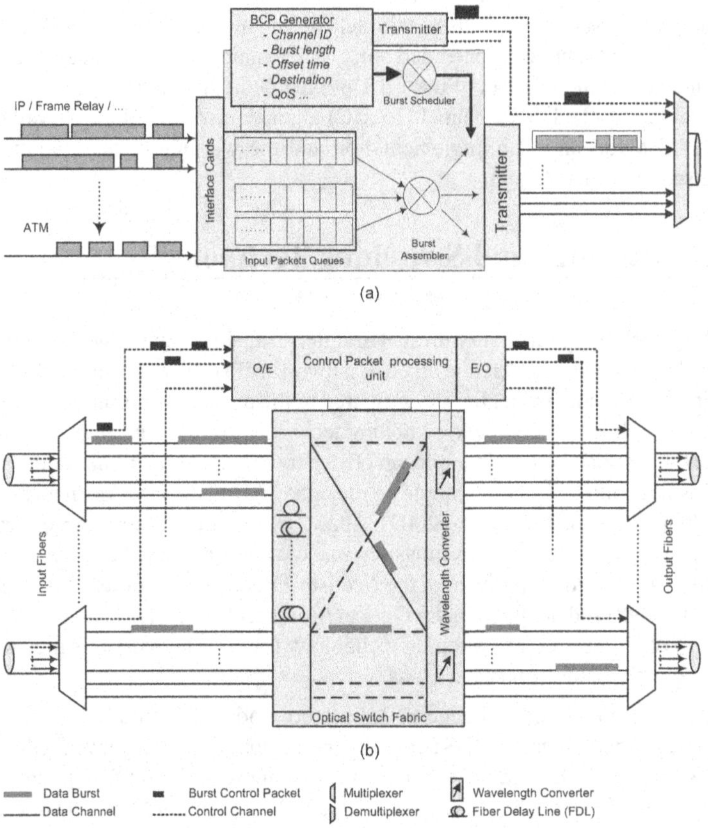

(a)

(b)

▬▬ Data Burst	■ Burst Control Packet	◖ Multiplexer	⬈ Wavelength Converter
── Data Channel	···· Control Channel	◗ Demultiplexer	◯ Fiber Delay Line (FDL)

- **Control packet processing unit:** For BCPs interpretation, channels scheduling, collision resolution, routing, and optical switching-fabric control;
- **Optical switching fabric:** To optically switch data bursts; And possibly *Wavelength converters* and *fiber delay lines (FDLs)*.

Data Burst Assembly

At the edge node, the burst assembly/disassembly process is implemented. A very important design parameter in OBS networks, the assembly process takes place at the ingress nodes. Burst assembly (burstification) is the process of aggregating a number of smaller transport units, for example, IP packets or ATM cells, into larger transport units called data bursts. Motivated by the need of optimizing the switching performance in the optical domain, larger transport units allow the switches to switch the same amount of data by handling less requests, since the ratio between the control information and transmitted data gets smaller. Furthermore, the efficiency of optical switching is improved due to the reduction in the mean inter-arrival time between the switched data units (bursts).

Generally, the assembly algorithms are based on a threshold that could be time, burst-length, or hybrid time-length threshold. In a single data burst, the assembled data units may belong to various upper layer traffic flows, and ultimately destined to different final destinations; however, the destination OBS egress node of all the data units must be the same. The arriving upper layer packets are stored in appropriate queues (according to their egress destination, QoS requirement, Class of Service (CoS)) in the burst assembler. A new burst is constructed and its control packet is generated when the threshold is reached. Obviously, the generated traffic will have variable burst length and constant inter-arrival time, if the algorithm operates only based on time as threshold; however, this may produce excessively large data bursts if the upper layer traffic streams are experiencing high loads. Conversely, if the algorithm operates based on the burst-length threshold, the inter-arrival time will vary, while the burst length is maintained constant. Optimally, a hybrid approach is used, that is, a combination of the time and length thresholds. In all cases, a minimum burst-length should be imposed to avoid too small bursts, which may cause the generation of too many control packets that may lead to traffic congestion on the control channels. A data burst is constructed when its length gets bigger than a pre-defined value, or when the maximum assembly time is reached; in the later case, data padding may be applied to bring the data burst to an appropriate length. Furthermore, a minimum burst-length should be imposed to avoid too small bursts, which may cause the generation of too many control packets that may lead to traffic congestion in the control channels.

More sophisticated assembly algorithms that trade-in the simplicity with the flexibility were proposed in the literature. For example The Adaptive-Assembly-Period (AAP) Algorithm, proposed by Cao, Li, Chen, and Qiao (2002). AAP analyzes current IP traffic statistics and change the values of thresholds accordingly, which can reduce the queuing delay in the edge nodes.

The data bursts disassembly (de-burstification) process is performed by disassemblers at the egress nodes upon the bursts' arrival. In the egress-nodes, the BCPs are processed and terminated, and the data bursts are disassembled to the initial data units. The data units are then forwarded to their final destinations.

QoS Support and Contention Resolution

The number of users (with different needs) and electronic applications (with different requirements) is growing exponentially on the Internet, causing the Internet to start suffering from its own success, in terms of bandwidth and service differentiation. Using optical infrastructure, the available capacity limits could be solved by bandwidth over-provisioning. However, because IP is a best-effort protocol, there is a need to incorporate QoS mechanisms and flow control capabilities.

OBS-QoS Mechanisms

A great effort has been directed to the QoS provisioning in the Internet, where many QoS mechanisms were introduced. However, the mechanisms that worked for electronic packet switched networks did not find the same success in optical networks, because of the lack of efficient optical buffers, which reduces the switches' scheduling capabilities. In this section, we will present an overview of the main QoS provisioning strategies proposed for OBS networks.

•   **Offset-Based QoS Scheme:** Offset-based QoS (Fan, Feng, Wang, & Ge, 2002) scheme adds an extra offset time to the basic offset between the BCP and its corresponding DB. The additional offset time, called QoS offset, is to compensate for the processing time of the BCP. The duration of such a QoS offset is varied, depending on the priority of the service class. This scheme is proposed for JET, whereby higher priority classes have larger offsets. With this scheme, if a low priority DB with no additional QoS offset time and a higher priority DB with a QoS offset try to make network resources reservation, the DB with the larger offset will be able to reserve resources in advance, before the low priority DB. In general, this will result in a lower burst loss probability of high priority classes compared to the lower priority classes.

Although the offset-based QoS scheme does provide an acceptable service differentiation, it is faced with some challenges that cannot be ignored. For example, DBs of high priority classes suffer longer waiting time (delay) than the data bursts of low priority classes. Furthermore, the scheme is non-preemptive that is, as long as low priority DBs can block optical paths, no complete isolation is achieved. Yet, starvation of low priority classes is possible if the offered traffic load of high priority bursts is high and not controlled.

•   **Active dropping-based QoS scheme:** In this scheme, a burst dropper (hardware) is implemented in front of every core node (Chen, Hamdi, & Tsang, 2001). Dependent on a dropping policy, some BCPs and their corresponding DBs are dropped before reaching the reservation unit. Therefore, the admission to the outgoing wavelengths is controlled, enabling the core nodes to locally control the offered load of certain service classes to maintain network resources for other service classes. Active Dropping-based QoS scheme intervene before congestion occurs, as the selective dropping of DBs is initiated according to the data traffic profile to guarantee that the higher priority classes have higher chances to make successful reservations. However, this scheme suffers from a major disadvantage which is the absence of feedback from the core nodes to the edge nodes, and thus traffic volume of different classes cannot be controlled. Furthermore, isolation between different traffic classes is not guaranteed. If the offered traffic load of a low priority class is significantly augmented, which increases the overall burst loss probability; burst loss probabilities of all classes are increased. Therefore, an additional traffic control mechanism is required.

•   **Segmentation-based QoS scheme:** In segmentation-based QoS scheme (Vokkarane & Jue, 2002), each data burst is subdivided into several independent segments. If DBs contend for the same network resources, the contention is resolved by discarding or deflecting some segments of one of the contending data bursts. The remaining part of the burst (truncated DB) will be then forwarded to the downstream nodes where it will experience either more shortening, be dropped, or be delivered to the egress node. Unfortunately, this scheme is implemented at the cost of increasing the size of the control packets, since the BCP should at least contain the segments number, the burst length, and the routing information.

Furthermore, the implementation of burst segmentation strategies is faced by some challenges and practical issues summarized as follows:

- **Switching time (ST):** ST is the time needed to reconfigure the switching fabric. ST depends on the design and implementation of the core node and on the used switching technology. ST may differ from one core node to another.
- **Data burst size:** Since the transmission of DBs depends on the transmission of their BCPs, the DB length should agree with minimum and maximum length requirements, to avoid congestion in the control channels. The same is true for the truncated burst (i.e., DB that lost some of its packets).
- **Segment Delineation:** Since the data bursts are transmitted all-optically, the segments' boundaries are transparent to the core nodes, and their sizes are not reflected in the BCP.
- **Fiber Delay Lines (FDLs):** As in Optical Composite Burst Switching (OCBS) (Detti, Eramo, & Listanti, 2002), FDLs are needed to delay the data bursts while their control packets are being electronically updated with the new burst size, which increases the electronic processing time needed before forwarding the control packet to the next node.
- **Trail-control messages:** Generated by the node where the DB has been truncated, the trailing control message is needed to indicate the data burst's new size to the downstream nodes, to avoid unnecessary resource reservation, and needless contention resolution actions.

Contention Resolution

In OCS, each traffic flow is supplied with the appropriate network resources, precisely with the necessary bandwidth. Therefore, flows would not contend for the same network resources in the core nodes of an OCS network. However, contention is a major problem in both OPS and OBS, which are based on multiplexing gain between the traffic flows. Typically, in electronic packet switching, this problem is solved using random access electronic buffers; however, this solution is far from being feasible in all-optical networks where optical buffering is yet to be a viable technology. In OBS, contention occurs when two or more bursts are destined to use the same channel from the same fiber (i.e., output port) at the same time. The contention can be resolved in one of three techniques. The contending burst can be optically delayed/buffered (time domain), converted to another channel in the same fiber (optical domain), or deflected to another output port (space domain).

- **Buffering:** One of the most prevailing factors that have motivated the development of OBS network is the immaturity of the optical buffering technology. Therefore, the use of optical buffers as a contention resolution technique in the OBS networks is less than feasible. Nevertheless, several proposals, and many research activities, were dedicated to the study of buffering techniques in OBS networks. Buffering is to delay or to queue contending bursts instead of dropping them. If optical-electrical-optical conversion is allowed (i.e., not an all-optical network) then random access electronic buffers can be used to buffer the burst for a long time. However, to implement an all-optical network (i.e., the data is maintained in the optical domain end-to-end), an optical buffering technique is needed. Optical buffering currently can only be implemented using Fiber Delay Lines (FDLs). The time that the bursts can be delayed is directly proportional to the length of the FDL. More efficient optical buffers can be realized through multiple delay lines of the same or different lengths, deployed in stages (Chlamtac, Fumagalli, Kazovsky, Melman, et al., 1996) or in parallel (Haas, 1993). Such buffers can hold DBs for variable amounts of time. Recently, designs of large optical buffers (Hunter, Cornwell, Gilfedder, et al., 1998; Tancevski, Castanon, Callegati, & Tamil, 1999) were proposed without large delay lines. However, in any optical buffer architecture, the size of the buffers and their flexibility is severely constrained by physical space and the effects of fiber dispersion. Therefore, fiber delay lines could be suitable for prototype switches in experimental environments, but not for real and commercial deployments.

- **Wavelength conversion:** WDM systems are multiple channel systems. Optical switches are connected with fiber links that are expected to carry hundreds of channels in the near future. This can be exploited to resolve traffic flow contentions. If two traffic flows contend for the same channel, one of the flows can be wavelength-converted to a free channel, and transmitted on the same link. It is clear that with this technique the contentions between data bursts in an OBS network can be minimized. However, using wavelength converters will increase the overall hardware cost of the WDM network, in addition to the complexity and technical issues associated with the wavelength conversion technology itself. Wavelength-conversion-enabled optical networks can be categorized to either: (1) networks with full wavelength conversion (any channel can be converted/shifted to any other channel); (2) networks with limited/fixed wavelength conversion (only limited/fixed channels can be converted); or (3) networks with sparse wavelength conversion (not all the network's nodes have wavelength conversion capabilities)

- **Deflection:** To delay (hold) data bursts, an alternative to the use of FDLs is the use of fiber links connecting the core nodes. When two bursts contend for the same output port, one will be switched to the correct output port, and the other will be switched (deflected) to any other available output port. Therefore, both bursts are given a chance to be switched instead of dropping one of them to resolve the contention. Because the correct output port leads usually to the shortest path (networking context) toward the destination, the bursts that are not switched to the correct output ports may end up following longer paths to their destinations. This technique is referred to as "hot-potato" routing. A drawback of this technique is the complexity associated with the calculation of the offset time of the deflected burst since it will travel on a different path with different hop count. Furthermore, the end-to-end high delays experienced by the deflected DBs may cause the DBs to be out-of-order at the destination, or trigger upper layers retransmission mechanisms. Additionally, deflecting data bursts because of local congestion may instigate global congestion. In the literature, deflection routing is studied on various network topologies, with and without FDLs.

In all the three aforementioned techniques, the data bursts are treated as single fused data units. However, there is another interesting OBS approach that suggests that the bursts should be dealt with as a combination of basic transport units called segments. Each of these segments may consist of a single packet or multiple packets. The segments indicate the possible partitioning points of a burst while the burst is traveling in the optical domain. With this approach, when a contention occurs, only the overlapping (time aspect) segments of the contending bursts are dropped, buffered, deflected, or converted to a different channel. It has been demonstrated in literature (Detti et al., 2002; Vokkarane, Jue, & Sitaraman, 2002) that the contention resolution techniques based on burst segmentation are efficient, and outperformed the traditional OBS with the "entire-burst-dropping" policy. Unfortunately the implementation of burst segmentation strategies is faced by some technical challenges, besides the complexity added to the algorithms and protocols on both edge and core nodes.

Flavors of OBS Networks

Besides the traditional definition presented at the beginning of this chapter, the following implementations of OBS can be found in literature; each implementation has its advantages and disadvantages.

- **OBS with fixed data burst length:** In this implementation of OBS, all data bursts have the same length. Its major advantage is the simplification of the switching technique. However, its disadvantage is the long queuing time of the upper layer packets if there is no adequate traffic load. An ineffectual solution to this disadvantage is data padding. This concept is closely related to the cell-switching paradigm where the transport unit is fixed in size.

- **OBS with two-way setup:** In this implementation of OBS, a burst will be transmitted only after having received a positive acknowledgement of its resource reservation request. Its advantage is the burst-blocking avoidance in the network's core nodes. However, the additional waiting time may cause buffers to overflow at the network ingress.

- **Mandatory FDL/Wavelength Converters in all nodes:** With the disadvantage of increasing dramatically the cost of the network, OBS could be implemented with core nodes that are capable to buffer the data bursts and/or convert them to any other wavelength. In this implementation some sort of store-and-forward routing for optical bursts is deployed, where each burst is delayed for a certain time until its corresponding control information is processed and an appropriate switching decision is determined, that is, the burst could be forwarded to an output port, converted to another wavelength, or simply dropped.

- **OBS networks for Ethernet:** Extending Ethernet services over OBS was proposed in Sheeshia, Qiao, and Liu (2002) as a more scalable and bandwidth-efficient implementation compared to the Ethernet over Synchronous Optical Network (SONET). The possible role that OBS will play in the development of 10-Gbit Ethernet (10GbE) metropolitan networks was investigated. OBS was demonstrated as an improved network resource-sharing platform and efficient transport for Ethernet traffic, particularly if it is coupled with the Generalized Multiprotocol Label Switching (GMPLS).

It is clear that OBS is a technology-driven paradigm; consequently, the architecture and the operational policies of the future OBS networks will be shaped by the upcoming developments in the multiplexing and switching technologies. The technology needed to generate and transmit more than 1,000 high-quality WDM channels with fixed wavelength spacing is already available. Furthermore, the Waveband Switching (i.e., switching multiple wavelengths as a single entity) is being researched. Therefore, the future OBS would be based on waveband-selective switching or other more advanced switching technologies. In the rest of the chapter, an attempt to streamline the OBS networks that are using burst segmentation techniques is presented.

Staged Reservation SCHEME (SRS)

The Staged Reservation Scheme (SRS) (Abid, Abbou, & Ewe, 2005) is introduced to streamline previous reservation protocols that are based on burst segmentation strategy, to increase the throughput of the core nodes, and to overcome some of the limitations associated with the burst segmentation concept (shown earlier). In SRS the data burst is divided into equal Data Segments (DSs). This is an indication to where the DB might be partitioned, while traveling in the optical-domain. The DSs have the same attributes and characteristics as any DB (i.e., each segment may range from one to several packets, and its length is reflected in the BCP). The control packets format was designed to be scalable to high transmission speeds, and to reflect the DSs' length in addition to the DBs' length.

BCPs Format in SRS

The burst control packet format in SRS is redesigned and changed from the traditional format to provide a constant transmission overhead and to make the BCP scalable to higher speeds, as it uses the *Flow Control and Reservation Bits* (FCRB) as the segments' length indicator instead of flags (Detti et al., 2002). The illustration shown in Figure 4 of the format of the BCP is briefly presented here.

- **FCRB field:** *Flow Control and Reservation Bits* field is created by the ingress-node to reflect the permitted segmentations. In the core-nodes, the SRS-length is multiplied by the number of 1_2 in FCRB to obtain the actual size of the corresponding DB. For

Figure 4. Data burst structure and burst control packet format in SRS scheme

example 0111_2 is an indication that the length of the DB (or truncated DB) is (3 * SRS-length), and it might be segmented into three segments. The size of FCRB is dynamic in that it may vary from one DB to another, and the burst assembly algorithm controls it.

- **Flag field:** The field is a sequence of bits with a recognizable pattern that identifies the end of the FCRB field (as its size is not fixed), and identifies the beginning of the SRE-length field.

- **SRS-length field:** The field contains the length of one DS. However, SRS-length combined with FCRB provides sufficient information about the DB's length and segmentation. To avoid congestion in OBS control-channel, SRS-length should comply with a minimum length (Detti et al., 2002), which is the minimum permitted data burst length transmitted over the optical links. The SRS-length may vary from one DB to another.

- **Other-Info fields:** The rest of the fields may contain routing information (e.g., burst destination address), offset time, and so forth.

By adopting SRS dropping policy, which will be described in the following subsection, if a contention is anticipated in the core-nodes, the resources allocation process will not be aborted (i.e., BCP is dropped and subsequently the corresponding DB is entirely discarded). Conversely, the FCRB field in the corresponding BCP is updated according to the resources that the core-node can provide (or free up). Hence, only the overlapping segments are dropped at the arrival time, allowing part of the DB to be transmitted (i.e., the data length that can be handled by the node at the arrival time) as shown in Figure 5. Since the BCPs are updated before forwarding them to the downstream nodes, to reflect the new DBs' length, the need for trailing messages is eliminated, and the contention is resolved at the BCPs level rather than at the DBs level.

SRS Dropping Policy

Beside the *Switching-Time* (ST), the dropping policy is based on the *Overlapping-Time* (OT), and the *Contention-Time* (CT) (i.e., the aggregated length (duration) of all the DSs that are entirely or partly overlapping minus the OT), as illustrated in Figure 5. The OT

Figure 5. SRS dropping policy with relation to CT, OT, and ST

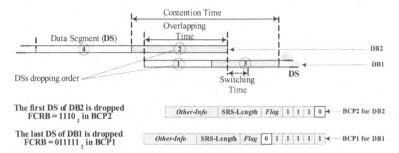

may span many DSs from the contending DBs. Therefore; the overlapping DSs are dropped alternately one-by-one from the contending DSs until the CT is reached. This guarantees a reasonable level of fairness between the data bursts (i.e., the number of discarded DSs is distributed among the contending DBs). The dropping policy rules are formulated in an algorithm that will be presented when the fairness in network resources allocation in the core nodes is discussed.

The contention, therefore, is resolved by performing the following three steps:

- Firstly, if *(OT + ST)* > *CT*, then a DS is added to the CT to efficiently contain the ST in the dropped DSs. The added DS is selected from the DB with the smallest SRS-length, or randomly if the contending DSs are equal in length. The ST is assumed to be much smaller than the duration of one DS.

- Secondly, if the "*SRS-length*" is the same for both contending DBs (i.e., the DSs are equal in length), then the dropping process starts from the DS at the tail of the first DB, not at the head of the contending DB. This gives fair chance to the packets to arrive to the destination in the correct sequence (assuming the retransmission of the lost packets).

- Thirdly, if the "*SRS-length*" is not the same for the contending DBs, then the dropping process starts at the DS of the shorter DB. The DS may be at the tail of the first DB or at the head of the contending DB (as it is deemed that the amount of transmitted data has higher priority than its order).

Fairness in Resources Allocation in SRS Core Node

A key parameter in the design of an OBS network is the maximum and minimum burst size, which is managed by the edge nodes using the assembly algorithms. This key parameter is entirely overlooked by the resource allocation schemes based on the burst segmentation concept, since no policies related to the size of the truncated burst (i.e., shortened data burst) are implemented, during the burst segmentation process in the core nodes. Furthermore, there is no fairness in allocating the network resources to the contending data bursts (usually form different sources), as all the segments are simply discarded from only one burst to resolve the contention.

A better solution would be selecting evenly (fairly) the segments to be dropped from both contending data bursts. Likewise, the truncated burst size should be monitored at the core nodes, and guaranteed to be larger than the Minimum Burst Length (MBL), which is the minimum length allowed into the network to avoid congestion in the control channels.

Besides fairness, data burst size, and implementation simplicity, any proposed technique should be designed to deal with the switching time, which is the time needed to configure the switching fabric (i.e., to switch an output port from one DB to another). To understand what follows, the following definitions are provided and illustrated in Figure 6.

- DB_O: Original Data Burst with Arrival time T_{OA} and Leaving time T_{OL},
- DB_C: Contending Data Burst with Arrival time T_{CA} and Leaving time T_{CL},
- TDB: Truncated Data Burst (i.e., a DB with dropped segments),
- N, M: Respectively, the number of segments in DB_O, DB_C,
- DS: Data Segment with Length DSL,
- R: the expected number of segments to be dropped from each data burst,

$$R = \left\lceil \frac{|T_{CA} - T_{OL}|}{2DSL} \right\rceil$$

When data bursts arrive to a core node, the technique performs three functions arranged in three main events. After an initialization (Table 1), the *Contention_Detection* (Table 2) event is performed; if a contention is detected, then R (number of segments to be dropped from the contending data bursts) is calculated, and the second event is executed. The second event named *Length_of_Truncated_Burst* (Table 3) is executed to guarantee that whatever is left from the data bursts after dropping some of their segments is good for transmission over the OBS network. In this event, if one of the truncated data bursts does not meet the MBL requirements, then the contention is simply resolved by dropping the shortest data burst in its entirety. However, the third event is executed if the truncated data bursts are larger than MBL. The *Even_Resource_Allocation* (Table 4) is used to resolve the burst contention by

Figure 6. Illustrations: (a) Segments dropping process, (b) DB structure in SRS-based QoS scheme

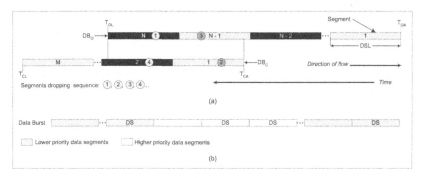

Table 1. Initialization

```
Initialization
/* Original data burst length. */
DBL_O = T_OL - T_OA = N * DSL
/* Contending data burst length.  */
DBL_C = T_CL - T_CA = M * DSL
/* Length to be dropped from each data burst. */
LTD = R * DSL
```

Table 2. Contention detection

```
Event :: Contention_Detection
/* There is a contention if the condition is true */
    IF ((T_CA - T_OL) < ST) THEN
```
$$R = \left\lceil \frac{\left| T_{CA} - T_{OL} \right|}{2DSL} \right\rceil \quad \text{/* calculate R. */}$$
```
        Execute: Length _of _Truncated_Burst
    END IF
End of Event
```

Table 3. Length of truncated burst

```
Event :: Length _of _Truncated_Burst
/* The truncated burst will be less than the allowed
burst length if the condition is true */
    IF ((DBL_O - LTD < MBL) || (DBL_C - LTD < MBL)) THEN
        IF (DBL_C < DBL_O) THEN
            /* DB_C is the smallest, therefore, dropped */
            Drop DB_C
        ELSE
            /* DB_O is the smallest, therefore, dropped */
            Drop DB_O
        END IF
    ELSE
        Execute: Even_Resource_Allocation
    END IF
End of Event
```

Table 4. Even resource allocation

```
Event :: Even_Resource_Allocation
/* Initialize counter */
i = 1
   DO
   {
   IF (i % 2 = 0) THEN
   /* DBc is reduced by one DS from the burst head*/
       TCA = TCA + DSL
   ELSE
   /* DBO is reduced by one DS from the burst tail*/
       TOL = TOL - DSL
   END IF
   /* Increase the counter i by 1 */
i++
   }
   WHILE ((TCA - TOL) < ST)
End of Event
```

discarding the overlapping segments *alternatively,* starting from the tail of the original burst, and then the head of the contending burst as shown in Figure 6(a).

SRS-Based QoS Scheme

Motivated by the SRS design, its dropping policy, and the use of the FCRB field, the SRS-based QoS mechanism is introduced. In this mechanism, the QoS requirements of the upper layer packets are defined based on their traffic class. Packets of the same class and destination are assembled into the same data segment, which will be labeled with a priority number accordingly. A data burst may contain data segments of the same or different priorities. Using an appropriate assembly algorithm, the data segments are assembled into data bursts in such a way that the lower priority data segments envelop the higher priority data segments as shown in Figure 6(b). To realize the SRS-based QoS scheme, both the edge nodes and core nodes must cooperate, using an assembly algorithm in the edge nodes and the SRS dropping policy in core nodes.

Assembly Algorithm

Although either timer-based or burstlength-based assembly algorithm could be used, it is preferred to use hybrid assembly algorithms. In the hybrid approach, first a burst length threshold is used in assembling the data segments; this allows the control of the data segments size, which must be fixed and restricted to a maximum length. (In some cases, data padding may be needed.) Second, in constructing the data bursts (from data segments) and to control the packets delay at the edge nodes, a timer threshold is used; that is, after a fixed time, all the data segments (could be of different priorities) destined to the same egress are assembled into a data burst. The data bursts are then transmitted to their destinations through the core nodes to undergo the SRS dropping policy.

FCRB for Congestion Control

In the course of discussing the QoS, congestion in networks appears to cause real problems by reducing the availability and the throughput of the network. Congestion is a complex phenomenon, and it occurs when the traffic load (number of bursts) on the network begins to approach the network capacity. Therefore, a congestion control mechanism is needed to maintain the number of the bursts being transmitted through the network within the limits at which the network performance is acceptable.

By using an explicit congestion avoidance technique, the edge nodes can use as much of the network capacity as possible, while reacting to the congestion in a controlled manner. In the proposed SRS-based QoS, an explicit signaling technique is used. In this signaling technique, the bits of FCRB are used to indicate explicitly the amount of data (i.e., the number of data segments in the DB) sent and the arrived amount. This signaling approach can work in one of two directions: forward (to notify the Egress), or backward (to notify the Ingress).

- **Forward signaling:** notifies the egress node that congestion procedures should be initiated where applicable for traffic in the opposite direction of the received bursts. It indicates the number of the dropped data segments, and that the received burst has encountered congested resources. This information could be sent back to the source node, and the end system will exercise flow control on the traffic sources at the higher layers (e.g., TCP).
- **Backward signaling:** notifies the ingress node that congestion procedures should be initiated where applicable for traffic in the same direction as the sent bursts. It indicates the number of data segments dropped, and that the sent burst has encountered congested resources. The ingress node will then lower the number of data segments sent in each DB to be equal to the number of data segments that could get through the network to the destination. Then the number of data segments is augmented progressively until the maximum size of the data burst is reached, or until the FCRB field reports congestion.

Summary

The network infrastructure has a decisive role in the success of any e-services provider. The next-generation network infrastructure is expected to be reliable, efficient, and supported by robust QoS schemes. The success of IP, with its flexibility, and the advent of WDM technology, with its advantages, are behind the widespread interest in selecting the IP/WDM internetworking model to build an All-optical Internet. Eventually, the next-generation network will be an all-optical Internet where the traffic flows are optically transmitted, switched/routed, tuned/amplified, and buffered.

The OBS is a major candidate to be deployed as the switching paradigm for the Next-Generation Optical Internet. OBS is flexible, manageable, and offers a good balance between OPS and OCS. Furthermore, OBS is amenable for improvement and expansion whenever the developments in optical technology permit.

In this chapter, a broad discussion on optical switching is presented. Many architectural and design aspects of OBS were reviewed, including burst assembly, signaling and reservation protocols, and QoS provisioning. At the end of the chapter, the recent work in OBS schemes is covered; however, the OBS paradigm remains an open field for more research and improvement.

References

Abid, A., Abbou, F. M., & Ewe, H. T. (2005). Staged reservation scheme for optical burst switching networks. *IEICE Electronics Express, 2*(11), 327-332.

Amstutz, S. (1989). Burst switching—An update. *IEEE Communication Magazine,* 50-57.

Baldine, I., Rouskas, G., Perros, H., & Stevenson, D. (2002). JumpStart: A just-in-time signaling architecture for WDM burst switched networks. *IEEE Communications Magazine, 40*(2), 82-89.

Callegati, F., Cankaya, H. C., Xiong, Y., & Vandenhoute, M. (1999). Design issues of optical IP routers for Internet backbone applications. *IEEE Communications Magazine, 37*(12), 124-128.

Cao, X., Li, J., Chen, Y., & Qiao, C. (2002). Assembling TCP/IP packets in optical burst switched networks. In *Proceeding of IEEE Globecom.*

Chen, Y., Hamdi, M., & Tsang, D. H. K. (2001). Proportional QoS over OBS networks. In *Proceedings of IEEE GLOBECOM 2001, San Antonio.*

Chlamtac, I. , Fumagalli, A., Kazovsky, L. G. , Melman, P. et al. (1996). CORD: Contention resolution by delay lines. *IEEE Journal on Selected Areas in Communications, 14*(5), 1014-1029.

Detti, A., & Listanti, M. (2001). Application of tell and go and tell and wait reservation strategies in an optical burst switching network: A performance comparison. In *Proceedings of the 8th IEEE International Conference on Telecommunications (ICT 2001), Bucharest.*

Detti, A., Eramo, V., & Listanti, M. (2002). Performance evaluation of new technique for IP support in a WDM optical network: Optical composite burst switching (OCBS). *IEEE Journal of Lightwave Technology, 20*(2), 154-165.

Dolzer, K. (2002). Assured horizon—A new combined framework for burst assembly and reservation in optical burst switched networks. In *Proceedings of the European Conference on Networks and Optical Communications (NOC 2002), Darmstad.*

Dolzer, K., Gauger, C., Spath, J., & Bodamer, S. (2001). Evaluation of reservation mechanisms for optical burst switching. *AEÜ International Journal of Electronics and Communications, 55*(1).

Fan, P. , Feng, C., Wang, Y., & Ge, N. (2002). Investigation of the time-offset-based QoS support with optical burst switching in WDM networks. In *Proceeding of IEEE ICC: Vol. 5* (pp 2682-2686).

Gauger, C., Dolzer, K., & Scharf, M. (2002). Reservation strategies for FDL buffers in OBS networks. In *Proceedings of the IEEE International Conference on Communications.*

Ge, A., Callegati, F., & Tamil, L. S. (2000). On optical burst switching and self-similar traffic. *IEEE Communications Letters, 4*(3), 98-100.

Haas, Z. (1993). The "staggering switch": An electronically-controlled optical packet switch. *IEEE Journal of Lightwave Technology, 11*(5/6), 925-936.

Hu, G., Dolzer, K., & Gauger, C. M.. (2003). Does burst assembly really reduce the self-similarity. In *Proceedings of the Optical Fiber Communication Conference (OFC 2003), Atlanta.*

Hunter, D. K., Cornwell, W. D., Gilfedder, T. H. et al. (1998). SLOB: A switch with large optical buffers for packet switching. *IEEE Journal of Lightwave Technology, 16*(10), 1725-1736.

Kulzer, J., & Montgomery, W. (1984, May). *Statistical switching architectures for future services*. Paper presented at ISS '84, Florence.

Mukherjee, B. (1997). *Optical communication networking.* McGraw-Hill

Qiao, C., & Yoo, M. (1999). Optical burst switching (OBS)-A new paradigm for an optical Internet. *Journal of High Speed Networks, 8*(1), 69-84.

Qiao, C., & Yoo, M. (2000). Choices, features, and issues in optical burst switching. *Optical Networks Magazine, 1*(2), 37-44.

Renaud, M., Bachmann, M., & Erman, M. (1996). Semiconductor optical space switches. *IEEE Journal on Selected Topics in Quantum Electronics, 2*(2), 277-288.

Sadot, D., & Boimovich, E. (1998). Tunable optical filters for dense WDM networks. *IEEE Communications Magazine, 36*(12), 50-55.

Sheeshia, S., Qiao, C., & Liu, U.J. (2002). Supporting Ethernet in optical-burst-switched networks. *SPIE the Journal of Optical Networking, 1*(8/9), 299-312.

Suzuki, M., Otani, T., & Hayashi, M. (2003). Transparent optical networks. In *Proceedings of 2003 5th International Conference: Vol. 1* (pp. 26-31).

Tancevski, L., Castanon, G., Callegati, F., & Tamil, L. (1999). Performance of an optical IP router using non-degenerate buffers.In *Proceeding of IEEE Globecom '99, Rio de Janeiro, Brazil* (pp. 1454-1459).

Tancevski, L., Yegnanarayanam, S., Castanon, G., Tamil, L., Masetti, F., & McDermott, T. (2000). Optical routing of asynchronous, variable length packets. *IEEE Journal on Selected Areas in Communications, 18*(10), 2084-2093.

Turner, J. S. (1999). Terabit burst switching. *Journal of High Speed Networks, 8*(1), 3-16.

Verma, S., Chaskar, H., & Ravikanth, R. (2000). Optical burst switching: A viable solution for terabit IP backbone. *IEEE Network, 14*(6), 48-53

Vokkarane, V., Haridoss, K., & Jue, J. (2002). Threshold-based burst assembly policies for QoS support in optical burst-switched networks. In *Proceedings of the SPIE Optical Networking and Communications Conference (OptiComm 2002),* Boston (pp. 125-136).

Vokkarane, V., & Jue, J. (2002). Prioritized routing and burst segmentation for QoS in optical burst- switched networks. In *Proceeding of OFC* (pp. 221-222).

Vokkarane, V., Jue, J., & Sitaraman, S. (2002). Burst segmentation: An approach for reducing packet loss in optical burst switched networks. *IEEE International Conference on Communications,* 5, 2673-2677.

Wei, J. Y., & McFarland, R. I. (2000). Just-in-time signaling for WDM optical burst switching networks. *Journal of Lightwave Technology, 18*(12), 2019-2037.

Wei, J. Y., Pastor, J. L., Ramamurthy, R. S., & Tsal, Y. (1999). Just-in-time optical burst switching for multiwavelength networks. In *Proceedings of the 5th IFIP TC6 International Conference on Broadband Communications (BC '99),* Hong Kong (pp. 339-352).

Xiong, Y., Vanderhoute, M., & Cankaya, C. C. (2000). Control architecture in optical burst switched WDM networks. *IEEE Journal on Selected Areas in Communications, 18*(10), 1838-1851.

Xu, L., Perros, H. G., & Rouskas, G. N. (2001). Techniques for optical packet switching and optical burst switching. *IEEE Communications Magazine, 39*(1), 136-142.

Yao, S., Dixit, S., & Mukherjee, B. (2000). Advances in photonic packet switching: An overview. *IEEE Communications, 38*(2), 84-94.

Yoo, M., Jeong, M., & Qiao, C. (1997). A high speed protocol for bursty traffic in optical networks. In *Proceedings of the 3rd SPIE Conference on All-Optical Communication Systems, Dallas* (pp. 79-90).

Yoo, M., Qiao, C., & Dixit, S. (2001). Optical burst switching for service differentiation in the next-generation optical Internet. *IEEE Communications Magazine, 39*(2), 98-104.

About the Authors

Moh'd A. Radaideh is currently serving as advisor/IT expert at the Human Resources General Directorate of Abu Dhabi Police GHQ (ADP) in the United Arab Emirates. Prior to ADP, he served for about four years as academic coordinator of the Information Systems Program at the College of IT in the United Arab Emirates University. Prior to UAEU, he served as senior consulting engineer at Verity, Inc (now part of Autonomy) where he led more than 30 projects throughout the U.S., Canada, and Mexico. Prior to Verity, he served as staff software developer at IBM Canada. Dr. Radaideh holds a PhD degree in software engineering from McMaster University in Hamilton, ON, Canada, a Masters in project management from George Washington University, a Master degree in computer engineering from Jordan University of Science and Technology, and a Bachelor degree in electrical and computer engineering from Yarmouk University. Dr. Radaideh is a senior member of IEEE, a professional member of ACM, and an active member of IRMA. He has published tens of publications in international journals and conference proceedings. Dr. Radaideh serves on the editorial boards of several international journals, as well as on the program committees for several international conferences. During the past few years, Dr. Radaideh has received several awards, including the Best Interdisciplinary Research Project award from UAE University, and the Best Track Chair award from IRMA, 2005.

Hayder Al-Ameed has MSc, OCP, MCP, DB2 Admin qualifications. Al-Ameed is an experienced engineer in computer systems and software engineering. He got his MSc. degree in computer science from the University of Technology/Baghdad. He has intensive academic experience in several universities of different countries. He participated into more than many projects. He has played a variety of roles such as consultant, team lead, system administrator, database designer, and programmer, in addition to providing consulting services for the IT departments in many private and state companies and organizations. Mr. Al-Ameed is pursuing his PhD degree at the University of Bradford, UK.

★★★

Abid Abdelouahab holds a Graduate degree in mathematics and a Masters Degree in information systems. At present, he is pursuing a PhD degree at Multimedia University. He is a certified e-commerce consultant. Previously, he had worked as senior software engineer, then as a consultant at Telecom Malaysia. Currently, he is a lecturer at the Faculty of Information Technology at Multimedia University. His current research interests include optical switching techniques, and IP-over-WDM networks architecture and design.

Fouad Mohammed Abbou received his MSc degree in 1995 from Delft University of Technology, Netherlands, in electrical engineering. He obtained his PhD in 2001 in electrical engineering from Multimedia University in Malaysia. He joined the Faculty of Engineering at Multimedia University as lecturer in 1997. Since 2001, he has been a multimedia advisor at Alcatel Network Systems, Malaysia. He is currently Alcatel associate professor at Multimedia University. His research interests include optical communication networks, optical switching, and optical devices. He has published more than 40 papers in international journals and conferences.

Romana Aziz got a Bachelor of Science in electrical engineering from the University of Engineering and Technology, Lahore, Pakistan. She completed her Master of Science degree in information systems engineering from the University of Manchester Institute of Science and Technology, UMIST, UK, and then went on to complete her PhD from UMIST in computation in the area of decision technologies and information systems. She has worked for ten years in a large public sector research organization in Pakistan. She joined academia in 1999 and has been the head of the computer science department at the Barani Institute of IT, University of Arid Agriculture, Rawalpindi. At present, she is an associate professor at COMSATS Institute of IT, a premier degree awarding organization of Pakistan.

Elarbi Badidi received his PhD in computer science in July, 2000, from Université de Montréal (Canada). He received his M.Sc. in computer science (1995) and B.Eng. in electrical engineering (1987) from École Mohammedia des Ingénieurs (Morocco). Dr. Badidi joined the College of Information Technology (CIT) of United Arab Emirates University as assistant professor of computer science in September, 2004. Before joining the faculty at CIT, he was the bioinformatics group leader at the Biochemistry Department of Université de Montréal. His research interests lie in the areas of Web services, middleware, distributed systems, bioinformatics, and distance learning.

Tapati Bandopadhyay is presently working as faculty member (IT & Systems) at ICFAI Business School, Bangalore and is pursuing PhD from ICFAI University. She has earned her B.E. from Jadavpur University, Calcutta, in 1995, with University Gold Medal, and has earned her M.S. in computer-aided engineering (Spl. in computer sciences) from University of Strathclyde, Glasgow, U.K. She has been an ODASS/DFID scholar with full sponsorship from the British Government for M.S. studies in which she procured the second highest record aggregate in 10 years of the program. She has two and a half years of industry experience in Tata Motors, Jamshedpur, India, in technical services and in GEC, Glasgow, U.K. on a software development project; she also has over six years of academic experience in reputed engineering colleges, and has published a number of books and papers. Her primary research interests include e-business, software engineering, and application of emerging information technologies to various business processes.

Thomas Biskup studied computer science from 1990 to 1997 at the University of Dortmund. He finished with "cum laude" and was granted both the Hans Uhde award and the German Software Engineering Price of the Denert Foundation. After working as an IT consultant he started to work on his Ph. D. thesis in 2000. In 2001, he co-founded the QuinScape GmbH (http://www.quinscape.de). He specializes in intranet and extranet systems, model-driven architecture, and model-driven software development. His thesis focuses agile methods and models in order to simplify requirements engineering with cooperative rapid prototyping approaches for non-technicians.

Oliver Braun studied computer science and business administration at the Saarland University of Saarbrücken, Germany. He made his PhD at the Department of Business Administration, especially information and technology management. Currently he is a research assistant and is writing his "habilitation" (a kind of post-doc lecturer qualification and the common way to become a professor in Germany). He is manager of the project "FiXplan - IT-Based Personal Financial Planning". At the Liechtenstein University of Applied Sciences, he is responsible for master courses in the field of enterprise modeling.

James Doran is an IBM distinguished engineer and chief architect of the On Demand Workplace, with the overall architecture responsibility for the On Demand Workplace portal for IBM, USA. He is also responsible for aligning our technology adoption of our internal portal with product direction. Additionally, Jim has been passionate in the adoption of autonomic technologies as a means to deliver efficient and effective infrastructure. He was named to his current position in August of 2004. Between 2000 and 2004, Jim was senior technical staff member responsible for our CIO Technology Lab. He led the process and technical design for implementing emerging technology pilots and proof of concepts for the CIO. Jim managed a team of engineers that authored several patents. Jim's technical leadership in this role has resulted in several large infrastructure services to be created by IBM.

Pablo Galdámez was born in Valencia, Spain, in 1971. He graduated from the Universidad Politécnica de Valencia, Spain, in computer science in 1994, and obtained his PhD degree in 2001. From 1995 to 2003, he was an assistant professor at his home university. In 2003, he became an associate professor, teaching distributed systems. Besides his activity as professor, he is a researcher at the *Instituto Tecnológico de Informática* (Valencia) where he leads the *Reliable Systems Group*. His research interests include distributed systems, high availability, and computer security, and he has authored more than 20 peer-reviewed technical papers.

Jorge Marx Gómez studied computer engineering and industrial engineering at the University of Applied Science of Berlin (Technische Fachhochschule). He was a lecturer and researcher at the Otto-von-Guericke-Universität Magdeburg, where he also obtained a PhD degree in business information systems with the work, "Computer-Based Approaches to Forecast Returns of Scrapped Products to Recycling". In 2004, he received his habilitation for the work, "Automated Environmental Reporting through Material Flow Networks" at the Otto-von-Guericke-Universität Magdeburg. From 2002 to 2003, he was a visiting professor for business informatics at the Technical University of Clausthal. In 2004, he became a full professor of business information systems at the Carl von Ossietzky University Oldenburg, Germany. His research interests include business information systems, e-commerce, material flow management systems, life cycle assessment, eco-balancing, environmental reporting, recycling program planning, disassembly planning and control, simulation, and neuro-fuzzy-systems.

Brian Goodman is a senior software engineer and certified IT architect with the Technology Strategy in the Technology Adoption Program. As a member of IBM's Emerging Technology and Innovation team, USA, Brian Goodman has been the principal architect defining technical direction for IBM's Technology Adoption Program, accelerating the process of identifying, developing, and transitioning innovation from the laboratory to internal applications and customer implementation. His expertise is primarily in innovation management, service-oriented architecture, autonomic application design, and high-performance Web applications. He is a prolific author and inventor, producing over 20 publications and more than two dozen patent filings worldwide. He earned a multi-disciplinary BA degree in computer science, psychology, and graphic design from Hampshire College, Amherst, Massachusetts, where his thesis centered on human-computer interface design for early childhood applications. He is based in Somers, New York.

Nils Heyer studied business information systems at the Technical University of Clausthal. Currently, he is a PhD student at Carl von Ossietzky University Oldenburg. His research interests include information systems, agent technologies, Web services, and Semantic Web technologies.

Maheshwar Inampudi is the lead IT architect for IBM's On Demand Workplace expertise location system (BluePages and several other intranet applications). Additional responsibilities include the architecture and solution design for several of IBM's internal offerings, as well as collaborating with the CIO office and IBM Research in helping design applications using the latest SOA methodologies. He helps showcase IBM's emerging technologies such as WebSphere eXtended Deployment (XD) and IBM's IntraGrid Grid Computing Architectures. Mahi improves process applying agile enablement of portfolio applications. Recent interests include leveraging emerging technologies, such as autonomic computing and grid computing. Between 2001 and 2003, Mahi worked as a consultant helping numerous customers, in the USA and Europe, design and build architectures involving the migration from legacy systems to WebSphere-based architectures.

A. F. M. Ishaq received his PhD in experimental physics from McMaster University, Canada, in 1972. In the late seventies, he switched over to computer system engineering. He is currently working as dean of faculty of information science and technology in Comsats Institute of Information Technology. He has a vast academic and industrial experience, and has been directly involved in a number of projects of national importance. He also heads Strategic Information Systems Research Group at CIIT. The group focus of research is to investigate how organizations can obtain better value from IS investments.

Pradeep Kumar holds B.Sc, B.Tech (Mech), PGDIE (NITIE), PhD (University of Delhi) degrees. He is serving as faculty coordinator, Doctoral Progarmme and Faculty, in information technology and systems at ICFAI Business School, Gurgaon. He has published and presented several research papers and articles in national and international journals and conferences. He has co-authored a book on computer application in management. He has served as an assistant vice president in information technology at Unit Trust of India and in a middle management position at Bharat Electronics Ltd. He has been nominated as reviewer for papers in the 4th International We-B Conference, Australia; 2004 and 2005 IRMA International Conference, USA, AMDISA SAMF 2004 Lahore, IIT2004 Dubai, 2005 Annual Conference of SWDSI and HICSS-38, Hawai; an ad hoc reviewer for the editorial review board of *IRMJ* and *IJECE*, USA; and a member of the editorial advisory board of the *Journal of International Technology and Information Management*. He is a member of various professional societies like IIIE, AIMA, CSI, IE (Australia), IE (India), and Federation of Business Disciplines (USA), IRMA (USA).

Yih-Jiun Lee is an assistant professor at the Department of Information Management of the ChienKuo Technology University, Taiwan. She recently got a PhD in computer science. Dr. Lee has more than five years of teaching and research experience. Her research interests include grid computing, electronic commerce, and mobile codes, especially on security issues.

Mohamed Vall O. Mohamed-Salem is currently an assistant professor with the University of Wollongong in Dubai. His current interests are in performance analysis and scalability issues, distributed systems, and software engineering. He held an IBM Canada Centre for Advanced Studies Fellowship and can be reached at salem@uow.edu.au.

Abou Bakar Nauman is working to complete his PhD in computer science at COMSATS Institute of IT, a prestigious and growing academic organization of Pakistan. He is an active member of Information System Group, and the areas of information systems failure and health informatics are of prime interest. He has obtained his M.Sc. in computer science from Baha-u-din Zakrya University, Multan, Pakistan. He has four years of experience in a multinational telecommunication firm in Pakistan.

Alex Pliaskin is a part-time lecturer in the School of Accounting and Finance at Victoria University, Australia. His background is in the electricity industry where he worked for over 31 years before retiring from that sector and coming across to academia. A certified practicing accountant, he also holds undergraduate degrees in politics and in computing. His works on Web portals have appeared in several publications, and he has had papers on this topic accepted at international conferences. He has also been involved in academic research relating to political issues and holds several senior advisory positions within the Australian Labor Party (Alex.Pliaskin@vu.edu.au).

Günter Schmidt studied business administration, industrial engineering, and computer science at the Technical University of Berlin. Since 1988, he has held positions as a professor of business administration, business informatics, and information and technology management at different universities. He serves on the editorial board of the Foundations of Computing and Decision Sciences, the IIE Transactions, the International Handbooks on Information Systems, the Journal of Scheduling and the Information Systems and E-Business Management.

M. Adel Serhani received his Master in computer science (Specialization Software Engineering) from the University of Montreal, Canada in 2002. He received the PhD degree in Electrical and Computer Engineering in 2006 from Concordia University, Montreal, Canada. He is currently an assistant professor in college of Information Technology, U.A.E. University, Al Ain, U.A.E. His research area is on Web Services Engineering that includes service selection and discovery, service lifecycle, QoS integration in SOA, End-to-End QoS management for Web services, QoS and Web services composition. He also worked on the application of artificial intelligence techniques mainly fuzzy logic to software engineering, object-oriented metrics, and software quality. He served as a member of committee program and/or reviewer in the following conferences (IIT'05, ISWS'05, IRMA'06, CSA'06, and IA 2006). He has published around 20 papers in conferences and journals. He has been involved in many projects during the last 6 years on the area of Software, Engineering, E-commerce, and Web services.

R. Todd Stephens is the technical director of the Collaboration and Online Services Group for the BellSouth Corporation, USA, an Atlanta-based telecommunications organization. Todd is responsible for setting the corporate strategy and architecture for the development and implementation of the enterprise collaborative and metadata solutions. Todd writes a monthly online column in Data Management Review, and has delivered keynotes, tutorials, and educational sessions for a wide variety of professional and academic conferences around the world. Todd holds degrees in mathematics and computer science from Columbus State University, an MBA degree from Georgia State University, and a PhD in information systems from Nova Southeastern University.

Toufik Taibi is an assistant professor at the College of Information Technology of The United Arab Emirates University, UAE. He holds a PhD in computer science. Dr. Taibi has more than 10 years of teaching and research experience. His research interests include formal specification of design patterns, distributed object computing, and component-based software engineering.

Arthur Tatnall is an associate professor in the Graduate School of Business at Victoria University, Melbourne, Australia. His PhD involved an innovation study where he made use of actor-network theory to investigate how Visual Basic entered the curriculum of an Australian university. His research and teaching interests include technological innovation, project management, electronic business, information technology in educational management, and information systems curriculum. He has written several books relating to information systems and published numerous book chapters, journal articles, and conference papers. He is currently editing an encyclopaedia of portal technology and applications (Arthur. Tatnall@vu.edu.au).

Ewe Hong Tat obtained his Bachelor of Engineering (Honors) degree from the University of Malaya, Malaysia, his Masters of Science degree in electrical engineering and computer science from M.I.T., USA, and his PhD degree from Multimedia University, Malaysia. He had worked before in Motorola Penang, Intel Penang, MIT's Research Laboratory for Electronics, and University of Malaya, and is currently the dean and also an associate professor at the Faculty of Information Technology, Multimedia University. In publication, he has published in books, international journals and conferences. His research interest includes microwave remote sensing, satellite image processing, networking, and wireless sensor network. He is also a senior member of IEEE.

Index